THE PERSISTENCE OF THE SACRED

GERMAN AND EUROPEAN STUDIES

General Editor: Jennifer L. Jenkins

The Persistence of the Sacred

German Catholic Pilgrimage, 1832–1937

SKYE DONEY

UNIVERSITY OF TORONTO PRESS
Toronto Buffalo London

© University of Toronto Press 2022
Toronto Buffalo London
utorontopress.com
Printed in the U.S.A.

ISBN 978-1-4875-4310-5 (cloth)   ISBN 978-1-4875-4311-2 (EPUB)
                                   ISBN 978-1-4875-4312-9 (PDF)

Library and Archives Canada Cataloguing in Publication

Title: The persistence of the sacred : German Catholic pilgrimage, 1832–1937 /
    Skye Doney.
Names: Doney, Skye, author.
Series: German and European studies ; 46.
Description: Series statement: German and European studies ; 46 | Includes
    bibliographical references and index.
Identifiers: Canadiana (print) 20220220263 | Canadiana (ebook) 20220220441 |
    ISBN 9781487543105 (cloth) | ISBN 9781487543112 (EPUB) |
    ISBN 9781487543129 (PDF)
Subjects: LCSH: Christian pilgrims and pilgrimages – Germany – Trier – History –
    19th century. | LCSH: Christian pilgrims and pilgrimages – Germany – Aachen –
    History – 19th century. | LCSH: Relics – Germany – Trier – History – 19th century. |
    LCSH: Relics – Germany – Aachen – History – 19th century. | LCSH: Trier (Germany) –
    Church history – 19th century. | LCSH: Aachen (Germany) – Church history –
    19th century.
Classification: LCC BX2320.5.G3 D66 2022 | DDC 263/.0424355 – dc23

We wish to acknowledge the land on which the University of Toronto Press
operates. This land is the traditional territory of the Wendat, the Anishnaabeg, the
Haudenosaunee, the Métis, and the Mississaugas of the Credit First Nation.

The German and European Studies series is funded by the DAAD with funds from the
German Federal Foreign Office.

Deutscher Akademischer Austauschdienst
German Academic Exchange Service

Support for this publication was provided by the George L. Mosse Program in History
at the University of Wisconsin-Madison and at the Hebrew University of Jerusalem.

University of Toronto Press acknowledges the financial assistance to its publishing
program of the Canada Council for the Arts and the Ontario Arts Council, an agency of
the Government of Ontario.

Canada Council
for the Arts

Conseil des Arts
du Canada

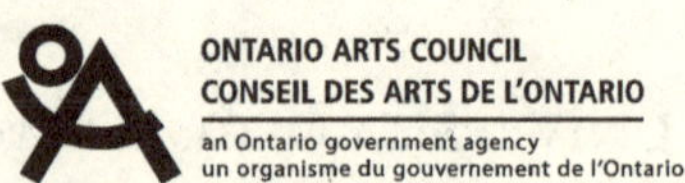

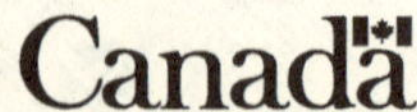

For three who believed in this book:
Bobbi Doney, Bob Johnson, Katherine Aaslestad

Every parting gives a foretaste of death, every reunion a hint of the resurrection.

— Arthur Schopenhauer

Contents

viii   Contents

Figures, Maps, and Tables

Figures

Maps

Tables

Acknowledgments

My first journey to the past was led by an outstanding historian: Katherine Aaslestad at West Virginia University. She introduced me to the key personalities of modern Europe and taught me how to navigate the foreign lands of the nineteenth century through documents and images. She also encouraged me to leave West Virginia and to continue my study of German history elsewhere. I was lucky that she continued to advise me and to remind me of the importance of asking the right questions. We are all much poorer for her passing this year.

Here in Madison I have had the privilege to meet and work with many brilliant historians. David Sorkin first got me interested in the history of European religion and the forms of sacred practices. Suzanne Desan's indefatigable engagement with this project has pushed me to sharpen the arguments and integrate new sources. Laird Boswell taught me to be patient with the writing process. Michael Shank's discussions were an invaluable source of encouragement and intellectual exchange. Lee Palmer Wandel urged me to read widely and to think about continuity. Rudy Koshar always reminded me to keep in mind the stakes for pilgrim participants. Without this intellectual community I would not have completed this book.

I am forever indebted to the George L. Mosse Program in History at the University of Wisconsin-Madison and at the Hebrew University of Jerusalem. Director Emeritus John Tortorice has acted as an unofficial advisor to many historians at both institutions and I am fortunate to be one of them. The Mosse Program sent me to Jerusalem where I began writing this project while studying with Professor Steven Aschheim. In Jerusalem, I further benefited from Daniel Hummel's steadfast commentary and willingness to discuss religiosity and religious experiences endlessly. Additional institutional support to complete this project came from the Fulbright Program, the German Academic Exchange Service, German Historical Institute, and the Mellon Foundation.

A very special thanks to the staff in Aachen and Trier for enthusiastically pointing me in the right directions. Dr. Dieter Wynands was always willing to discuss sources and helped me frame the chapters on miracle culture and *Andenken*. Stefan Nicolay noted key folders and the most striking images at the Bistumsarchiv Trier. This book further benefited from the guidance and dedication of archivists and librarians at the Archiv des Erzbistums Köln, Erzbischöfliche Diözesan-und Dombibliothek Köln, Bischöfliches Archiv Trier, Geheimnes Staatsarchiv Preußischer Kulturbesitz, Berlin, Landeshauptarchiv Koblenz, Stadtarchiv Aachen, Stadtarchiv Trier, Zentralbibliothek Aachen, and the Paulinus Verlag. Thank you especially to Stefan Nicolay (BATr), Dr. Beate Sophie Fleck (BDA), Dr. Birgitta Falk (DAA), Maria Schneiders (DAA), Dr. Samuel Hober (Paulinus), Bernhard Simon (SAT), Sandra Schumacher (Bistum Trier), and Jessica Hardenberger (ZBA) for kindly allowing me to include the images here.

It has been humbling to think back on all of the individuals who have offered essential and critical insights throughout the writing. Adi Armon, Sean Bloch, Suzanne Desan, Matthew Greene, David Harrisville, Daniel Hummel, Stephen Shapiro, and James Ungureanu all read the entire manuscript at different points. The book has also benefited greatly from the thoughtful comments from Melissa Anderson, Celia Applegate, Brad Baranowski, Athan Biss, Thomas Brodie, Eric Carlsson, Charles Cahill, James Coons, Jason Doerre, Eric Carlsson, Matthew Estel, David Fields, Katherine Guenoun, Kilian Harrer, Katie Jarvis, Eric O'Connor, Michael O'Sullivan, Johannes Paulmann, Cassandra Painter, Nicholas Perich, Terrence Peterson, Ute Planert, Zack Purvis, Ulrich Rosenhagen, Mark Ruff, Anthony J. Steinhoff, John Suvall, Steven Turley, Matthew Unangst, Kevin Walters, Jennifer Wunn, Matthew Yokell, Sunny Yudkoff, and Jeffrey Zalar. I hope that all of you will find your voice and recommendations reflected in the text. Thank you to everyone who has so generously given their time and energy through the seemingly endless procession of new versions of this project. Katherine Guenoun has been trying to get me to use commas for years, I have tried to get it right below. Any errors that follow are naturally my own.

Most importantly, thank you to J for joining me for the long journey to complete this book. I look forward to taking the next steps with you, Sigrid, and Elvia.

Skye Doney
Madison, Wisconsin
6 October 2021

Archive Abbreviations

AEK	Archiv des Erzbistums Köln
BATr	Bischöfliches Archiv Trier
BDA	Bischöfliches Diözesanarchiv Aachen
DAA	Domarchiv Aachen (PA – Propstarchiv)
GStA PK	Geheimnes Staatsarchiv Preußischer Kulturbesitz, Berlin
LHA Ko	Landeshauptarchiv Koblenz
SAA	Stadtarchiv Aachen
SAT	Stadtarchiv Trier
ZBA	Zentralbibliothek Aachen

Select Dates in German Catholicism: 1813–1939

Year	Events
1813	Johannes Ronge born at Bischofswalde (now Biskupów) in Upper Silesia, then part of the Kingdom of Prussia (now in Poland)
1815	Prussia assumes control of the Rhineland; religious freedom ensured in Patent of Possession
1817	Bavaria signs Concordat with the Vatican
1821	Bishopric of Aachen dissolved in the papal bull *De Salute Animarum*
1825	Prussian law on mixed marriages states that children are to be raised in the religion of their father
1831	Bartolomeo Alberto Cappellari (1765–1846) elected as Pope Gregory XVI
1832	Heinrich Hahn (1800–82), in Aachen, establishes *Missionsverein* that will become *Franziskus-Xaverius-Verein* Papal Encyclical *Mirari Vos* issued against transforming the Church
1834	Joseph Görres (1776–1848) publishes *Athanasius* in defence of Cologne Archbishop Clemens August von Droste-Vischering (1773–1845) and the rights of the Catholic Church against the Prussian state German historian Leopold von Ranke (1795–1886) publishes *A History of the Popes* critiquing the political role of the Vatican
1835	Clemens August von Droste-Vischering becomes archbishop of Cologne
1837	"Cologne Troubles" (*Kölner Wirren*), Droste-Vischering arrested for following papal instructions not to allow marriages between Protestants and Catholics without a guarantee that children would be raised in the Catholic faith
1838	*Historisch-politische Blätter* (Historical-political pages for Catholic Germany) founded in wake of Cologne Troubles King Ludwig I of Bavaria (1786–1868) requires soldiers to kneel in the presence of the Eucharist

(Continued)

Year	Events
1839	Droste-Vischering released from prison, but not reinstated as archbishop of Cologne
1841	Wilhelm Franz Sintenis (1794–1859) founds *Die Lichtfreunde* or Friends of the Light to bring together dissenting Protestants
1842	Wilhelm Arnoldi (1798–1864) becomes bishop of Trier (1842–64)
	Prussia resumes construction on the Cologne cathedral
1844	Johannes Ronge issues public critique of Trier pilgrimage in *Sächsische Vaterlandsblätter*
	Karl Borromäus (1820–74) founds the *Borromäusverein* in Bonn to advance Christian teaching through publication
1845	Johannes Kardinal von Geissel (1796–1865) selected bishop of Cologne (1845–65)
1846	Giovanni Maria Mastai Ferretti (1792–1898) elected Pope Pius IX
1847	Friedrich Wilhelm IV (1795–1861) issues the "Tolerance Edict," which allows religious disaffiliation
1848	*Piusverein* ("Pius Association") founded
	First meeting of Catholic Associations in Mainz (*erste Versammlung des katholischen Vereines Deutschlands*) – reflecting the growth of Catholic organizational life
	German Revolutions begin (1848–9) and lead to the establishment of the Frankfurt Parliament
1849	Friedrich Wilhelm IV refuses imperial crown offered by Frankfurt Parliament
	Papal encyclical *Nostis et nobiscum* argues that the 1848 Revolutions and attacks on papal territories were the fault of the Protestant Reformation
1852	Karl Otto von Raumer (1805–59), Minister of Educational and Religious Affairs, forbids Catholic missions to predominantly Protestant areas
1854	Pius IX proclaims the Dogma of the Immaculate Conception in *Ineffabilis Deus*
1858	Bernadette Soubirous (1844–79) experiences first apparition of the Virgin Mary – thousands of German Catholics eventually make pilgrimage to Lourdes
1864	Pius IX issues Syllabus of Errors (*Syllabus errorum*) against modern heresies, including pantheism, liberalism, socialism, communism, and natural Christian ethics
	Second Schleswig War, Denmark surrenders control of Schleswig and Holstein to Prussia and Austria
	Leopold Pelldram (1811–67) elected bishop of Trier (1864–7)

(Continued)

Year	Events
1866	Paulus Melchers (1813–95) elected bishop of Cologne (under arrest 1874–85)
	Austro-Prussian War, Prussia wins decisive victory at the Battle of Königgrätz on 3 July
1867	Matthias Eberhard (1815–76) elected bishop of Trier (1867–76); imprisoned March–December 1874 after refusing to pay Prussian fine of 10,400 thaler
1869	First Vatican Council begins in Rome
	Klostersturm: mob attacks Catholic orphanage in Berlin's Moabit neighbourhood
	"Ubryk Affair": Newspaper reports of nun Barbara Ubryk being held against her will in Kraków; mob attacks convent
1870	Papal infallibility proclaimed in *Pastor Aeternus*
	Centre Party (*Zentrum*) organized to defend Catholicism against increasing state-sponsored persecution
	Italian military assumes control of Rome – Pius IX declares himself a "prisoner of the Vatican"
1871	German Empire proclaimed in Versailles following Franco-Prussian War
	Kulturkampf begins
	Otto von Bismarck (1815–98) forbids Catholic priests from discussing political opinions from the pulpit
	Catholics constitute 34% of the Prussian Empire
	Bismarck abolishes Roman Catholic bureau in Prussian Ministry of Culture
1872	Bismarck declares before the Reichstag, "Do not worry, we do not go to Canossa," indicating his unwillingness to accommodate Catholic interests
	Religious schools subjected to state inspection
	Religious teachers removed from state schools
	Jesuit Order outlawed in Germany, Redemptorists and the Lazarist orders expelled
	Germany cuts diplomatic ties to the Vatican
	Expatriation Law makes it possible to expel undesired priests or to take away their citizenship
1873	May Laws enacted in Prussia
	Grant German government control over religious training
	Grant German government control over ecclesiastical appointments within the church
	Grant Catholic laity the right to leave the church via a secular judge
	German scientist and political activist Rudolf Virchow (1821–1902) describes "a great Kulturkampf" between Catholicism and Germany

(*Continued*)

Year	Events
1874	Ludwig Windthorst (1812–91) succeeds Hermann von Mallinckrodt (1821–74) as leader of Centre Party
	Centre Party doubles representation in the Reichstag after winning 77% of the Catholic vote
	Catholic Eduard Kullmann (1853–92) attempts to assassinate Bismarck in Kissingen
1875	Civil marriage obligatory throughout Germany
	Non-compliant clergy go into exile
	Non-compliant dioceses lose state financial aid
1876	Hundreds of Catholic priests imprisoned – more than 1,000 parishes without a priest
	Katharina and Lischen Hubertus, Margaretha Kunz, Susanna Leist, and Anna Meisberger report Marian apparition in Marpingen, Germany
	Görres Gesellschaft zur Pflege der Wissenschaft im katholischen Deutschland (Görres Society for the Support of Science in Catholic Germany) founded
1878	Pope Pius IX dies
	Vincenzo Gioacchino Raffaele Luigi Pecci (1810–1903) elected Pope Leo XIII
	In Prussia, only three of eight bishops remain in office
1880	Cologne cathedral construction completed – German Emperor Wilhelm I (1797–1888) attends dedication, while Bishop Melchers remains in prison
1881	Michael Felix Korum (1840–1921) selected bishop of Trier (1881–1921)
1885	Philipp Krementz (1819–99) selected bishop of Cologne (1885–99)
1887	Leo XIII declares that the Kulturkampf has ended
	Johannes Ronge dies
1891	Leo XIII issues *Rerum Novarum*, calling for "social Catholicism"
1898	Therese Neumann (1898–1962) born in Konnersreuth, Bavaria, Germany
1899	Hubert Theophil Simar (1835–1902) selected bishop of Cologne (1899–1902)
	Papal encyclical *Testem benevolentiae* issued against "Americanism" and argument that the church should adapt to its modern context
1900	Fulda Bishops Conference issues letter condemning Christian Trade Unions
	Catholic journal *Hochland* launched, first edition appears in 1903
1902	Antonius Fischer (1840–1912) selected bishop of Cologne (1902–12)
	Papacy decides that Christian trade unions allowable where already established

(*Continued*)

Year	Events
1903	*Katholischer Deutscher Frauenbund* (Catholic German Women's Association) established in Cologne
	Giuseppe Melchiorre Sarto (1835–1914) elected Pope Pius X
1910	Pope Pius X issues *Sacrorum antistitum* and requires Catholic clergy to take an "Oath against Modernism"
1912	11% of the Zentrum deputies in the Reichstag are clerics
	Felix Kardinal von Hartmann (1851–1919) selected bishop of Cologne (1912–19)
1914	First World War begins
1917	Last paragraphs of the Jesuit Law repealed
	Three children report apparitions of the Virgin Mary in Fátima, Portugal
	Catholic Church forbids séances in response to growing German interest in the occult
1918	First World War ends
	Adolph Hoffmann (1858–1930), Prussian Minister of Culture, orders all religious objects removed from Prussian classrooms
1919	Catholic Church forbids theosophy out of anxiety that it will promote pantheism
1920	Karl Joseph Kardinal Schulte (1871–1941) selected bishop of Cologne (1920–41)
	Abbé Argence Vachère reports a picture of Christ weeping blood in his Aachen apartment
	Adolf Hitler announces the 25-point National Socialist Program
1922	Ambrogio Damiano Achille Ratti (1857–1939) elected Pope Pius XI
	Franz Rudolf Bornewasser (1866–1951) elected bishop of Trier (1922–51)
1923	France and Belgium occupy the Ruhr after Germany fails to make reparation payments stipulated in the Treaty of Versailles. Belgian soldiers headquartered in Aachen.
	Destabilization of the value of the mark, accelerated hyperinflation
1924	Bavaria finalizes Concordat with the Vatican
1925	France and Belgium withdraw soldiers from the Ruhr
1926	Therese Neumann reports first stigmata experience
	Vatican condemns Action Française political movement
1929	Prussia finalizes Concordat with the Vatican
	Wall Street Crash
	Lateran Accords between Italy and the Vatican to settle the "Roman Question"
1930	Heinrich Brüning (1885–1970), Centre Party chairman, becomes chancellor
	Bishopric of Aachen reconstituted, led by Bishop Joseph Heinrich Peter Vogt (1930–7)

(*Continued*)

Year	Events
1932	Baden finalizes Concordat with the Vatican
	Catholic episcopate bans National Socialist German Workers' Party (NSDAP) armbands in Mass, bans membership in NSDAP
	Franz von Papen (1879–1969), Centre Party politician, appointed chancellor
1933	January, Catholic episcopate removes ban on NSDAP armbands and party membership
	5 March, Cologne-Aachen votes 35.9% for the Centre Party
	23 March, Centre Party supports the Enabling Act after the Reichstag Fire
	28 March, Catholic Church withdraws formal ban on voting for NSDAP
	29 March, German bishops drop prohibition on joining the NSDAP
	5 July, Centre Party votes to dissolve itself
	20 July, Franz von Papen concludes Concordat negotiations with the Vatican
1934	February, Catholic Church places Alfred Rosenberg's (1893–1946) *Der Mythus des 20. Jahrhunderts* on the Index of Forbidden Books
1935	National Socialists restrict Catholic press and lay organizations
	1935–7 Nazi trials against hundreds of priests and nuns for foreign currency violations, homosexuality, and pedophilia
1936	November, NSDAP halts attempt to remove crucifixes from public schools in Oldenburg
1937	March, Pius XI issues *Mit brennender Sorge* (With Burning Concern) to German Catholics, denouncing myth of "race and blood"
	Marian apparition witnessed by four girls in Heede, Germany
1938	February, Nazi Party closes Catholic youth groups in Cologne
	9–10 November, Kristallnacht, Catholic episcopate does not speak publicly about attacks against German Jews
	Hermann Joseph Sträter (1866–1943) elected bishop of Aachen (1938–43)
	Pope Pius XI develops the *Humani generis unitas*, a draft for an encyclical condemning antisemitism, racism, and the persecution of Jews; the encyclical is never officially issued
1939	Prussia, Bavaria, and Württemberg abolish denominational schools
	Eugenio Maria Giuseppe Giovanni Pacelli (1876–1958) elected Pope Pius XII (1939–58)
	Second World War begins

THE PERSISTENCE OF THE SACRED

Introduction

Physicians could not heal Frau Willmann.[1] She contracted pneumonia in February 1929. She came so close to death later that spring that her priest in Mutterstadt, Germany, administered the last rites. Willmann survived, but she was chronically tired and physically weak. She had constant pain in her left leg and needed a cane to walk. Doctors tried to relieve her discomfort. They prescribed sand baths and diathermy treatments. Willmann followed their advice and travelled to healing centres in search of relief – to Bad Dürheim for four weeks in 1929, to Bad Reichenhall for six weeks in 1930, and to Ludwigshafen for five weeks in 1931. None of these expensive treatments worked and so her doctors decided that her condition was incurable. Declared a lost cause by physicians, Willmann sought out extra-medical assistance.

In 1933, Willmann travelled with twenty other pilgrims from Mutterstadt to Trier to visit the Holy Coat of Jesus. Four years after her first bout with pneumonia, Willmann now weighed only thirty-seven kilograms. The 180-kilometre journey was extremely arduous. She travelled without permission from her doctors and prayed to Mary for help and strength: "Dear Mother of God, help me." By the time her pilgrim group arrived in Trier, Willmann was too fragile to walk with her Mutterstadt procession to their staging church, *Jesuitenkirche*, where they would wait for their appointed time to process to the cathedral. Instead, her husband helped her skip the queue and together they went directly to revere the Holy Coat of Jesus. In doing so she participated in a centuries-old tradition. Since 1512 pilgrims had gathered before this sacred garment. And by 1844, the relic had an established international reputation for bringing about physical transformation and miraculous corporeal restorations.

Early the following morning between five and six, Willmann returned to the cathedral. Church officials allowed sick individuals who obtained prior permission to touch the Holy Coat before the cathedral opened. Two priests sat to the right and left of the Coat to regulate and facilitate access. Willmann touched the relic twice, dropped her cane, and was healed. That same Sunday afternoon, she travelled back to Mutterstadt. News of her miraculous cure preceded her and a large crowd greeted her train. The conductor had difficulty escorting Willmann off the platform through the throng of curious onlookers.

For millions of pilgrims in Germany over the course of a century, pilgrimage offered possible answers to the mysteries of sickness, life, and death. This book explores the religious world views of Europeans who, like Frau Willmann, travelled to Trier and Aachen, two cities in Western Germany, between 1832 and 1937. Who were they? What did they believe? The opening chapters examine specific forms of religious practice: prayer, song, procession, the cult of miracles, and the items pilgrims acquired – *Andenken* – during their travels. These varied forms of religiosity are treated separately in order to highlight what was consistently important for the participants over the course of a century. As much as possible, I let pilgrims explain their hopes, expectations, and concerns. Doing so gives voice to those who believed there were places where they could access the divine through sacred terrestrial objects.[2]

After considering the sacred landscapes of pilgrims, the second half of the book turns to public criticism of pilgrimage and how church leaders responded. Trier Bishop Wilhelm Arnoldi (1798–1864) could not anticipate the severity of the critique he faced for coordinating a pilgrimage to the Holy Coat of Jesus. In 1844, a defrocked Silesian priest – Johannes Ronge (1813–87) – protested against the ongoing Trier pilgrimage. He was incensed by clerical support for the Holy Coat and disavowed public claims of bodily healing through the relic. Ronge wrote that Arnoldi and his colleagues pandered to superstition and harmed Christendom. Disgusted with his co-religionists, Ronge established a new Christian sect, the German-Catholics.[3]

Ronge's broadside touched off a vigorous pamphlet debate across Germany about the place of Catholicism in society, the possibility of miracles, and the nature of God. Local church leaders subsequently sought to regulate what pilgrims said about their bodies. Rhenish clergy required evidence from physicians and priests of pre-existing conditions. Ronge's schism ultimately failed and his movement faded, but after 1844 clergy modified how they talked about the origins and sacred potential of relics. This clerical reaction points to the complicated ways clergy responded to the nineteenth century. They were not necessarily guardians of unmediated tradition and conservatism.

To recover the history of Catholic pilgrimage over this century I draw on a range of sources, including films, photographs, postcards, correspondence, publications, and even a pipe engraved with the Aachen relics. An array of church and community leaders responded to the thousands of inquiries pilgrims sent before travelling. Clergy – often joined by local politicians, professors, or architects – staffed Pilgrimage Committees to plan events and to coordinate logistics with regional and national authorities. In addition to correspondence, pamphlets written by clerics, laity, and theologians point to the major concerns of church thinkers about pilgrimage practices. Taken together, the texts, images, and sounds created by participants and organizers point to multiple – at times competing – Catholic understandings of the relationship between relics and religiosity, between modernity and faith, and between humanity and God.

The Relics and Cities

It was one of the earliest Christian pilgrims, the former Roman empress St. Helena, who Trier tradition maintains brought back the Holy Coat of Jesus from Palestine.[4] The Holy Coat is a faded, reddish-brown garment. Jesus would have worn the garment externally, held around his waist by a belt (see image 0.2).[5] According to Trier Catholics, the Coat appears twice in the Gospels. In Matthew 9:20–22, a woman suffering from constant haemorrhage touched the Coat as Jesus passed by and was healed. In John 19 Roman soldiers decided not to cut up the Coat, but instead to cast lots to determine which of them could keep it. Both of these moments remain significant to pilgrims because they indicated that the relic was never cut into smaller pieces and that it could always heal the sick. Trier pilgrims encountered the Coat only in the cathedral. They walked past the altar and up the ambulatory, where the relic was exhibited. Depending on the year, pilgrims like Willmann could either touch the relic themselves or have a devotional item (*Andenken*) pressed against the fabric of the relic by a cleric. For many travellers, the Coat and their personal devotional items offered unprecedented proximity to the lives and bodies of the Holy Family.

Pilgrims travelled to Aachen to visit several different relics but believed the most important of these were the four items stored in the Marian Shrine. The first, the "Garment of the Blessed Mother," of white linen, has the form of a tunic or dress when unfolded. The second, the "Swaddling Clothes of Jesus," made of camel or goat wool, appeared before pilgrims unstained and dark brown. The "Loincloth of Jesus," the third Marian Shrine relic, woven from coarse linen, resembles a trapezoid when unfolded. The final major Aachen relic, the "Decapitation Cloth of John the Baptist," or beheading garment, is a long rectangle bordered on all four sides with fine damask. The main body of the decapitation cloth is linen.[6] Clergy rarely unfolded these last three of the Marian Shrine relics. Pilgrims encountered them as folded rectangles, bound by coloured silk. During the Aachen pilgrimages, bishops hung the relics either in or outside the cathedral for crowds to view (see image 0.6).

Over the course of a transformative and tumultuous century, mass groups of pilgrims made their way to Aachen and Trier to view the five relics. Both cities are located in Western Germany near the French border. When crowds assembled in the Aachen cathedral square in 1832, Prussia had already administered the Rhineland for nearly two decades. The 1830s signalled the coming of age of a new European generation without memories of the Old Regime.[7] The region was increasingly integrated into greater Prussia; for instance, in 1834 the *Zollverein* (customs union) simplified trade across borders. That same year, German Protestant theologian Friedrich Schleiermacher died, and those who followed him worked to understand his attempt to reconcile orthodox theology with contemporary thought.[8] In 1835, the Catholic Church stopped officially opposing the Copernican system and removed publications by Copernicus and Galileo from the Index of Forbidden Books.[9]

In this context, the Aachen 1832 pilgrimage celebrated an episcopal hope for a new era of political stability and peaceful political coexistence with predominantly Protestant Prussia. This was not to be the case. By 1837 tensions between the Rhenish clergy and the Prussian state flared to the point that Cologne Bishop Clemens August Droste zu Vischering was arrested for refusing to sanction "mixed marriages" between Protestants and Catholics without a guarantee that the children would be raised Catholic. These "Cologne Troubles," contemporaries noted, revealed the limits of Catholic cultural integration.

Aachen pilgrimages continued to intersect with dramatic political transformations over this 105-year period. The city displayed its four relics at seven-year intervals and hosted fifteen events between 1832 and 1937. Aachen was fairly consistent in attendance, with its two most successful pilgrimages taking place in 1881 and 1925.[10] Around 800,000 pilgrims arrived in 1937 in a potent statement about the continued significance of traditional religiosity, despite Nazi efforts to orient Catholics away from the church and towards the state.

In moments of extreme uncertainty and political instability, including during the Second World War, Aachen clergy kept the *Marienschrein* relics safely stowed until they could again be displayed openly. The 1916 pilgrimage, to take place during the First World War, was cancelled as a result of unpredictability at the front. The 1923 Aachen pilgrimage was delayed two years in response to France's military occupation of the region. And more recently, the 2021 pilgrimage was postponed to 2023 because of the COVID-19 pandemic.

Between 1832 and 1937 Trier hosted three pilgrimages to the Holy Coat of Jesus, in 1844, 1891, and 1933.[11] Each event occurred under a different government: Prussia, Kaiserreich, and Third Reich. With each pilgrimage, Trier attracted more pilgrims; their numbers peaked in 1933, with over two million in attendance. This event coincided with the signing of the *Reichskonkordat* between the Vatican and the Third Reich. Far from establishing a stable legal basis for Catholic associational life in Trier as the episcopate hoped, tensions between the nascent Nazi regime and Catholic authorities proliferated in 1933. Clergy were unable, for instance, to ban the wearing of party uniforms during the event. In their correspondence, pilgrims noted that their fellow believers had difficulty crossing into the new Third Reich because there were new, complicated border policies and rules about currency exchange.

After 1937 the Trier and Aachen episcopate delayed further pilgrimage until after the end of the Second World War. In 1945, Aachen displayed relics in a bombed-out cathedral. But the damage to infrastructure, fatigue from six years of fighting, and disorientation from occupation greatly limited participation. Trier never again attracted the over two million pilgrims of 1933. This study thus ends when Catholic Church membership and weekly Mass attendance were at their peak and before the Allies subdued the region.[12] The postwar pilgrimage story is a different narrative of new forms of clerical adjustment including increasing Christian ecumenicism and interfaith dialogue, and waning pilgrimage participation.[13]

Rethinking Modern German Pilgrimage

The century of pilgrimages preceding Frau Willmann's encounter with the Holy Coat of Trier problematizes several longstanding historiographic assumptions about German Catholicism. In the first place, scholars have viewed European pilgrimages primarily through the eyes of political and cultural authorities, including monarchs, authors, and state and regional officials.[14] Deploying political sources, historians have demonstrated that German Catholics mobilized over the course of the nineteenth century, and that Catholics increasingly supported their confessional Zentrum political party in response to state-sponsored persecution.[15] Confessional newspapers and Zentrum political speeches indicate how German Catholics worked to defend their faith against hostile regional and national leaders. A focus on the political nature of Catholicism has also produced important studies on Chancellor Otto von Bismarck's Kulturkampf and the imagined boundaries of Germanness in the nineteenth century. The emphasis on political Catholicism has demonstrated important interconnections between Catholic activism and the development of the Zentrum.

Yet this top-down view can be perilous, not least because it tends to emphasize the anti-Catholic aspects of the German liberal world view. Liberals were anxious about the place of the Catholic population in the newly united Germany and often assumed that Catholics were inherently conservative, reactionary, and disloyal.[16] They pointed to the Catholic desire to include Catholic Austria in a *Großdeutschland* as a key reason the 1848 Revolution failed.[17] Prussian authorities questioned the trustworthiness of German Catholics and wondered whether an individual could be German and still heed papal encyclicals.

Beyond the anti-Catholic sentiment reflected in bureaucratic or political sources, a focus on Catholic political concerns can wrongly conclude that Catholic leaders represented the will and hope of Rhenish Catholics or that they dictated the experiences and world view of pilgrimage participants. For example, both Wolfgang Schieder and Jonathan Sperber present the 1844 Trier pilgrimage as indicative of clerical control over laity because the event was "strictly and bureaucratically organized from the top down."[18] Sperber highlights the fact that in 1844 pilgrims no longer staggered along the roadside "as individuals or in small groups under questionable lay supervision" but were now led by priests "in strictest order and discipline."[19] Clergy organized the pilgrimages, and at first glance it does seem that these church shepherds had their flock well in hand.[20] The events between the 1830s and 1930s did not devolve into protests, revolutions, or unfettered mass violence. In general, they proceeded in an orderly fashion and included impressively choreographed public processions.

At the same time there were limits to this top-down organization and supervision. As we shall see, travellers did not necessarily welcome coordination, or regulation from above. They did not always obey or even read the instructions carefully crafted by the Pilgrimage Committees. Indeed by the 1930s, Trier organizers were vexed and overwhelmed by the volume of unregistered individual pilgrims who arrived to see the Holy Coat. Everyone was supposed to sign up beforehand, and clergy were unprepared for thousands of pilgrims arriving unannounced every day.

And even as clergy revisited their teachings on pilgrimage, the history of relics, and miracles over the course of the nineteenth century, their revised, or modern, homilies, tracts, and even prayers did not significantly shift what pilgrims said about their sacred objects. In some cases, pilgrims rejected revised clerical instruction about their relics. For those seeking a miraculous restoration of their body, priestly emphasis on the "symbol" of the Holy Coat or of Jesus's swaddling clothes did not temper pilgrim expectations that they would encounter an authentic garment from the Holy Family.

The tension between pilgrim hopes and clerical theology offers still another caveat to the myth of a unified German Catholic milieu, or sub-society. The milieu approach originally stressed rigid clerical leaders who, when faced with the pressures of revolution, persecution, and nationalism, turned to Rome for guidance on how best to resist the political and cultural movements that threatened Catholic orthodoxy.[21] In actuality, clerical leaders in the Rhineland solicited advice from both church and secular authorities as they worked to determine the possible authenticity of their sacred objects. What they learned in turn influenced what they taught pilgrims about the history of relics.

A close examination of individuals travelling to see relics and the clergy organizing pilgrimage indicates that in many ways German Catholicism in the Rhineland was heterogeneous, not monolithic. Clergy instructed pilgrims how to behave and how to be devout, often in the weeks before relics were exhibited in Trier and Aachen. But participants made practices like prayer, singing, and even procession their own. The Rhenish Catholic Church accommodated divergent theological understandings about pilgrimage and religious practice.

Aachen and Trier pilgrim demographics reveal new problems with the feminization of religion thesis.[22] Launched initially as a prism through which to understand Protestant religious observation in the United States, historians have deployed this framework to discuss male disenchantment with Judaism, Protestantism, and Catholicism.[23] Following the Enlightenment, the French Revolution, and the tumults of political and economic instability, European men attended weekly religious services less frequently, were more reluctant to become clerical leaders, and found fulfilment outside the local Christian community: in political parties, national movements, pubs, or associational life.[24]

This book reinterprets male religious participation and identity over the century. Men may not have been at Mass every week, but they still demonstrated their religiosity in other important ways. In Aachen and Trier, they stood guard while relics were out for display. They wanted to be seen in public spaces as protectors of the sacred. Male associations jostled for prominent positions in public processions through their communities. When the Nazi Sturmabteilung (SA) assumed control of guarding the Holy Coat and regulating crowds in 1933 Trier, Catholic shooting society (*Schützenverein*) members voiced their annoyance that their traditional role as guardians of the sacred had been usurped.

In addition to wanting to publicly position themselves as Catholic, men engaged in the cult of miracles in greater numbers than historians have realized. Men were more likely to request time with a relic than they were to subsequently proclaim themselves healed.[25] Sick pilgrims had to travel to the relics, and for many the painful journey was an act of atonement and an essential element of the miracle experience. For many men, relics remained an important alternative to contemporary physicians. This private pursuit of physical healing offers insight into the complicated nature of male Catholic identities.

German pilgrims highlight the tangled relationship of gender, religion, and power in the nineteenth and early twentieth centuries. Female cure-seekers consistently make up the majority of miracle claims, but their ability to corroborate their own bodily experiences independently declined over this century. In the 1840s, female participants in the cult of the miracle could testify to their own physical restoration. But by the next Trier pilgrimage such individual testimony was insufficient to claim God's intervention through relics. For instance, in 1891 Trier Bishop Michael Felix Korum (1840–1921) forbade publications on miracles during that pilgrimage for three years so that his office could investigate claims of healing. And by the 1930s, professional men – priests and physicians – were required to confirm changes in female Catholic bodies. This "masculinization of truth" intersected with increasing professionalization among both clergy and medical professionals.[26]

Finally, in the context of Rhenish pilgrimages, the following analysis points to the varied ways German Catholic leaders framed their faith as professional, respectable, and *bürgerlich*. Priests and bishops faced enormous internal and external pressure to publicly present Rhenish Catholicism as respectable, reasonable, and even Germanic.[27] As pilgrimage detractors – including Johannes Ronge and university faculty in Bonn – questioned the historical authenticity of the Coat of Trier and the theological merits of pilgrimage, Rhineland priests responded by seeking out new sources of secular authority to confirm the status of the Coat of Trier. They conducted fibre analyses on the garment in order to demonstrate its origins and authenticity. After 1844, clerics also ensured that any miraculous claims could be corroborated and that they occurred privately behind closed doors, early in the morning and out of sight. Recall that Frau Willmann arrived at the cathedral at 5:00 in the morning to touch the Holy Coat. Many of these decisions should give historians pause about describing clerics as reactionary conservatives.

Practising Pilgrimage

Pilgrims arrived in Aachen and Trier in ever greater numbers between 1832 and 1937, through the violence of revolution, warfare, and economic collapse. Relics remained foci of pilgrim practices and clerical instruction throughout this century. Over five generations, individuals largely observed the rites of the preceding pilgrimage. Contemporaries, both organizers and critics, noted the enduring continuity of such practices as evidence of the timelessness (or backwardness) of Catholicism. And there is indeed ample evidence for continuity; clergy highlighted the same passages from scripture during each event, and processions followed the same routes through the cities. The correspondence and publications of Catholic participants and organizers reveal the enduring and multifaceted ways that pilgrims to Aachen and Trier understood this divine presence.[28]

The first three chapters therefore thematically explore the activities of pilgrims who continued to visit Rhenish relics despite the fierce debate about relic authenticity. By addressing unique religious practices individually, I note the remarkable persistence of religiosity through successive German political regimes.[29] Overwhelmingly the participants wrote about their personal difficulties and their hope that their physical, mental, and spiritual suffering would be lessened after visiting the Holy Coat of Trier and the Marian Shrine in Aachen. On the road, in trains, on boats, the prayers and songs of travelling Catholics emphasized the temporal exception of pilgrimage and relics: the practice and objects endured despite the rapidity of technological, social, and political change.

Participation included many activities, such as travelling, writing letters, praying, and still other forms.[30] Emma Figulla, for example, offers a glimpse into the variety of ways pilgrims engaged with the Rhenish relics. She wrote to Trier pilgrimage officials in 1933 from Ratibor. She asked them to touch her golden ring to the Holy Coat. The ring had belonged to her deceased father. She wore it every day after he died. For the previous nine years Figulla suffered from an unnamed bone, joint, and tendon disease. She was exhausted and did not have the strength to personally attend the Trier event. But she heard an inner voice reminding her of her father's ring and urging her to send it on to Trier.[31] After a period of relative strength, she acted on this interior urge. "God can heal me from a distance," she wrote, "as he healed the servant of the centurion Cornelius."[32] She sent her father's ring on faith with stamps so that it could be returned. Figulla could not physically attend the pilgrimage but did not believe this lessened her participation in or her proximity to the divine. The ring acted as a substitute pilgrim. It could touch the Coat for her, make the circuitous journey, and bring divine presence back to her in Ratibor. Pilgrims to Trier and Aachen, like Figulla, gave *place* a meaning, and defined what value their journey, the relics, and the visited cities held.

Travellers and petitioners like Figulla held a variety of theological understandings of the role of relics. Pilgrims who wrote to clerical officials discussed their immanent hopes for their encounter with the Holy Coat of Trier or the Aachen relics in the Marian Shrine. Frau Willmann was sick and hoped to be healed.[33] Others described their spiritual and material crises. For many, the trip to these churches had high stakes: to save a loved one's soul, to find work, to protect a family in times of uncertainty. Despite efforts of clergy to frame the significance of relics, pilgrims were adept at coming to their own conclusions that did not necessarily correspond to the homilies they might hear in Aachen and Trier. This gap between clerical teaching and pilgrim expectations increasingly widened after the disruptions of 1844.

Relics in Doubt

The bureaucratic procedures Frau Willmann encountered in 1933 were the culmination of shifting clerical teachings about relics since 1844. In one telling letter, Anton Joseph Binterim, a clergyman in Düsseldorf, wrote to Jakob Marx, a professor at the Trier Catholic seminary, about how to defend the authenticity of the Trier Coat.[34] Binterim confided that it was a matter of course that the Holy Coat could heal. After all, the Coat's biblical significance was clear for anyone who cared to pick up the New Testament. If Jesus's garment could make the blind see and restore the ability to walk while he wore it, then it was logical that this healing potential persisted into the nineteenth century.[35] Even so, Binterim continued, would Marx please write back with information about the earliest historical sources about the Coat. Binterim went on to write a pamphlet in support of the Coat's authenticity.

Binterim's enquiry reflected an emerging consensus among Catholic elites that pilgrimage critics would not be silenced with arguments dependent on scriptural passages or church tradition. This shift, away from popular pilgrim views of the divine nature of the relics and towards their origins in *Urgeschichte* (prehistory), points to how clergy accommodated and co-opted theological critiques and how they attempted to make popular religiosity palatable to their fellow Germans.

The last three chapters of this book follow public attacks on pilgrimage and how clergy like Father Binterim responded. Faced with ridicule and chastised for not embracing a positivist understanding of history and science, clergy turned away from traditional understandings of their sacred objects. While still revering these five relics, Rhenish church leaders sought scientific explanations and justifications for pilgrimage. This "turn outward" in the realm of religious practices forced clergy to grapple with changing medical practices, new forms of experimentation, and historical criticism.

Before Rhenish clergy were ready to confront what the legacy of revolution and occupation meant for popular piety, Johannes Ronge forced their hand in 1844. Ronge was the most notorious critic of the Trier episcopate and the continuation of traditional religiosity after the Enlightenment. But he was not alone. Additional denunciations came from anti-Catholic public intellectuals like Johann Gildemeister (1812–90) and Heinrich von Sybel (1817–95) and from additional former clergy like Johann Czerski (1813–93). Together this sceptical generation questioned the veracity of relics and the place of Catholicism in post-revolutionary society. Thus in 1844, the cultural positioning of Rhenish Catholicism remained precarious. Ronge and others like him acted as a catalyst for clerical shifts outlined in the final chapters.

Clergy confronted internal and external challenges to relics, even as they faced increased responsibilities after French Revolutionary armies pillaged religious orders throughout the Rhineland and the subsequent 1802 secularization of religious life. It now fell to local churchmen to organize religious life without the network of charitable and teaching orders. Beyond these challenges, the church was understaffed in urban centres as the population grew much faster than enrolment in seminaries. In Trier, Bishop Arnoldi strove to find a balance between ultramontanism and the realities of Prussian pressure on the leadership of the church.[36] Bishops like Arnoldi had to tread a difficult path out of the challenges of the French Revolution and into a tenuous future as a religious minority.

At the beginning of the nineteenth century clergy encouraged reports on miracles. In 1844, for instance, Arnoldi helped publicize reports of cures in the *Luxemburger Zeitung*.[37] But clerical explanation for the origins and merit of relics shifted after 1844, and new teachings led to changes in pilgrimage policy. By 1933, sick pilgrims like Willmann needed elaborate proof from a physician before they could visit the Holy Coat. Clergy monitored miracle claimants for years before publishing official lists of corroborated miracles and divine mercies. Clerical restrictions placed on relic access opened a gap between popular, lay beliefs and the clergy. Wary of being mocked and wanting to avoid scandal, Rhenish church leaders simultaneously restricted what pilgrims could say about God's presence and expanded their acceptable sources of truth to include non-Catholic, secular medical specialists.

Clergy thus moved away from tradition-based or biblical explanations of relic origins.[38] For church officials, authenticity could no longer be backed by solely scriptural evidence like Matthew 9:20–21, "And a woman who had been suffering from a haemorrhage for twelve years, came up behind Him and touched the fringe of His outer garment; for she was saying to herself, 'If I only touch His garment, I will get well.'" Beginning in the mid-nineteenth century, clergy used extra-biblical sources to explain the authenticity of relics. They added new proofs to their pamphlets and homilies, including archaeological evidence and elaborate fibre analyses. The final chapter addresses how clerical rhetoric about relics moved from these objects being literal garments from the lives of Jesus, John the Baptist, and Mary, to being symbols of Catholic unity.

This book reveals the ways in which German Catholics like Figulla, Willmann, and Binterim adapted to the post-1844 period by exploring what pilgrims and clergy wrote about public religious practice.[39] In their correspondence, Catholic pilgrims describe their understanding of sacred objects and explain their reasons for travelling to Aachen and Trier between the 1830s and 1930s. They left their homes in pursuit of highly varied goals, but were united in their belief that God bestowed blessings through the four objects in Aachen and the Coat in Trier. As pilgrims continued to affirm their belief that the Holy Ghost and the Holy Family acted through terrestrial objects, the Rhenish episcopate tempered their teachings on miracle and relics. Clergy introduced barriers between travellers and relics in order to stave off criticism that German Catholicism was antiquated and backward. Priests and bishops worked to avoid embarrassment, but their new rhetoric – that relics were symbols, not necessarily authentic – failed to resonate. By exposing the growing gulf between pilgrim expectations and clerical instruction, this book reveals the contested and highly textured nature of the German Catholic "milieu" over one hundred years. It also excavates how some Catholics attempted to resolve the perennial tension in Christian thought about the interrelationship of nature, the body, and the divine.

Map 0.1. Modern Germany
Source: University of Wisconsin Cartography Lab.

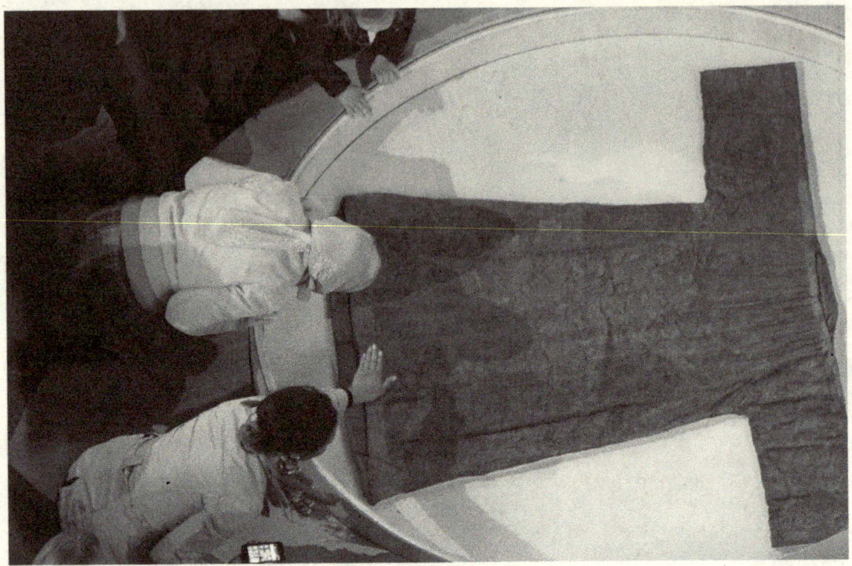

Figure 0.1. Kneeling pilgrims touch and kiss the Holy Coat shrine, 12 May 2012. The Coat measures 156 cm across the top of the garment, 102 cm across the bottom, and is 147 cm long. The sleeve openings are 29 cm wide.[40] Source: H. Thewalt/Bistum Trier.

Figure 0.2. Opening the Marian Shrine (*Marienschrein*) during the *Heiligtumsfahrt*, Aachen, 2014. Source: © Domkapitel Aachen; photo by Andreas Schmitter, Aachen.

Figure 0.3. *Andenken* from 1895 pilgrimage, showing the Marian Shrine, and the four main relics down the centre of the image. The Garment of the Blessed Mother is 153 cm × 132 cm, measured from sleeve to sleeve.[41] The Swaddling Clothes of Jesus measure 68 cm × 94 cm.[42] The Loincloth of Jesus is 127.5 cm × 151 cm.[43] The John the Baptist Decapitation relic is 282.2 cm × 131.5 cm. Source: Stadtbibliothek Aachen, Sonderbestände, Dkk 14 Heil (20388048).

Figure 0.4. The Weihbischof (auxiliary bishop) of Paderborn (*left*) displaying one of the four Marian relics from a cathedral gallery. Together with an attendant he here uses sticks to keep the relic in place. Note the size of the crowd below. n.d.
Source: Domarchiv Aachen (DAA), Domkapitel 4.1.1.31 1 Plakat, Ausweiskarten, Pilgerbüchlein, Fotos.

Figure 0.5. Trier cathedral ambulatory, 1933.
Source: Bischöfliches Archiv Trier (BATr), Abt. 100, Nr. 0002.

1 What They Practised: Prayer, Songs, and Processions

Bishop Stephan Ackermann and 1,000 pilgrims greeted a six-metre-tall, three-ton, steel representation of the Holy Coat of Trier on 20 April 2013.[1] Pilgrims to Trier were invited to write their name or a message on a steel letter *A* which was then welded to the larger *Schaff-Rock* sculpture. The proceeds from this practice went to the Bishop's Fund for the Unemployed (*Bischöfliche Solidaritätsfonds für Arbeitslose*).[2] The construction of the *Schaff-Rock* provided several steel workers with fifty to sixty hours of labour.[3] The *Schaff-Rock* was designed to be a tribute to both the German Catholic commitment to labour and the Trier relic. Visitors to Trier could visit a permanent representation of the Holy Coat, regardless of whether or not there was a pilgrimage. Now the Coat symbolically watched over the city from the Markusberg, with the pilgrim participation literally fused to its surface. Here the Coat was abstracted, represented in colossal proportions, made up as a sign of unity, socio-economic solidarity, and ecumenical togetherness.

As in 2013, clergy taught travellers to Trier and Aachen how to behave as pilgrims between 1832 and 1937. For instance, in 1933, pilgrims from Bonneweg, Hollerich, were issued a first-person flyer titled "What Every Pilgrim Must Know," instructing readers on how to conduct themselves during the journey: "During the trip I stay with [the] group as much as possible, I participate in the joint rosary or sing a religious song with fellow pilgrims."[4] Not only were the Bonneweg pilgrims urged to stay together, they were also told what to silently pray as they walked past the Coat. "In the cathedral I see at the end of the middle aisle the Holy Coat. With great devotion I draw closer to the Holy garment and pray silently in my heart, 'Oh Jesus, let out your blood and your pain, it is not wasted on me, a poor sinner!'"[5] These 1933 pilgrims were instructed to think viscerally about the execution of Jesus, the divine sacrifice made for them. The Coat linked them to that event because

Figure 1.1. Pilgrims sing from their Pilgrim Books, 1933. BATr, Abt. 100, Nr. 003, "und singen die Pilger aus dem Pilgerbüchlein."
Soruce: BATr, Abt. 100, Nr. 003.

Figure 1.2. Pilgrims sing while waiting to enter the Trier cathedral for the opening ceremony, 2012.
Source: Holly Wade, 12 April 2012.

Jesus wore it during his life and ministry, even until the final moments before he was nailed to the cross. In 1933, song and prayer helped to keep order in the crowded city. Schmitt, a teacher who helped with the event, outlined the standard pilgrim experience, which included "religious preparation during normal congestion in the Jesuit Church.... [U]nder song and prayer the procession moved toward the cathedral."[6] Pilgrims made themselves heard; their prayers and songs regulated their movements through the city and fostered a sense of community. Prayer helped to keep the pilgrims focused on the purpose of their journey, to honour Christ, Mary, and John the Baptist via their garments.

In addition to the audible practices of prayer and song, Catholics claimed sacred places by marching. In the Rhineland, this practice was not limited to the pilgrimage years. Indeed, Catholics in Aachen held at least one major procession every year, the *Frohnleichnams-Prozession*, or Corpus Christi Procession. During this event, over forty local associations and organizations marched behind the Eucharist.[7] In addition, the city held processions on momentous occasions, such as the Rosary Sunday procession on 12 September 1915. This event was both to celebrate the *Gnadenbild der Mutter Gottes* (Blessed Statue of Mary) and to pray for protection during the First World War.[8] On Rosary Sunday, Aachen Catholic participants prayed specifically for the wounded, for honourable victory, and for a favourable peace in Germany. German Catholics often made processions outside of their churches and cathedrals.

Like Corpus Christi processions, the pilgrimage cortège began and ended at the cathedral. Also, like Corpus Christi, the closing processions at Aachen festivals meant bringing sacred objects into profane space.[9] Corpus Christi processions involved contests for public space, such as whether or not to disrupt public transportation to accommodate large processions. Aachen and Trier clergy had to secure permission for their events. In Aachen, pilgrimage organizers required approval of both local and district police to host the event and to carry out the public closing ceremony. Similarly, in 1891 Trier, Bishop Korum requested state approval for increased train activity to carry pilgrims from across Germany to the Holy Coat. However, Catholic processions were about much more than the use of public space. A procession visibly delineated insiders and outsiders and momentarily transformed public, shared spaces into sacred places.

Through an examination of their prayers, songs, and processions, this chapter reconstructs the sacred landscapes of pilgrims and clerics. The following traces pilgrim practices from interior (silent prayers) to exterior (public processions) to show, first, the varied meanings of pilgrimage. Travellers pointed to their motivations for visiting Aachen and Trier in their prayers and in their songs. They left home to find physical healing, for help with their finances or relationships, to ask for forgiveness, for adventure, and out of curiosity. Second, Rhenish religiosity illustrates how Catholics transformed public spaces into sacred places. Pilgrims took an active role in constructing the pilgrimage experience and did not always follow clerical instructions. What did pilgrims do? How did they travel to Trier and Aachen? And, upon arrival, what did they sing, pray, and expect? Over the course of a century, Rhenish pilgrimage experienced a technological revolution in one sense: from small groups walking together to thousands of individuals driving private automobiles and arriving via train. At the same time, there are striking continuities in Catholic public religious practices and pilgrimage processions in the century between 1832 and 1937.

Getting There: The Pressures of Pilgrimage Success

Newspapers and officials generally estimated how many people visited the Trier and Aachen relics on given days. This imprecision has resulted in several years without reliable pilgrim totals. For instance, several Aachen city estimates were completed by taking a count of individuals who came through the city gates. The peak Aachen pilgrimage occurred in 1881, after a decade of the Kulturkampf, when about one million pilgrims attended the event. The slump during the 1930 pilgrimage can be explained by the economic crisis that struck Germany; the resultant unemployment and uncertainty made travel difficult for potential pilgrims. Tables 1.1 and 1.2 summarizes the number of participants for each event.

Walking was an essential aspect of the Rhineland pilgrim experience.[10] In 1844, entire communities took to the road to visit the Holy Coat. As he approached Trier, Charles Edward Anthon described large processions "composed of the inhabitants of a single town or village, but their numbers were sometimes very great, often amounting to five or six thousand, and the distance from which they came such as to make some trial of their constancy."[11] These communal marches contained men, women, rich, and poor. Children dressed in white carried crucifixes or crosses at the head of the procession. Pilgrims hoisted banners of regional or Catholic significance at the front of the multiple columns.[12] The rest of the procession group followed, ideally in ascending age order, with the most elderly towards the end of the column. Priests marched alongside the winding procession train. In 1846 Aachen, officials assumed that people would walk because it was summer and the weather was favourable.[13] In 1902 a group walked from

Table 1.1. Number of participants for each event, Trier

Year	Attendance
1844	563,000*
1891	1,013,000[†]
1933	2,031,000[‡]

* The estimates for 1844 vary. Johannes Ronge, a contemporary, guessed there were about 500,000. Wolfgang Schieder, an historian, estimated the total to be around 450,000 because, he argues, individuals were likely counted multiple times. See Schieder, "Church and Revolution," 66.

[†] See appendix 2 for daily pilgrim totals.

[‡] See appendix 3 for daily pilgrim totals. Estimates usually run around 500,000 for 1844, 1 million for 1891, and 2 million for 1933. These more precise figures are taken from BATr, Abt. 90, Nr. 173, 346. An alternative total of 2,190,121, with a daily average of 44,700 appears in the statistical analyses in BATr, Abt. 90, Nr. 173, 609. Again, these figures are contested. For example, in 1891 the figure of 996,400 (with 672,000 coming from the Trier diocese) appears in BATr, Abt. 90, Nr. 173, 343. This count attributes the figure of more than one million to people seeing the Coat multiple times because they stayed overnight in Trier. But most accounts in the 1890s set the total at over one million. The increase in pilgrim numbers was reported throughout the city. Trier's city slaughterhouse kept track of how many animals the city butchered between 1 July and 10 September 1933 and estimated that 359,865 more kilograms, or 4,769 more animals, were consumed in Trier from 1 July to 10 September 1933 than in 1932. BATr, Abt. 90, Nr. 173, 461–2.

Niederlandenbeck to Aachen, roughly 190 kilometres.[14] Before the 1930s, most pilgrims arrived in Trier and Aachen as part of planned processions.

Processions were opportunities to publicly affirm and renew faith. For instance, in 1902 Franz Zander, vice president of the Aachen Catholic Workers Association, asked that his group be allowed to visit the Marienschrein.[15] He explained that the Workers Association had participated in 1895 and wanted to continue that tradition. For Zander, workers needed to be part of the *Heiligtumsfahrt* because they faced spiritual risk. "We hope [you are] the more likely to grant our request as indeed the working class is especially at risk for the dangers of faith and immoral heresies."[16] Zander thought that his 1200–1500 workers needed spiritual "strength and encouragement."[17] Through participation, by marching together to view the four Aachen treasures, Catholic workers, "from mature men to youth," would remember their faith and draw "new courage and strength" from the procession. Moving towards the relics, as a group, could return Catholics to their "neglected" and "holy religion" that was unrelentingly assailed by worldly temptation.

Table 1.2. Number of participants for each event, Aachen

Year	Dates	Attendance (figures, descriptions)
1832	9–24 July	15 July, 50–60,000, daily about 25,000*
1839	10–24 July	"Not so many people in city since the French Revolution army"[†]
1846	10–31 July	500,000 attended with Cologne Bishop von Geissel[‡]
1853	9–24 July	800,000 total, 36,000 at closing ceremony[§]
1860	9–24 July	16 July, 65–70,000, 15 July, 65,000, 22 July, 52,000[ǁ]
1867	9–24 July	119,000 by train, 60–65,000 each Sunday[#]
1874	10–24 July	700,000 total, 100,000 on busy days, both Sundays 150,000**
1881	9–24 July	1,000,000 total, 17 July, ≥ 90,000, three Sundays ca. 156,000[††]
1888	9–24 July	800,000 total, 15 July, 80–100,000, 24 July, 50–60,000[‡‡]
1895	9–24 July	421,925 total, 306,000 by train alone[§§]
1902	10–24 July	553,486 total[ǁǁ]
1909	9–28 July	774,483 total[##]
1916	First World War	No pilgrimage
1923	French Occupation	No pilgrimage
1925	10–26 July	ca. 775,000,*** 1,000,000 total
1930	10–27 July	ca. 400,000 total, 331,761 by train alone[†††]
1937	10–25 July	800,000 total; 120,000 attended final procession, 20,000 marched in the final procession[‡‡‡]

Note: See also appendix 5: "Pilgrimage Dates."

* "Inland," *Aachener Zeitung*, Montag, 16 July 1832; Lambertz, *Aachener Heiligtumsfahrt*, 10.

[†] Lambertz, 12.

[‡] Lambert, 22.

[§] "Deutschland," *Fliegende Taube*, 29 July 1852, No. 31: "daß die ganze 14 tägige Feier, trotzdem sich wohl an 800,000 Menschen zur Verehrung der hl. Reliquien eingefunden haben"; "Aachen, 25. Juli," *Aachener Zeitung*, Dienstag, 26 July 1853.

[ǁ] Lambertz, *Aachener Heiligtumsfahrt*, 34; "Aachen," *Fliegende Taube*, 10 August 1860; *Fliegende Taube*, 20 July 1860.

[#] Lambertz, 37; "Umschau," *Aachener Sonntagsblatt*, Sonntag, 21 July 1867, No. 29. *Aachener Zeitung* records 68,000 people coming on 12 July; see "Lokal-Nachrichten. Aachen," Sonntag, 14 July 1867. According to the article, 68,000 was equivalent to the population of Aachen in 1867, and on 19 July, there were no fewer than 60,712 people, perhaps as many as 100,000. See "Lokal Nachrichten. Aachen," *Aachener Zeitung*, 20 July 1867.

** Lambertz, 46; "Lokal-Nachrichten," *Echo der Gegenwart*, Sonntag, 19 July 1874, Bl. 3; "Zur Aachener Heiligthumsfahrt," *Sonntagsblatt der Germania*, 14 July 1895, No. 28.

[††] Lambertz, 50; "Lokales. Aachen," *Aachener Zeitung*, 18 July 1881. *Echo der Gegenwart* estimated that there were over 100,000 on 17 July. See "Aachen, 18 Juli," *Erstes Blatt*, Dienstag, 19 July 1881. "Zur Aachener Heiligthumsfahrt," *Sonntagsblatt der Germania*, 14 July 1895, No. 28.

[‡‡] Lambertz, 57; "Heiligtumsfahrt 1888. Aachen, 16. Juli," *Echo der Gegenwart, Erstes Blatt*, Dienstag, 17 July 1888; "Lokal-Nachrichten. Aachen, 25. Juli," *Politisches Tageblatt, Erstes Ausgabe*, Donnerstag, 26 July 1888.

[§§] Lambertz, 65; "Heiligthumsfahrt 1895 + Aachen, 25 Juli," *Echo der Gegenwart*, Freitag, 26 July 1895, *Erstes Blatt*.

[ǁǁ] "Aus Aachen und Umgebung," *Politisches Tageblatt*, 25 July 1937. Of these, the newspaper estimated that 225,942 individuals made the pilgrimage on foot. See also "Aachen," *Fliegende Taube*, Aubel-Mittwoch, 30 July 1902, No. 61. Lambertz has the total at 567,966, which he takes from the Polizeiberichte.

[##] Lambertz, *Aachener Heiligtumsfahrt*, 78. The 1909 and 1895 figures come from *Echo der Gegenwart*, Samstag, 16 October 1909, Bl. 5. This 1909 figure could have been lower, according to *Echo der Gegenwart*. See also correspondence with the Polizeiverwaltung, DAA, PA 66, "Aachen, 5 Februar 1925." The 1925 *Fliegende Taube* estimated 1909 participation to be closer to 2 million, 1,750,000. See "Kirchliches: Die Schlußfeierlichkeiten der *Aachener Heiligtumsfahrt*," *Fliegende Taube*, Samstag, 1 August 1925.

*** Lambertz, 87. See "Kirchliches: Die Schlußfeierlichkeiten der *Aachener Heiligtumsfahrt*," *Fliegende Taube*, Samstag, 1 August 1925: "Am letzten Tage der Heiligtumsfahrt war der Verkehr wieder besonders lebhaft. Der Gesamtbesuch der Heiligtumsfahrt ist amtlich noch nicht endgültig festgestellt, doch dürfte er die Ziffer von 1909 1,750,000, mindestens erreicht, wenn nicht überschritten haben."

[†††] Lambertz, 94, 97.

[‡‡‡] Lambertz, *Aachener Heiligtumsfahrt*, 103. Here Lennartz discusses other figures offered from other sources, including 500,000 and 450,000. However, 800,000 is most often used and that is why it is cited here. Selung, *Heiligtumsfahrt Aachen 1937*, 86–8.

For all of the time spent travelling, pilgrims were only briefly in proximity to the relics. In 1860, Provost Dr. Grossman and the Pilgrimage Committee notified pilgrim groups before their arrival that individuals would move continuously through the cathedral: "These processions [after leaving their station churches] alternately praying and singing through the great so-called Wolf Door [of the cathedral], [walk] up on the right side of the choir, then slowly, but without lingering, pass in front of the shrines, then [walk] down on the left side [of the choir] and through the so-called Kramer-door out of the church."[18] Pilgrims were not supposed to pause in front of the relics. For the majority of travellers, viewing sacred objects was a tiny fraction of their total experience.

Pilgrims encountered the relics in the context of established sacred space. In a typical Aachen pilgrimage, clergy displayed the relics from the cathedral's outdoor gallery during the morning. Various groups and regional towns had their own days to make special processions to see the relics. These processional orders were published in the local papers and posted in the towns of departure. The assigned groups had first access to the Wolf Door (*Wolfstür*) at 1:00 p.m. when clergy moved the relics from the cathedral balcony to the church interior. In 1874, several groups marched each day of the pilgrimage aside from the last day on 24 July. Thus, on 23 July the Sisters of Holy Francis, the Franciscan Orders, and the deanships of Siegburg, Uckerath, Blankenheim, and Steinfeld had access to the relics.[19] All four of these cities are in the Rhineland, and the farthest trip was 300 kilometres for the pilgrims from Steinfeld.

The Pilgrimage Committees struggled to accommodate procession leaders' requests and to maintain an efficient timetable of arrivals and departures. In 1909, J.W. Fischer planned to lead a processional group from Cologne to Aachen. He informed Canon Bellesheim that he anticipated the group would arrive around 8:00 a.m. His procession, Fischer continued, would report to the station church St. Michael, where he anticipated that they would sound the bells to announce their arrival. Fischer foresaw no difficulty in going to see the relics after his group prayed in St. Michael's Church.[20] In his response to Fischer's postcard, Bellesheim informed the Cologne cleric that none of his intended itinerary was possible. In fact, the cathedral would be closed on the desired morning because at 9:00 a.m. the sick were admitted into the church to touch the relics. Bells were also not allowed to sound at random in the city. Bellesheim explained that there was an established daily routine in place that had been approved by the police. The Cologne group would have to conform to that schedule. Apparently wary that Fischer might not get the message, Bellesheim also wrote that he would ask the priest at St. Michael's Church to pass on the same information when they arrived.[21]

To help regulate the flow of pilgrims to the cathedrals, both Aachen and Trier developed "station churches" (*Stationskirchen*) beginning in the 1840s. These "station churches" acted as staging areas for large processions. Pilgrim groups were assigned a local parish church and assembled inside before processing to the main cathedral. In 1846 Aachen, after a group viewed the four relics, pilgrims returned to their designated church to celebrate.[22] From there they either went home or to their local lodgings. In 1891 the Trier Pilgrimage Committee designated pilgrims not in a procession as "single pilgrims" (*Einzelpilger*). These *Einzelpilger* assembled at the Jesuit Church and were allowed to make processions throughout the day to the cathedral to view the Holy Coat. Thus, even if these unanticipated individual pilgrims made it into the city without a clerical guide, they still had to wait for a priest to take them from the Jesuit Church to the relic. To ease crowding, *Einzelpilger* arriving by train were asked to avoid congested areas and to use North Alley for their walk to the Jesuit Church.[23]

Buses, automobiles, and efficient rail connectivity made the participation of over two million 1933 pilgrims possible. On 1 September 1841 Cologne was linked to the wider Prussian train network, and in 1843 joined the Belgian network.[24] By 1860 Aachen was also added to the Prussian rail network. In 1860, Father Andreas, from Düsseldorf, led the Marian Sodality procession to Aachen. This group took the train from Düsseldorf to Kohlscheid and walked the remaining eight kilometres. By using multiple forms of transport, Düsseldorf pilgrims avoided a ninety-kilometre walk from Düsseldorf to Kohlscheid while preserving a procession before and after viewing the relics.[25] Train companies offered reduced prices based on group size. The Prussian railway – *Königliche Einsenbahn Direktion* – required 1881 Aachen groups to have at least thirty participants and to travel both to and from Aachen in order to qualify for a 50 per cent price reduction.[26] These special fares led to increasing numbers of pilgrim participants. In 1902, one newspaper stated, "In a century no Heiligtumsfahrt has drawn more pilgrims as in this year."[27] Trains made participation affordable and more accessible, but Germans still had to choose to get on the trains and to buy discounted tickets.

Pilgrims also purchased pilgrimage packages through private Catholic travelling companies. Whether on train or ship, these pilgrim itineraries emphasized the devotional element of the pilgrimage. Cologne pilgrims in 1933 had access to a private *Schiffswallfahrt* (ship pilgrimage). Participants travelled to Trier from Tuesday, 22 August through Thursday, 24 August 1933. They held Mass both below and on deck, complete with music and songs. Their first night they stopped in Bornhofen and held an evensong service. On the second day, the Cologne pilgrims again boarded their ship at 6:45 a.m. They held Mass on board before they arrived in Koblenz. From Koblenz they took a chartered train for pilgrims to Trier. While in the city, they not only venerated the Coat of Jesus, but also the legs of St. Matthew in the St. Matthew Basilica in Trier. Afterwards, they headed back to Koblenz and then returned to Bornhofen for an evening candle procession. On Thursday, they held Mass in the Bornhofen Grace Church and boarded their ship back to Cologne. The price was 19.75 Reichsmarks and included the train and ship fare, music, the Trier pilgrim badge (*Pilgerabzeichen / Trierer Domabzeichen*), printed prayers, and other paraphernalia, such as official pilgrimage postcards.[28] Children under fourteen only had to pay half price. Pilgrims also had the option of buying a Rhine panorama that was colourful, showed the river, and had "elegant text."[29]

New modes of transportation, including buses and automobiles, made it very difficult for the Trier episcopate to manage the 1933 pilgrimage. Church officials repeatedly asked pilgrims to travel in registered groups. After a parish enquired about attending, the Pilgrimage Committee requested additional information: when they would arrive and depart, how many cars they would have, the number of pilgrims in their group, whether or not a priest led their group, and, if possible, from which street they would approach the cathedral.[30] Once the Pilgrimage Committee had a sense of the size of the group they sent the parish priest instructions that included their station church, the time of their procession into the cathedral, and their scheduled time of departure.[31] After the 1933 event was underway, however, the Pilgrimage Committee learned that this system was ineffective because it relied on pilgrim groups writing in to announce their arrival. The Trier Pilgrimage Committee looked to local clergy to help minimize the number of *Einzelpilger* by discouraging individual travelers. Cathedral Vicar Fuchs, for example, asked that Fräulein Lucie Ruffert, from Eckersdorf, contact Father Drzyzga, in Schomberg/Oberschlesien, because he was coordinating a pilgrimage group to Trier from 15 to 20 August.[32] Despite these efforts, 1933 had the largest turnout of individual pilgrims and unregistered small groups of pilgrims.

Clergy struggled to cope with the volume of *Einzelpilger* travelling by bus and automobile in 1933.[33] These individual pilgrims are direct evidence for the growth of automobile travel in Germany from the pre–First World War period to the Weimar Republic.[34] They also point to new individual attitudes towards pilgrimage that developed between 1891 and 1933. Rather than taking to the roads, rails, and rivers with

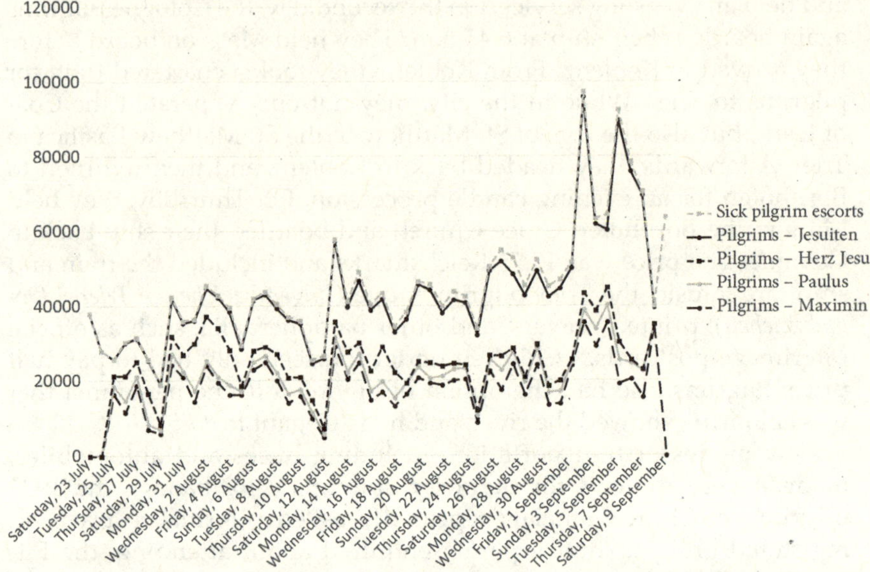

Figure 1.3. Number of pilgrims by station church, 1933.
Source: Data from BATr, Abt. 90, Nr. 173, 489. This is a reproduction of a hand-drawn
line graph that appears at BATr, Abt. 90, Nr. 173, 615. But data for both charts come from
p. 489, a large sheet that details the number of pilgrims and processions each day of the
1933 event.

their parish community, those who could afford it preferred to make
their own way to Trier. The chart above reveals the steady increase in
the number of unregistered pilgrims (*Jesuitenkirche*) through the 1933
pilgrimage. Unsurprisingly, the chart also indicates that the peak days
of pilgrimage were Saturday and Sunday.

In her 1933 diary, Cäcilie, who hosted individual pilgrims and volunteered for the Women's Stewards (*Frauenordnungsdienst*), complained
about the large number of *Einzelpilger* in the city. For her, the logistical quagmire could be blamed on the *Einzelpilger* "whose number was
not previously assessed."[35] Cäcilie hosted several visiting pilgrims in
her home. Two of her guests, from Freiburg, arrived as *Einzelpilger*. She
urged them to try to make the 5 a.m. Jesuit Church procession. They
dressed warmly and took food with them when they left. When the
two women returned much later that day, they complained bitterly that
overcrowding from the thousands of unscheduled *Einzelpilger* arriving
at the church had become life-threatening. The conditions were especially dangerous for children and the elderly.[36]

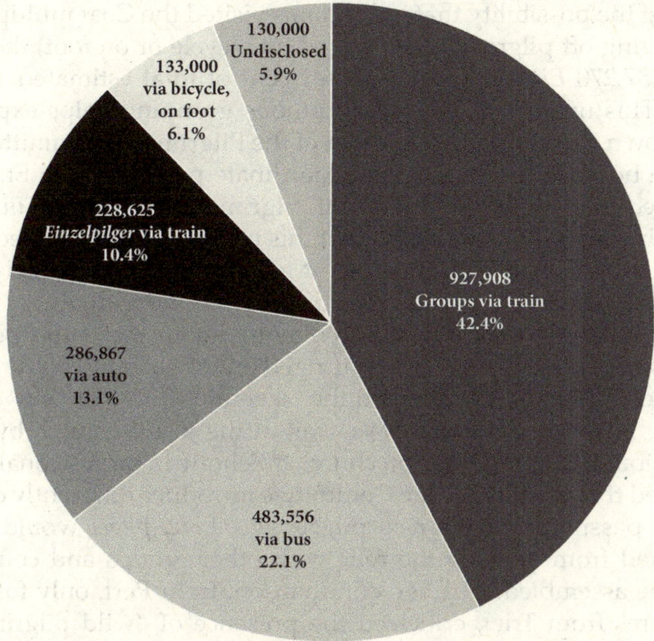

Figure 1.4. Pilgrim modes of transport, 1933.
Source: BATr, Abt. 90, Nr. 173, 489.

Clergy preferred that pilgrims attend the pilgrimage as part of a procession. Cardinal Karl Joseph Schulte, in Cologne, had priests read out a statement to this effect on the Feast of the Ascension, a holy day of obligation: "The Trier Pilgrimage Committee desires that pilgrims only visit Trier in closed, priestly-led processions, but not in small tourist groups."[37] As in pilgrimages past, parishes received train discounts if they went via the Trier Pilgrimage Committee and Cologne Diocese. The cardinal established a temporary office, led by General Secretary Schroeder, to coordinate special trains (*Sonderzüge*) from Cologne to Trier. These *Sonderzüge* included reduced prices from the National Railways (*Reichseisenbahn*).[38]

The Trier Pilgrimage Committee kept detailed records of how pilgrims arrived to the city.[39] Because travellers were classified by mode of transportation, it is difficult to get at a definitive counting of the *Einzelpilger*. However, evidence from correspondence suggests that, individuals and small groups who came by car and about half of bus pilgrims neglected to register before arrival. Taken together (completely ignoring the possibility that individuals visited the Coat multiple times and leaving off pilgrims who arrived by bicycle or on foot) there were about 757,270 *Einzelpilger*, or, 35 per cent of total estimated 1933 pilgrims. This unanticipated and enormous grouping helps explain the breakdown in procession schedules of the Pilgrimage Committees. Nik. Mohr, a bookbinder who helped coordinate pilgrims from St. Paulus, estimated that about one-quarter of pilgrims in 1933 were *Einzelpilger*, or roughly 500,000. Mohr noted that this type of pilgrim arrived in Trier primarily by bus and automobile.[40] Mohr's observations likely underestimated *Einzelpilger* by a quarter of a million individuals.

Local volunteers complained frequently about these unexpected attendees because their presence infringed on the sacrality of the pilgrimage. The St. Maximin staff noted that several "shifty" or "sly" (*schlaue*) pilgrims avoided the *Einzelpilger* wait at the Jesuit Church by joining processions out of their station church.[41] Schmitt, a professional teacher, proposed that the Pilgrimage Committee introduce differently coloured pilgrim passports for the next pilgrimage. *Einzelpilger* would then be prevented from viewing the relic with other groups and could more easily be assembled.[42] Father Windhausen, from Perl, only forty-eight kilometres from Trier, criticized the presence of "wild pilgrims" and waiting in line for a long time. Windhausen had a particularly unpleasant interaction with three youth from Mainz who had joined his procession without permission. Windhausen tried to get the SA (*Sturmabteilung*) security guards to remove them, but it was a security guard who had put the interlopers in with his group in the first place. Father Windhausen's complaints only meant that the youths were able to go into the cathedral before his procession, "victorious and deliberate." Why, he asked, did the Pilgrimage Committee do nothing against these "savage pilgrims"? "This is no pilgrimage" the priest continued. True, there were massive numbers attending the event, but he doubted they were gaining much spiritual benefit from their participation.[43] Vicar Fuchs responded to Windhausen and thanked him for his frank observations. The Trier cleric confessed that the Pilgrimage Committee had overlooked the possibility of mass individual travel from the outset, though he hoped that Windhausen had seen the new press announcements. Those pilgrims arriving by bus and car were now being issued special tickets. Of course, Fuchs conceded, it would not be possible to stop all confusion during the pilgrimage.[44]

The three-quarters of a million *Einzelpilger* set off hours of delays for pilgrims who had appointed times to visit the Holy Coat. Deputy Leader (*Stellvertr. Leiters*) Georg Rudolf, for example, noted how tickets were supposed to soothe the minds of pilgrims who stood in line:

"You do not wait in vain. No one can press forward" or jump the line because of the ticket.[45] But this aspirational system routinely collapsed into chaos, especially during busy weekends. Magda Müller, a volunteer, described the last few weeks as a blur of unending pilgrims: "And so it goes, day after day and without a break and without ceasing. More and more people come, the evenings are getting later and sometimes you want to give up hope when the crowds have no end."[46] Anton Loch, a teacher, wrote to officials, "With large crowds of pilgrims it happened very often that the procession had to stop and wait for hours in front of the barrier. Then the leader had a lot of trouble to prevail so that his procession was allowed through the barrier and into the cathedral square."[47] Father Nicolay from Thörnich wrote to Trier officials to protest that processions that arrived after his group were allowed into the cathedral before him. He did not understand why pilgrims who had arrived with no procession were also allowed to gain access to the Coat. Nicolay was supposed to meet with a group of young people from his parish who had driven to Trier. However, the young parishioners decided they did not want to wait in line and managed to go through the cathedral and return home before Nicolay even got into the church.[48] Father Gerhartz from Densborn (Eifel) agreed. The risk of waiting for hours, he explained, should be on the pilgrims who arrived unannounced in their cars, not on scheduled processions.[49] The mass of people was so intense that the police and the SA had to regulate processions entering the Cathedral Square.

Overwhelmed Jesuit Church leaders had no choice but to send large processions, at times containing 4,000–5,000 people, on to the cathedral even though they knew that they would have to wait outside for hours before they got to the entrance.[50] Georg Rudolf noted that "our beautiful procession plan" rarely worked for those coming from the Jesuit Church.[51] Ideally, the *Einzelpilger* were to be released at set times and allowed to go to the cathedral. However, when they arrived at the Cathedral Square, there were processions already waiting in line to view the relic. This meant that the *Einzelpilger* procession leader had to offer an "energetic performance" so that the scheduled procession could join the queue to enter the cathedral. Furthermore, the *Einzelpilger* were considered an "annoying side effect." Their appearance at the Cathedral Square often set off "great restlessness" within other groups whose members had already waited a long time.

Johann Jansen travelled to Trier from Cologne on 28 August 1933. He wrote to pilgrimage officials to explain his failed pilgrimage. Jansen made his way to Trier via Koblenz and arrived in the morning. He secured a ticket to be part of the 4 p.m. *Einzelpilger* procession from the

Jesuit Church to the cathedral. At the Cathedral Square, however, he grumbled that "we stood only 1. 2. 3. hours and were by then not even on the actual Cathedral Square." At 7:45 p.m. the last train connection from Trier to Cologne departed, so Jansen had to leave the city without even seeing the Coat. To add insult to injury he ran into a group of people he knew at the Trier train station. They had arrived later in the day and were able to gain access to the cathedral.[52] Jansen was upset that he had lost the time and money and not been able to venerate the relic: "Is this fair treatment?"[53] Another pilgrim, who only signed as "One for many" (*Eine für viele*) noted that they had to stand in the street for four to five hours and got badly sunburned.[54]

The Jesuit Church staff, under the subheading "Here an honest word!," informed the Trier Pilgrimage Committee of their many difficulties during the pilgrimage. They had too few priests, too few seminarians, too few leaders, and too few prayer and song leaders.[55] There was not enough space on busy days for mustering processions even when Jesuit Church coordinators took over the adjacent two schoolyards.[56] In short, the Jesuit Church office believed that if they had more help and room, especially on peak days like Sundays, a great number of their logistical problems could have been alleviated. Still another *Einzelpilger* coordinator complained that the Pilgrimage Committee should not have shut out individual pilgrims between 1:00 p.m. and 5:00 p.m. Doing so had created chaos on Sundays, and they would have been better served by reserving this time for the unregistered pilgrims.[57]

Thus in 1933 Trier, the sheer number of participants threatened pilgrims' ability to concentrate on the Holy Coat. For Jesuit Church coordinators, the large number of pilgrims placed in each procession meant that the solemnity of the event was lost. People shoved one another, and those at the back of the Jesuit Church processions could neither hear nor follow along with the prayers and songs emanating from the front of the procession.[58] Georg Rudolf also worried that the spiritual focus of the pilgrimage was lost in the crowds. The Jesuit Church procession leaders had to shuffle pilgrims around to keep things in order. Then, at the outdoor services, the priest's words "echoed in the great square" and went "unheard in the wind."[59] Wilh[elm] Pfoh echoed these concerns: "[If] one gathered the *Einzelpilger*, those who arrived in Trier by train or car, in particular at station churches [so that they could] hear a homily and prayers in their native language, the religious goal of the pilgrimage would be better fulfilled."[60] In 1933 Trier, the primary tension was between individual pilgrims and groups, efficiency and piety.

The Pilgrimage Committee did their best to respond to the outraged letters from both priests and pilgrims. For example, on Sunday, 20 August,

Table 1.3. Jesuit Church procession ticket numbers

Procession time	Total tickets	Ticket nos.
5:00 a.m.	1,000	1–1,000
5:20 a.m.	1,000	1,000–1,999
5:40 a.m.	1,500	2,000–3,499
6:40 a.m.	1,500	3,500–4,999
7:40 a.m.	1,500	5,000–6,499
9:40 a.m.	3,000	6,500–9,499
Noon	1,500	9,500–10,0000 / A1–A999
1:00 p.m.	1,500	A1,000–A2,499
5:00 p.m.	1,500	A2,500–A3,999
7:30 p.m.	1,500	A4,000–A5,499
9:30 p.m.	500	A5,500–A6,000

Source: Data from BATr, Abt. 90, Nr. 100.
Note: "A" indicated afternoon tickets.

they posted a large pronouncement for *Einzelpilger*. In the flyer, the Pilgrimage Committee stated their aim of issuing tickets to regulate the number of *Einzelpilger* moving towards the Holy Coat throughout the day.

However, setting aside certain times and tickets proved inadequate. The mass of pilgrims already on the Cathedral Square made the job of the *Einzelpilger* procession leader very difficult.

Observers were divided over whether or not the popularity of the pilgrimage threatened Catholic sacred practices. Herr Quins noted the piety of these visitors: "A great number of the *Einzelpilger* took care to prepare themselves by receiving the sacraments before visiting the Holy Coat. One can well say that the church and the altar rail [*Kommunionbank* (sic)] in the early morning hours were never empty."[61] Quins also noted that individual pilgrims were discriminated against when they tried to get into the cathedral; some of them had to wait over a day for access. This situation was especially absurd for Quins because *Einzelpilger* undertook a more expensive trip than those who rode the discounted trains (*Sonderzüge*). Georg Rudolf was surprised at the resilience of the Trier pilgrims: "Most of the pilgrims came with the right attitude, not as spectators, but as pilgrims." Rudolf explained that as pilgrims they were able to endure the hardships they encountered.[62] In other words, he did not think physical suffering from walking and standing hours on end hindered pilgrims from experiencing the spiritual elements of their journey.

Pilgrimage volunteers, attendees, and police all noted that 1933 was a departure from previous Rhenish pilgrimages. Traditionally pilgrimages reaffirmed a communal commitment to the Catholic faith. The influx of individual pilgrims, made possible by new modes of transportation, threatened the sanctity of the pilgrimage. Their unanticipated presence, combined with the summer heat, the confusion of procession schedules, and the increased security all made focusing on the Coat difficult. In their correspondence to pilgrimage officials, pilgrims lamented the fact that the public spaces were so contested. During the preceding opening and closing ceremonies, clergy and laity came together to march through Aachen and Trier. By carrying relics through their cities, Catholics transported divine presence out of the cathedral into public space.

Public Commemoration: Packing and Unpacking Relics

Opening and closing ceremonies brought together a range of Rhineland Catholics in a public celebration of shared religiosity. Aachen church officials organized the first major city-wide and publicly advertised procession to commemorate the opening of the pilgrimage in 1874.[63] The 1874 Opening Day Parade included sixteen groups, which were divided on the basis of flag and ribbon, including the Aachen Reading Association and the Sacraments Brotherhood.[64] The 1888 pilgrimage opened on 9 July at 7 p.m. with a massive procession. The Opening Day Large Pageant (*Eröffnungstage Großer Festzug*) consisted of thirty-two separate participant groupings. These troops were drawn from several different clubs, including the Gesellschaft Constantia, Quirinusverein, Piusverein, and local choirs. The procession continued the tradition of incorporating varied professions such as bakers, hair stylists, carpenters, and butchers. These participants marched through the Aachen streets four abreast, with the exception of singers, who moved through the city eight across.[65]

The Aachen opening processions grew larger over time and reflected the increasing importance of Catholic associational life after the Kulturkampf. Fifty-seven separate groups went on procession in 1895. Like in 1888, though, the number of designated groups does not capture the full number of associations, as there were twelve different units under "the Burtscheid Associations." After 1874, diverse clubs and affiations processed behind clergy and the relics: Brewer Guild, Welder Guild, and Barrel-Maker Journeyman League.[66] In 1902, at least sixty-three different groups marched through Aachen, including the "ox and pig butchers, bakers, painters and house painters."[67] In 1909, there were forty-two different groups, but they now reflected a specifically Catholic identity: St. Mary's Church Choir, Charlemagne Shooting Guild, Youth Congregation of St. John, Artisans Association of St. Joseph,

Men's Congregation, etc. In other words, at the 1909 Opening Day Procession the associations, clubs, and guilds that processed through the city of Aachen were largely the same as those of the nineteenth-century processions, but now took on names that reflected their Catholicism. For example, in 1909, unlike in 1888, professional associations either self-identified as Catholic – Catholic Workers and Artisans Association Aachen I, Catholic Teachers Association – or with a particular saint, such as the Workers Association of St. Joseph.[68] This shift towards Catholic labels further illustrates the importance of being seen as a supporter of the community relics.[69]

Clergy worked closely with local municipal authorities to coordinate procession routes and to ensure the safety of pilgrim crowds. Aachen Prelate Dr. Bellesheim sought Police President Hamm's approval of the 1909 closing procession route. The adopted path went from the cathedral, down Annastraße, Löthergraben, Jakobstraße, Markt, Großkölnstraße, Komphausbadstraße, Peterstraße, Friedrich Wilhelmplatz, Kapuzinergraben, Kleinmarschierstraße, Schmiedstraße, and Fischmarkt before returning to the Aachen cathedral.[70] Aachen clergy continued to use this basic route through 1937.[71] During the 1937 closing procession, the crowds were so large that the police had to muster at major intersections to ensure order, including the corners of Annastraße/Löhergraben and Löhergraben/Jesuitenstraße.[72] Ultimately, the *Bistumsblatt Passau* noted that approximately 20,000 men, one cardinal, and four bishops walked during the closing ceremony. This massive procession drew around 120,000 onlookers.[73] Like 1933 Trier, the 1937 Aachen pilgrimage attracted notable attendance.

Alongside Catholic associations, social elites consistently participated in the Aachen and Trier pilgrimage closing ceremonies. In 1874, Pilgrimage Committee member Dr. Schlünkes responded to ticket requests from the Regierungs Präsident, local lawyers, the Charlemagne Association, principals of schools, local clergy, the postal director, the district court president, the commercial court president, and the president of the Chamber of Commerce, among others.[74] Like individuals, large groups had to request tickets if they wanted to attend the opening ceremony, closing ceremony, or participate in the reliquary processions. In 1902, Cathedral Canon Bellesheim informed club and association leaders that they would receive tickets that allowed them to participate in the closing ceremony.[75] The 1933 Trier Pilgrimage Committee invited local priests, professors, the postmaster, the Reichsbank director in Trier, the mayor (who offered seven spots to the Nazi Party city council faction), the school principal of Kaiser Wilhelm Gymnasium, the director of the Provincial Museum Trier, the District Leader (*Kreisleiter*) of

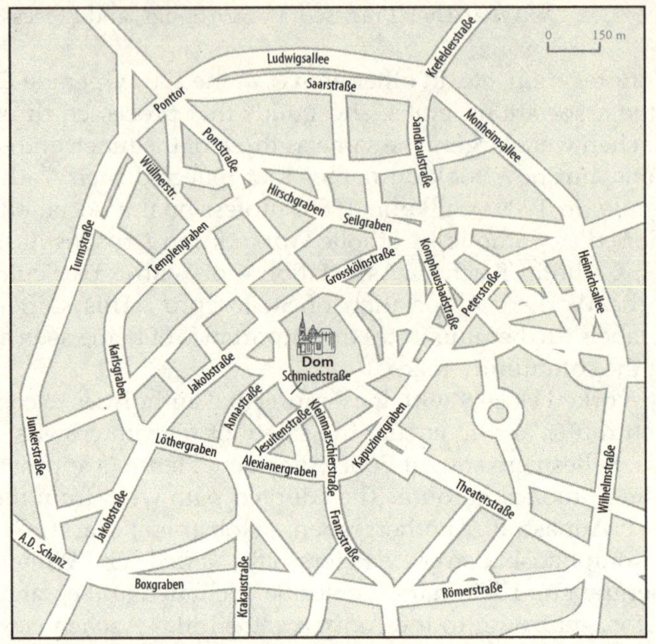

Map 1.1. Aachen *Altstadt* (old city).
Source: University of Wisconsin Cartography Lab. From ZBA, 1965 envelope, 65.1218, 1–11, *1965 Heiligtumsfahrt Aachen*.

Figure 1.5. Cardinal Schulte of Cologne (*centre*) during a 1930 procession.
Source: DAA, PA 81.

Figure 1.6. Bishop Bornewasser of Trier (*wearing white mitre*) holding up the Loincloth of Jesus for assembled crowds in Aachen.
Source: DAA, PA 81.

Figure 1.7. Reliquary procession, Aachen 1930.
Source: DAA, PA 81.

the Trier Nazi Party, local physicians, the director of the provincial institution for the deaf, Ortsgruppe Director of the Trier-Mitte Nazi Party, the City Police Director, abbots of local monasteries, etc.[76] These guests lent their prestige to the pilgrimage ceremonies.

Taking into account the highly diverse social makeup of participants, church officials worked diligently to map out the processional order.[77] In 1888, a music corps preceded the Aachen Charlemagne and Katharina Guard organizations. These were followed by groups carrying the relics of Leo and Charlemagne. Throughout the twenty-eight different organizations, choirs, musical groups, and relics punctuated the procession.[78] German Catholic leaders came out in force, including abbots, prioresses, parish priests, and bishops from across Western Europe. Relics rested literally on priests' shoulders reverently carried in elaborate reliquaries, illuminated with torch light and blessed with incense as they made their way through the city and back to the cathedral.

Processions not only offered Catholic organizations and leaders an opportunity to parade; they also brought sacred objects into public spaces (see appendix 7 for the procession order of the 1867 Aachen closing ceremony). In figure 1.8, local clergy hoist three "Charlemagne group" relics: the Charlemagne Bust (*Karlsbüste*) containing part of his skull, the Leo Bust (*Leosbüste*), and the Charlemagne Shrine (*Karlsschrein*) containing Charlemagne's leg bones.[79] Interspersed between relic groupings, different organizations and choirs sang and prayed as they wound their way through Aachen's old city. In 1888, the Male Congregations accompanied the Charlemagne Shrine, which contained the few remaining bones of the emperor. Any bishops present, in full vestments, accompanied the other main cathedral reliquary, the Marian Shrine, which housed the four Aachen relics between pilgrimages. Each bishop carried smaller relics and was flanked by two chaplains.[80] Clergy bore other small relics, including the Philip II chapel and the Karl IV chapel.[81] In addition, they exhibited several smaller relics, such as the Lothar cross; one of Charlemagne's talismans: a medallion of two crystal spheres containing hair of the Virgin Mary; and an heirloom (*Erbstück*) of Pepin the Short (Charlemagne's father), which was said to be a gift from either Pope Zacharias or Pope Stefan.[82] The closing procession in 1933 honoured the committees that made the event possible, including the art, sick, press, Mass, and finance committees.[83] Following these groups marched the honour guard of several churches, the cathedral choir, and the Mass attendants of the station churches.

During closing ceremonies, clergy and laity oriented themselves towards the Aachen and Trier relics. Like those in Aachen, Trier processions followed a circular pattern, beginning and ending at the cathedral.

Figure 1.8. Carrying the Charlemagne Shrine (*Karlsschrein*) out of the Aachen cathedral, 1909.
Source: DAA, DAA Andenken, 1909.

After exiting the church, the bishop led pilgrims along Fleischstraße, Brückenstraße, Jüdemerstraße, across the Viehmarkt to Neustraße, Brotstraße, then continued onto Grabenstraße and Palaststraße before returning to the cathedral.[84] In 1844, at the closing ceremony Bishop Arnoldi led participants through the street, singing out "Herr, Großer Gott!" as they walked. The 1844 Trier closing ceremony lasted two hours and was preceded by a candle-lit procession. Like Aachen, Trier included many religious and professional organizations. The Bachelor Sodality, for instance, contained forty-three firefighters, seven shoemakers, nineteen butchers, and Trier sailors.[85] Individual members of associations, like the Sailors Union (*Schiffer Gewerkschaft*), purchased their own candles at the cathedral for the event.[86]

A detailed description of closing ceremonies further reveals the experiences of Rhenish pilgrims. Both cities had formalized practices for honouring their objects before sealing them away at the close of a pilgrimage. In 1933, Bishop Franz Rudolf Bornewasser (1866–1951) praised and knelt before the Coat. He treated the Coat like the Eucharist. Bornewasser blessed the Holy Coat and passed around it with incense.[87] He then applied the incense with rehearsed choreography. First the bishop bent himself in the direction of the relic while the assembled pilgrims remained kneeling. After briefly kneeling himself,

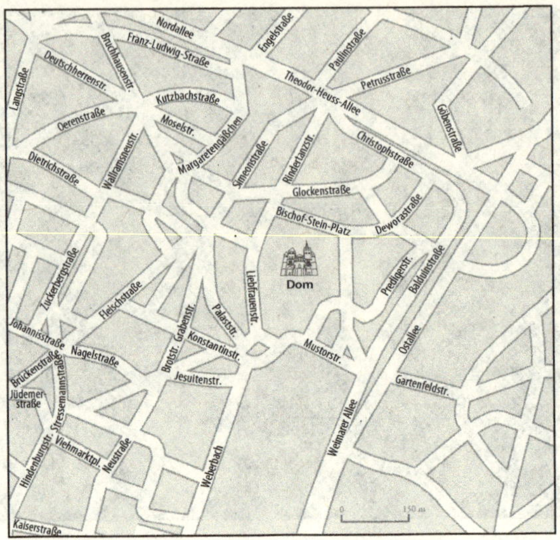

Map 1.2. Trier *Altstadt* (old city).
Source: University of Wisconsin Cartography Lab, based on the map "Stadtplan,"
Paulinus: Die Tageszeitung zur Wallfahrt, Trier, 13 April 2012, 16.

Bornewasser crossed the relic with a reliquary containing a piece of Jesus's cross. He kissed the censer and knelt with the Coat to his right. When he stood, the bishop began an elaborate interaction with the Coat. "Give up censer. Kiss: first censer, then hand. Genuflect before and after [waving] incense over the Coat. Take the censer. Kiss: first hand, then censer. Descend from altar."[88] The bishop began the closing ritual with a Pontifical Mass and a homily. The assembled then sang the "Te Deum" and a song to honour the Holy Coat. During the second song the bishop once again applied incense and began to cover the Coat. Finally, the pilgrims present followed the bishop in singing the first two verses of "Großer Gott wir loben Dich."[89] The 1933 Pilgrimage Committee had elaborate directions for the Credo, another round of incense, for reading the Gospel, and for what to do following the homily. Reverence was not to be improvised.

The Aachen closing ceremonies closely followed the schedules of preceding pilgrimages. For example, in 1860 Aachen, following the 8:00 a.m. Mass on Tuesday, 24 July, pilgrims had one last opportunity to look upon the relics. At 5:00 p.m. the cathedral doors were closed and the bells sounded to summon the musicians and singers. By 5:30 p.m. the mayor, city officials, municipal authorities, and invited clergy gathered in the cathedral. They sat in the choir, with the four Aachen relics spread on the table. The leaders faced outwards towards the main cathedral door, the Wolf Door. Together, these men began to sing Psalm Cantate 95, "Sing to the Lord a new song, sing to the Lord all the earth."[90] Meanwhile, guards opened up the doors and allowed pilgrims to fill the church. Cathedral officials stepped forward to the altar, accompanied by two acolytes and two assistants. As the song continued, these clerics blessed the relics with incense and stood aside for the sermon. Afterward, the officials and those assembled sang Psalm 148 Laudate Dominum, "O praise the Lord from the Heavens," accompanied by the organ.[91] After singing, clergy lifted up the relics for all assembled to see. They then put the relics back onto the altar on the dais and wrapped each relic in new silk for storage for the coming seven years. Priests carried the relics to the sacristy to be resealed. They were flanked by city officials holding candles. While the relics were wrapped and stored, the assembled crowd sang alternatively the "Salve Regina," accompanied by the orchestra, and the "Laudate Dominum," led by the organ. Finally, with the relics stored, the officials and assembled sang out the "Te Deum," "We praise thee O God." At this point fireworks (*Böller*) went off and the church bells of Aachen sounded the official closing ceremony of the pilgrimage. Officials gathered around the altar to sign the "Closing Protocol" verifying that the relics had been stowed and resealed. Official signatures verifying the integrity of the relics were common for Aachen. In 1874, the mayor and city officials helped to pack away the relics by verifying that they had not been tampered with and by affixing a seal to the relic silk.[92] The organ continued to play as the faithful left the cathedral and returned to their homes "in silence and devotion" (*in aller Stille und Andacht*).[93] They had sanctified the city for another seven years.

Talking with God: Pilgrimage, Praises, and Petitions

With scripted and spontaneous prayers, pilgrims identified themselves audibly as members of a Christian community. Participant petitions communicated their hopes and concerns as they made their way towards Trier and Aachen. Prayer was essential for preparing travellers to encounter the divine in the relics. As one student recalled in 1933, "It was in the afternoon, around 5:30 p.m., that we went singing and praying into the cathedral."[94] By praying, pilgrims focused their attention on why they made the journey to view the Holy Coat and Marian Shrine. Aachen pilgrims received an indulgence in February 1853 from Pius IX for attending that year's pilgrimage. To receive the indulgence pilgrims needed only to travel to the cathedral and perform prayer with devotion.[95]

Prayer was a central component of pilgrimage ceremonies. In Aachen, prayer was scheduled into the pilgrimage protocols. In 1874, "these processions go, alternating with prayers and songs, by the great so-called Wolf Door into the cathedral."[96] When Aachen clergy opened Charlemagne's reliquary for analysis in 1906 the process began with a prayer.[97] And when Charlemagne's bones were once more laid to rest, the clergy began the resealing ceremony in prayer.[98] In 1933, pilgrims had prescribed songs and prayers in hand before departing for Trier. The Pilgrimage Committee worked hard to make sure priests registered their groups ahead of time so pilgrims would have recommended prayers for their procession.[99] All pilgrims were instructed to pray. The sick, for instance, were not passive when they were presented with the Loincloth of Jesus in Aachen, but were expected to pray the rosary to prepare themselves before a cleric touched them with the cloth.[100]

Beyond sick pilgrims, prayer was a life-and-death practice for Rhenish Catholics during the First World War. On 3 August 1914, as the war broke out across Europe, Aachen clerics opened the Marian Shrine to ask Charlemagne, Mary, John the Baptist, and Jesus for protection and guidance during the coming conflict.[101] At 8:00 a.m. on 11 May 1915, just four days after a German U-boat sank the *Lusitania*, Aachen clergy again opened the reliquary to pray over the relics. They hoped that God would protect them during the uncertainties of the war. After confirming that the relics were intact and had not been disturbed since the last consultation, the mayor, city council members, the provost, and other clergy offered their prayer while standing over the exposed relics. Their petition radiated out from the cathedral: "May God, through the powerful intercession of our holy patron saint, the patroness, the Blessed Virgin Mother of God Mary, St. John the Baptist, and St. Emperor Charlemagne protect our church (*Münster*) and our city Aachen, our beloved Emperor and King Wilhelm II and the whole German Fatherland, and in the future graciously protect them and preserve them from harm."[102] The assembled city officials and clergy huddled around the Marian Shrine and invoked divine protective presence. God would hear their prayer, offered so close to his son's swaddling clothes, and would preserve their own sons and their city from the well-known horrors of combat that raged in the opening months of the conflict.

Clerics also offered prayers, in lieu of funds, for individuals who asked for financial assistance from the profits of the pilgrimage. To Frau Hubert Serve, in Jünkerath, Domkapitular Fuchs explained that the diocese was rich in prayer, but short on monetary resources in 1933: "On behalf of His Episcopal Grace I am writing to you in response to your letter dated 30 July. It is unfortunately not possible to fulfill your request. You are in error if you believe that money is abundantly flowing currently in Trier. We, leaders of the pilgrimage, are happy when we can cover the large expenses of the pilgrimage. There has also been such a torrent of petitions that the fulfillment of these requests cannot even be imagined." Many Catholics looked to the Trier event for financial assistance in their moments of trouble, but had to content themselves with divine petitions: "His Episcopal Grace will gladly remember you and your deceased father in prayer."[103]

For some clergy, prayer not only protected but could be mobilized against societal division. In 1933, Trier officials publicly clarified that prayer was unifying. Father Ekkelhard, a Franciscan from Paderborn, called on Trier officials to make the Coat a symbol of German unity: "During the Exhibition the Coat could be held in an irenic, solemn sermon with subsequent devotion about the reunification of Germany. Especially considering that the Coat is a symbol of unity, it must be so good to talk about the unity of faith and to mainly pray the same."[104] Ekkelhard went on to call for the Catholic people to rise up in a "prayer crusade" (*Gebetskreuzzug*) to this effect. In response, Domkapitular Fuchs avowed that any political rallies were not connected to the Coat because Trier officials coordinated devotionals themselves.[105] Furthermore, as a Franciscan priest, Ekkelhard should have refrained from politicizing the relic.[106] As the Holy Coat was not a civic symbol, Fuchs instructed that devotions directed towards the relic should be channelled to the heavenly, not the earthly city.

In the 1930s, as National Socialism restricted Catholic associational life and openly challenged church doctrine, clerics focused on the power of prayer, and their petitions often contained allusions to storms, tempests, and combat. Weihbischof Sträter closed out the 1937 Aachen pilgrimage by praying, "Let a storm of prayer roar up to the sky for our every need, for our families, for our beloved country, for our Holy Church!"[107] For Bishop Bornewasser, pilgrim prayer set loose a storm of grace from heaven: "This is a singing and praying day and night, this is a cyclone from the heart. I thank God that I am able to tap into this current of grace."[108] In 1937, Provost Sträter viewed the pilgrimage as an opportunity to bombard heaven: "[The Aachen pilgrimage is] a valuable opportunity to send to heaven a tempest of prayers for church, for *Volk*, for Fatherland from hundreds of thousands of people."[109] Bishop Bornewasser's 1933 prayer was that the pilgrims be both protected and take the journey as a foretaste of eternity. "Oh Christ, you Divine King of the nations, bless all who make the pilgrimage to the Holy Coat under the sign of the cross. The Trier journey was to be a guide to their entire life path, may it also guarantee a happy journey into eternity."[110] The pilgrimage did not end in Trier, but continued even after pilgrims died.

Pilgrims prayed both on their way to Aachen and Trier, while in the cities, and on their way home. In the 1937 "Homily Sketch for the 1937 Aachen Pilgrimage," officials described the pilgrimage as "primarily a matter of prayer."[111] And through prayer, pilgrims drew closer to the sacred centre of the relics. The author of the "Homily Sketch" affirmed God's omnipotence, but also taught pilgrims that there were places in the world where God was more accessible: "There are venerable and sacred sites where the prayer fervency is stronger, the grace greater." The sheer number of participants lent legitimacy to pilgrim petitions. Mass participation led to increased prayer efficacy: "Rarely in life [do] you get such a deep religious feeling as when thousands make common cause, in full confession of their faith." The unity of pilgrim prayer created a "prayer tower" that "must penetrate the sky."[112] Catholic theology taught that one could talk to God instantly from anywhere and about anything.[113] At the same time pilgrim pamphlets and prayers stressed that being physically near a garment that God's son had worn meant that a prayer carried more weight, or that the message had to travel a shorter distance to reach the divine. "The devotional prayers in the Cathedral Square were a wonderful way to prepare one's heart for the visit to the Holy Coat," wrote Father Saffrath from Aachen. Saffrath went on to ask that the Pilgrimage Committee continue to remember him and the Roman Church in their prayers during the exhibition.[114]

Prayer reaffirmed German Catholic identity throughout this century. In 1925, the clergy prayed, "We thank you for the great unmerited grace that we are Catholic" after they stored the relics.[115] And, in this prayer, God was present for Catholics. The divine healed sick pilgrims and listened to the cries of the afflicted: "We prayed, and you, from Heaven, heard our entreaties."[116] In 1937, parishes and communities that organized a special train to get to and from Aachen also prepared leaflets that explained the train timetable, included a map of the old city, and, in some instances, procession organizers inserted prayers for the journey. On these rail journeys, pilgrims prayed for the pope, their bishops and priests, their parents, and their youth and children. But they also prayed for the German *Volk*, the Catholic *Volk*, the unity of faith; Catholics in Mexico, Russia, and Spain suffering for their faith; all stray believers; all sick, afflicted, or harried; the departed; and for favourable weather. In short, pilgrims prayed about all aspects of their lives: their climate, their family, their spiritual leadership, and the body of believers – those healthy and sick, near and far, believing and unbelieving, dead and alive. As pilgrims travelled to Trier they offered up their prayers physically nearer to the divine manifested in the Holy Coat.

Trier officials sought to avoid open confrontation with the SA keeping the peace; this included delineating Trier sacred place as German.[117] Non-German pilgrims could pray in their native language but not necessarily out loud in Rhineland public spaces in the 1930s. Thus the Trier Domkapitular let the Montigny-les-Metz parish pray in French. Even though the Pilgrimage Committee produced a French edition of the 1933 *Pilgerbuch*, Chaplain Leroy still enquired as to whether or not his group of 600 pilgrims could pray together in French. Fuchs's response was cryptic. Yes, the group was allowed to pray in French in their station church, St. Maximin, presumably during Mass. However, Trier clergy did not answer whether or not the pilgrims could parade about the town praying in French. That same year, Trier clergy denied the Unio Cleri procession's request to sing in French.

Prayer was part of the sacred economy wherein pilgrims purchased remembrances and devotional items (*Andenken*) during their pilgrimages.[118] These *Andenken* often featured short reflections and prayers for recitation. In 1844, Jakob Marx observed at least 160 stands throughout Trier that sold devotional objects and prayer booklets.[119] In 1925, when *Kühlen Kunst* proposed an *Andenken* prayer booklet to Vicar Brüll in Aachen, they wanted help choosing the best prayers and images. That same year, the Aachen Xaverius press marketed their *Pilgrim Guidebook* as having "prayer exercises for all parts of pilgrimage, including a sick prayer."[120] *Andenken* often included short prayers. In 1937, one *Andenken* featured silk used to wrap the swaddling clothes of Jesus and included the prayer, "Jesus! Du bist mein 'Du'! Du bist aber auch mein 'Ich' und unser 'Wir'!" (Jesus! You are my "you"! But you are also my "I" and our "we"!).[121] There was high demand for prewritten prayers, and this fact is reflected in lists of items for sale to those who made the pilgrimage journey.

Though pilgrims purchased *Andenken* that contained suggested praises and petitions, many understood the act of communicating with God as sacred and set apart from commerce. One anonymous pilgrim wrote in to Trier to alert clergy to a problem during the processions. While a pilgrim group from the Koblenz Catholic Women's League prepared to enter the cathedral, they were disturbed by a young man. The interruption was particularly despicable to the women because they had their heads bowed in prayer and song. Their meditative pose did not deter the youth. He boldly walked up to each of them and pressed a piece of paper into their hands. His missive was an advertisement for wine and included a list of available vintages and their prices. While the

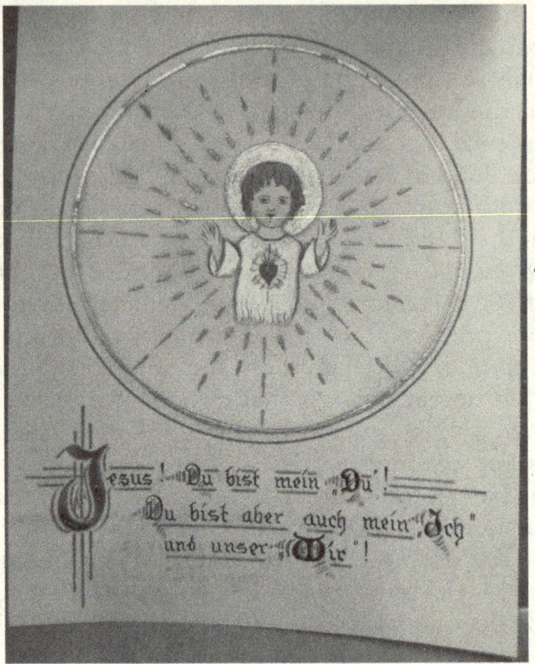

Figure 1.9. Swaddling Clothes *Andenken*.
Sources: DAA, Domkapitel 4.1.1.31. This *Andenken* also appears in Domkapitel 4.1.1.7.

perturbed pilgrim understood times were hard in 1933 and conceded that Trier citizens had a right to try to earn some extra money during the pilgrimage, she also found interrupting prayer to be an inexcusable violation of sacred space.[122] A prayerful pose ideally communicated that the individual was not to be bothered as she was engaged with the Coat and the divine. Prayer transported a pilgrim into "sacred time" and out of economic or commercial time. The offending flyer-dispenser violated sacred space and illegally crossed the border between sacred and profane.

Prayer also facilitated physical healing. Charlotte recalled that it was when her niece, the Countess Droste zu Vischering, prayed in front of the Trier Coat in 1844 that her health problems disappeared.[123] This prayerful aspect of the Droste zu Vischering miracle story was central in the many retellings of her experience. In 1909, nuns from San Francisco asked for confirmation of their understanding of what happened to the Countess: "She stopped, and always supported by her crutches remained there for some time, standing quite still and nearly motionless, hiding her face in her hands and performing a silent prayer. Suddenly she dropped her crutches."[124] In 1933, Cologne Vicar General Dr. David approved prayer cards for sick pilgrims. These index-card-sized objects included a prayer to Jesus, to Mary, and a prayer of St. Teresia of the *Kinde Jesu* Order. St. Teresia was sure that "Jesus wants to attract far more through suffering and testing, than by working and preaching the soul itself."[125] Jesus tested the sick, but not without purpose; such trials were to bring glory to God and attract the unbelieving. On the back of the card, pilgrims were urged to unite with Mary in her suffering at the foot of Jesus's cross.[126] Prayers fostered unity and a community of belief. Prayer cards were portable and helped link pilgrims back to the sacred centres of Aachen and Trier.[127]

Prayer at the sacred centre transcended geographic boundaries. For Peter, son of a vineyard owner and a parishioner of Pastor Steffens, prayer overcame the obstinacy of a haricot bean he had inadvertently lodged in his ear.[128] Peter lived with the bean for some time. Occasionally it would work its way to the edge of his ear canal, but when he tried to remove it, he invariably pushed it farther back into his ear. On 19 August 1844, though, his mother was in Trier before the Holy Coat and prayed for her son. At that hour, noon, the bean fell out: "The bean was covered in earwax and surrounded by a solid crust that formed around it – the hard shell of the bean was in decay."[129] Pastor Steffens was proud to report further that the prayer had cured Peter of his painful condition and that he could now hear "like every other person, very well."[130]

Peter's mother was not unique. Pilgrims saw the Rhineland relics as sites of prayer, places to gain a better understanding of the divine and to have their petitions heard by God the Father and His son, Jesus. Maria Fröhlich, an 1844 pilgrim, recorded her own prayers throughout her diary, including a prayer to help her prepare to see the Coat: "Open up, O Lord, my mouth, to praise your holy name, and purify my heart of all perverse and impure thoughts, facilitate my understanding, light a zeal in me, that I may worthily, attentively, devoutly, and fully bring my prayer, that it will be examined in the sight of your divine majesty, through Christ our Lord, Amen."[131] Prayers often reflected the petitioner's desire to live a virtuous life.

Pilgrims and clergy consistently cited prayer as a means of overcoming geographic limitations. Through prayer individuals could travel to Aachen and Trier without ever leaving their homes. In 1860, the bishop of Speyer could not make it to Aachen but promised to send his laity and to join his prayers with the "pious prayers of the many thousands" of attendants.[132] In 1895, the bishop of Fulda promised to attend if he could, and to pray that the Aachen festival would lead unbelievers to the Catholic Church.[133] Walburga, of Ingoldstadt, sent the Trier Pilgrimage Committee five marks in 1891 so that they would pray for her at Mass. Her circumstances, including caring for seven children, prevented her from physically travelling to Trier.[134] In 1902, the bishops of Osnabrück and Münster promised to entreat the Lord on behalf of the event, even though they could not travel to Aachen.[135] In 1933, one seventy-year-old female pilgrim feared being crushed to death trying to gain entrance into the cathedral. Because she could not get to the Coat, she went to Josefskirche to pray the rosary instead. These would-be pilgrims made indirect pilgrimages to the Trier Coat.[136]

Maria Gertrud, an Ursuline abbess, wrote her own litany to honour the Coat in 1933. For Mother Gertrud, the Coat was an opportunity to simultaneously affirm her orthodoxy and praise the unique sacrifice of Christ for sinners: "Jesus, begotten Son of God, you have tightened the robe of our morality." Jesus wore not just the Coat, and the "robe of morality," in Gertrud's prayer, but also the "garb of humility"; the "Coat that healed"; the "atoning cloth doused in blood"; the "transfigured, white Coat of Tabor"; the "Coat of immortality"; the "garb of our mortality"; of divine humility; and the "robe of glory."[137] The seamless relic represented many aspects of Christ's divinity and Catholic theology for Gertrud. The Coat in Trier brought Mother Gertrud into contact with many aspects of Christ's lived experience.

Jesus, as a historical actor, remained physically part of the Coat. Like Mother Gertrud, pilgrims petitioned his presence: "Lend us the grace," and "grant us the sentiments of the faithful servant who does not want to be better dressed than his master."[138] Mother Gertrud wrote several other prayers and songs for the pilgrimage. The Trier Pilgrimage Committee thanked her for the contribution and the cathedral clergy that they hoped to use the donated funds for a publication and they further noted that the cathedral choir director (*Domkapellmeister*) was circulating her devotionals widely.[139] The Coat, as it existed in 1933, represented the humanity of Christ: "You wear the clothing of your land and of your people."[140] The act of getting dressed featured prominently in Mother Gertrud's prayers: "You have taken all of our sickness upon yourself and you carry all of our pain."[141] Catholics had a duty to honour the Coat linked to Jesus's triumphant entry into Jerusalem: "The people spread their clothes on the path. They cut down branches from the trees and strewed them at his feet."[142] The long journey of Jesus's Coat from Jerusalem to Trier was in part paved with the lesser garments of Christ's followers.

In Trier, pilgrims found a powerful connection to Christ's suffering and death. Jesus's blood flowed out of the Coat to pilgrims. Together they prayed, "O Jesus, Redeemer of the World, in your death angst, your garment soaked with bloody sweat; it was your divine blood [the Coat] drank on the path to the cross."[143] Pilgrims found in the bloodied Christ a cleansing and purifying experience. They "washed their robes white in the blood of the Lamb."[144] Christ's suffering and bloody body was often the focus of prayers in the 1930s. Bishop Hilfreich, of Limburg, compared a trip his friend made to Palestine with his pilgrimage to Trier. On the Mount of Olives and at Golgatha, one could only kneel and pray because of the spiritual significance of the place. Similarly, pilgrims to Trier were in proximity to a site of divine torment. The Coat transported them to the Crucifixion and linked them to the past: "Before the Cross itself, this Coat was the last sacrifice of the Saviour, as he was robbed of his clothes."[145] The bishop of Ermland prayed that "the blood of Christ would come to all good people, that all people, through the blood of the Redeemer will find great healing and great grace."[146] Blood saved and pilgrims communed with the blood of their redeemer through prayer.

Pilgrimage was an act of atonement.[147] Through prayer, pilgrims communicated with Jesus to request their redemption. In 1933, directly across from the cathedral on Windstraße sat a Prussian-era prison, the *Königlich-Preußisches Gefängnis*. Cäcilie, a pilgrimage volunteer, recalled that late one night the prisoners were allowed to visit the Holy Coat. The participating inmates first made confession. The following morning, at 4:00, they processed across Windstraße and into the cathedral. As they crossed the street, they wore "bourgeois Sunday clothes" in order to appear respectable should pilgrims chance to see the odd parade. Three priests led them with a flag and cross. Cäcilie noted that they were covered "in prayers as they went up to the choir [where the choir sat in the cathedral] and prayed as they went up the stairs to the Holy Coat."[148] As each prisoner passed the Coat he made a deep bow. Afterwards they participated in a thanksgiving Mass in the prison. For Cäcilie, all were pilgrims if they followed the proper protocol. In this case, looking respectable, praying, and showing reverence towards the Coat were the most important aspects of pilgrimage. Prayer, combined with bowing, indicated humility and a desire for forgiveness.

Yet participants and observers differed over the significance and merit of praying in the proximity of holy relics. Clerics emphasized the power of divine petition and pilgrims sought salvation, healing, and recovery through prayer. Pilgrimage critics cited Catholic teachings and maintained that prayers offered up near the Holy Coat were no more efficacious than those prayed elsewhere. For critic Johannes Ronge, prayers directed to the Trier Coat constituted sacrilege: "If the Trier pilgrims shout: 'Holy Coat, Pray for us!' so it is and it remains idolatry."[149] For Ronge, there was nothing special about being in Trier. The divine was evenly dispersed, concentrated in no particular location.

Contrary to Ronge's position, in 1891, Johannes Joseph, bishop of Luxemburg, announced his support for Korum's pilgrimage call. In the Luxemburg diocesan newspaper, pilgrims were instructed about the pilgrimage and how to make themselves ready for the journey. If Luxemburg pilgrims wanted spiritual benefit they were taught that "to attain this indulgence, it is sufficient that you have received before the commencement of the pilgrimage the holy sacraments in any church, and then in the Trier cathedral you pray vocally, about five Lord's Prayers."[150] Prayer was not the only audible practice of pilgrims. They also sang loudly as they travelled to Aachen and Trier. By doing so, the sojourners transformed profane terrestrial locations into sacred place.

Those Who Sing, Pray Twice: The Songs They Sang[151]

Singing set pilgrim participants apart in their communities and made a direct claim on public spaces. In September 1844, as pilgrims from Züsch, about forty kilometres from Trier, made their way home, they encountered harassment and obstruction from their neighbours. As the roughly 400 participants returned to the town in the evening of 9 September 1844, they loudly sang and prayed. When they approached the Protestant church, they found the roadway blocked by large stones.[152] Observers disagreed over what transpired following their encounter with the improvised barricade. Some witnesses heard Protestants screaming at the pilgrims and calling out to them as though they were horses or decrying their worship as devilish. Others only heard children yelling that the Catholic priest was insane. Some did not think that stones blocked the path at all, or that they had been moved right after the procession, or that there were only two rocks stacked one on top of the other.[153] Jakob Klos, a thirty-six-year-old Catholic seminarian, heard Arend Sattler mock and threaten participants from his front door as he walked past.[154] Louisa Weber, a Protestant, twenty-nine years old, recalled hitting her foot on a stone that was in the middle of the road and having great pain afterwards.[155] And Johann Georg Dupre, a Catholic, heard a mocking voice ask why the Catholics were stumbling if they had an inner light that burned brighter than lanterns.[156] Ultimately, the stones and comments caused no lasting harm for the procession – nobody was severely injured.[157]

Nevertheless, pilgrimage forced confrontation or compromise in German communities where Catholics and Protestants lived side-by-side. When state and regional officials considered the Züsch incident, they were not certain whether any crime had been committed. They could not verify whether reports that Protestants splashed Catholics with water were true. In the end, authorities in Berlin and in Koblenz decided that there was insufficient cause to investigate the Züsch controversy any further. Officials attributed the episode to fanatical confessional bickering.[158] Importantly, though, Züsch Protestants allegedly attacked Catholics because they were singing and praying – a protest against having to hear pilgrimage in action. The transient procession and ephemeral songs were a claim on otherwise neutral space: the road. Religious acts could turn the road into a Catholic place. Even so, the Züsch incident does not necessarily mean tense relations between Protestants and Catholics were universal in Rhineland in the 1840s. Steffens, in Enkerich, felt that the orderliness of the 1844 processions left a favourable impression on Protestants: "The processions are well received in Protestant localities, [it] is twice as nice, and makes me happy that this has happened."[159]

Pilgrims created, learned, and sang a wide variety of songs and melodies concerning the relics in Aachen and Trier. They sang at Mass before leaving their hometowns, while walking or riding to their destination, and in the public squares and in the cathedrals of Aachen and Trier. Some of their songs never went out of style but persisted as essential aspects of the Aachen and Trier events. These included the "Te Deum" at the closing ceremonies and "Großer Gott, wir loben Dich" (Great God, we praise you) at the opening events. Other songs related to the relics rose and fell in popularity. For example, in the official Trier hymnbook, the number of songs directly related to the Trier relic peaked in 1846 with five songs and declined over the next 130 years (see table 1.4).

Two of the 1844 songs were included in the diocesan hymnal all the way up until the 1955 edition. They were then removed in favour of a new song to commemorate the 1955 pilgrimage (see also appendix 4: "Holy Coat Songs in Trier Hymnal, 1846–1955").[160]

Pilgrims, including the Züsch procession, used singing and prayer to prepare themselves for a liminal encounter with relics. In 1844, a Frenchman travelling along the Mosel River wrote about a group of twenty pilgrims on his ship. These twenty prayed the rosary and other prayers before singing "holy songs." Other individuals in the boat joined in when they recognized the tunes.[161] Jakob Marx viewed singing aboard pilgrim ships as an important bonding experience. He

Table 1.4. Songs in Trier hymnbook about the Holy Coat
(*Diözesangesangbuch*)

Year	No. of songs
1846	5
1871	3
1892	3
1955	1
1975	0

Source: Data from Heinz, "Die Lieder vom Heiligen Rock."
Note: For a list of the Trier Diözesangesangbuch songs, see
appendix 4, "Holy Coat Songs in Trier Hymnal, 1846–1955."

noted how groups from Koblenz tended to sing vespers during the trip and even as they disembarked.[162] In another 1844 article, the *Rhein und Moselzeitung* described Koblenz pilgrims leaving work early to board four ships to Trier, singing "Herr Großer Gott! Dir danken wir!" during the journey.[163] The 1933 *Reiselieder* or "travel songs" reflect the importance of movement and of being oriented towards the divine. Songs focused on the actual journey and are rife with travel terms: sojourn, hurry, draw near, to walk, paths, and return. Regardless of the changing political context, pilgrims highlighted the veracity of relics through their songs.

The Züsch incident was emblematic of how pilgrims on foot were noted for the volume of their singing. Jakob Marx recalled a parish group that sang the "Te Deum" so loudly that bystanders could not help but fixate on the group and recorded that "no eye remained dry."[164] Another group from Cologne arrived at Trier by foot and singing in 1844.[165] A priest reported to Marx that his pilgrim group had sung while walking through the night. The priest thought that singing in nature was an important emotional aspect of pilgrimage.[166] For many pilgrims, singing as a group proved to be a highlight of their experience. Maria Fröhlich, whose Neuwied parish travelled to Trier in September 1844, kept a diary of her pilgrimage and made note of all the songs her group sang along the way: "It was a delightful trip. We sang and prayed."[167] In 1844, Cathedral Deacon Sauer gave sixteen members of the Bachelor-Sodality permission to loudly pray and sing over the relic while they helped guard the Coat overnight.[168] Hubert Peters, in August 1933, requested permission from the Pilgrimage Committee to print his own song about the Trier Coat, set to the tone of "Singt dem König Freudenpsalmen." His request was denied and, unfortunately, his lyrics were not included with his letter.[169]

Participants prayed and sang loudly to reflect their joy at both being present with fellow pilgrims, and at viewing sacred relics. The dynamics of prayer, often projected and uncontrolled, were also an important symptom of an impending encounter with divine presence. In 1844, Katharina Petsch explained to Trier officials that before her body was healed she "tried to pray aloud" without success.[170] After touching the Trier Coat, Petsch was able to exclaim a prayer of thanks: "Ach, my Saviour!"[171] In the 1853 Aachen pilgrimage program, point nine explained that "pilgrims, during the filling [literally: 'with the tightening'] of the church will alternatively pray and sing loudly."[172] That same year in the clerical outline for the opening of the Marian Shrine, Aachen officials called for "loud praying and singing" as they laid out the relics and exhibited them for the first time.[173]

Published pilgrim songs reflected changing clerical rhetoric surrounding Rhineland relics, from authentic biblical objects to symbols of Catholic unity. In one 1839 song, Aachen pilgrims sang of relics worn by John the Baptist at his beheading. The Cloth originated in a faraway land and was brought back to Aachen by Charlemagne for his beloved capital and its inhabitants. Similarly, in 1844, Trier pilgrims were called to rush to the city to view the ancient relic worthy of adoration. Jesus had worn the Coat and instilled in it a sacred aura that was able to heal the bleeding woman in Mark 5. Because the Coat was present with Jesus on the Mount of Olives at the transfiguration and during his trial, it contained a divine agency. The Coat healed in the Gospel when the faithful simply touched the hem, and it retained the power to intercede in the lives of pilgrims. In "Song to the Holy Coat," the pilgrim should anticipate life-altering transformation during the journey: "Think, what was, what even today / He has done for our Salvation. / Rejoice, pious! Tremble, sinner! Begin a new life" (see appendix 1 for full lyrics).

Pilgrim songs defended Catholicism against political and theological enemies. Following the Kulturkampf, pilgrims sang out against their spiritual opponents. Songs now emphasized themes of triumph and consolation. Pilgrims aggressively created sacred place by calling out the divine judgment that awaited their persecutors. The cathedral doors now stood open, and the enemies of pilgrimage were defeated. God was on the side of pilgrims: "Oh he feels, that God is present, / And through God is help and grace." Songs reinforced Catholic identity against outside challengers. Critics of pilgrimage came in for heavy mocking in 1881:

Whether the enemy with stupid brains
Names it [the Coat] baubles and deceit

> Whether the unbeliever jeers and disclaims,
> Truly the simplemindedness is yours.
> Such as burns and drools for evil.[174]

Pilgrims continued to sing about overcoming their foes into the twentieth century. In 1933, a group on procession to Trier sang, "The world also likes to quarrel, to mock us always again anew, / We stand at all times, true to our bishop." In another travel song, "Let the world call us foolish, / for them all that is holy lies."[175] Pilgrims walked the road of virtue because they possessed the true Christendom. They pleased God, Mary, and Jesus by hastening along the pilgrim path.

Pilgrimage songs established insiders and outsiders: "Rejoice, pious! Tremble, sinner! / Begin a new life."[176] This is most clear when the lyrics distinguish "the world" from "us": "The world also likes to quarrel, to mock us," and "we defend ourselves against Hell in a blind, wild rage."[177] And, like the prayers above, these songs reinforced a *German* Catholic identity. Fuchs explained in a letter to Dr. Hennequin in Metz that he hoped there were no hard feelings when he denied the Unio Cleri request to sing a French song during their procession. Fuchs assured Hennequin that he respected the procession, but it was not possible to permit such a display within the cathedral.[178]

Clerics were keenly aware of the importance of song as part of pilgrim experience. In a circular to the pilgrim group leaders who were ordering special trains to Trier, the 1933 Trier Pilgrimage Committee explained the centrality of the *Pilgerbücher* for participants: "The pilgrim book is an indispensable means for achieving uniform praying and singing and thus to deepen the spiritual pilgrimage in the individual and the community of believers. To prevent any abuse by repeated uses, the pilgrim book is endorsed by a date stamp on entering the Cathedral Square."[179] Pilgrims could not gain access to the Trier relic without carrying in a copy of approved prayers and songs to honour the Coat.

Singing sacralized space and created a pilgrim experience between 1832 and 1937. At the same time, song themes and emphases responded to the shifting historical context of Rhineland pilgrimages. Songs stressed Catholic triumph after the Kulturkampf. After 1844, clergy promoted songs that described relics as symbolic reminders of the Holy Family. For Jakob Marx, singing taught God's love, and pilgrims came together to experience a sense of community through shared activities like song and prayer.[180] In this sense song transcended any potential differences among participants: "Everyone felt comfortable with one another."[181] Pilgrims sang and prayed to honour God, Jesus, Mary, John the Baptist, for unity, for their own hardships. Not all felt comforted, though. Eternal damnation awaited anyone who persecuted pilgrims following the pathways to Aachen and Trier.

Conclusion

Through elaborate processions at the beginning and end of pilgrimages, clergy, Catholic politicians, and Catholic laity carried relics through their cities. The opening and closing ceremonies in Aachen and Trier were thick rituals, with each action planned and laden with meaning.[182] Deacons, sub-deacons, the presbyter, and honorary deacons (*Ehrendiakone*) carefully choreographed their interactions with relics.[183] These events dedicated the town and the cathedral to Jesus, Mary, and the saints. Closing ceremony processions disseminated divine presence in the public arena.

In the mid-nineteenth-century, pilgrims increasingly sang about the relics as symbols rather than as authentic historical artefacts. Through liturgy, clergy taught that relics were reminders of Christian piety rather than literal-historical belongings of the Holy Family. In the 1867 song "Welcome Song for Holy Loincloth," the lyrics emphasized the Loincloth of Jesus soaking up His blood during the Passion. But the Loincloth also reminded pilgrims that the sacrificial death of Jesus was the origin of divine compassion and of their salvation. In 1891 Trier, Jesus as the saviour, rather than His Coat, became the focal point in songs: "Think on Him [Jesus] and his deeds, / He who took our guilt on Himself, / Bleeding and died for the world's salvation." The emphasis on the individuals who wore the relics continued in 1895 Aachen: "Oh that I could embrace you / Just as the swaddling clothes, / As close as they are to you."[184] And by the 1930s, drawing towards the Trier Coat meant crossing to the divine: "God! we confidently draw near to you, ... / you in the Coat of glory."[185] Pilgrimage sanctified, the practice brought the participant closer to eternal salvation: "lead us to salvation," "salvation of Christendom," "we confess without trepidation." The transition from artefact to symbol was gradual, even as the songs never actually denied the *possibility* of authenticity.

These Rhenish pilgrimages contain continuities of religious practice – prayer, procession, song – but were not events out of time. The number of participants in Trier consistently increased between 1832 and 1937, but Aachen, because it hosted an event every seven years, was more susceptible to European events. Thus, there was no Aachen pilgrimage during the First World War, nor during the subsequent French occupation of the Rhineland. Aachen also saw a slump in participation during the Great Depression. Rhineland clergy had to balance the perpetuation of tradition with shifting political regimes. After the NSDAP came to power in 1933, Cathedral Canon Fuchs found compromise with the National Socialist regime. Fuchs ultimately allowed the SA to manage pilgrimage security, but limited party armbands at the closing ceremony and denied the Hitler Youth the right to march in their uniforms.

For the pilgrims over this one-hundred-year period, prayer was about communicating with the divine in the moment of a rare relic display. Prayer sanctified one for the journey and provided an audible and metaphysical means of connecting to God during and after the sacrifice of pilgrimage. Rhineland Catholics used praying, singing, and marching to create sacred landscapes and to transform spaces into significant places. Through prayer, pilgrims prepared themselves for their encounter with divine presence in Aachen and Trier. Participants prayed for healing, forgiveness, and strength. With song, Catholics laid claim to the topography wherever they travelled. Catholics sang while on ships, trains, and on the road. The next chapter examines how sick pilgrims united bodily with Rhineland relics and further explores how cure-seekers understood their physical relationship to the divine. After preparing themselves through song and prayer, ill pilgrims sought out sacred objects in order to restore their physical health.

Over the course of several weeks, seventeen-year-old Countess Johanna Droste zu Vischering lost the ability to walk. She first felt an ache and then a numbness in her right leg. In the spring of 1842, the pain spread to both of her legs and they began to curve and warp. By August she required crutches to move. Vischering travelled from her hometown of Münster and sought relief at the baths in Kreuznach. She consulted her local doctors and the physicians at the spas. Finding no lasting cure, she finally decided to visit the Coat of Trier in 1844. To prepare herself for the journey she took communion and met with her priest. On 31 August 1844 she received permission from Bishop Arnoldi to touch the Holy Coat of Jesus. Her grandmother then helped her into the cathedral. After touching the relic, Vischering prayed for several minutes in front of the Coat.[1] Suddenly the countess covered her face with her hands and began to weep. She shouted out, set aside her crutches, and got to her feet, aided by her grandmother. The pilgrims around her were shocked and moved to tears.[2] After further prayer, Vischering walked out of the cathedral unaided for the first time in three years. She left her crutches behind as an offering to Jesus for her physical restoration. Vischering returned to the cathedral the next day to thank God again for the miracle and as a testimony that she was fully cured.[3]

Vischering's story became the focal point of a fierce pamphlet debate centred on the question of whether or not she was truly healed in Trier. Her supporters claimed that the Catholic Church now had irrefutable evidence that God acted through relics to show favour to the faithful. Detractors, both Protestants and Liberals, were outraged that in an age of Enlightenment, and that after the French Revolution, the church would continue to peddle superstition. For opponents it was obvious that the incident had been staged. Vischering was at best a hysteric, critics explained, and the emotional outburst before the Coat brought a moment of temporary clarity. It was only a matter of time before she reverted to her crutches.

Historians of nineteenth-century German Catholicism have mirrored the dichotomies of the Vischering pamphlet debate and recreated a division between Catholics and Liberals.[4] With an eye to the impending Kulturkampf, mid-nineteenth-century pilgrimages were a political staging ground in which the Catholics and Liberals began to stockpile armaments for the inevitable confrontation in the 1870s and 1880s.[5] Historians have been too willing to side with Vischering's detractors and explain her miracle as being "best understood as the product of neither supernatural intercession nor deliberate deception, but of the power of suggestion, or the cathartic effect produced by faith and heightened expectation of a cure at a time of unusual emotional excitement."[6] But Rhineland miracle claims were a central component of the Catholic experience. For the participants, pilgrimage facilitated an encounter with the divine.

Examining the world of Rhineland miracles means posing new questions. Previously scholars have asked, "What is gained by claiming a cure?" or "How can we account for the mentality of an individual claiming physical change?" Such questions lead to problematic answers, some of them psycho-historical. "Many of the nervous symptoms displayed by the 'cured' women and girls of Marpingen and Mettenbuch can also be plausibly seen as a response to the reality or prospect of relentless toil and hardship, as a form of flight into illness," noted David Blackbourn in his examination of Marpingen.[7] This line of argument risks caricaturing Catholic participants: "[The] majority of cases where inferences about occupation are possible suggest that the families of miners, peasants, or small traders were involved."[8]

A close study of pilgrims to Aachen and Trier challenges the notion that those seeking cures were overwhelmingly impoverished, female, and elderly. Men were much more willing to seek out a cure in Trier and Aachen than historians have realized. Their underrepresentation in literature is due to the fact that Catholic men would seek a cure but were far less likely than Catholic women to publicly proclaim themselves healed after touching a relic. Yet even as women sought confirmation of divine intervention, between the 1830s and 1930s they were accorded less and less authority to corroborate such claims. By the 1930s, a woman's testimony about her body required masculine confirmation: from a relative, male physician, or clergyman. This "masculinization of the truth" delineated the gendered boundaries of who could speak about divine presence.

Put simply, the question that guides the following analysis is, "Who were the cure-seekers and what did they say about relics?" From pilgrimage to pilgrimage the number of requests to visit Rhineland relics for medicinal purposes increased. Pilgrims hoped to find divine presence that would penetrate and modify their bodies. For the Catholic pilgrims seeking cure, this was not merely a "remnant" of "medieval experience" but a powerful world view that persisted well into the twentieth century. Pilgrims believed that God could break into the world at will and manipulate nature.[9] This chapter explores how cure-seekers understood their religious practices. Here, what most matters is not whether or not a miracle took place.[10] Rather, the emphasis will be placed on the interaction of pilgrim bodies and religious practice.[11]

Participants in Aachen and Trier describe being first separated during the journey as a subset of pilgrims seeking cures and as a group looking for a physical encounter with the relic.[12] The sick pilgrim then went through a transition. Participants noted sensations of hot and cold, weeping, collapsing, or fainting. Finally, they were incorporated back into their community as whole members: women now capable of resuming their daily tasks or men able to return to work or to go back into the field to harvest. For example, after Vischering's cure in 1844, healing in Trier began to follow similar reports of weeping and fainting, and certainly leaving crutches behind was an important aspect of the cult of cure after Vischering dramatically cast her crutches aside.[13]

The Trier and Aachen Catholics who experienced healing in this chapter are of course no longer available to complete psychological evaluations about their propensity to absorption and cannot be surveyed on their openness to trance, hypnosis, or dissociation.[14] Also problematic for this study, anthropologists have emphasized repeated exposure as a mechanism for acquiring knowledge about appropriate behaviour.[15] There were only three Trier pilgrimages between 1832 and 1937, and Aachen hosted an event only every seven years. The irregularity of the events suggests there was not enough continuity to develop the skill of healing or to learn a "cure script."

Rhineland Catholics inhabited a world permeated by sacred centres.[16] The sick hoped to experience both the eternal and the temporal. They described moving across, transforming, and overcoming the boundaries of their body through divine intervention. Pilgrim understandings of the body, sickness, health, and God converged in the Coat of Trier and the four Aachen relics and reflected the persistent belief that these objects were sites of sacred presence.[17] In Aachen and Trier, individuals suffering from physical and spiritual ailments expected to find relief. Before turning to pilgrim encounters with sacred relics, this analysis first examines the demographics of those seeking physical and spiritual restoration.

The Cured and Cure-Seeking

Although men were less likely than women to publicly claim a miracle, they visited shrines and relics for physical restoration. Scholars agree that the individuals who went on pilgrimage and sought a cure in the nineteenth and twentieth centuries tended to be lower-class women and children. For example, Robert Orsi, in his analysis of letters sent to the shrine of Blessed Margeret of Castello in the 1980s, noted that "evidence in the letters suggests that the correspondents are mainly lower class" and "most correspondents are women."[18] In Germany, the most detailed analysis of this religious practice is that of David Blackbourn, who examined forty-five cases in which the person claimed to be cured. As Blackbourn explains, his 1880s sample size accounted for roughly 10 per cent of those claiming healing in Marpingen. He drew the cases from miracle reports in the *Trierische Zeitung* and from the archives. He selected claims in which he knew the name and sex of the cure claimant; in twenty-eight of these he knew the pilgrim's age, and in all but four he knew from which town the cure-seekers originated.[19] Historian Ruth Harris drew her examples from 127 cured who were present at the 1897 procession of cured. Off these only 10 were men.[20] In both cases, historians based their analyses on those claiming to be healed.

In the early nineteenth century, female Catholics claimed to be healed much more frequently than men. Within the 1844 pamphlet literature there is a wide variety of miraculous healing lists. For example, one anonymous pamphlet cited *Luxemburger Zeitung* articles to compile a list of eleven cured (see table 2.1).

Here only two of the cured are male and only one is an adult.[21] Other pamphlets proposed twenty-three cured, of which only three were males.[22] Still others presented a list of nineteen cured, with only two men being relieved of physical suffering.[23] Within the pamphlet literature related to the 1844 Trier pilgrimage, women were much more represented than men among the healed.

However, by the end of the nineteenth century the ratio of men to women increased. In Bishop Korum's list of approved miracles, six of the eleven were male, although three of the males cured were children (table 2.2). Korum refused to confirm as miraculous certain illnesses, including "sadness," "persistent vomiting," and "nerves." While plenty of the "mercies" claimants had insisted on an outward, physical transformation, like the "miracles," Korum was unconvinced by the evidence he was

Table 2.1. Miraculous healings, 1844

Name	Age	Town	Illness
Unnamed child	Not listed	Limburg	Blind
Female			
Appolonia Porn	9	Olkenbach	Rickets
Daughter of Johann Schell	12	Gutenthal	Contraction of left leg
Regina Morscheidt	14	Kürenz	Hoarse voice
Countess Johanna von Droste zu Vischering	19	Münster	Contraction of left leg
Anna Josephine Wagner	19	Alsen	Epilepsy
Catharina Drolait	24	Ressonville	Fever, lameness, seizures
Susanna Müller	44	Saarburg	Gout
Katharina Petsch	45	Konz	Stroke
Male			
Joseph Heinz	11	Berncastel	Lost voice
Mathias Mieler	51	Bontenbach bei Rhaunen	Pain in left leg

Source: Data from Ernest, *Bericht über die wunderbaren Heilungen.*

Table 2.2. Miraculous healings, 1891

Name	Age	Town	Illness
Female			
Ursula der Franziskanerinnen	Not listed	Waldbreitbach	Elbow
Helena Daniel	14	Recht	Eye pain
Magdalena Weinachter	34	Nieder-Kontz	Joint pain
Frau Peter Stinner geb. Wüst	38	Brachbach	Abdominal
Schw. Stephanie Popp	≥60	Trier	Growing nodule
Male			
Peter Eul	1	Bürdenbach	Weakness
Johann Wecker	4	Berlin	Intestines
Joseph Wendling	4	Gemar in Elsaß	Spine decay
Joseph Petri	24	Erkeln in Westfalen	Cramps
Jakob Holzapfel	32	Caldenhausen	Lameness
Johann Hoffmann	40	Tholey	Lupus

Source: Data from Korum, *Wunder und göttliche Gnadenerweise.*

offered. The bishop validated these experiences but offset such "mercies" as a separate category. Women are by far the majority when Korum's undefined "divine mercies" – those incidents that the bishop was reticent to call "miraculous" – are combined with his list of "miracles."[24]

By the 1930s, ill pilgrims to Aachen and Trier had to first acquire a sick pass (*Krankenkarte*) to access relics during designated times set aside by

Table 2.3. Miraculous mercies (*Gnadenerweise*), 1891

Name	Age	Town	Illness
Male			
Michael Florange	Not listed	Trier	Left eye
Johann May	4	Weiler	Feet malformed
Emil Herb	12	Pforzheim	Foot rheumatism
Johann Baptist Steinbach	12	Schillingen	Heart trouble
Daniel Mahoney	≥30	Westminster	Lower back
Kaspar Speich	48	Linz	Right hand
Johann Schäfer	58	Herschwiesen	Dropsy
Female			
Franziska Papenhoff	Not listed	Heisingen	Abdominal distress
Katharina Will	5	Dorweiler	Going blind
Anna Reding	7	Berdorf-Luxemburg	Lameness
Margaretha Schwartz	17	Berdorf-Luxemburg	Stomach
Anna Maria Fink	20	Naunheim	Body weakness
Elisabeth Felten*	22	Waldbredimus	Vomiting
Stephanie Fleig	22	Baden	Nervous system
Hektorine Hogenbill	25	Ueckingen	Ulcer
Angela Rörsch	27	Cahren	Aphonia
Elisabeth Schmitz	29	Loogh	Sadness, hysteria
Gertrud Gilles	33	Polch	Eyes and ears
Angela Weis	35	Ittel	Spinal cord
Eva Maaßen	36	Haaren b. Aachen	Nerves
Susanna Strupp	37	Wawern	Heart trouble
Margaretha Riewer	39	Strohn	Persistent vomiting
Schw. Edmunda	40	Waldbreitbach	Lameness
Frau Förster Hahn	42	Laubach	Uterus
Apollonia Franziska Allendorf	42	Wicker	Inverted uterus
Barbara Lichtmeß	55	Waldweiler	Gout in knees

Source: Data from Korum, *Wunder und göttliche Gnadenerweise*.
* Waldbredimus is in Luxembourg. Her sickness is classified as "hysterical vomiting."
Korum, 48–151.

cathedral clergy. Prior to the 1930s, these pilgrims needed only to bring a note from a physician confirming that they were sick and an attestation from a cleric stating they were in good standing. In 1933, the Trier Pilgrimage Committee introduced a standardized medical form and required that sick pilgrims have a physician fill it out before they could visit the relic one-on-one. Sick pilgrims filed formalized applications and answered questions about their gender, age, job, point of origin, and ongoing illness.

In the 1930s, cure-seekers tended to be middle-aged and in their thirties or forties. In 1933 Trier, roughly one-third of the cure-seekers were men. More cure-seekers visited 1933 Trier than any preceding

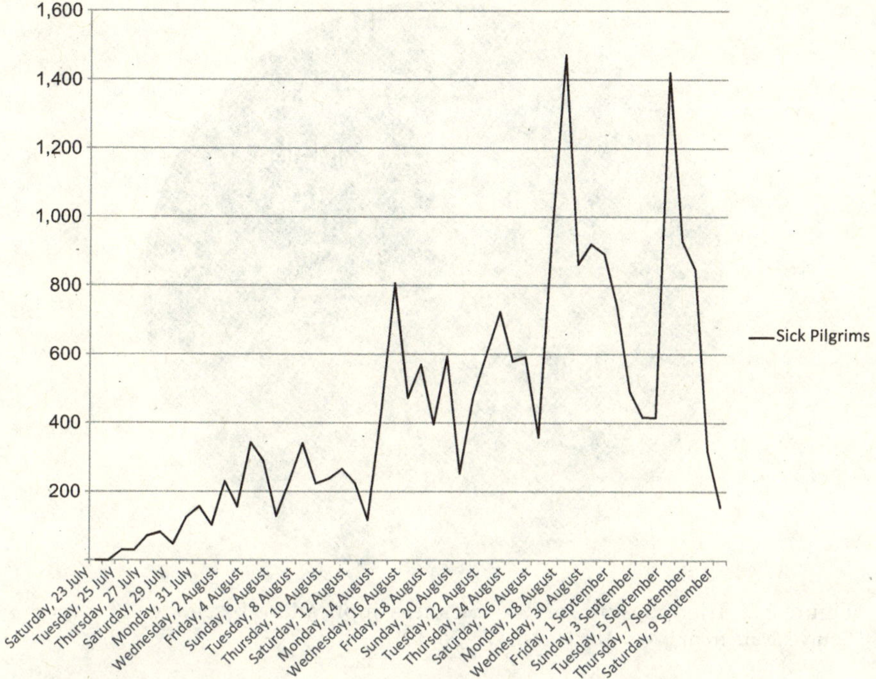

Figure 2.1. Sick pilgrim daily visits to Trier, 1933.
Source: Data from BATr, Abt. 90, Nr. 175–Nr. 191.

pilgrimage. The 1933 Pilgrimage Committee conservatively estimated that 21,126 sick pilgrims visited the Coat for a cure.[25] They were accompanied by at least 63,681 attendants, individuals who escorted the ill pilgrim into the cathedral. Each sick petitioner averaged three assistants.

Taking 1933 as a benchmark, male requests or desires for cure were much higher in the nineteenth century than is reflected in an analysis of only publicized cures; perhaps as high as one-third of those seeking cures were men. Unlike 1937 Aachen, where pilgrims often included their salutation on the application, doctors tended to simply mark *M* or *F* for the Trier Pilgrim Committee. Therefore, for this pilgrimage, it is simpler to break the entirety of the applicants into these binary groups. Within the sample size, 3,617 applicants are clearly labelled *M* or *F*. The male-to-female ratio can be seen in figure 2.2. What is most striking here is again that males make up nearly a third of the applications.

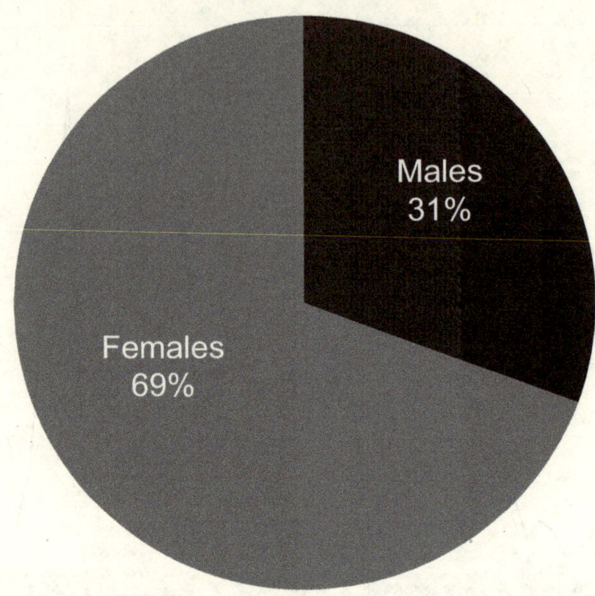

Figure 2.2. Trier pilgrimage, 1933: Sickness applications by gender.
Source: Data from BATr, Abt. 90, Nr. 175–Nr. 191.

It is more challenging to analyse women's social standing in Trier, for lack of salutations, but the age information is much more complete, with 2,276 female and 1,024 male applicants having a clearly stated birth year or age. Average adult pilgrims seeking a cure were thus somewhere in their mid-thirties to mid-forties. Parents brought children for cures, but these were a small percentage (21 per cent of male applicants, 7 per cent of female) within the overall cure-seeking population. The children tended not to be very young but between the ages of eight and twelve when they arrived in Trier.

Although a clerical note was not necessary to view the Holy Coat in 1933, as it had been in the nineteenth century, many pilgrims brought notes from their priests as a form of insurance to prevent Trier officials from denying them access to the cathedral based on church standing. Male cure-seekers comprise roughly 30 per cent of the 672 notes from priests in 1933 corroborating the illness of the petitioner.[26] Once again, the gender data are best expressed in terms of salutation. These clerical notes also reveal that men were not reluctant to ask their priest to evaluate their religiosity.[27] Even so, like in the nineteenth century, men were still unlikely to claim a cure in the 1930s. Of eighty-three cures clergy investigated in 1933, only eleven were men, or 13.25 per cent.[28]

Table 2.4. Trier pilgrimage: Age analysis by gender (all entries), 1933

Gender	Sample size	Age		
		Mean	Median	Modal
Female	2,276	40.07	41	47
Male	1,024	31.41	30	11

Source: Data from BATr, Abt. 90, Nr. 175–Abt. 90, Nr. 199-70.

Table 2.5. Trier pilgrimage: Age analysis by gender (≥ 12 years old), 1933

Gender	Sample size	Age		
		Mean	Median	Modal
Female	2,108	42.66	43	47
Male	810	37.75	36	12

Source: Data from BATr, Abt. 90, Nr. 175–Abt. 90, Nr. 199-70.

Table 2.6. Trier pilgrimage: Age analysis by gender (11 years old only), 1933

Gender	Sample size	Age		
		Mean	Median	Modal
Female	168	7.48	8	9
Male	214	7.41	8	11

Source: Data from BATr, Abt. 90, Nr. 175–Abt. 90, Nr. 199-70.

Table 2.7. Trier pilgrimage: Notes from priests, 1933

Salutation	No. (%) of petitioners
F	262 (39.46)
Frau	106 (15.96)
Frl.	41 (6.17)
Herr	23 (3.46)
Kind	62 (9.34)
M	154 (23.19)
Schw.	3 (0.45)
Wwe.	13 (1.96)
Female	425 (70.60)
Male	177 (29.40)

Source: Data from BATr, Abt. 90, Nr. 134a-134b.
Note: The total sample is 664 except for female and male, which is 602.

Priests did not consistently include the age of petitioners; therefore it is best to defer to the medical testaments cited above.[29]

Of the original Trier sample size of 3,625 sick pilgrim requests, 3,018 clearly indicate their *Beruf*, or professional position of the applicant. Pilgrims responded to this part of the medical history questionnaire (*Fragebogen*) with highly varied answers, ranging from "child" to the specific administrative court director (*Verwaltungsgerichtsdirektor*). Sick pilgrims fall into eight categories (see table 2.8).[30]

The old middle class included professions such as handicrafts, commerce, agriculture, military officers, pig herders, florists, and policemen. Germans who worked for hourly wages constituted the working class: cement workers, field hands, factory employees, etc.[31] Salaried employees, white-collar workers, and civil servants (*Beamtentum, Berufsbeamtentum*) formed the backbone of the new middle class, which included clerical leaders and sales personnel.[32] The *Rentnermittelstand* lived on fixed incomes and suffered the most economically during the Weimar crises of hyperinflation and the depression: pensioners, rentiers, widowers, and disabled veterans. "Church" here includes all individuals dedicated to advancing the life of the Catholic Church: chaplains, monks, abbots, and nuns.[33]

Overall these occupational data reveal that no single economic group or class, aside from the unemployed, dominated requests to touch the Holy Coat. The unemployed in Germany had been suffering since Franz von Papen cut unemployment benefits in June 1932 as he sought to cater to business interests and the extreme right. Chancellor von Papen's economic policies failed to jump-start the German economy, and unemployment reached a peak of six million people out of work, an increase of 150 per cent between 1930 and 1932.[34] Although unemployment had declined by the 1933 Trier pilgrimage, millions of Germans continued to search for positions in an unpredictable economy.

Fully one-quarter of requests to touch the Holy Coat came from the German middle classes. In 1933 Trier more members of the old middle class (466) sought time with the Trier Coat than the new middle class (227). In other words, Trier officials received nearly twice as many requests from the old than from the new middle class. Taken together, 25.51 per cent of requests to touch the Holy Coat came from the middle class, or more than twice the number of working-class petitions. Thus 1933 Trier was very different from 1876 Marpingen, where David Blackbourn found that the bourgeoisie were underrepresented.[35]

Trier's sick required a note from a doctor that specified their affliction before they could gain time with the Coat. Of the sample size, 3,447

Table 2.8. Trier cure-seekers by profession, 1933

Profession	% of applications
Unemployed (*Berufslos, Erwerbslos, Arbeitslos*)	33.96
Wife (*Ehefrau, Hausfrau, Frau*)	16.70
Old middle class	15.44
Working class	10.07
Child (*Kind*)	8.28
New middle class	7.52
Middle-class pensioners (*Rentnermittelstand*)	5.14
Church	2.88

Source: Data from Childers, *Nazi Voter*.

pilgrims had clearly stated illnesses on their applications. The table in appendix 6 offers an extensive list of the common complaints. For the sake of clarity, the table maintains the phrasing used by 1930s physicians to diagnose patients who wanted to visit Trier. Pilgrims suffered from a wide range of ailments that reflected the limits of what doctors could heal in the early twentieth century. Appendix 6 consolidates illnesses to give a clearer picture of disease concentrations. The "lungs" designation, for instance, includes the varied ailments of emphysema, bronchitis, shortness of breath, lung pains, atrophy, bloody lungs, pulmonary trouble, and lung carcinoma. Similarly, categories such as cancer, heart, and stomach contain a wide range of more specific physican diagnoses.

Due to the required medical form, Trier diseases tended to be much more specifically described than Aachen ailments and reveal a range of physical complaints among the cure-seekers in the 1930s. Here I have broken these into four broad categories (for specific ailment complaints see appendix 6: "Trier Pilgrimage Sick Pilgrim Complaints, 1933"). The first group, "General pain," included suffering, arthritis, and illness petitions. Pilgrims also sought to regain full use of their senses. Best described as "Incurable sensory," these forms included blindness, deafness, and paralysis (lameness, multiple sclerosis, etc.). A third tier of diseases, "Internal," is composed of dysfunctional/ malfunctioning internal organs: heart, kidney, lungs, bladder, liver, "blood," stomach, and gall bladder. Another concentration of diseases, "Unpreventable conditions," includes heart attack, stroke, polio, flu, sterility, alopecia, and epilepsy. A fifth grouping, "Unspecified ailment," included painful sensations or chronic pain, most often diagnosed as cramps, war wounds, operation accident, headache, joints, bones, and so on. A final group, "Mental illness," was diversely

Table 2.9. Aachen categorical totals, 1937

Salutation	No.
F	479
Frau	1,257
Frl.	582
Group	33
Herr	358
Kind	241
M	198
Pfarrer (priest)	1
Schwester (sister)	94
Wwe. (widow)	111
Undifferentiated requests	46

Sources: Data from DAA, 4.1.1.18, Krankenkarten A–C, 4.1.1.19, Krankenkarten D–G, 4.1.1.20, Krankenkarten H–K, 4.1.1.21, Krankenkarten L–P, 4.1.1.22, Krankenkarten Q–Z.

represented with dementia, senility, paranoia, nerves, nervousness, schizophrenia, psychosis, and the contemporary diagnoses of "idiocy," "imbecility," and "hysteria." Interestingly, by the 1930s, medical practitioners began to abandon "hysteria" and terms like *"Frauenleidend"* (woman suffering) in favour of more specific diagnoses related to mental health and women's reproductive organs (e.g., ovarian cancer, sterility).

1937 Aachen

In the archive for the 1937 Aachen pilgrimage there were at least 3,410 requests for a *Krankenkarte* to see the relics. On the last day of the 1930 Aachen pilgrimage more than 1,000 sick pilgrims visited the relic, and during the preceding Thursday over 1,500.[36] In 1937, in just the first four days, 8,000 sick visited the Aachen relics.[37] However, there were many more individuals than the 3,410 who submitted petitions for one-on-one time with the four sacred garments. Letters were often sent in for a group of three people or for both a mother and her child. The following analysis draws on these requests and separates out cure-seeking pilgrims by their salutations: Frl. (single woman), Frau (married woman), Wwe. (Witwe, widowed woman), Schw. (Schwester, sister, member of a female religious order), Kind (child), and Herr (Mr.). Where possible, requests are classified through inference, such as an *F* to Christine Schmitz and Johanna Wolff and an *M* to Matthias Herzog and Hermann Püsken. The tables do not include instances where there is only a last name, the first name is illegible, or the names of the members of a group

Table 2.10. Aachen totals from the 33 group requests, 1937

Requests	No.
Male	86
Female	438
Undifferentiated requests	649

Sources: Data from DAA, 4.1.1.18, Krankenkarten A–C, 4.1.1.19, Krankenkarten D–G, 4.1.1.20, Krankenkarten H–K, 4.1.1.21, Krankenkarten L–P, 4.1.1.22, Krankenkarten Q–Z.

Table 2.11. Aachen totals by category (categorized + group), 1937

Salutation	No. (%) of petitioners
F (479 + 438)	917 (23.85)
Frau	1,257 (32.69)
Frl.	582 (15.14)
Herr	358 (9.31)
Kind	241 (6.27)
M (198 + 86)	284 (7.39)
Pfarrer (priest)	1 (0.03)
Schw. (sister)	94 (2.44)
Wwe. (widow)	111 (2.89)
Total	3,845 (100)

Sources: Data from DAA, 4.1.1.18, Krankenkarten A–C, 4.1.1.19, Krankenkarten D–G, 4.1.1.20, Krankenkarten H–K, 4.1.1.21, Krankenkarten L–P, 4.1.1.22, Krankenkarten Q–Z.

request are not specified.[38] Within these parameters the sample size appears in table 2.9.

In many instances, within the group requests, it is possible to distinguish men from women and to learn how many *Krankenkarten* each group required. These data are broken down in table 2.10.

At least 4,540 individuals wanted to be cured by the Aachen relics in 1937.[39] By combining these group requests with the categorical dataset and removing the indistinguishable individuals, the totals appear in table 2.11.

Finally, by lumping the categories together into *F* (F + Frau + Frl + Schwester + Wwe), *M* (M + Herr + Pfarrer), and Kind it becomes clear that women comprised 77 per cent of those interested in having one-on-one time with the relics (table 2.12).

The 1937 cure-seeker percentages indicate a decline in male requests for cure from 1933 Trier. They also mirror Blackbourn's analysis of those claiming cures at Marpingen (78 per cent of his cases were female; 22 per cent were male).[40] The decline in male participation from 1933

Table 2.12. Aachen totals by adult and children, 1937

Categories	No. (%)
Adult	
Female	2,961 (77.01)
Male	643 (16.72)
Children	241 (6.27)
Total	3,845 (100)

Sources: Data from DAA, 4.1.1.18, Krankenkarten A–C, 4.1.1.19, Krankenkarten D–G, 4.1.1.20, Krankenkarten H–K, 4.1.1.21, Krankenkarten L–P, 4.1.1.22, Krankenkarten Q–Z.

cannot be attributed merely to the fact that the sources do not distinguish children, because even if one were to assume all the 1937 Aachen children were male, this would still only add up to 22 per cent and represent a nearly 10 per cent decline over four years.

There are a few possible explanations for the decline in male participation over the course of the 1930s. First, the Coat of Trier was better known as a relic that heals. Stories of its miraculous healings circulated widely after 1844. Second, there was a notable drop in unemployment between 1933 and 1937. In January 1933 nine million Germans were out of work, and by January 1935 this number was reduced to around four million, meaning fewer men had leisure time to participate.[41] Third, men may have been reluctant to proclaim themselves diseased when the National Socialist regime increasingly labelled the sick as useless eaters and an intolerable burden on society. Perhaps Catholic men had, to some degree, internalized National Socialist notions of masculinity as standing above the church.[42] On 18 October 1935 the Nazis created the Law for the Protection of the Hereditary Health of the German People, which "provided for the banning of a marriage where one of the engaged couple suffered from an inherited disease, or from a mental illness."[43] Germans who were considered "hereditarily diseased" could not receive marriage loans and could be prevented from marrying. In this climate men may have thought twice about publicly identifying themselves as ill.

In the 1937 Aachen *Krankenkarten*, there is detailed age information for 308 of the applicants. These data reveal a notable swing upward in the average age of sick pilgrims in 1937, from an average age of forty-three to fifty-four years old for women, and from thirty-eight to forty-eight years old for men. This age shift also may have been affected by National Socialist notions of health, race, and hereditary disease. As in 1933 Trier, children tended not to be infants or ill babies, but between eight and nine years old.

As in the preceding century, pilgrims sought refuge from a number of diseases in 1937, including child lameness, cramps, gout, asthma,

Table 2.13. Age of applicants, Aachen 1937

Salutation	Sample size	Age		
		Average	Median	Mode
F	45	47.72	50.50	58
Frau	91	53.50	54.00	43
Frl.	57	46.10	47.00	47
Herr	40	48.20	49.00	52
Kind	42	8.99	8.00	8
M	12	37.38	33.00	53
Schw.	6	64.40	63.00	63
Wwe	15	63.69	63.50	74
Total	308			

Sources: Data from DAA, 4.1.1.18, Krankenkarten A–C, 4.1.1.19, Krankenkarten D–G, 4.1.1.20, Krankenkarten H–K, 4.1.1.21, Krankenkarten L–P, 4.1.1.22, Krankenkarten Q–Z.

Table 2.14. Age of applicants by adult and children, Aachen 1937

Categories	Sample size	Age		
		Average	Median	Mode
Adult				
Female	214	51.30	52.00	58
Male	52	45.59	48.50	64
Child	42	8.99	8.00	8
Total	308			

Sources: Data from DAA, 4.1.1.18, Krankenkarten A–C, 4.1.1.19, Krankenkarten D–G, 4.1.1.20, Krankenkarten H–K, 4.1.1.21, Krankenkarten L–P, 4.1.1.22, Krankenkarten Q–Z.

eye troubles, afflictions (*Gebrechen*), general illness, and epilepsy. Of the 3,410 *Krankenkarten* requests, 3,154 pilgrims (92.49 per cent) specified the disease they believed the Aachen relic could help them overcome. Like the data from 1933, table 2.15 breaks these diseases down into larger groups where possible. For example, any injury characterized by spasms or seizures (*Anfall, Schlaganfall, Aufbringung*) is simplified to "seizure," or varied complaints about pulse, heart rate, or heart pain are categorized as "heart"; similarly, bronchitis (*Bronchitis*), breathlessness (*Atemnot*), asthma (*Asthma*), and tuberculosis (*Tuberkulose*) all fall under "lungs." The most common requests were for relief from general "sickness," 2,585, (*Krankheit, Kranken*) and unspecified "suffering," 89, (*Leidend*).[44]

By the 1930s pilgrims spoke with medical precision and gave specific names to their ailments. During this decade, many of the

Table 2.15. Pilgrimage illness complaints by type, Aachen 1937

Illness	No. of complaints	Original description
Sickness	2,585	*Krank*
Suffering	89	*Leidend*
Heart	66	*Herz*
Legs	58	*Beine*
Nerves	56	*Nerven*
Eyes	47	*Augen*
Lungs	29	*Lungen*
Head pain	26	*Kopf/Kopfschmerzen*
Blind	21	*Blind*
Stomach	18	*Magen*
Ears	17	*Ohren*
Arms	12	*Arme*
Epilepsy	12	*Epilepsie*
Gout	10	*Gicht*
Rheumatism	10	*Rheumatismus*
Accident	8	*Anfall*
Breast	8	*Brust*
Kidneys	8	*Nieren*
Back	7	*Rücken*
Child sickness	7	*Kind*
Diabetes	6	*Zuckerkrankheit*
Joint	6	*Gelenk*
Liver	5	*Leber*
Surgery	5	*Operiert*
Woman suffering	5	*Frauenleidend*
Spiritual ailment	4	*Geist*
War wounds	4	*Krieg*
Blood	3	*Blut*
Phlebitis	3	*Venenentzündung*
Sciatica	3	*Ischias*
Paralysis	2	*Körperlähmung*
Cramps	2	*Krämpfe*
Bladder	1	*Blase*
Skin	1	*Haut*
Speech	1	*Sprachfehler*
Arthritis	1	*Arthritis*

Sources: Data from DAA, 4.1.1.18, Krankenkarten A–C, 4.1.1.19, Krankenkarten D–G, 4.1.1.20, Krankenkarten H–K, 4.1.1.21, Krankenkarten L–P, 4.1.1.22, Krankenkarten Q–Z.

nineteenth-century complaints about hysteria and unknowable sufferings disappeared from pilgrimage rhetoric. Pilgrims in the 1930s endured a wide variety of illnesses, but above all they were concerned about ambulatory sicknesses that restricted their ability to freely move. Many cure-seekers had specifically modern problems, including injuries from car accidents and industrial work-related wounds or disfigurements. While there were still many seeking relief from "blood disease," "illness," and "nerves," pilgrims knew to name their afflictions in medical terms with a specificity and standardization that could only have come from increased contact with physicians and growing awareness of contemporary medicine.

At the same time, the 1930s pilgrimages reveal a number of continuities from the nineteenth century. The average sick pilgrim remained an adult somewhere between thirty and fifty-five years old. This suggests that the individuals had suffered from their pains, aches, lameness, or other illness for an extended period. Likely they had already visited the doctor (in the case of Trier, they had at least once) and not found relief. Pilgrims, in the 1930s, especially desired to be cured of diseases that reduced their quality of life, or threatened to shorten their lifespan. Although this numerical analysis does not allow for insights into the mentality of the petitioners, it is clear that Catholic belief in the ability of relics to enable an encounter with the divine persisted into the National Socialist period, and that this belief was not polarized among the very young and very old, the poor or the rich, men or women, but actually appealed to a wide range of German Catholics with health problems.

Men were not as underrepresented in both 1933 and 1937 as they were in nineteenth-century miracle accounts. Although men did not often proclaim themselves cured, they pursued miraculous interventions more frequently than historians have realized, suggesting these cure-seekers preserved Catholicism as part of their identity.[45] The diseases that plagued pilgrims were not gender-specific. The biggest complaints – vision, lameness, suffering, stomach, and heart – cut across boundaries and greatly overshadowed gendered diagnoses such as cervix, uterus, and *Frauenleiden*, which comprised only a handful of petitions. Cure-seekers saw the relics as being linked to the bodies of Jesus, Mary, and John the Baptist. That divine connection could overcome the limits of contemporary physicians and restore broken bodies.

Pilgrims believed their suffering was interconnected with the potential for divine intervention. Pilgrimage became a test of faith; if participants were lame, they could secure a cure by bearing the hardship of the journey. For example, Margretha Keinsler was fifty-five years old and suffered from gout. She watched her legs turn "lightning blue" over time and was bedridden for up to two weeks at a time.[46] The gout eventually spread to her hands and breasts. She travelled to visit a hospital in Bliescastel, where physicians unsuccessfully attempted to stop the disease by slicing open the wounds. She visited Trier on 4 September 1844 and could barely stand from her swollen feet and legs. Müller brought her before the Coat, and after touching it, she had to sit down because she felt as though she were floating.[47] When she got up the next day, her legs were more powerful and she regained mobility in her fingers. Doctors could not help Margretha and they advised her not to travel. When she did consult physicians, the proposed cure of cutting open her many wounds was worse than enduring the condition. She believed that if she could reach the divine presence of the Coat, God would renew her ambulatory ability. She numbered among the many who fixated on diseases that reduced their mobility. Five of the eleven miracles proclaimed as authentic in the *Bericht* for 1844 were related to lameness. This trend continued into the 1930s. In 1933 Trier, "lameness" and "legs" were the third and fourth greatest requests, behind "heart" and "lungs." At the 1937 Aachen pilgrimage, "legs" were only behind "pain" and "heart" as the principal complaints. Cure-seekers believed that if they could somehow get to the relic, they could find healing. God had challenged them with immobility, but if they could get to Him they would find relief and independence.

The Threshold of Divine Presence

Pilgrims claiming to have been healed left vivid accounts of their experiences in Aachen and Trier. In their narratives, cure-seekers tended to make four consistent points about the Rhenish miracle experience: (1) there are limits to what science and physicians can accomplish, thus cure narratives stress that modern medicine has reached the end of its capabilities; (2) there are physical sensations that accompany experiencing the divine presence; (3) there are results from directly touching the relics or from being in their proximity, namely, a cure or physical and/or emotional transformation; (4) after encountering the relic one must give appropriate thanks. Pilgrims recounting their experience usually included all four of these components in their story. However, there was no script that pilgrims followed, and miracle narratives recounted highly personal experiences between the 1830s and the 1930s. What follows is an examination of several cure narratives through the century, each emphasizing at least one of these four essential elements.[48]

In 1844, the *Ehrenwache*, or local volunteers who guarded the relic and watched over pilgrims, gave written testimony about each cure they witnessed.[49] Local press and pamphleteers used these reports in order to corroborate miracle stories. The *Ehrenwache* testimony reveals two crucial aspects about the 1844 encounter with the Coat of Trier: the centrality of witnesses to confirm events, and the necessity of physical action to trigger a cure. For example, in the testimony recounting Countess Droste zu Vischering, the *Ehrenwache* first established that six reliable individuals were present, including a sailor, private secretary, butcher, and innkeeper.[50] Each testified that the Countess approached the Coat with her grandmother and a small entourage. After going before the Coat and praying, she dropped the crutches. Her grandmother and General Vicar Müller helped Droste zu Vischering out of the church. Thus, for the *Ehrenwache* it was not the physical contact with the Coat but the moving through the cathedral and prayer leading up to the encounter that brought about physical restoration.[51] Pilgrims sang about Droste zu Vischering's cure narrative in a popular song:

Freifrau von Droste zu Vischering	Countess von Droste zu Vischering
Freifrau von Droste zu Vischering	Countess von Droste zu Vischering
Zum Heil'gen Rock nach Trier ging;	Went to the Holy Coat of Trier;
Sie kroch auf allen vieren,	She crawled on all fours,
Das tat sie sehr genieren,	She did this very embarrassed,
Sie mußte auf zweien Krücken	She relied on two crutches,
Durch dieses Leben rücken.	To move through this life.
Sie sprach, als sie zum Rocke kam:	As she came to the Coat she spoke,
Ich bin auf allen vieren lahm,	I am on all fours – lame,
Du Rock bist ganz unnähtig	You, Coat, are completely seamless
Und ganz entsetzlich gnädig,	And completely gracious,
Zeig mir dein Gnadenlichte!	Show me your light of grace!
Ich bin des Bischofs Nichte.	I am the bishop's niece.
Da gab der Rock in seinem Schrein	There was the Coat in its shrine
Auf einmal einen hellen Schein;	And suddenly a bright glow;
Das fuhr ihr durch die Glieder,	That went through her limbs,
Sie kriegt das Laufen wieder,	She regained her ability to walk again,
Sie ließ die Krücken drinnen	She left the crutches inside
Und ging vergnügt von hinnen.	And walked delightedly outside.
Freifrau von Droste zu Vischering	Countess von Droste zu Vischering
Noch selb'gen Tag zum Tanze ging.	That very day went dancing.
Dies Wunder, göttlich grausend,	This miracle, divinely sent
Geschah im Jahre tausend-	Happened in the Year one thousand,
Achthundert-fünfundvierzig,	eight hundred, and forty-five
Und wer's nicht glaubt, der irrt sich.[52]	And whoever does not believe, is wrong.

The year is incorrect, but the song nevertheless reveals the popularization of the cult of the Coat. Here the Countess is healed by being near the Coat. Her proximity to the sacred centre is enough for the mystical glow to flow out of the relic and into her troubled limbs.

Like the *Ehrenwache* testimony of Droste zu Vischering, the story of eleven-year-old Catharina Schell emphasized the power for pilgrims of being adjacent to the Coat. Schell visited the Coat on 7 September 1844. She had suffered from gout since Christmas 1843. Her stepmother hoped the child would find relief through pilgrimage. At 8:00 in the morning Schell entered the cathedral, trembling in her crutches. As she came before the Coat she fainted and was carried out of the church. Schell approached the Coat again, and after praying with her stepmother she once more fainted. When she recovered she stated that she no longer needed her crutches, walked out, and continued to improve afterwards.[53] Once more, the *Ehrenwache* established that others were present as witnesses, including Schell's stepmother and Anna Maria Gehren, whose husband was the mayor of Rindenberg. Similarly, fifty-one-year-old Mathias Mieler, who suffered from a contracted left leg for two years, was healed after simply walking past the relic.[54] Here again it was the *presence* of the Coat that healed. Schell and Mieler were in proximity to objects linked to the bodies of the Holy Family and were overwhelmed. They crossed through the experience to emerge free of gout and crutches and transformed into new individuals.

However, proximity to the relic was not always enough to initiate physical change in the faithful. Twenty-one-year-old Maria Sibilla Müller suffered from a malformed hand and stiffness in her arms, a condition that began around Christmas 1842. Twice she came before the Coat and convulsed and fainted. Her sister helped her to secure permission to touch the relic, with the hope that physical contact would bring about a complete healing. When they arrived at the cathedral, Maria and her sister realized they had misplaced the bishop's permission form. Still clergy allowed her to touch the Coat. As soon as Maria brushed the relic she felt her strength returning. She prayed for thirty minutes and afterwards felt completely restored. Her previously black-and-blue hand began to heal.[55] Even though the relic initially overpowered Maria, it was only by touching the garment that she was physically transformed.

For German pilgrims, healing could bring ecstasy, or what Mircea Eliade has termed a "return to Paradise" characterized by "the overcoming of time and History."[56] In 1867, Franz Lauschet wrote to Aachen authorities to report the cure of a twenty-one-year-old woman from Friesenrath.[57] Lauschet explained how the woman suffered from a nervous disorder that sent her into uncontrolled screaming fits on the floor. These episodes left her with bloodied hands, ankles, and knees. The frequency of the attacks brought on a contraction of her knees, so that she had to lean forward to walk. In the five months leading up to the 1867 exhibition her condition worsened to the point that her confessor asked Lauschet to help the unnamed woman travel to the relics of Aachen. In the cathedral a priest touched Jesus's Loincloth to her head, and as he did so she prayed, "Son of David have mercy on me."[58] Lauschet took her out of the cathedral to a nearby plaza. Together with a priest he continued to pray over the girl. They told her not to lose heart and that God might yet help her. Dramatically, and only after Lauschet thought she would die, or, at the very least that he would have to carry her back home, the woman stood up straight, said she was healed, and proceeded back to the church. Lauschet called out to her, "Where are you going?" She replied, "I must give thanks, I must give thanks." Once more in the cathedral she prayed a series of Our Fathers and the rosary, and concluded with additional recitations of the Lord's Prayer. For the cured, this experience was a restoration, a return to the paradisal form. In the liminal moment, at the point of the Loincloth touching her head, she called on Jesus to have pity on her and to restore her hand.[59] For the healed, this paradisal moment was a temporary transcending of her body. She was momentarily brought to the presence of Jesus and restored.

Frau Willmann first became ill in February 1929, suffering from pulmonary disease and requiring a cane to move about. Standing before the Holy Coat in 1933 did not restore her body. After securing permission to touch the garment from the Pilgrimage Committee, Willmann made her way into the cathedral on Saturday morning and had a visceral experience in the presence of the Coat: "[I felt] alternatively hot and cold. I was seized by severe pain and broke out in sweat. I felt a rush of blood to my head and thought I would suffer a stroke and die.... All of this happened after I first touched the Coat. Then suddenly I felt a strong jolt.... With the second touch I inwardly stated, 'Dear God, stand with me!' Then I felt I was healed.... I wept, but without that I would have had the feeling that I had to cry!"[60] Willmann was so drawn to God in those moments that the encounter defied description. Those around her immediately noted she was changed. After the miracle, Willmann became a local celebrity; indeed, residents of Mutterstadt waited for her at the train station, where she showed her grandson she could now jump.[61]

An Overwhelming Encounter

The cured were often physically and emotionally overcome by their divine encounter. They cried out in ecstasy or pain, fell to their knees, gripped their body tightly, wept openly, and shuddered. Crying out or screaming was a central component of mid-nineteenth-century pilgrimage. In his observations about the pilgrimage, Jakob Marx noted that one often heard cries of "Oh God!" when individuals approached the Coat.[62] The first and most famous exclamation came from Droste zu Vischering; as word of her miracle spread, it became common for people to scream out in the Trier cathedral. Jacob Oppenhäuser, father of the cured Madgalena Oppenhäuser, reported that his daughter was unable to contain herself after being healed of lameness. After the cure she shouted, "I will not ride, Father! I am now healthy and can walk, I will walk with the procession. Take me with you, Dad!"[63] The cured experienced extreme joy and enthusiastically proclaimed themselves restored after their encounter with the relics.

For some, their experience with the relics involved a shuddering or shivering. Heinrich Meier, thirty-two years old, from Herne, was able to touch the Coat in August 1933 with the intention of healing the swelling in his feet and knees. One hour later, Meier noted, "In my legs, in the knees and ankles, a a [*sic*] cold shiver went through my body."[64] Fifty-one-year-old Frl. Hepting travelled to Trier in 1933 because she had been bedridden for the previous six years. Hepting was taken into the cathedral, where a priest prayed before the relic and each of the sick was given an opportunity to see the Coat. Hepting explained to the *Neue Augsburger Zeitung* that following the prayer, "I felt a lightness throughout my body that I cannot explain. It was like a shudder. My legs felt tighter, it was as if suddenly they were strong and I could walk."[65] The following morning one of the nuns volunteering at the hospital found her walking around and physically restored. In order to assuage sceptics, the *Augsburger Zeitung* included a picture of Hepting and the sister (see figure 2.2). Like Droste zu Vischering, Catharina Droleit, twenty-four years old, had a stiff right leg. She could not get around without the assistance of a cane or friends. On 29 September 1844 she visited the Coat. Herr Edinger, a member of the cathedral guards (*Ehrenwache*) on duty that morning, reported that after Droleit touched the relic she "cried loudly." Similarly, another witness reported that she yelled so loudly "that you could hear the shouts below the church."[66] Droleit, after five minutes of prayer before the relic, was able to bend her knee and leave the cathedral without her crutch or her friends supporting her.

At the local level in 1844 Trier, there was no clear "feminization" divide between male and female pilgrims. In recounting their own physical cures, men were less likely to describe uncontrolled emotions. For example, they were less likely to cry out when they touched the Coat. Mathias Mieler and Jacob Heinz, the two most famous males cured, did not weep before the Coat or after touching the relic. At the same time, male pilgrims were at times deeply moved by their journeys. Jakob Marx watched a man enter the cathedral openly weeping. The observed pilgrim gave a large donation and stated it was for "the reversal of a large sin."[67] Pilgrim experiences were highly individuated and it is difficult to generalize on the basis of gender.

Fainting was common among the cured. Josephina Wagner passed out for five to eight minutes after touching the Coat in 1844. Wagner suffered from falling sickness and daily attacks as a result of abuse from her stepfather as a child. She spent fourteen days walking to Trier unaccompanied. After arriving she continued to deteriorate, but when she touched the relic her symptoms subsided. Johann Olk reported to the Pilgrimage Committee that she stayed in Trier ten more days, she gave thanks at Mass, and he never saw her hurt again.[68]

Pilgrims believed that they first had to prepare themselves to encounter God in the relics. When Maria Anna Keiss arrived in Trier she made confession and took communion. Her family could not afford shoes when she was a child. As an adult her feet were so damaged that Keiss needed crutches to move around. Living barefoot, Keiss believed, had also triggered the gout plaguing her lower extremities. Following communion and confession, she went to the cathedral and was allowed to touch the Coat. She described how she temporarily felt a "power" before the relic. As she descended the first altar stair with her crutches, she paused. Later she recalled a force within her that lasted as long as "several Our Fathers." Following her encounter with the Coat, Keiss entered sacred time, not measured in minutes or seconds, but in units of prayer. At the second step Keiss sensed that her legs were healed and continued down without her crutches.[69] For cure-seekers, the relic created or allowed a physical manifestation of the divine liminal encounter. Pilgrims, like Keiss, often viewed their healing as a multi-step process.

By the beginning of the twentieth century, the enduring nature of Rhineland relic miracles was an essential aspect of pilgrim narratives. The prioress of a Carmelite order in San Francisco wrote in 1909 to verify her version of the Droste zu Vischering cure. In this account Droste zu Vischering wept and wailed prior to touching the garment:

Aided by her grandmother and the other lady, the Countess mounted the right staircase leading to the choir and approached the saint Relic. Before she stopped, and always supported by her crutches, she remained there for some time, standing quite still and nearly motionless, hiding her face in her hands and performing a silent prayer. Suddenly she dropped her crutches, spoke a few words to her grandmother, and without any help she knelt down, audibly weeping and praying. Her followers as well as the assembled pilgrims did the same. After about five minutes the

Countess rose, and by the suffragan bishop, Dr. Müller, was led to the right side of the saint's Tunic, where the Canon de Wilmowsky was sitting. Here the Countess, continually weeping and praying, knelt again, and her right hand directed by Monsg. de Wilmowsky, touched the saint's Tunic. She remained kneeling before the Relic for five to eight minutes, then the Countess rose, this time without any help of her assistants, turned swiftly, and at her grandmother's arm, treading flat on both soles of her feet, she descended the left staircase, a liveryman bearing the crutches after her.[70]

Everyone in the cathedral knelt down to praise God in one accord for the miracle. Despite this flourish, not mentioned in the 1844 accounts, the 1909 version from the United States closely resembles the testimony given by those around Droste zu Vischering in 1844. The climax of re-telling was coming before the presence of the Coat. The actual touching brought the cure, but Droste zu Vischering was already exhibiting the symptoms of crossing a threshold before Wilmowsky guided her hand to the Coat. Furthermore, it is revealing that by 1909, the sisters focused on the permanence of the healing: "And the next day, for the first time, and afterwards at Kreuznach and Münster, [she] was examined by some highly celebrated medical men, such as Dr. Hansen at Trier, Dr. Prieger at Kreuznach and Dr. Busch at Münster. On September 1st the Countess left Trier for Kreuznach, where she continued to make use of the waters for a fortnight. All to whom she had formerly been known there, were filled with wonder, when they saw her walking without crutches."[71]

The healing power of the Coat persisted long after a pilgrimage and, like the *Andenken* recipients, cure-seekers believed they did not necessarily require direct contact with the relics to find physical restoration. In 1830, Trier resident Rosalia wrote to her brother Anton to report that their mother was healed from her unnamed sickness relapse after holding onto a picture of the Coat. This *Andenken* was touched to the relic in 1810 and played a pivotal role in her recovery.[72] Rosalia initially expressed concern that the three images she had of the Coat would be too small for the job, but, in the end, her health improved. Another example of this second-hand sacrality: Father Breitz wrote to Jakob Marx explaining his encounter with Johann Müller II, whose three-year-old son was sick. The child suffered from tumours and could not rest, and, in turn, the parents had been unsuccessfully trying to help him for nine months. They took their son to Trier and had his cap touched to the Coat. By the time they got home the tumours had cleared and the child was peaceful.[73]

Germans went on pilgrimage hoping for physical, spiritual, and emotional cures. Individuals walked for several days or through the night in order to seek the healing potential of Trier and Aachen.[74] For pilgrims, cures came as a chance to remodel their lives, to transcend the limitations of their physical bodies. Pastor Steffens in Enkerich wrote to the bishop in Trier in November 1844 to explain some of the changes he witnessed among his parishioners. One woman, "who led a most unchristian life," had to visit the Coat three times. On the third her vision was restored as she was looking at the relic that Jesus wore.[75] This was a case of a sudden cure and was delivered for her salvation. Steffens explained that she was blind before and did not have enough faith – but on the third visit she was restored in response to her perseverance and belief. Similarly, Katharina Petsch was relieved of the paralysis on the right side of her body only after visiting the Coat twice, initially to look upon the relic, and then to touch it. Petsch was healed after learning it was possible to physically encounter the Coat, having learned about Droste zu Vischering's experience after arriving in Trier. She viewed her recovery as having parallels to Christ's sufferings. He carried a cross to Golgotha; she bore her cane to Trier. She understood her recovery as a blessing received because she was able to visit both the 1810 and 1844 Trier exhibitions.[76] Petsch was repeatedly near the Coat, and that proximity to the sacred transformed her body.

Encountering the relics, and in some cases simply hearing about the miracles, brought peace to Rhineland Catholics throughout the century. Angela Altringer described to the Pilgrimage Committee how "fear and unease" left her after she saw the Coat in 1844.[77] Altringer was also physically restored, but her letter places greater emphasis on the emotional healing that came with completing the pilgrimage. In 1935, eighty-year-old E. Wurzer wrote to her pastor, explaining that she had been ill since she had fallen down and hoped the year would bring her a good death. Wurzer was cheered by the fact that her sister had been doing better since the 1933 pilgrimage and because she heard that a completely paralyzed Protestant woman, who was told she would never survive the journey, was fully healed after visiting Trier.[78]

Parents hoped that encountering the relics would lead to a better future for their children. In 1844, Johannes Michael Dreher and his wife brought their son to Trier because he was sickly and weak and required crutches to move around. The Dreher parents had great hope that touching the Coat would give their child new strength. After his son touched the Coat, Johannes Dreher wept to see him walk unaided. He shed more tears of thanks for God above and for Bishop Arnoldi for letting his ill son touch the Coat.[79] Similarly, eleven-year-old Jacob Heinz came to Trier with his mother and was healed of speechlessness. Heinz was a unique case, as his affliction came on him after initially visiting the Coat and so his mother had to return to Trier for him to be healed.[80]

Pilgrims were willing to risk much for a chance to encounter the divine through the Rhineland relics. Maria Müller of Bacharach had been suffering since she was twelve from dropsy and kidney disease. Thirty-six years later Müller lived her life confined to her bed and in consistent pain. She decided that she would go to touch the Coat, despite warnings that she should not leave her bed for an hour, and certainly should not brave the four-hour car ride from Bacharach to Trier. Despite the warnings, Sister Gisela agreed to escort her to the cathedral and the relic. On the way to Trier, Müller confided in Gisela, telling her, "Either I will receive help from the Coat or the Saviour will take me."[81] In the cathedral, Müller cried out and collapsed after touching the relic. Before Dr. Bellmann could get her to the descending stairs, he pronounced her dead.[82] Afterwards physicians in Trier stated she had suffered from a heart attack. The Trier Domvikar notified Müller's cousin, explaining that Müller received one of her preferred options in Trier: death.

Journey metaphors abound in descriptions of healing. Pilgrims focused on movement. This preoccupation is manifest in the previous discussion of ambulatory cures related to lameness, legs, and feet, and is prevalent in pilgrim testimonies. Margretha Keinsler, in a report to the 1844 Pilgrimage Committee, described how her legs turned blue and her blood thickened. She was not able to wear boots or shoes and had to go barefoot because of the pain and swelling.[83] Keinsler's sickness worsened until she could not go to church or leave her house. When doctors could not help her, she decided that only by making the painful trip to Trier would there be any hope of relief. In the cathedral Keinsler could not stand because her feet had swollen from the journey. Two men assisted her when she could no longer carry herself. The next day she visited the Coat again, this time without her crutches, and she was healed over the following night. Similarly, in 1925 Aachen, Father Lenartz wrote to a colleague to report the healing of Frau Schnitzler's leg. After visiting no fewer than eight doctors she was still not able to get around on her own. However, after touching the Aachen relic she was healed over the next two days. Lenartz was happy to report "the woman can walk."[84] In both cases, the journey itself brought on the cure. Travellers were purified through pain; they believed it necessary to cross into divine space on their own power before they could find relief.

The cured wrote to Trier and Aachen to give thanks. Frau Maria Amo from Prüm, fifty-four years old, offered thanks for healing seven years after her 1888 cure. Amo suffered from an unknown disease for seventeen years that caused festering wounds to form all over her body.

Neither regional nor local doctors could cure her, so she travelled to Aachen in 1881 to touch the relic, but she did not have the required clerical permission. Amo had to wait seven years until the 1888 exhibition, during which the bishop granted her access. The morning after touching the Aachen Loincloth, the bandages she used to bind the sores on her arm were dry.[85] Amo stated that she wanted to say thanks and that she had remained healthy and had not needed to visit any physicians since 1888. As part of her thank offering, Amo again made the pilgrimage in 1895 with her son, who hoped to find relief from his weak hearing.

Joh. Kessler wrote to Trier officials in 1936 to give thanks for his 1933 miracle, which included a vision after touching the Coat. "As I touched the Coat and withdrew my hand," he recalled, "something of the Coat hung on my hand. I wanted to look out at the cathedral, which shone in a beautiful white-blue colour and was empty of people, until the bishop blessed me and told me, 'Go in peace my son.'"[86] Kessler, a pensioner from the Rhineland, had suffered from difficulty walking, a consequence of his career as a miner and soldier. After he touched the Coat, Kessler's condition improved to the point that he no longer needed to be carried. He could independently move with the assistance of two canes. Although only partially recovered, he was so thankful that he again made the seventy-three-kilometre journey from Elversberg with his crutches to offer praise to Jesus and Mary for his renewed strength and mobility. Another cure-seeker, Frau Minna Brenner, had suffered from debilitating back and abdominal pain during menstruation since she was sixteen. Brenner consulted multiple physicians and endured two operations to help relieve the pain. She was prescribed opium, but it only brought temporary relief, so that she relied on her sister to help run the household and to take care of her child. Brenner decided to go to the Trier Coat in 1933. After she touched the relic the pain persisted, but subsided after she had refreshment and received the Eucharist. In the end she was independently mobile and free of physical suffering.[87] Her recovery testimony contained an implicit criticism that the medical prescriptions of tampons, douches, opiums, and surgeries were nothing compared to the physical contact with Jesus's garments.

In another 1933 case, Eugenie Klaffschenkel thanked Mary for providing her with a physical transformation. Klaffschenkel was led to the Trier cathedral at three o'clock in the morning. Although she was taken through an alley to make the journey shorter, by the time she arrived she was weak and drenched in sweat. Upon entering the cathedral, she felt a change that made it possible for her to walk up the altar stairs unassisted. Afterwards she went the entire day without her cane and had

Figure 2.3. Frau Lippert with priest and pilgrimage coordinator after being cured, 1933.
Source: BATr, Abt. 90, Nr. 132.

a restored appetite. Klaffschenkel believed Mary had taken pity on her and restored her ability to walk.[88]

Conclusion

By the twentieth century, the Trier Coat was an international symbol for physical restoration. Reports of the 1844 miracles continued to influence pilgrim attitudes into the 1930s. Pilgrims circumnavigated clerical and scientific attempts to verify cures by choosing to believe cure narratives, or by not bothering to report their own healing, or by taking part of the sacral power of the relic to sick loved ones by bringing them an *Andenken*. "What is modern about modernity?," William Egginton has asked.[89] In the nineteenth- and twentieth-century German-Catholic miracle culture there are quintessential elements of modernity, such as increased access to the relic made possible by new transportation, and

Figure 2.4. Frl. Hepting with nun who found her walking after six years.
Source: BATr, Abt. 90, Nr. 129, 110, *Neue Augsburger Zeitung*, 12 Sept. 1933,
"Schwerkrank nach Trier – genesend zurück," no. 204.

scientific descriptions of diseases and bodies, but such technology and
discourse were accompanied in the Rhineland by a strong continuity
of belief in miracles. German Catholics pursued the healing power and
divine presence of Rhenish holy sites into the Third Reich.

The stakes were high during the 1930s cures. While National Socialists debated eugenics and who belonged to the "Aryan" community,
the Catholic Church required the sick to bring forms from their doctors that enquired into the health of other family members. The church
wanted to ascertain whether a condition was chronic throughout one's
family, as that would be an even stronger testimony to the curing and
restorative authority of the Coat. Similarly, as the Nazis condemned
the chronically sick, Germans with inherited medical conditions, and
the developmentally disabled as "useless eaters," the church publicly
offered them a place of honour. While remaining sceptical and hesi-
tant, remembering the public relations disasters of the 1840s, the church

continued to minister to the sick while at the same time requiring stricter proof that they were ill and would benefit from touching the Aachen or Trier relics. For the church, those designated as a drain on German society by the Nazis, beyond the assistance of modern medicine, were the best candidates for a miracle.

In 1933, Bishop Dr. Antonius Hilfreich of Limburg/Lahn delivered a homily to several hundred assembled pilgrims in Trier. In his message Hilfreich covered familiar ground for the pilgrims – the Coat brought them closer to its original owner, Jesus had bled on the garment, and it could heal. Hilfreich reminded the faithful that they were composed of two elements: body and spirit, and spirit is the higher of the two. The bishop urged the pilgrims to not just see the Coat with their physical eye but to turn to it with their spiritual eye and see that the saviour of the Gospels was before them.[90] Hilfreich emphasized an important shift in clerical opinion about relics from the 1830s to the 1930s: a move from bodily and physical emphasis to stressing the spiritual healing, reconciliation, and symbolism. This clerical turn is the subject of chapter 5. The next chapter examines another important aspect of pilgrim practices: the purchasing, creating, and exchanging of pilgrim remembrances, or *Andenken*.

3 The Sacred Economy

Pilgrim salami, lighters, pens, pins, chocolates, cookies, sweat towels, magnets, bookmarks, paperweights, cigarette lighters, T-shirts, hats, pilgrimage wine – these were just some of the available items for purchase by travellers to the 2012 Heilig Rock Wallfahrt in Trier, Germany. There is a long-standing tradition within Western Germany of religious journey, and of pilgrims buying or manufacturing their own *Andenken* (remembrances) or *Abzeichen* (badges) to mark their journey to a Catholic site. The sacred economy had two components. It was monetary and included the buying and selling of physical objects. But it was also a spiritual economy that was predicated on the belief that God, through a divine plan, left a piece of the eternal on the earth to aid the faithful. Within this sacred economy the wealth, worth, and merit of a sacred object was determined by the physical proximity to the relics in these towns. Even as the number of objects available increased in diversity between 1832 and 1937, pilgrims continuously thought of their *Andenken* and *Abzeichen* as part of the holy, a connection to the sacred – not mere trinkets or souvenirs.[1] At the same time, this sacred economy expanded geographically, in the sense that an increasing number of Catholics around the world were able to participate in the holy marketplace, which was always centred in Trier or Aachen – foci of German Catholic piety and religious journeys within the Rhineland.

In *Andenken* pilgrims found a way to bring the sacred presence of Rhineland relics home.[2] Pilgrims believed pilgrimage objects could change their lives. *Andenken* recipients – from Rhinelanders to Brazilians – believed they could interact with and be part of the holy through the religious objects, which included medals, relic silk, and rosaries.[3] Participation in the sacred economy required that pilgrims undergo a *presentification* whereby they were bodily linked to an object, which could bring healing, relief from suffering, conversion to loved ones, or even employment.[4] Pilgrims related to *Andenken* physically. In their letters to Aachen and Trier clergy, they recorded how *Andenken* remained present in their lives after they completed pilgrimages.[5]

Between 1832 and 1937, Rhineland clergy worried about the aesthetics of *Andenken* and the meanings such objects conveyed. They wanted to avoid any reproduction that would damage the holy reputation of their sacred relics. Trier clergy in 1933, for example, worked to define the parameters of "authentic" *Andenken* and to ensure pilgrims did not buy "kitschy" objects that were not sufficiently reverent towards the Holy Coat. Here again clerical regulation diverged from pilgrimage expectations.

Trier and Aachen pilgrim correspondence also reveals the importance of *Andenken* for European Catholics. Travellers make no mention of a slackening of the sacred, nor do they complain that their *Andenken* were cheap reproductions.[6] For the pilgrims to Aachen and Trier, the devotional objects derived their authenticity from their proximity to the relic. Here one can think of *Andenken* value in terms of concentric circles with a Rhenish relic at the centre – the closer an item came to the middle, the more it was worth in the sacred economy.[7] Thus a rosary purchased in Trier or Aachen was more prized than one acquired at a non-pilgrimage location, and an item that physically touched a relic was most highly valued.

Even as items became more standardized and were mass-produced, the significance pilgrims assigned to their devotional items did not significantly change over time.[8] Why did travellers to Aachen and Trier purchase depictions of the relics? How did they describe objects they purchased to commemorate their journeys?[9] In general, historians have grouped the varied items for sale at religious sites with the merchandise found at touristic destinations. Underlying this link is the ongoing debate on whether or not pilgrimages and tourism are similar activities in the modern period.[10] As scholars have woven this discussion into analyses of consumption, they tend to point out that objects made available to pilgrims in the nineteenth and twentieth centuries were produced, shipped, and, some have contended, consumed in the same way as the increasingly available knick-knacks at touristic destinations.[11] One scholar has gone so far as to call the items for sale to pilgrims in Lourdes – "the souvenirs, bottled water, and inexpensive religious trinkets" merely the "vulgar … mumbo jumbo" of commercialism.[12]

Scholars of German pilgrimage often compare German practices with those of Lourdes, France – where Bernadette Soubirous experienced a Marian apparition in 1858 – in order to note the similarity of devotional objects across Europe. David Blackbourn uses an example of a German who was appalled by what he found at Lourdes at 1876, to begin his discussion of the commercialization of Marpingen. In Marpingen, the entire community commercially mobilized after the Marian apparitions. Innkeepers and bar owners offered accommodation, townsfolk improvised bed and breakfasts, hawkers tried to sell medals, tradesmen attempted to sell Marpingen water, drunks tried to sell dirt from near the apparition site, and so on.[13] In France, mass marketing of devotional objects risked diluting their authenticity. As Suzanne Kaufman writes, "[A] traditional Christian pilgrimage site and its sacred objects are endowed with both a sense of sacred aura and miraculous power by their association with a unique divine power: Jesus, Mary, or a saint. This sacred aura and miraculous power was thrown into question at Lourdes by the mass-marketing of the shrine and its goods."[14] While emphasizing sources related to vendors illuminates an important aspect of commerce and pilgrimage – the generation and distribution of *Andenken* – these documents reveal little about how pilgrims related to the items.

In Trier and Aachen, pilgrims found great overlap in devotional objects, such as medals, postcards, and rosaries. Yet the form of the *Andenken* was ultimately superficial. It is in the local manifestations of these "ideal types" that one gets a better sense of what was important to pilgrims historically, how Catholics saw themselves and depicted themselves, and how relics were venerated. Dismissing the different forms of *Andenken* as trivial souvenirs misses the multifaceted ways that pilgrims found significance in their devotional objects. For example, in the case of Aachen and Trier, pilgrims hoped to acquire part of the silk used to wrap the relics between exhibitions. These *Andenken* were few and treasured by their possessors, much like travellers to Lourdes prized bottles of water from the grotto where Mary appeared. Letters sent to Pilgrimage Committees in Germany offer an intimate view of the sacred economy as it was constructed, understood, and imagined by participants.

Increased Diversity of Objects Available

As the variety of objects available to pilgrims increased in the mid-nineteenth century there was less evidence of pilgrims creating their own items. This decline in homemade objects was the result of two factors. First, clerics began to intervene in the sacred economy. Second, for pilgrims it became more convenient to acquire items on site because of the growing selection of objects available and the corresponding upsurge in independent vendors. Availability combined with church endorsement of certain items negated the need to produce one's own remembrance. Of course, purchasing *Andenken* from religious journeys was not new to the nineteenth century or unique to the Rhineland. In Trier, historians have found pilgrim objects dating to the fourteenth century.[15] Aachen also has a rich history of sixteenth-century pilgrimages, including detailed woodcuts by German printer Arnt van Aich that taught the history of the relics in the Aachen cathedral.[16] Van Aich's images remain an important part of the Aachen pilgrimage tradition; for example, they were used to create mementos of the 1965 pilgrimage.[17]

Before pilgrims had ready access to mass-produced objects, they were highly creative in generating their own items to mark their passage to Trier or Aachen. The surviving remembrances from the eighteenth century are crafted, handmade, and often embroidered. In addition, pilgrims were eager to customize household objects, such as pipes, to recall the relics of Aachen. These self-made items reflect participants' desire to bring part of the sacred home and to have a tangible reminder of their encounter with the relics. The sacred economy drew its strength from this willingness to generate personal *Abzeichen* and *Andenken* at a time when the Rhineland church leadership had not yet embraced the sale of remembrances as a legitimate part of a pilgrimage.

At the beginning of the nineteenth century, the array of objects available to pilgrims when they arrived in Aachen and Trier was limited. Through the 1830s and into the beginning of the 1840s, pilgrims frequented unofficial vendors. In the 1840s pilgrims developed several new ways of demarcating their homes as "pilgrim homes" to commemorate their journeys.[18] Pilgrimage wall hangings were not new to the mid-nineteenth century, but the range of designs and increased availability were novel. In Trier, for example, Elizabeth Dühr has identified thirty-seven separate wall-applicable and embroidered images from 1810 and sixty unique remembrances from 1844.[19] The number of surviving mountable images nearly doubled between these two Trier pilgrimages.[20] These hangings not only helped the pilgrims remember their participation in 1844, but also announced to visitors that the family participated in the event and sympathized with the relic.

The office of the bishop of Cologne gave permission for official pilgrimage items to be sold in Aachen only in 1846. They included pictures, rosaries, and medals; consent came with the caveat that Aachen was to ensure that the vendors were honest and upright individuals.[21] Even then, Aachen officials did not design any official medal or pin, nor did they interfere in the aesthetics of the objects. Clerics focused on preventing fraud. The 1846 Cologne approval of the sale of official *Abzeichen* and *Andenken* helped Aachen catch up with 1844 Trier in

Figure 3.1. Handmade Trier *Andenken*, "Touched the Robe of our Lord J.[esus] Ch.[rist] on 4 May 1765."
Source: Stadtarchiv Trier: SAT, Sam 106, 1–14 in SAT (Bilder vom hl. Rock).

what was available to pilgrims.[22] Like the Trier wall hangings, the 1844 pilgrimage had more than double the number of *Andenken* from the previous 1810 exhibition.[23] These expanded *Andenken* included medals, lithographs, printed images, and models of the cathedral itself. It was also in 1844 that the Trier church leadership first issued official thank-you or commemorative *Andenken* to the honour guard who watched over the relic for the duration of the event.[24]

In the twentieth century, pilgrimage organizers, vendors, and participants continued to expand the selection of objects available and widen the variety of previously offered items. In 1902, for instance, pilgrims to Aachen could easily acquire coloured postcards that venerated all or only one of the four key Aachen relics, such as a postcard of Mary's Tunic or John the Baptist's Beheading Cloth.[25] In the first decade of the twentieth century, pilgrims from France and the Low Countries purchased and mailed out postcards in French and Dutch.[26] Leading up to the First World War, vendors offered highly varied postcards that

Figure 3.2. *Andenken*, "Touched the Holy Coat of Jesus Christ on 4 May 1765."
Source: BATr, Abt. 90, Nr. 514, A 44; Foto: Rita Heyen (AKD).

showed the major Aachen sites and affirmed the role of Charlemagne as patron of the relics and city. Pilgrims eagerly purchased the new postcards and sent word home of their participation. For example, in 1902, Aachen pilgrim Maria Flattery wrote back to the Trier region and asked Ms. Gretchen Stephany to give her love to their four friends.[27] Unfortunately, most surviving postcards contain no messages and are simply addressed to a friend or relative back home. Even so, the increase in options and first appearance of addressed postcards in 1902 and 1909 reveal a desire to share the journey with those who could not participate and an eagerness to convey some of the images the pilgrim was exposed to in Aachen with friends and family.

The push for new forms of postcards came from parties outside the Aachen church leadership. In 1902, the Aachen *Stiftsprobst* (church secretary), following repeated requests for access, first allowed photographers to enter the cathedral in order to capture pictures of relics and of

Figure 3.3. Sealed and approved image of the *Heilig Rock* relic, 1844, given to Stephan Luccas, a sailor in the honour guard (*Ehren Wache* [*sic*]) who stood watch over the relic and pilgrims in 1844 Trier. The cathedral appears in the bottom right corner, and the Porta Nigra in the bottom left.
Source: SAT, "1844 Ronge."

the opening ceremony. He granted permission with the understanding that the photographers would use the resulting images to make *Andenken* for pilgrims.[28] Similarly, in 1909, as a result of the increasingly successful pilgrimages, there was demand for a new Aachen cathedral treasury where the relics could be placed on permanent display. In order to accommodate the new treasury, the Aachen leadership had to remodel part of the cathedral. One company, Engos und Export Handelsfirma, based in Cologne, wrote to the *Stiftskapitel* and explained how they had made *Andenken* for the Cologne cathedral by attaching stone debris to postcards. Engos and Export asked if they could carry out a similar project for the 1909 pilgrimage and use the rubble from the treasury construction as part of a 1909 *Pilgerandenken*.[29] The resulting postcard incorporates images of the cathedral, Charlemagne, the

Figure 3.4. Trier wall hanging *Andenken*, 1844.
Source: SAT, Sam 106, 1–14 in SAT (Bilder vom hl. Rock).

relics, and a piece of the Aachen Münsterkirche. Pilgrims could now take home, or send a loved one, a piece of the church that housed the four Aachen relics.[30]

Following the interruption of the First World War, Aachen resumed pilgrimages in 1925. After the armistice, Aachen was under Belgian occupation and experienced food shortages, inflation, and demonstrations against the high price of groceries. Aachen lost 3,278 soldiers in the war, and at its end 12,109 men were out of work.[31] Vendors and church officials in Aachen sold postcards that reflected the hardships and losses since the 1909 festival. These *Andenken* no longer depicted cartoonish renderings of Charlemagne and the relics. Artistic postcards were now in black-and-white and featured angels with downcast eyes, holding relics above the cathedral, rather than regal depictions of Charlemagne and the city.[32] Aachen, as a physical location, was no longer the focus but was contextualized as beneath the dying Messiah. Artists of illustrated postcards focused increasingly on John the Baptist, Mary, and the death of Jesus rather than on the cathedral. In these new images,

Figure 3.5. "Remembrance card" available to Aachen pilgrims, 1846,
emphasizing the Tunic of Mary: "The white tunic of the Virgin Mary, which she
wore as she gave birth to the saviour of the world." Charlemagne, "Carolus
Magnus," appears above the tunic. Two unnamed clerics keep watch, on either
side the relic. The figure on the right blesses the garment, while the figure on
the left points to his crosier as a reminder that the Catholic hierarchy approves
of the relic. Beneath the image, the *Andenken* states that the pilgrimage is taking
place under the supervision of Bishop von Geissel from Cologne.
Source: DAA, Domkapitel A4.1.0.1 Allgemein Karton.

the relics were not depicted as objects apart, and instead showed them
as the pilgrims believed they were used: wrapped around a crucified
Christ, or with John the Baptist as he instructs a crowd. Pilgrims in 1925
and 1930, in addition to the early twentieth-century photos of bishops
with relics and crowds before the church, could now purchase stark
images of single objects related to the pilgrimage: the lock used to seal
the reliquary, the stand the reliquary rested upon, the cathedral devoid
of pilgrim crowds.[33]

By the 1920s, Trier and Aachen church authorities developed official
Abzeichen and pamphlets for travellers. In Trier, pilgrimage coordinators
went so far as to require that every traveller buy the church-sponsored

Figure 3.6. Aluminium Aachen *Anhänger* to be used as jewellery, n.d. Two angels hold the four *Aachen* Heiligtümer. The *Anhänger* came in a variety of designs, including rounded medals and glass-plated *Andenken* on wood that could be mounted on walls or doors.
Source: DAA, Domkapitel A4.1.0.1 Heite Allgemein Karton.

1933 Trier *Wallfahrt* pendant and pilgrim booklet for thirty pfennige before entering the cathedral. Pilgrims now had to physically separate and identify themselves as members of, or participants in, the religious festival and sacred economy. In an effort to avoid overcrowding, prior to entering the line to enter the cathedral in 1933, it was required that pilgrims' booklets first be stamped with the date by a security guard. In 1937, Aachen pilgrims needed to wear their official *Andenken* and fill out their personal information in their pilgrim "passport" before gaining access to the cathedral and relics.[34]

For participants, these mandated items became lifelong reminders of their pilgrimage experience. Seventy-eight-year-old Rosemarie Geiter attended the 1933, 1959, 1996, and 2012 Trier festivals and told reporters that she still had her 1933 *Abzeichen*.[35] Emma Krämer, eighty-seven

Figure 3.7. Pilgrim pipe depicting the four Aachen relics.[36]
Source: DA'A, Domkapitel A4.1.0.1 Heite Allgemein Karton.

years old from Orenhofen, also attended the previous three pilgrimages and brought her 1933 *Pilgerbuch* and *Abzeichen* with her in 2012.[37]

Pilgrimage officials went to great lengths to assure that potential pilgrim pamphlets and official *Abzeichen* were fairly priced. The leader of a 1925 Dekanates Hochneukirch pilgrim group instructed his participants to first purchase a *Pilgerbuch* for fifty pfennige because it contained the pertinent songs and prayers they would sing on the way and in the Aachen cathedral. In the same circular, pilgrims learned that they would have limited leisure time and could expect to pay the same price, around fifty pfennige, for a cup of coffee.[38] In 1933 Trier, Cathedral Canon Fuchs notified Dr. Braun, leader of the Trier School Board, that even schoolchildren needed the thirty pfennige *Pilgerbuch* and *Abzeichen*; but Fuchs also stated that the priests of the Trier diocese would be asked to help cover this small cost for the poorest children in the

Figure 3.8. An Aich image showing drops of blood on Jesus's loincloth during the crucifixion, 1965.
Note: Thanks to Professor Dieter Wynands for bringing Aich and this *Andenken* to my attention.
Sources: Bischöfliches Diözesanarchiv Áachen (BDA), Sammlung Gebetszettel, Erinnerungsbildchen, A483.

school system.[39] The secretary of the bishop of Trier noted in a letter to Julius Graff that "in every parish there are enough people who can afford to give thirty pfennige to a poor individual."[40]

The pilgrimage organizers did not charge high prices when they developed official pamphlets, passports, and *Abzeichen*, and they expected the Catholic community to financially assist would-be pilgrims who could not afford mandatory documents or badges. Pilgrimage Committees did not make large profits from the items sold to pilgrims. For example, in 1933 pilgrims had the opportunity to buy a silver or a gold *Abzeichen*, in case they wanted to distinguish themselves or desired something more imposing than the standard thirty-pfennige option. In the sales of *Goldabzeichen* the Committee made a net profit of sixty-one Reichsmarks and on the silver fifty-five.[41] On

Figure 3.9. Postcard, now available in both French and German, 1902.
Source: Stadtbibliothek Aachen, Sonderbestände, Dkk 14 Heil (20388056).

the *Pilgerbücher* and *Abzeichen* themselves there was a far more notable profit: 84,262 Reichsmarks for the *Abzeichen* and 58,782 for the *Pilgerbücher*. Taken together, this is a net gain of 143,004 Reichsmarks. The 143,004 Reichsmarks, divided by the total number of 1933 pilgrims, 2.2 million, indicates that the Committee netted only seven pfennige total per pilgrim for both the *Pilgerbücher* and *Abzeichen*. These surpluses were put into covering the organizational costs of the pilgrimages.

The official 1930s *Andenken* and booklets were the culmination of a larger attempt by church officials to control the distribution and design of pilgrim remembrances. In 1891, Dr. Joseph Keil, of a local printing press, wrote to Dompropst Dr. Scheuffgen to ask if his press could distribute images of the Coat at ten pfennige. Keil wanted to ensure there was an authentic, high-quality picture of the relic available to pilgrims at an affordable price.[42] In Trier, Domkapitular Nikolaus Irsch approved and rejected proposed goods for the 1933 festival.[43] Vendors coveted a

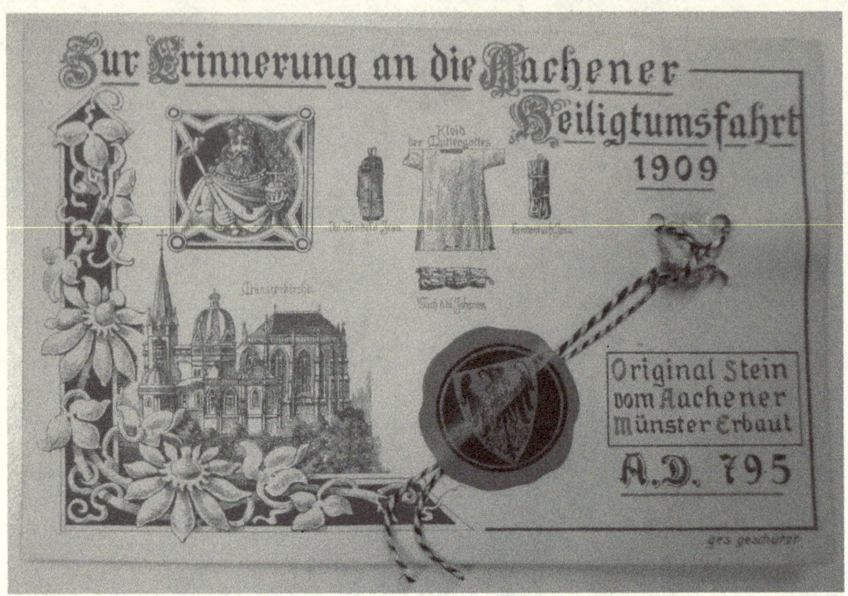

Figure 3.10. Postcard with piece of cathedral stone attached, 1909. This postcard again reveals the centrality of Charlemagne, who hovers in the top left corner. Source: DAA, PA 65 a.

seal of approval from the *Wallfahrtsleitung* (Pilgrimage Committee), because pilgrims to Trier were instructed to acquire their *Andenken* only from stands and stores that the Pilgrimage Committee recommended. In correspondence with potential vendors and manufacturers, Trier officials conceptualized an "authentic" *Andenken*.

For Irsch, a proposed *Andenken* must be tasteful, have artistic merit, and appropriately revere the Heiliger Rock of Trier.[44] However, potential sellers struggled to discern what was both reverent and artistic. Frau Peter Becker offered a hand-painted image of the Coat, for example, but was rebuffed because the work did not resonate with Irsch and the Art Committee.[45] Willy Rieble, from Stuttgart, had his design rejected on the grounds that it lacked any artistic beauty.[46] Otto Becker and Franz Plantz had their *Andenken* denied because they distorted the realistic appearance of the Coat and made it appear "ugly."[47] Another rejection from the Art Committee, to Gustav Braendle of Pforzheim, complained about the aesthetic of the design, calling the text careless, the image of the Coat impotent, and the connection of the Coat and Jesus's cross unsatisfactory.[48]

Figure 3.11. Jesus crucified, with the loincloth. The cathedral is still present but is dominated by the image of the relic-in-action.
Source: DAA, PA Nr. 67 a.

Irsch was particular about what he did not want to see available to pilgrims, including malformed angels. In a notice to Vereinigte Staniolfabriken, Irsch wrote that their request for approval of an *Andenken* card was being disallowed because the arms of the angels did not realistically correspond with their torsos and because the angels had a "languishing, sweet" expression on their faces.[49] However, if Staniolfabriken could overcome the angel's corporeal shortcomings, they could reapply for Irsch's seal of approval. Artists who tried to accommodate too many elements of the Trier pilgrimage also faced the wrath of Irsch's rejection letter. Adolf Winkel proposed an image of Constantine holding the Coat, blessed by the Holy Spirit and flanked by the Porta Nigra and cathedral of Trier. Irsch determined that it was not possible to smoothly blend Romanesque, early Gothic, and modern elements in a single image and was surprised Winkel did not notice that himself. Irsch further decided that for an artist like Winkel it would be

Figure 3.12. Official *Abzeichen* for Aachen pilgrimage, 1937.
Source: DAA, Domkapitel A4.1.0.1 Heite Allgeim Karton.

no problem to quickly create another more aesthetically pleasing *Andenken*, which he could then resubmit for approval.[50]

Of the 127 *Andenken* (statues, cards, medals, images) proposed, only fifty-seven or 45 per cent were approved by Irsch and the Art Committee in 1933.[51] Before sending on their submission, one firm, Gesellschaft für christliche Kunst, wisely asked what exactly Irsch and the Art Committee wanted in an *Andenken*. In their response, Irsch and the committee did not define "artistic merit" but suggested they knew it when they saw it. Approved items were well designed, included the words "Trier 1933," might situate the relic in its historical context (most often at the crucifixion of Jesus or with St. Helena bringing the relic back from Jerusalem), and portrayed the Coat in a prudent, non-cartoonish fashion. Church officials promoted images of the Coat in its natural, red-brown colouring. The Coat could be displayed with images of Jesus, or representations that made clear it was Christ, through the Coat, who was revered.[52] But it was not enough only to incorporate these suggested

Figure 3.13. Adolf Winkel's rejected *Andenken* proposal. The Andenken reads, "That you have shed your blood for us."
Source: BATr, Abt. 90, Nr. 136, 344.

elements. Firma Franka in Düsseldorf proposed a series of aluminium plaques that could be mounted on walls, showing St. Helena displaying the Coat. Irsch signed off, on the condition that they adjust the font and ensure the writing was not so close to the image itself.[53] Hamm, a sculptor, also received permission to sell his statues of St. Helena with a cross and the Coat, but only if he inserted the text "Display of the Holy Coat of Trier 1933" at the base.[54] In contrast, Josef Thesing had no difficulty getting his postcard of the Coat at Jesus's crucifixion approved – ostensibly because it was tasteful and put the relic in its first-century context.[55] Similarly, Ludwig Bonertz of Karlsruhe was complimented for his approved work. For Bonertz, Irsch went so far as to call his picture of St. Helena and St. Agritius flanking the Coat and cross "visionary" and "naturalistic."[56]

Church officials like Irsch worked to establish the grounds of legitimate *Andenken* by carefully curating which objects enjoyed official church approval. Irsch established "authentic" as those items that were tasteful, solemn, non-kitschy, and conveyed the sacred presence of the relics.

Figure 3.14. Josef Thesing's approved postcard. In this ivory relief, Roman soldiers gamble for the Holy Coat of Jesus. The Trier cathedral in the background stands ready to receive the object. The most famous Trier ivory relief was originally thought to depict St. Helena bringing the Coat into the city.
Source: BATr, Abt. 90, Nr. 136, 316.

Irsch was a tastemaker and believed that "good" *Andenken* were readily apparent to the viewer.[57] The devotional objects had to capture the essence of the relic and facilitate an encounter with the divine. These hoped-for holy moments could not be attained if *Andenken* resembled souvenirs one could acquire on secular journeys. The items were important because they were mediums between this world and God.[58] In order to ensure each pilgrim had access to a credible *Andenken*, church officials intervened in the market, establishing the aesthetic qualities of what entered the sacred economy. Thus church officials viewed the early twentieth century, with the new array of items available for purchase by pilgrims, as a potential threat to legitimate images and items. For officials, it was not that authenticity had changed from the nineteenth century, but that new forms of mass production threatened to overrun official clerical messaging about relics. The church had to ensure pilgrims encountered objects that conveyed the solemnity of the garments.[59]

In response to the growing danger of counterfeit goods in the sacred economy, clerics not only more actively shaped the appearance of objects, but also sought to control the public spaces where vendors sold *Andenken*. Aachen and Trier clergy worked to ensure that the ever-increasing number of pilgrims were not scammed and had access to a genuine *Andenken*. Church officials found that they had much more influence over what was sold and purchased than over where vendors set up their stalls. Clergy lacked the secular power to banish objects from their cities that they defined as kitschy or cheap.

Selling the Sacred: Authentic and Counterfeit Andenken

Church leaders worried about not just the form of *Andenken* but about where such objects were sold. Pilgrimage Committees turned to Aachen and Trier municipal authorities for help, but came up against the limits of their jurisdiction. Pilgrimage Committees had little authority to limit the commerce of the ever-growing number of vendors and hawkers at pilgrimage events. While it is sometimes impossible to get a full picture of the number of *Andeken* vendors between the 1830s and 1930s, the surviving evidence points to an overcrowded marketplace. In his notes on the 1844 exposition, Jakob Marx counted at least 167 large and small stalls.[60] Combined with his observations in other parts of Trier, Marx estimated there to be at least 400 improvised shops throughout the city with *Andenken* available to passing pilgrims.[61]

Already in 1844, Trier city officials intervened in the economy during the pilgrimage, such as by posting that bread made during the event could not be diluted with "disadvantageous substances."[62] Trier police also prohibited butchers and bakers from increasing the price of their goods during the festival. Most importantly, Trier police took control of where vendors could set up shops: "Vendors cannot set up stands or erect tables in any other open plaza, other than those referred to below, in no street, in no promenade, most especially on no street corner, with the purpose of selling food or wares. Vendors cannot disturb the free passage of the streets and plazas or the established businesses of the citizens."[63] The buying and selling of sacred objects was limited to parts of the city the police deemed safe and appropriate.

Similarly, in Aachen, throughout the nineteenth century the police were central in regulating commerce and public space. Police presidents decided which routes pilgrim groups would take through the city and where merchants could and could not sell their wares. In 1881, 1888, 1895, and 1902 the police presidents took action against price gouging, forbade local shops from setting up stands that charged higher prices for food and drink from what they charged in non-pilgrimage times.[64] In addition, vendors now needed police permission to set up their stands: "Without police permission there should be no stands, tables, benches, chairs, or anything else hung or set up that would inhibit the free passage of the streets and plazas."[65] Police promised to arrest and jail violators immediately.[66]

By the early twentieth century, citizens consistently asked for permission to set up shops near their houses. In 1902, a certain L.N. asked Pilgrimage Committee member Propst Buschmann for permission to carry on a family tradition. As L.N. explained, his ancestors set up a stand in the space next to their house on the main Münsterplatz to sell items to the passing pilgrims.[67] That same year Ignas Lange, a cathedral choir member, enquired about managing a stall on the Chorusplatz, near the cathedral, from which he could sell *Andenken*, devotionals, and rosaries.[68] Lange asserted that he had run this stall in 1888 and 1895. Sick individuals did not always want a special visit to the relics. Jos. Willmar, a tailor, asked instead for permission to set up a stand near the cathedral so that he could sell devotional objects and medals, presumably to help pay for his medical bills.[69]

Similarly, in 1909 Adolf Busch explained to the Aachen *Stiftskapitel* that his store was cut off from pilgrims leaving the church because there was a barrier erected between the cathedral and his house.[70] Busch proposed setting up a series of stands, 2.5 x 3 metres, at his own expense, from which he could continue to trade during the event. Busch also asked whether or not he could put up benches for pilgrims and paint his house shortly before the pilgrimage began. In his response, Propst Buschmann rejected the stands as outside his authority, but approved the benches and deferred the painting decision to his colleague Velten.[71]

Aachen and Trier church officials continued to work with the local police to control the selling of wares into the 1930s pilgrimages. Aachen Stiftsvikar Müller reached an agreement with police superintendent Beyer in 1930 about commerce during the affair. Accordingly, stands were prohibited on the Fischmarkt, Katschhof, Domhof, and upper portion of the Münsterplatz, but residents on the Fischmarkt, Katschhof, and Münsterplatz could apply to the police to sell devotional items from their windows.[72] The Trier mayor and police announced that during the display of the Holy Coat from 23 July to 3 September 1933, only certain areas of the city were designated for stands.[73] Any who wished to set up a kiosk or stall had to apply to the police and include information on how much space they required and what they intended to sell.

Any application that was not received before 15 May 1933 or that did not have the pertinent information was immediately cast aside.[74]

Clerical authorities had no power to pursue or prevent merchant abuses within the sacred economy. In 1933 Trier, Gutschmidt, a bank director from Cologne, warned Domkapitular Fuchs that he witnessed pilgrims buying large numbers of rosaries and *Andenken* and filling up suitcases with their purchases. Gutschmidt suspected these rogues intended to sell the wares illegally. Fuchs thanked Gutschmidt for the tip and affirmed that the Trier church strongly opposed such practices. Fuchs noted that the goods might be for family members only, but the church would keep an eye out for potential wrongdoing.[75] There was no mention of future punishment or suggestion that Fuchs could take preventive actions beyond being wary of scammers. In 1937, Maria Funk wrote to the Caritasdirektor Müller to complain about an *Andenken* she acquired while in Aachen. In its response the Pilgrimage Committee was curt, stating that such matters had nothing to do with them because the police regulated the stands set up during the pilgrimage.[76]

Gutschmidt was not the only one to overestimate the authority of the 1930s Aachen and Trier pilgrimage committees. Vendors failed to spot newspaper notices that provided information about how to acquire space and incorrectly assumed the Committee had the authority to decide whether or not they could set up stands and tables in the city. Despite the public notices about police authority, the Trier Pilgrim Committee received dozens of requests for permission to establish tables, seating, or stalls in 1933.[77] In a response to Peter Franken Firm, who enquired about setting up small chairs for pilgrims to rent while the relics were displayed from the Aachen cathedral gallery, Fuchs confessed that he had to turn the matter over to the police, because "the city has taken over the pilgrim seating procedure."[78] Similarly, the Committee could not change decisions reached by the civil authorities, much to Vitus Föhr's dismay. Föhr resented that he was assigned a spot on the Trier Jesuitenplatz to sell his non-devotional objects.[79] He wanted a place behind the cathedral, near the cathedral museum, but was informed that would not be possible, and his best bet was a place on Maximinplatz. While trying to get a space on Maximinplatz, a different firm took over his Jesuitenplatz spot. Unfortunately for Föhr, he now had no ideal space to sell his items. The Pilgrimage Committee was not able to help him, because stall locations were beyond their control, and now Maximinplatz was full – there were no more stalls available in high-traffic areas.[80] Unprecedented attendance in 1933 made it exceptionally difficult for Föhr and other vendors to secure public space to market objects.

Even Domkapitular Fuchs and the Pilgrimage Committee required police permission to set up stands for pilgrims. In a letter enquiring about public notices, Fuchs asked for access to the plazas around three Trier churches – Herz Jesu, St. Paulus, and Jesuitenkirche – so that the Committee could distribute *Pilgerabzeichen* and pilgrim books required for entry into the cathedral. Mayor Weitz's office granted the request by giving Fuchs permission to set up two stalls, at the three churches and at the cathedral.[81] The mayor explained that the stall space was selected to satisfy the Committee's needs without impeding the circulation of pilgrims through the city.[82]

The Trier Pilgrimage Committee warned pilgrims, even before they departed, to be cautious when purchasing devotional objects. Each pilgrimage group that reserved an attendance date was sent instructions on the pilgrimage schedule and a map of the city. Within these directions was a special note on buying objects while in Trier. Pilgrims were instructed to "exercise extreme caution" and were reminded that the Trier officials had approved certain objects as appropriate for pilgrim reflection.[83] Trier participants were asked to buy from established vendors who had a Pilgrimage Committee endorsement and to not acquire items from "wandering hawkers."[84] In 1933, a month before the Trier pilgrimage even began, Trier local Nicolas Lenz wrote to the mayor to express his disgust at the vendors who were ruining the aesthetic of the city. For Lenz, the new vendors were an insult to the city because their presence implied that the locals were disorderly and peddlers of kitsch. Indeed, Lenz warned that if Mayor Weitz did not take action, his administration would be held accountable when the population of Trier set fire to the "dirt shacks."[85] Lenz called on the mayor to come down to the market to witness the insulting presence of the filthy stands (*Schmutzbuden*) and respond as a wise civil servant before it was too late and the people took matters into their own hands.[86] The mayor's office approved the establishment of stands, but did not regulate their aesthetic. Lenz's complaint went unanswered.

Pilgrims were exposed to unapproved vendors despite clerical approval and disapproval of specific stands. The Pilgrimage Committee faced criticism about its own volunteers and their relationship to local vendors in 1933. In a summary report about his experience as an assistant during the event, J. Lirvas pointed out the problematic relationships that pilgrim guides developed with local businesses. In response to the large number of 1933 participants, the Committee set up a volunteer corps to guide large groups from train stations and local churches to the cathedral. As Lirvas observed, "*Andenken* salesmen paid guides

Figure 3.15. Selling *Andenken* in Trier, 1933.
Source: BATr, Abt. 100, Nr. 0004, Bd. 2.

to lead pilgrim groups by their stands."[87] Lirvas confessed that the issue was likely unavoidable, as innkeepers, car renters, and bookstores similarly offered incentives to guides if they brought their groups or directed pilgrims to their business. Despite the recommendations required from the Committee to sell items and the police regulation of locations, *Andenken* salesmen still found ways to circumvent local authorities and expose pilgrims to their wares.

By the twentieth century, Trier and Aachen church officials worked to regulate the physical remembrances that participants acquired when on pilgrimage. But their authority was limited to church property. Irsch wanted pilgrims to buy and trade only with those items that favoured the history of the relic (St. Helena and Constantine), its relationship to the city, and its role in the life of Jesus. He stressed that *Andenken* containing these elements would help pilgrims best recall their journey and the church tradition surrounding the Holy Coat. But pilgrims were unconcerned with the aesthetics of *Andenken* and assigned merit to such objects on the basis of how close they came to the divine presence of the Rhineland relics.

Purchasing the Sacred

What did pilgrims say about their devotional objects? Why did they buy *Andenken* in Aachen and Trier? In 1874, in an article on the chaos of the foot traffic of passengers at the Aachen train station, one reporter described the disorderly rush of pilgrims to the nearby vendors. Participants wanted to acquire last-minute items such as pilgrim books or rosaries before heading home.[88] These 1874 pilgrims did not pause to consider whether or not each stand was clerically approved.[89] Between the 1830s and the 1930s, pilgrims requested and acquired objects for similar reasons: for healing or for earthly assistance. German Catholics, and Catholics abroad, understood that the acquisition of items displaying the Trier and Aachen relics, or *Andenken* blessed by the bishop or commissioned by the Pilgrimage Committee, had transcendent power in their lives.

Aachen and Trier pilgrims employed *Andenken* to cross an experiential threshold; their transcending was a commonly understood possibility, as even those who could not attend recognized the potential power within a remembrance. The *Andenken* acted as a contact point between the sacred and the temporal. Officials determined what items were available, but recipients ultimately interacted with them in their own ways, most often as an embodied link to Jesus, John the Baptist, or Mary.[90] For pilgrims writing to church officials in Trier and Aachen, *Andenken* were not solely about commemorating journeys, but also relayed commanding forces in their lives with the potential to heal bodies, repair careers, and bless interpersonal relationships.

The closer an object was to the Rhineland relics, the more powerful it became for pilgrims, or the more value it held in the sacred economy. In 1844 Trier, as pilgrims approached the Holy Coat, they went up a set of stairs to the top of the altar. Up to this point they walked in a double line, but as they got to the stairs they merged into a single line. Pilgrims had the opportunity to have an object touch the hem of the Coat: "On either side of the reliquary are stationed ecclesiastics, one of whom receives from each passer-by their rosaries or medals ... brings them into immediate contact with the hem of the garment, and then returns them to the owners."[91] As we have seen, those who failed to bring their own *Andenken* could purchase one in town. The most popular items included medals, rosaries, and images of the Coat.[92] The practice of touching items to the relic continued through the nineteenth century and into the twentieth.

In 1933, Trier organizers had problems with the massive number of objects that pilgrims dropped and left behind as they went through the veneration line. Director Menke wrote to Domkapitular Fuchs, beseeching him to create a new system, because the items left behind were causing an irresolvable lost-and-found crisis for the police. Pilgrims were bringing items to touch the Coat, but the quick tempo of the line meant that many items were left behind, resulting in baskets full of displaced rosaries, medals, and devotionals. Menke demanded that new instructions be placed in the Catholic press organs throughout Germany, the local churches, and on the plaza, leading up to the cathedral line. Pilgrims were told that they must tie together their assorted devotional objects.[93] Fuchs complied with the suggestion because it was important to keep the line moving through the cathedral as smoothly as possible.

Those unable to physically attend Aachen and Trier pilgrimages still hoped to access the sacred presence of the relics. Pilgrims first began submitting mail-order requests for devotional items in the mid-nineteenth century, and this practice became increasingly popular into the 1930s. Already in the 1840s pilgrims who could not make the journey asked to participate through indirect contact. For example, in 1845, a couple requested an image of the Trier Coat to strengthen their eldest daughter.[94] This trend continued through the nineteenth century: Elisabeth, a self-described poor woman, assured the Aachen pilgrimage committee in 1881 that she only wanted pieces of the silk to help her grow closer to God. She planned to ask for the pieces in person but was too afraid. She hoped that her request would be granted, because obliging her would show that the power, grace, and light from Jesus were present in the pilgrimage.[95] For Birgid Rooney, of Castle Clayney, Ireland, the Trier relic was the last stage of a recovery from nervousness and other afflictions. Rooney had spent over twenty days at Lourdes, where she acquired an object she now sent to the bishop of Trier. Rooney expected "to be restored to perfect health" after the sacred power of Lourdes was combined with that of Trier.[96] Pilgrims viewed the silk as a means to confidence, emotional well-being, and a link to the divine.

Whether travelling or not, devotees of the Rhenish pilgrimages desired items that had physically touched the relics. Again, the efficacy and worth of an item was determined by how close it came to a relic, or, for the pilgrims, its proximity to Jesus, Mary, or John the Baptist.[97] Within their requests, pilgrims explained their financial hardship or personal reasons for not being able to personally attend. This was the case even when letters are received from nearby German-speaking areas such as Austria or Bavaria. The most commonly requested *Andenken* was a piece of relic silk, the cloth used to wrap either the Trier or the Aachen relics. Each time church officials revealed the relics for veneration, the silk they had been stored in was removed and used to make cards for pilgrims. Before putting the relics away at the end of an exhibition, they were stored in new silk. Possessing a piece of this relic silk was an honour. In 1860, Princess Carls hh. visited Aachen and was allowed to help display the relics to pilgrims from the outdoor gallery. Before she left Aachen, pilgrimage leadership gave her four pieces of the silk used to wrap the relics as a gift.[98] In this same year, pieces of the cloth were sent out to bishops across Germany, including to Cologne, as a reminder of the pilgrimage.[99] In 1867, the mayor of Aachen asked for pieces of the relic silk for himself and his colleagues.[100] Both civil and church authorities coveted pieces of the relic silk. Recipients sought grace within and via the *Andenken*, wanting divine presence or "the unrepresented way the past is present in the present," not mere replications or representations.[101]

Laity also requested and were given pieces of this silk. In 1874, H. Riedel of Aachen asked for four pieces of the relic silk for his personal use.[102] In this same year, J.N. Racke offered to buy new silk (for fifteen thalers) for the end of the pilgrimage, in exchange for four small pieces of the cloth.[103] Similarly, Herr Mathey from Rensdorf was pleased to receive pieces of the cloth by post after his 1874 request.[104] Even after pilgrimages had concluded, the bishops and leadership received requests for pieces of relic silk. Agatha Miszkowski, from Berlin, requested a piece of Trier cloth for her priest in 1936, three years after the 1933 pilgrimage concluded. Miszkowski explained that the priest's sister had sent him an *Andenken* that was touched to the Coat, and the priest treasured the gift. Weihbischof Fuchs was able to comply with the request, but asked Miszkowski to be content with only a very small piece, because the cloth was almost all gone.[105]

In the twentieth century, pilgrim interest in owning items that were physically near the relics, such as relic silk, exploded. In broad terms, these requests can be divided into two categories: temporal and spiritual. Temporal requests expected that possessing an *Andenken* would better one's worldly position. Spiritual requests were to bring emotional healing. For example, the Schwestern vom armen Kinde Jesus asked Aachen Prälat Bellesheim for a piece of the silk in 1909. The sisters wanted as many *Andenken* with the cloth they could get to benefit their "numerous community."[106] In another example, Eileen O-Harell, from Dublin, wrote to Bishop Korum in search of physical healing: "My brother, sister, and I are most anxious to obtain some article that has touched the Relic of the Holy Coat. We feel so sure of good health if we can only succeed in getting some relic that has touched the Holy Coat. It is not possible for us to make the journey there, circumstances and illness prevent us. I trust my Lord Bishop that you will grant me this request. I enclose an offering of 1£ in thanks."[107] Also in the twentieth century, pilgrims were less geographically limited; requests now came to Aachen and Trier from across the Atlantic, Asia, and all over Europe. The sacred economy benefited from faster shipping, growing interest in international news, and more reliable national postal services.

At each pilgrimage, pilgrims sought *Andenken* to restore their physical health. Rosina Benitz, a German-speaker from Erie, Pennsylvania, wrote Trier in 1891, because she was plagued by headaches, the flu, and eye troubles. Benitz believed these ailments originated from an unnamed sin she committed in 1848. Since returning to her faith, she learned about the 1844 Trier cures and hoped that if Bishop Korum would send her two or three *Andenken* it would help restore her relationship with God, and thus relieve her physical suffering.[108] Mrs. K. Kelly, from San Francisco, also asked for "a card from the Holy Land. Please have it blessed also pray for my Family."[109] For Kelly, it was key that whatever the bishop sent be blessed on the Holy Coat altar because the *Andenken* was for her "deformed daughter." Mary Murphy, from Glasgow, Scotland, in 1933, asked for a medal that touched the relic, explaining, "I am an invalid and would be very happy to receive such a relic."[110] Germans also requested *Andenken* to aid in physical restoration. Margaretha Probst asked Bishop Korum to send a medal to Herr Benefiziat in Tölz, near Munich. Probst explained that Benefiziat had been lame on the right side of his body for three years and could not make the trip. For Probst, the medal would help bring Benefiziat back into the fold of the church, if only the bishop would pray for him at Mass.[111]

Not all pilgrims elaborated on why they wanted the *Andenken*. Gillespie, a woman from Canada, posted an advertisement in the *Catholic Record London*, in which she requested Bishop Korum send her an item from the 1891 Trier pilgrimage.[112] Walburga Reinhart from Ingolstadt, Bavaria, also did not specify why she wanted an image. Reinhart could not attend because she had seven children and did not know anyone in Trier she could room with when she arrived.[113] In 1933, Sister Mary Zita, based in Cleveland, Ohio, asked for permission to send in her own objects and promised to pray for Trier if she was obliged: "Your Lordship this is the request will you please give me permission to send some goods to be made up into scapulars that is the fine scapulars of the Sacred Passion of our blessed Lord. Will you dear good Bishop permit these pieces of goods to be touched to our Blessed Lord's tunic which He wore on his sacred Person and to other precious relics which you may have and I will promise I will pray for you every day"[114] The Pilgrimage Committee in Trier was more than happy to fulfil Sister Zita's request, so long as she sent in some money for the return shipping.[115] Zita's successful request inspired the Ursuline sisters of Cleveland to send in a medal and case to be touched to the Coat.[116]

For J.A. Menth, a first-generation child of two German immigrants in Cleveland, the Coat represented home, a link to the German-Catholic community left behind. In 1891, for his parents, Menth asked that Korum send him two *Andenken*, two rosaries, and two small crosses that touched the Coat. Menth's parents had emigrated from Bausendorf, Kreis Wittlich, only forty-eight kilometres from Trier. Together, they had gone to see the Coat twice in 1844 but now they lived in the United States and could not attend the event.[117]

Catholic belief in the healing power of the Rhenish relics drew broad and diverse international attention. James P. Molygan from Atalissa, Iowa (Muscatine County) wrote to Weihbischof Fuchs in 1935 after he heard about the 1933 Trier pilgrimage. Molygan asked that they pray for him in Trier because he was out of work and had health problems:

> Kiss the Holy coat and make a novena to the Lord that I can get a good home of my own soon and get a good wife so i can have someone to care for me. Can you offer up a good mass to cure up this prostrate gland and blader trouble on me as i haft to beg how is your charity can you help me some can to cure me up in good health. Send me a bit of the holy coat so i can tuch it and kiss it. as it is a dogs life the way i haft get a long. So cure me up of this trouble i am a good catholic and Right by all. tuch and kiss the holy coat in my favor so i can get well so i can get a good study job of work at once in a good PLaCE and get good wages i want to get a good home of my own so i wont haft to work by the day all my life kiss and tuch the holy coat FOR me that i can get a good home soon.[118]
>
> Friend in the Lord as i will as a favor of you all. as i am a poor man and no home as i am so poor and hard up. as i haft to beg, as i am out of work so long i am a good catholic and do right by all. Take pity on me and PRaY to the Lord that i can get a good study job of work in a good place pray that i can get good wages as i need it bad. answer soon.[119]

Molygan's phonetic spelling, grammar, and punctuation suggest he had not completed schooling and was likely impoverished. Having lost his job and now his health, he sought out divine intervention through the Trier Holy Coat. Fuchs was happy to oblige and prayed for Molygan during Mass. He also sent him a piece of the silk that was used to wrap the Coat between 1891 and 1933.[120] Like Molygan, Fred Hallem from England believed that acquiring an *Andenken* that had made contact with the relic would bring him work: "Be so kind to send me some small holy picture that had touch [*sic*] the Holy Coat and for me to receive Holy Communion on receiving it I feel I should get work."[121] The Coat represented divine potential for Catholics worldwide; it offered a chance at a fresh start, a new job, and hope for a better future.

Some Catholics understood the Trier Coat *Andenken* as a path to convert their loved ones. John Hughes of Mobile, Alabama, could not attend the pilgrimage, but wrote to Trier to request a "little Relic a Chaplet or Crucifix that touched the Holy Garment" for "my Darling Wife who is not of our Faith. Pray for her that the Almighty God may soften her heart, convince her of her error and guide her Footsteps that she may be converted to our Holy Faith."[122] For Hughes, the Coat had the power to change his wife's confession, just by being near her person.

As the pilgrimage attendance grew and peaked in the 1930s, the Pilgrimage Committee was overwhelmed. Clergy were not always able or willing to fulfil requests. In 1933, Milly Brosda from Nordhorn/Haan explained that she learned about the new pilgrimage from the *Krefelder Zeitung*. Brosda's mother had a rosary that was touched to the Trier relic, but her father lost it during the First World War. Brosda asked if they could send a different rosary to the Committee, have it touched to the Coat, and returned. In their response, the Committee denied Brosda's rosary request, noting that a large pilgrim group from the Hildesheim diocese was scheduled to visit Trier. Brosda should instead send a rosary with a trusted pilgrim in that group.[123]

Catholics outside of Trier and Aachen could get access to *Andenken* through unofficial intermediaries. Some individuals requesting *Andenken* distributed, and in some cases may have sold, the received goods. For example, Josef Fleck stated he had already received and distributed over 100 *Andenken* and that he had 80 more on the way from his friend in Trier.[124] Fleck further requested that the Trier Pilgrimage Committee send him a picture of Helena for his church, so that he could remember his trip to Trier. Js. Smyth of Wine Tavern, Ireland, was given twenty-one medals that touched the Coat in 1891. Smyth explained that after receiving the medals he was besieged with requests, from Jackman, a Franciscan priest; from his wife; four other priests; and nuns working in his community. Smyth apologized and asked for an additional twenty-one medals. Smyth also wrote that he gave away some of the medals to the French nuns at St. Kestowed because they previously gave him water from Lourdes.[125] Rhineland *Andenken* were in high demand, and these items were part of a larger, Europe-wide trade in remembrances. Unfortunately, the Smyth and Fleck correspondence is an extremely rare glimpse into how Rhenish objects could swap hands in a trade-based sacred economy. J.B. Wijs, from Amsterdam, attended the 1909

Aachen event and wrote back when he got home to ask for a piece of the cloth used to wrap Mary's shroud. Wijs intended to give it to his sister for her twenty-fifth birthday.[126] Catholics outside of Germany and France revered *Andenken* that were in contact with known relics or pilgrimage sites.

Catholics made requests for whole parishes who could not make the journey to Trier or Aachen. Friar Francis Jerome of Honesdale, Pennsylvania, explained in 1933, "As I have read in American papers that your Lordship has this Sacred Relic (Holy Coat) enshrined in your cathedral, so I thought by writing to you, we could obtain from your Lordship a particle of this Sacred Relic." The acquisition of this piece of the Holy Coat was not for Jerome himself but "for the veneration of the faithful." The Pilgrimage Committee declined cutting off part of the Coat and instead offered to touch an object of his choosing to the relic, so long as it arrived before the final day in August.[127] Nobody, clerics included, had access to the divine presence of the relic once the pilgrimage period concluded and the Holy Coat was sealed in its reliquary.

Andenken petitioners often sought the objects not for themselves but for friends and family. Maria-Magdalena Pfluzer, from Seifershan, asked for a picture of the Trier relic to be touched to the Coat and sent to her in 1933. Pfluzer wanted the object for an unnamed man.[128] She explained that she had already had many Masses said for this individual but they had not been successful.[129] In Pfluzer's letter, it is not clear whether her loved one was suffering physically or spiritually, but she requested discretion from the priest.[130]

Church leaders only touched devotional objects to the relics. Fritz Winter wrote in August 1933 to the Trier officials and asked that they touch a draft of an important contract to the Coat. Winter made a solemn vow to God that he would help a penniless young person study theology if the contract came through and made it possible for him to pay for someone's schooling.[131] In their response the Pilgrimage Committee sent the unblessed contract back, apologized, and said that they "only touch *Andacht* objects [*Andachtgegenstände*] to the Holy Coat."[132]

In 1933, a shortage of relic cloth and high demand helps to explain the Committee's preference for touching objects pilgrims sent in to the Coat. As thanks to the 4,500 volunteers, the Trier Pilgrimage Committee used the silk to make plaques commemorating each person's service to the community and church. When the Deutsche Mittelstandhilfe asked for silk in September, Fuchs informed them that, after the 4,500 volunteer plaques, "if any silk remains it is reserved for clergy and Holy Orders."[133] Bishop Bornewasser also issued images of himself to notable pilgrims. For example, Bornewasser wrote Father Hilterscheid in Zewen after the bishop read an article about a ninety-six-year-old woman who had attended the 1844, 1891, and then the 1933 pilgrimages. As thanks for the woman's devotion to the Coat, Bornewasser issued the faithful pilgrim an image of himself.[134]

Even after the pilgrimages ended, potential pilgrims sent in requests for items that were touched to the Coat of Trier. In 1933, the Pilgrimage Committee responded to this problem by establishing a second-degree sacral proximity. In November, two months after the closing ceremony, Helen Croft of Lancashire enquired about touching a piece of linen to the Coat, because she could not afford to come to Germany in person.[135] Similarly, Yolanda Giordano from Campinas, near São Paolo, asked that Bishop Rudolph have mercy on her and send her a piece of the relic silk.[136] In response to these two requests, Trier officials stated that the Coat was put away and they did not know when it would next be revealed. Even so, they were able to touch the sent materials to a piece of cloth that was used to wrap the Holy Coat.[137] Therefore, their *Andenken* were twice removed from the relic, but this practice still allowed those who could not personally visit Trier, and only heard about the event after the fact, access to the sacred economy. God's presence could not be constrained by timetables or geography.

Conclusion

Andenken remained a central component of nineteenth- and twentieth-century German Catholic religiosity. Aachen and Trier clergy consistently received requests from a wide range of individuals both within and outside of Europe. The allure of the divine presence surrounding Rhenish relics attracted the sick, the impoverished, the unemployed, bishops, aristocrats, and mayors.[138] Within their letters it is clear that pilgrims had great expectations for the *Andenken* and were convinced that objects brought into physical contact with the sacred, through a relic, could heal their bodies, repair their relationships, and improve their worldly position. For Catholic pilgrims, objects took on a sacrality upon contact with the Coat of Trier or the four relics of Aachen. Thus, cloth that was used to wrap a relic for seven or for thirty years was greatly prized, given to important pilgrims who could not attend, volunteers who sacrificed their time, and those in the direst situations.

The sacred economy brought together municipal authority, church hierarchy, vendors, and the pilgrims. Rhineland clergy ultimately had little control over how pilgrims understood their objects or where they were sold. Increasingly the items available for pilgrims to purchase were standardized and mass produced. Pilgrims had less need to create their own objects to wear on the pilgrimage or to hang on their wall to commemorate the journey after the mid-nineteenth century. They now had easy access to affordable postcards and other celebratory items. This expansion was partly due to the Pilgrimage Committees' commending, or at least approving, certain items and requiring official *Abzeichen* and booklets to gain access to the relics. It was not until the twentieth century that pilgrims were required to physically mark themselves as participants with official pins, in a tradition that continues in Trier to the present. Despite the seismic shifts around the form of *Andenken*, pilgrims consistently described these objects as gateways to the celestial. *Andenken* allowed a pilgrim to experience the divine presence in the world. The act of touching an object to a relic had sacral power, because doing so could sanctify the faithful and bring them spiritually closer to Jesus and the Holy Family.[139]

In *Andenken* pilgrims found a connection to Jesus, John the Baptist, or Mary. Many of them believed that this link to the relics could transform bodies and transcend physical illness. The value of currency in the sacred economy was determined by proximity to sacred sites, verification by clerical authorities, and the expectations of pilgrim participants, both those who went to Trier or Aachen and those who could not attend but wanted a physical connection to the event. In other words, the *Andenken* underwent "presentification" for the pilgrims, in which participants understood themselves as being intellectually, spiritually, and bodily oriented towards the divine via their acquired items.[140]

Pilgrim acquisition of *Andenken* and the varied meanings derived from these sacred objects triggered the most severe cricisim of Rhenish pilgrimage. Johannes Ronge, in 1844, labelled the Trier pilgrimage a medieval superstition. For Ronge and his supporters, nineteenth-century Catholicism had no room for the cult of miracles or *Andenken*. Ronge sought to create a new Christianity, the German-Catholics, in order to restore the true church free of popular religious practices. The next chapter addresses Ronge's critique, which accelerated shifts in clerical teachings about the relics in Aachen and Trier.

4 Rending Religiosity: Johannes Ronge and the 1840s Trier Controversy

The Fury of Conviction

On 25 October 1887 Johannes Ronge (1813–87) died while travelling by train with his family from Budapest to Vienna. Forty years earlier, he had been hailed as Germany's "second Luther" who would bring a Reformation of reason to the Continent. He was also condemned and vilified as the Antichrist, a defrocked priest bound for an eternity in hell. At the time of his death, however, Ronge was remembered primarily as a man who failed to deliver on his promises to forge a new Christianity. Reflecting on his life, the *Deutsch Protest[ant] Blatt* wrote that Ronge was an overly ambitious man whose charisma was insufficient for the task he set himself: "His will and desire was certainly greater than his skill," and "upon consideration of his life path and his work one gets the impression that he was restless, tormented by a task that was too high and too great [for him]."[1] Ronge's meteoric rise to fame in the 1840s was followed by decades of disappointment, years that included excommunication, exile, and alienation.

When Ronge died he was still evangelizing for his new Christian faith, the "German-Catholics," which he founded in 1844 to protest the pilgrimage to the Holy Coat of Trier. Ronge's open critiques of Trier Bishop Wilhelm Arnoldi set off a public debate about the Catholic Church – centred on pilgrimage, relics, and the role of tradition – that continued to resonate through the nineteenth century. Thus, in 1891, Ludwig Henning, a fellow critic of Trier pilgrimage, triumphantly reminded his readers that 600,000 people left the Catholic Church in 1844 because of the sham display of the Coat of Jesus. "One would think that 1844 would have been the last pilgrimage," he noted, but no, already in 1887 Bishop Felix Michael Korum declared his intention once more to show the Trier relic. With the planned pilgrimage, Henning continued, the Enlightenment of the nineteenth century was endangered. Reason was suspended during the upcoming six-week-long display of the Trier Holy Coat. For Henning, Ronge had laid bare the hypocrisy of the Trier pilgrimage, including the inauthenticity of the Coat. German-Catholic supporters believed that, thanks to Ronge's trenchant criticism in the 1840s, the established Christian churches were coming to an end. Catholicism had staked its final survival on a futile confrontation with the sciences and would lose everything.[2]

Ronge's confrontation with popular Catholic religiosity shook the upper echelons of German Catholicism and inspired a virulent pamphlet war throughout German-speaking Europe. On one side stood Ronge and his supporters. They contended that the worship of relics was paganism, an anti-biblical practice that exposed the rotten foundations of the Roman curia and demonstrated the Catholic Church's greed. By breaking with the church over the validity of miracles and relics in the "Enlightened" age, Ronge called into question whether traditional Catholicism could withstand European cultural change after the French Revolution.[3]

Opposite them, Bishop Arnoldi, Catholic theologians, and clergy depicted Ronge as a betrayer of his faith. Ronge divided not only Catholicism but also German society. He was an uninformed, bitter man who was not intelligent enough to complete Catholic seminary. For Trier supporters, the struggle against Ronge was intertwined with the future of Catholicism. If they could make Ronge not-Catholic, or label him "Protestant," they could preserve the practice of pilgrimage and veneration of relics as sound Christian doctrines.

Clergy became increasingly defensive of their religious practices in response to the Ronge incident. Church officials redressed the potential for relics to heal bodies by reining in public declarations of miraculous transformations. At the same time, clerics began to present their relics as genuine artefacts of the first century, or, at the very least, suggested such church treasures were *potentially* genuine. Thus, even as church leaders strongly refuted Ronge on scriptural and theological grounds, they tacitly recognized or acknowledged Ronge's critiques.

Ronge and his detractors battled over how to authentically access the sacred and gain eternal salvation. Ronge's success would have meant the disestablishment of *Andenken* and the refutation of Rhenish relics as sites of miraculous healing. Catholic clerics fought to uphold divine presence – God in the world, manifest in the Trier Coat. During the Ronge debate, clergy presented the Coat as a literal, authentic garment of Christ. However, by the end of the nineteenth century, clergy became much more cautious and emphasized the symbolic significance of Rhineland relics.

Ronge's schism helped widen a developing rift in Rhenish Catholicism between pilgrim participants and clerical leadership.[4]

Ronge's Life

Johannes Ronge was born in Breslau on 16 October 1813 to Michael and Hedwig(a) Ronge, the second son of seven children. Ronge studied in Neiße before he returned to Breslau to study Catholic theology during the 1836–7 winter semester. In March 1841 he began work as a chaplain in Grottkau.[5] The following year Ronge was put on suspension from the priesthood after he anonymously published an article that was critical of Rome's interference with the selection of clergy in Breslau. He took a position as a private tutor in Laurahütte, 200 kilometres from Breslau. There he read Feuerbach and Hegel and provoked the ire of his superiors for teaching these texts. He had to leave his tutoring position as a result of the controversy surrounding his curriculum.[6]

Out of a job and disillusioned with the priesthood, Ronge again sat down to write, but this time he challenged what he saw as the materialistic excess of the pilgrimage to the Holy Coat of Trier. The opening shots in the Holy Coat of Trier pamphlet war came when Ronge publicly attacked Bishop Wilhelm Arnoldi on 1 October 1844 in the *Sächsische Vaterlandsblätter*.[7] As he explained, he was speaking out in order to give voice to the "millions" who, like him, were disgusted by what they heard was happening in Trier.[8] Ronge was succinct in his descriptions of what he found most repugnant about the "unworthy pageant" of Trier.[9] The pilgrimage was too fanatical and superstitious, "the busy commerce of the city, and even the harvest labours of the field were silent – everything like this world's occupations and concerns were all alike neglected, to give pomp and emphasis to the sad spectacle of men's faith deceived and led astray by a piece of an old garment."[10] Ronge presented two broad critiques of pilgrimage: that it was heresy and superstition, and that it was a fraud to enrich the local German Catholic authorities.[11]

On 4 November 1844, Ronge left Laurahütte to stay with his brother, Franz. Four months later, on 1 March 1845, he led a service as the pastor of a "universal Christian church" in Breslau.[12] On 9 March, he was appointed priest within his movement.[13] And by the end of 1845, Ronge led a congregation of 7,000 in this capital city of the German-Catholics.[14] They developed new creeds, including, "I believe in God the Father who by his almighty word created the world and rules it in wisdom, justice and love; in Jesus Christ, our Savior [who by his teaching, his life and his death redeemed us from sin and slavery]; in the [working of the] Holy Spirit [on earth], in a holy general Christian Church,

Figures 4.1. and 4.2. Depictions of Johannes Ronge from pamphlets by Robert Blum and J. Vecqueray.[15]
Sources: Blum, *Johannes Ronges offenes Sendschreiben*, 2; Vecqueray, *Der Aufruf des Herrn Joh. Ronge*, title page.

forgiveness of sins and life everlasting."[16] Ronge then spent the rest of his life promoting his new sect throughout Central Europe.[17]

By December 1844, the official church paper for the southern Rhine and Hessen informed its readers that Ronge was no longer a Catholic priest. In fact, he had already been suspended in Silesia in 1843: "All Catholic priests, as previously his cohort and fellow students, chaplains, disowned him, and had no more community with him."[18] Ronge, the Silesian bulletin assured the faithful, was now barely a Christian, only retaining the irrevocable baptism into the faith that a Christian convert to Islam or Judaism would also never lose. Ronge was on equal footing with those who renounced Christianity in favour of a separate monotheistic faith.[19]

Despite these retroactive denunciations, Ronge's assault on the Trier hierarchy led to momentary fame and a speaking tour in 1845. He was greeted as a hero in Potsdam at the tomb of Friedrich the Great.[20]

Supporters in Berlin established an "Association for the Support of the German-Catholic Congregation" to financially bolster Ronge's cause.[21] Although he received warm welcomes in Ulm, Offenbach, Frankfurt am Main, Weimar, and Königsberg, Ronge encountered problems beginning in Oberschwaben, where farmers blamed him for their weak potato crop. Afterwards, a crowd attempted to hurl Ronge into the river in Koblenz. Even in his own hometown, Bischofswalde in Neiße, Ronge was shouted down as locals pelted him with a hail of stones in June 1845. During this encounter Ronge's brother was bloodied and a local policeman suffered wounds to his head.[22] From there Ronge's situation continued to deteriorate. One night in August, while he was staying in Tarnowitz in Oberschlesien, the church bells summoned the locals to his hotel. The crowd hurled rocks at the building and called *"Ronge raus!"* ("Ronge out!"). Although police and local officials eventually gained control of the mob, Ronge still had to sneak out of town at five in the morning.[23]

The Ronge schism came as a surprise to Catholics in part because the critique originated from a self-professed Catholic priest who lashed out at Catholic religious practices with theologically informed arguments. Ronge's former superiors in Silesia were particularly angry that he had dared to name them his colleagues and signed his anti-Trier letter as "a Catholic priest."[24] Ronge refused to back down or withdraw his criticisms. He was ultimately excommunicated in December 1845.[25] Two months later Ronge developed his own twenty-two-point creed, which he announced after German-Catholic meetings on 11 and 16 February 1846.

Ronge's February 1845 declaration codified his criticisms of Arnoldi and contemporary Catholicism. Ronge signalled his complete departure from the church in the first article: "We declare ourselves free from the Roman bishop and all of his subjoinders."[26] Further tenets of the German-Catholic faith included the right to knowledge and free thought, scripture as the foundation of Christian belief, and the denial of spiritual authorities' right to interfere with research into and interpretation of scripture. For obvious reasons, Ronge wanted to avoid a hierarchical structure with the power to excommunicate. German-Catholics maintained that there were only two sacraments: baptism (they affirmed infant baptism), and the Lord's Supper. German-Catholics received communion in both kinds (bread and wine) but regarded this act as symbolic. They rejected transubstantiation of the Eucharist and the need for confession as part of the sacrament of the Lord's Supper. Ronge and his followers also banned mediators between humanity and God (besides Jesus), fasting, and feast days. The only holidays were to be those of the nation, and the only laws came from the state as well. The congregation selected the pastor in the German-Catholic community, although the services barely deviated from the Catholic Mass. Finally, new members could join by simply reciting the new creed in front of the congregation. Many of Ronge's reforms echoed those of sixteenth-century reformers, most notably his affirmation of only two sacraments. F. Treumund, a Protestant supporter of Ronge's break with Rome, concluded his account of the early history of German-Catholics by wondering if Protestantism had just won another group of fellow believers. He identified a kindred spirit in Ronge.[27]

Ronge continued to work on establishing the German-Catholics as a movement after 1845. However, his calls for the Christians of Europe and America to wake up, throw off papal tyranny and Roman hierarchy, and establish a new Kingdom of Christ on earth went largely unanswered in the Rhineland. After 1848 Ronge fled to England, where he stayed until 1861.[28] Upon his return to the Continent, Ronge found a changed German-Catholic community. While he was in exile, in 1859 the German-Catholics joined with Protestant dissenters in the *Bund freier religiöser Gemeinden Deutschlands* (Federation of Free Religious Communities in Germany), which was part of a larger "Free Religious" movement that stretched to the United States. Ronge worked within this new framework, but in a diminished capacity. He acted as a speaker and as an assistant who helped coordinate kindergartens.[29]

Ronge left an ambiguous legacy for German-Catholics. He presented himself as a new, nineteenth-century prophet who would reunite Germany under a single faith. But the theological revolution did not supersede established Protestant and Catholic traditions. By 1863 Ronge was back in Germany and tried to reinvigorate his movement by supporting Italian general and nationalist Giuseppe Garibaldi (1807–82) and war with the Vatican.[30] The Ober-Procurator of the Rhineland acknowledged that the Prussian regime could punish Ronge for breaking censorship laws with his publications but advised that would only unnecessarily make Ronge a martyr. It was best to continue ignoring him.[31] That same year, the Königlicher Landrath (royal district administrator) dismissed Ronge as "nearly forgotten" in a letter to the Königliche Regierung (Royal Administration) in Trier.[32] By the time he died on the train in 1887, Ronge had outlived his movement.

Ronge's Anti-Trier Writings

In 1844–5, Ronge was keen to reveal the unchristian and superstitious nature of Arnoldi's event. He made this critique via three separate observations in his anti-pilgrimage tracts. First, the event was fanatical, because the focus of the cult was so obviously forged. Arnoldi, as bishop, must have known that in the Gospels the Roman soldiers responsible for Jesus's execution divided his clothes at the foot of the cross. Jesus's executioners drew lots to decide who would take home Christ's Coat. Arnoldi promoted the worship of a spurious piece of cloth that could not possibly have changed hands from Roman soldier to Christian sympathizer in the first century CE. Second, the bishop ignored the Gospel prohibition against worshipping images or relics. By calling for the pilgrimage, Arnoldi set Christendom back – he was reverting to European paganism. Third, Arnoldi willfully corrupted Jesus's central teaching: "Do you not know? – as bishop you must know that the founder of the Christian religion did not leave his disciples and followers his Coat, but his spirit."[33] Jesus's legacy was spiritual and not tactile.

Much like his anti-Christian argument, Ronge's point that the event was a scam or con appeared in several different forms. Arnoldi, he asserted, was getting personally rich from the 500,000 pilgrims, most of whom came from "lower classes, already in great poverty, depressed, ignorant, stupid and superstitious and partially degenerate."[34] Rather than focusing on their all-too-real material problems, these pilgrims wasted resources to enrich the Catholic hierarchy.[35] Worse, the pilgrims lost days of work and got sick from the trip when they should have been focused on their livelihoods.[36] Ronge asked, "Is it not unforgivable that as bishop you accept gold from our hungry and poor people?"[37] Arnoldi worsened the living conditions of the impoverished and superstitious Rhinelanders while also covering the "German name" in shame by promoting relics.[38] Ronge clarified that Germans had been immune to this particular form of religiosity prior to the thirteenth and fourteenth centuries. The crusades polluted Germany's "religious atmosphere" and helped to place the German people in bondage to the church hierarchy.

Ronge explained away reports that the Holy Coat could heal pilgrims. The cult of miracles epitomized Roman Catholic superstition and stupidity. For example, Ronge dismissed the claims that Countess Johanna Droste zu Vischering was cured after visiting Trier. He described the dramatic account a "simple story" and "a rather better than average specimen of the popish miracles of the continent."[39] Ronge included a medical explanation for what happened to the Countess. She had not exercised the diseased limb for many years, and when she saw the Coat she became ecstatic. In her fit she stretched and bent the limb, which in turn relaxed the muscles and provided temporary relief.[40] Without corroborating evidence, Ronge assured his readers that the Countess had since relapsed and was "we believe, now using the crutches, which had been too hastily hung up in the cathedral as a thank-offering for her marvelous restoration."[41]

Ronge signed off his 1844 broadside with an appeal in the name of the German people to resist Catholic leadership on the grounds that the Coat was simultaneously inauthentic and a forgery. The Catholic history of the Coat illuminated the "effects which superstition and idolatrous adoration of relics have worked among us."[42] The history of the tangible Coat blinded Catholics to the true essence of Christ: his mystical presence among the faithful.[43] Thus, Ronge maintained that the Coat was a product of human hands, unintended for worship, inauthentic, illegitimate, and ultimately tyrannical.

The Catholic Response

Ronge's denunciations struck a nerve because he called for a complete break with Rome. Catholic authors stressed that pilgrims were properly trained in the New Testament and that widespread biblical literacy cut off Ronge's criticisms of pilgrims as superstitious and ignorant. Furthermore, the pilgrims knew that they could worship God anywhere and that they did not have to travel to Trier to access the divine. Mauritius Moritz, a priest and teacher, turned in his *Open Reply* to 2 Corinthians 11:13–15 to explain why Ronge had to be excommunicated, "Such people are false apostles, deceitful workers, masquerading as apostles of Christ. And no wonder, for Satan himself masquerades as an angel of light. It is not surprising, then, if his servants also masquerade as servants of righteousness. Their end will be what their actions deserve."[44]

As Catholic sympathizers responded to Ronge with a flurry of tracts and counter-arguments, they were uncertain whether to attack Ronge's biography or limit themselves to his arguments. Professor Doctor Schmitz wrote Bishop Arnoldi from Regensburg to caution that "the unfortunate Johannes Ronge and his shame should not be particularly mentioned, for this misery has already been too often named."[45] Indeed the pilgrimage, a great public show of church unity should be enough to convince Catholic pilgrims that Ronge's writings were baseless. Schmitz lamented the fact that other commentators, especially Moritz, levelled more personal attacks against Ronge. He viewed Moritz's approach as "shameful and untimely, but in any case, well-meant."[46] Catholics had to address Ronge, but they could do this by pointing to the massive attendance and order of 1844. Schmitz believed that there was no need for Moritz's narrative about Ronge's personal life and failure as a priest.

Catholic pamphleteers ultimately concentrated their criticism on Ronge's sweeping statements about the New Testament and early church history. Against Ronge, Jakob Marx maintained the veracity of the Coat of Trier and the biblical foundation of his faith. Marx was a professor at the Trier Catholic seminary. He helped Arnoldi coordinate the pilgrimage and worked closely with the bishop.[47] Marx concluded his account with a quote from Luke 8:48: "Woman, thy faith hath saved thee!" Joseph Ritter, a cathedral canon, directed his pamphlet to a "non-academic" audience and made it his goal to answer one question: "Is the cult of relics reasonable for a Christian?"[48] Ritter noted that in Acts 3 Peter healed a lame beggar by telling him to walk and by helping him stand up. Later, in Acts 5:12, "The apostles performed many signs and wonders among the people." These passages established the possibility of miracles emanating from saints. Christians should honour the items they left behind. Franz Heide, also Catholic, grounded his understanding of relics in Acts 19:11–12: "God did extraordinary miracles through Paul, so that even handkerchiefs and aprons that had touched him were taken to the sick, and their illnesses were cured and the evil spirits left them."[49] Heide noted that such miracles, through the garments of the saints and prophets, happened to orient people towards God and show God's authority.[50] For Mauritius Moritz, Acts 21 was the key passage, wherein Paul makes a pilgrimage to Jerusalem.[51] All of these authors worked to counter Ronge by rooting their religious practices in the biblical history of the early church. Ronge planned to throw out tradition, so the Catholic authorities countered the suspended priest on his own scriptural terms.

For Catholic pamphleteers, the fact that Jesus himself established and promoted the medium of relics in the Gospels was even more important than the relic-affirming chapters in the Acts of the Apostles, and in St. Paul's letters. For example, anti-Ronge writers often cited Matthew 9:18–26:

> While he was saying this, a synagogue leader came and knelt before him and said, "My daughter has just died. But come and put your hand on her, and she will live." Jesus got up and went with him, and so did his disciples. Just then a woman who had been subject to bleeding for twelve years came up behind him and touched the edge of his cloak. She said to herself, "If I only touch his cloak, I will be healed." Jesus turned and saw her. "Take heart, daughter," he said, "your faith has healed you." And the woman was healed at that moment.

Catholic commentators pointed to this story as definitive proof that the Coat had miraculous authority.[52] Like the 1844 pilgrims to Trier, the woman in Matthew only had access to the hem of the Coat, but that was physically close enough to Jesus to change her life. Similarly, after reporting the miracle of his parishioner Susanna Beth, Father Berig of Cochem concluded that it was imperative that Trier release its report confirming miracles in order to stop Ronge and his polemic against the church. Furthermore, Berig believed that a report on the healing power of the Coat would be a deathblow to the opponents of the Trier pilgrimage.[53]

Jesus promised that he would always be present with his followers, pamphleteers noted. Moritz, for example, pointed to Matthew 28:19–20: "Therefore go and make disciples of all nations, baptizing them in the name of the Father and of the Son and of the Holy Spirit, and teaching them to obey everything I have commanded you. And surely I am with you always, to the very end of the age." For Moritz, Jesus's promise to always accompany his followers foreshadowed the Coat and was a tangible reminder that Jesus had lived in the world. Moritz also cited John 21:17, wherein Jesus commanded Peter to feed his sheep. As Peter was the first pontiff, Catholic traditions were indirectly approved by Jesus. At the end of his Gospel discussion Moritz cautioned that religion was much more than the mind, more than knowing facts or scripture.[54] Despite the scriptural assurance, Ritter acknowledged that he was not certain what happened to Jesus's garment after he was executed. But it was entirely possible that John the Apostle or Mary somehow eventually acquired it from the Roman soldiers.[55]

If the Gospel writers did not clarify what happened to the Coat after Jesus's execution, the authors did approve of pilgrimage. Jesus called pilgrims to leave their homes. Johann Peter Neumann stressed the promise of Mark 10:29–30 that those who follow Jesus and leave "home or brothers or sisters or mother or father or children or fields for me and the gospel will not fail to receive a hundred times as much in this present age: homes, brothers, sisters, mothers, children and fields – along with persecutions – and in the age to come: eternal life."[56] Not only did Jesus call on his disciples to be in motion, he also promised that doing so brought divine blessing. Jesus approved of the financial sacrifice that accompanied leaving home. Neumann pointed to John 12, where Martha anointed Jesus's feet with expensive perfume, a great monetary forfeiture. Here Ronge was likened to Judas, who decried the cost of the perfume, or, for Ronge, the cost of travelling to Trier. Neumann used these Gospel passages to defend pilgrims giving donations within the cathedral; economic sacrifice was equal to the physical toil of walking to Trier.[57]

Ronge's attacks on pilgrimage practices like donating money, commentators maintained, paradoxically demonstrated that Catholicism was diligently pursuing proper worship. Moritz concluded his treatise defending pilgrimage with John 15:20 and Matthew 5:11: "Remember what I told you: 'A servant is not greater than his master.' If they persecuted me, they will persecute you also. If they obeyed my teaching, they will obey yours also," and, "Blessed are you when people insult you, persecute you, and falsely say all kinds of evil against you because of me."[58] Ronge was more than the fulfilment of persecution prophecy, though. Franz Gerhard Vecqueray, another Ronge opponent, closed with 1 John 4:1 and accused Ronge of being a false prophet sent by Satan to confuse the faithful.[59] Franz Heide, who cited Revelation 13:5–6, argued that Ronge was the "beast" who "opened its mouth to blaspheme God, and to slander his name and his dwelling place and those who live in heaven."[60] Ronge damned himself when he criticized divinely ordained pilgrimages.

Pamphleteers took aim at Ronge's assertion that for the first three hundred years of Christianity there were no images or relics in Christian practice. Authors pointed to several Church fathers – including Polycarp, Joseph of Arimathea, Irenaeus, Hieronymus, Tertullian, St. Augustine, St. Stephen, Origen, Vigilantius, Ignatius, and Chrysostomos – to justify pilgrimage.[61] Polycarp was bishop of Smyrna and executed for refusing to offer sacrifices to honour Roman Emperor Marcus Aurelius in the 160s.[62] After he was burned at the stake (or stabbed, or killed by wild animals, depending on the pamphlet) for disobedience, his bones were brought back to Smyrna and buried. Immediately afterward Christians from the area began to make pilgrimages to his bodily remains. Why, Dr. J.H. Reinerding, a Gymansium teacher, asked Ronge, would Christians carry his bones back to Smyrna when there was perfectly good dirt in Rome?[63] Because venerating saints' dead bodies was already an established tradition before the third century. Stolz wrote that on the anniversary of Polycarp's death, the Christians of Smyrna made a procession to honour his body and sacrifice. Like these second-century Christians, the pilgrims of Trier continued to venerate God via relics.[64] Coupled with the Polycarp example, pamphleteers repeatedly stressed that it was not Polycarp's remains as such that early Christians venerated, but the divine *presence* that gave Polycarp the courage to face execution for his belief in Jesus and Christian monotheism.

Pilgrims naturally visited Polycarp's body in order to recall his martyrdom. Everyone – Protestant, Catholic, or even Ronge – participated in relic adoration of some form. Franz Heide pointed to the example of a dying mother and her child. Even after the mother passed away, the child, knowing there was no life in her, kissed her dead hand anyway. Along the same lines, the child instinctively holds onto a physical remembrance of his mother, such as a picture or image. For the child, this item could quickly become his most prized treasure.[65] Humans intuitively kept objects in order to recall the departed.

Authors extended this "intuition" argument beyond immediate family members to make their next major point: everyone, including Protestants and Ronge, venerated notable dead individuals. Thus, C.F.B. Franksmann defended the Coat by citing the auction prices of Martin Luther's personal items in the eighteenth century. If Protestants venerated Luther's Bible, pocket watch, marriage bed, or catheter, then they could not fault Catholics for honouring Jesus's garment.[66] Joseph Hillebrand stressed that Catholics had no problems with Protestants keeping images of Luther or honouring their founder.[67] Wilhelm Volk noted how even Protestants made pilgrimages to the Wartburg while singing and that they treasured books that Luther once owned.[68] Hilarius Jocosus Geron complained that Luther and Calvin's followers would have even honoured their underwear.[69] Another author likened the practice to naming a street "Martin Lutherstraße" and asked for understanding.[70] Non-Catholics did not just honour Luther's underwear, but Rousseau's nightcap and Voltaire's underpants as well.[71] Again, pamphlet writers maintained, this linking of memory to physical items should have been common sense to Ronge.

If Ronge-sympathizers remained unconvinced that relics were an instinctive part of human remembrance, it ultimately did not matter to Catholic commentators, because the Council of Trent upheld sacred objects as legitimate.[72] Theologians at Trent declared that martyrs' bodies and items were worthy of honour because they acted as divine vessels for the Holy Spirit. God filled martyrs and saints with grace and allowed physical items to remain in the world to strengthen the faithful.[73] The Council of Trent also affirmed that it was not the objects themselves that had merit, but God acting through the relics.[74] For Reinerding, the fact that Trent upheld relics and images after the Protestant Reformation made Ronge all the more absurd. How could Ronge think he was wiser than over 100 priests in the final Trent meetings, or smarter than all the living bishops, priests, and 180 million laity?[75] Although Reinerding carefully laid out a defence of relics, he accused Ronge of inciting confessional strife because everyone knew the history of iconoclasm and how images and relics had created a fundamental rift between Catholic and Protestant Christianity during the Reformation.[76]

Beyond theology, Austrian officials worried about Ronge's message and its potential political harm to the empire. In November 1844, Carl Ernst Jarcke (1801–52), Metternich's press secretary in Vienna, wrote to Trier officials and asked for a copy of Marx's history of the Coat.[77] Jarcke contended that Ronge's words existed in two separate spheres: spiritual and temporal. The spiritual consequences were minor; the church only needed to look at the pilgrimage itself and reaffirm the meaning of relics to the laity. The potential temporal fallout was more ominous, however. He believed the Prussian government had to be fair and protect Catholics from defamation.[78] Catholic pamphleteers and state officials were thus both concerned about the temporal and spiritual fallout from Ronge.

As news of Ronge's anti-pilgrimage article spread through Rhenish parishes, Catholic clergy sought out official government and church responses. Catholic clerics unsuccessfully petitioned the Prussian government to censor Ronge and the *Sächsische Vaterlandsblätter*. They warned both Trier and Berlin that temporal intervention was necessary if the regime wanted to maintain religious peace. As early as October 1844, Catholic priests wrote to Trier to learn what was being done about Ronge. Dean Schneider, supported by ten other priests from Ehrang, urged the Trier Domkapitel to turn to the Prussian King for assistance. Schneider feared that the Ronge letter, which he warned was spreading to more newspapers in the Rhineland, including the *Mannheimer Abendzeitung* and *Elberfelder Zeitung*, threatened the dearly bought peace between Christian confessions.[79] The Catholic faith, and leaders like Arnoldi, deserved state-sponsored protection from "most sickening attackers" like Ronge.[80]

Similar to Ehrang, the priests in Berncastel were outraged about the treatment of Catholics in the press. They urged the Trier Domkapitel to either secure protection from the king or to petition competent state authorities to defend their faith: "Our holy Catholic Church is ill-treated by the daily press, how her sanctuaries were put into the mud, the church's ancient dogma and venerable ceremonies are attacked and disfigured."[81] Sixteen priests in Prüm signed another protest letter in November 1844 to call for immediate action. They contended that nothing would be gained from tolerating the Ronge letter. "With deep anxiety we ask what will result from such commotion? The desired German unity? The offered brotherly love without distinction of confession? No!"[82] The king and the Bundestag had to act to uphold the laws of toleration, to stop the fires of hate before it was too late. The deans and priests in St. Goar urged Trier to appeal to the king on the basis of equal treatment. Trier required the monarchy to treat Catholics with only the same respect given to Protestants. If a Protestant cleric had lashed out in the press, would the article have been suppressed? Why should the situation be different for Catholics? The Prussian law guaranteed the position of German Catholics and an unbiased application of the censorship laws. In short, St. Goar leaders desired redress and the rights "granted to the Protestant Confession every day."[83]

Priests acted surprised that in the 1840s the Catholic confession was abused so openly in Central Europe. Lentz, in Neumagen, recounted how the Trier mayor refused to allow an article against Jews to be published in the *Trierische Zeitung* and asked why "this excessive proliferation of such malicious attacks against the church, its institutions, its customs, and even their most sublime servants in public" was tolerated by the civil authorities.[84] In Hermeskeil, the clergy listed goals and grievances about the Ronge situation, including a respectful request that the law be equally applied to all religious groups. They further affirmed that Arnoldi was hardly outside the law, because civil authorities had approved the pilgrimage before it began. These priests concluded by asserting their belief in a free press, with the caveat that all sides (presumably Ronge and the church) must receive a fair hearing.[85] The Daun priests wrote a song for the Protestant king, in order to persuade him to defend the Catholic Church and existing laws:

Es möge Versorge getroffen werden,	Provision should be made
daß weder in Preußer, noch in	That neither in Prussia, nor in
der übrigen Bundes staaten die	The rest of the federal states
Rechte der katholischen Kirche	Rights of the Catholic Church
ungestraft gekränkt, daß vielmehr	[are] offended with impunity, but rather
die deshalb bestehenden	
Gesetze gehand habt werden mögten [*sic*].	Treated according to the already existing laws.[86]

In Daun, church leaders were most upset that newspapers did not offer positive views of Catholicism and ran only negative articles. They worried that enemies of Catholicism could strike without consequence, leaving a skewed view of the church for the newspaper readership.

In their letter from Wittlich, five priests asked the state to free the church from the hindrance of the censor so they could respond to Ronge, especially since the government chose not to stop Ronge's public attack on the religious status quo.[87] The Trier Domkapitular received similar letters from clerics in Kelberg, Mayen, Engers, Bisdorf, Meisenheim, Cochem, Merzig, Saarlouis, Bitburg, and Kreuznach. Historian Alf Lüdkte has shown that the anxiety these priests expressed had merit. Beginning in 1789, Prussian officials grouped Catholic priests with "apprentices, journeymen and day labourers, servants and maidservants, beggars and vagrants ... mobile Jewish salesmen." For Prussian officials, all of these groups were worthy of observation and "permanent distrust."[88] Catholic priests contended that they were not a threat and believed they were entitled to state assistance in reining in Ronge, because the former priest was a menace to Prussian peace. Priests spread news of Ronge's infamy in order to warn fellow clerics.[89] For Ronge's part, he thought that the biblical and political criticisms levelled against him were baseless and dodged his key critiques about sacrilege and idolatry.

Ronge Responds to Pamphleteers in Early 1845

Ronge responded to his Catholic critics, again in the *Sächsische Vater-landsblätter*, in January 1845.[90] He now defined the German-Catholic movement by negation. His new confession was at its core *not* Catholicism. He scoffed at the various names given him by Catholic pamphleteers: "Judas," "demagogue," and "false prophet." The Catholic hierarchy and the Jesuits made the Pharisees seem like harmless children. "The chief priests and the priestcraft of the Jews devoured only the Jewish nation," he wrote, "but you have the unfortunate fate of many nations of Europe on your hands."[91] For Ronge, Catholicism was darkness, fog, servitude, and deceit. In turn, he offered Central Europeans light, sunshine, freedom, and truth.

Ronge chose not to respond to the specific theological criticisms of his movement. Instead, he expanded upon his original arguments. Maintaining his Gospel focus, Ronge now likened Arnoldi to a money changer in the ancient Jerusalem Temple. He was surprised that the Catholics were unfamiliar with Matthew 21:12–13: "Jesus entered the temple courts and drove out all who were buying and selling there. He overturned the tables of the money changers and the benches of those selling doves. 'It is written,' he said to them, 'My house will be called a house of prayer,' but you are making it 'a den of robbers.'" For Ronge, no matter how much emphasis Catholics placed on the good of the pilgrimage, they simply could not overcome the fact that Arnoldi took money from impoverished pilgrims.[92] Arnoldi, like the Temple accountants, turned religion into a financial transaction and thereby gutted its spiritual core.

Ronge reaffirmed his belief that the devotion around the Coat was simple idolatry. He rejected explanations about the symbolism of the Coat as "drivel" from "some [who] have sought to refute me!" Despite all the wit of the canons and church doctors, "[even with] their cunning and their rhetoric … they cannot reverse common sense."[93] Dr. Ritter, whom Ronge directly targeted on several occasions, could not deny the fact that one of the pilgrim songs, sung for all the world to hear, included the lyrics "Holy Coat pray for us."[94] Despite clever turns of phrase about the symbolism of the Trier relic, for Ronge, this devotion was unchristian and an untenable belief for the German-Catholic movement. There would be a divine reckoning for the Catholic clergy. Ronge declared himself "a very simple man, without wealth, without power, a man who has no other home than the hearts of his friends and the greater part of the people that you abuse."[95] The excommunicated priest declared his willingness to die for the cause of the imminent "priestly revolution" that would sweep away the Roman sympathizers.

Ronge presented no detailed revolutionary program, however. Instead he offered Catholics a series of stark choices: "Roman or German, servant or free, hypocrisy or truth, hierarchy or Christianity."[96] To help readers choose their allegiance, Ronge sought to reveal the "truth" about pilgrimage and Catholic history. He firmly believed the historical record would lead Germans to abandon the Catholic Church. He held Catholicism accountable for the Thirty Years' War, Poland's descent into bloody disorder, and the butchering of Spain and France in recent memory, presumably meaning the Napoleonic Wars.[97]

Ironically, Ronge accused the Catholic hierarchy of collusion with the state in enforcing censorship of the press and imprisoning those who spoke out against religious abuses. This was a remarkable accusation, as the Trier clergy pressured Prussian authorities to censor and imprison Ronge without success. The criminal offences of the church hierarchy were legion, if often undifferentiated, but Ronge hammered home his 1844 accusation that pilgrimage was debauchery. Pamphleteers spoke of peaceful processions, but that was only to cover up the loss of virtue among the laity.

Ronge could not articulate a positive definition of what his movement meant, and ultimately this inability cost the German-Christians momentum. Two years after the pamphlet conflict began, on 2 January 1846, Bishop Arnoldi reported that there were only two small communities in his bishopric that still had German-Catholics: Saarbrücken and Kreuznach.[98] By 1850, as one historian has stated, the German-Catholics lost their historical significance.[99]

German-Catholics and Their Supporters

Ronge was the loudest voice in a chorus of attacks on Trier pilgrimage and Catholic practices. Adolf Glaßbrenner (1810–76) composed an anti-pilgrimage play that was set in Trier. Glaßbrenner sought to liberate the people from superstition and spark their interest in democracy and emancipation. He, like Ronge, denounced the Catholic Church, miracles, and the money brought in during pilgrimage.[100] German politician Robert Blum (1807–48), in solidarity with Ronge, wrote that German Christendom was in a "fight between light and darkness."[101] In this conflict Ronge served as the resplendent guide. Blum, the editor of *Sächsische Vaterlandsblätter*, further supported Ronge's theological positions and his critiques by reprinting Ronge's article as a stand-alone pamphlet.[102]

Johann Czerski (1813–93) also left the Catholic priesthood to establish a new Christian sect in 1844.[103] In March, the western Prussian Catholic hierarchy transferred him to Schneidemühl in eastern Prussia. Two months later, Czerski's superiors suspended him from the priesthood for living with a woman.[104] In August, Czerski officially declared that he was no longer a member of the Roman Catholic Church. On 19 October 1844, in Schneidemühl, Czerski began a new form of Catholicism, called the *Christlich-Apostolisch-Katholische-Gemeinde* (Christian-Apostolic-Catholic-Community). Czerski refused to recant his new teachings, including his rejection of clerical celibacy, and was subsequently excommunicated from the Catholic Church.[105] Officially outside the church, Czerski married and was re-baptized as a member of his *Christlich-Apostolisch-Katholische-Gemeinde* sect in December 1844.[106] Czerski initially supported Ronge and most of Ronge's proposed reforms of the Catholic Church. The two met in January 1845 to reach a theological agreement. However, after Ronge issued the Breslau Confession in Leipzig in 1845, Czerski broke with the German-Catholics.

Czerski espoused his own creed, which he published in Schneidemühl on 19 October 1844.[107] Czerski affirmed the existence of one God, whose son was Jesus. He also denounced papal control of the Catholic Church, established a Mass in German, denied the existence of Purgatory, and administered the Lord's Supper with both bread and wine. Czerski contested Ronge's German-Catholics on two points: the number of sacraments, and the role of Jesus. For Czerski, there were still seven sacraments, as laid out within Catholicism: these included baptism, confirmation, Lord's Supper, confession, priestly ordination (though he made no mention of other Holy Orders), marriage, and the last rites.[108] Against Ronge, Czerski stressed Jesus's authority within the church over that of the Holy Spirit in his eleventh statement of faith: "We firmly acknowledge that Christ alone is the head of His Church and His Vicar on earth [is] the Holy Spirit."[109]

Despite their distinct creeds, both pro- and anti-Ronge pamphlets flattened Ronge and Czerski's peculiarities in order to create a single anti-Catholic antagonist.[110] One anonymous author included a section "Ronge, Czerski, and Company."[111] Here the author described both ex-priests as blind and stubborn, possessing "an almost limitless ignorance."[112] Hilarius Jocosus Geron also linked the two and cited the *Frankfurter Journal* to criticize their "minor personal skills."[113] Johann Leonard Pfaff addressed his anti-reform poem to Czerski and Ronge and blamed both for fomenting anti-Catholic hatred and poor theological knowledge.[114] This linkage was not limited to the critics. Gustav Eschirn, for instance, saw Czerski as dependent on Ronge, following through with his reforms only after Ronge established a viable German-Catholic community in Breslau.[115] The fact that Ronge was not the only critical ex-priest further explains the explosion of Catholic pamphlets and adamant calls for governmental intervention. Like the German-Catholics, the *Christlich-Apostolisch-Katholische-Gemeinde* lost momentum in the latter decades of the nineteenth century and faded into obscurity.

The Reception of German-Catholicism

News of the Ronge controversy spread swiftly and pamphlets on the topic sold quickly. The *Lyser und Ronge* tract, for example, sold 300 copies within a few weeks.[116] The Leipziger Reclam-Verlag sold 50,000 copies of Ronge's anti-pilgrimage letter in just fourteen days.[117] By 1847, Ronge's movement included 70,000–80,000 followers in 230 communities.[118] At its height, the German-Catholic movement included 300 separate communities with over 100,000 members.[119] In 1848 in Saxony, the German-Catholics were numerous enough to be recognized as a regional religious community.[120] Anti-Ronge pamphleteers rushed to offer counterarguments to this deluge of Rongean criticism.

Catholic laity were often exposed to anti-Ronge arguments. Several pamphlets against Ronge's positions were actually priests' published homilies. Jakob Marx noted that in 1844 homilies, pilgrims to Trier were warned about "liberalism" and "unbelieving hearts."[121] One priest blasted the "new Enlightenment, new *Bildung* … new Humanity" of the nineteenth century. Priests taught that Ronge was a spokesman of "unbound" and shortsighted philosophies that threatened Catholic beliefs and institutions.[122]

Church publications, including weekly bulletins and diocesan newsletters, instructed the faithful on how best to respond to German-Catholic teachings. Through the 1840s and on into the twentieth century, German laity learned about Ronge and his movement from German clergy. Unfortunately, lay dispositions are not readily available for analysis and were not as prominent in the public sphere (or the archives) as the pamphlet debates between Trier supporters and critics. The authors of several anonymous pamphlets styled themselves as non-members of the clergy, as "a Catholic," "a Catholic layman," or "a pilgrim from Koblenz."[123] Yet these perspectives were the minority and, while often anonymous, they tended to show a remarkable grasp of Christian history and the writings of theologians such as Aquinas, Polycarp, or Origen. This expertise suggests at the least some scholarly training.

In addition to diocesan publications and pamphlets, the debate between Ronge and German clergy about the origins and credibility of the Trier Coat appeared in popular literature. In December 1844, Leipzig-based satirical *Charivari* mocked the Trier relic by depicting it as a plain jacket hung up over Trier. The editors also included a poem by

Figure 4.3. Trier Coat, *Charivari*, December 1844.
Source: Oettinger, "Die streitenden Röcke Gedicht," 1845.

Figure 4.4. Pro-Ronge satire. Ronge's trumpet blast dislodges the clerical
stork and breaks the chains of Catholicism. Note the sheep participating in the
event below.
Source: SAT, "1844 Ronge."

Figure 4.5. Ronge's new German-Catholic faith dislodges old authorities, including clergy, nobility, and the Holy Coat of Trier. Having seen the light of German-Catholicism, the laity now flock to Ronge's movement.
Source: SAT, "1844 Ronge."

Figure 4.6. On the divine scales, Ronge's "Open Letter" outweighs the Holy Coat and the church's excommunication. Note also that Ronge's missive has toppled the papacy.
Source: SAT, "1844 Ronge."

S. Zed in which three competing coats claimed to be the true garment of Jesus. The first posed a question to the other two: Am I the correct coat because I was present for the first miracle of Jesus at the feast of Canaan? No, asserted the second, the true garment, itself, has been approved as authentic by the papacy. The final coat noted that it was present for Jesus's ascension on the Mount of Olives and sarcastically quipped that Jesus left it behind to do miracles on the earth. At the end of the poem God looked down and laughed at the eccentricities of humanity. God wondered why Catholics chose the Trier relic and not some other garment, like the Cologne coat.[124]

In addition, Ronge was satirized throughout the Rhineland. He appeared alternatively as a religious reformer and a heretical demon. For instance, in figure 4.4 Ronge sounds the trumpet of truth. His alarm calls attention to the large sacks of money flowing out of the Trier cathedral. In the foreground, laity and clergy are depicted as sheep, passively following the wolfish pope in the top left corner.[125] In figure 4.5, Ronge dispels both the Coat and Catholic clergy with the force of his words in the "German-Catholic confession." Truth, winged and armed with sword and shield, stands guard over the German-Catholic church and its respectable citizens.[126] Finally in figure 4.6, the weight of Ronge's words outweighs the Holy Coat and the proclamation of Ronge's excommunication. All of the assembled clerics are unable to balance the scales of tradition and reformation. The pope is tossed off his seat and falls backwards. The pope's mitre pretiosa tumbles off his head, exposing his bald pate. Having also dropped the keys of Peter, symbol of his office, the leader of the Catholic Church is further menaced by a descending sword of truth. Ronge's words reveal that the pope does not control the gates of heaven. Having cut down the rotten tree of Rome, Ronge and his followers water the new tree of truth.

The cartoons, Marx, and *Charivari* writings indicate that pilgrims to Trier had multiple means of accessing the debate about the origins and tradition of the Trier relic. The sheer number and variety of pamphlets suggest Catholics were often exposed to the opinions of both Ronge and his detractors. Furthermore, pamphlet authors directly addressed a popular audience. Mauritius Moritz blasted Ronge's "hateful fantasy" that the pilgrims to Trier were ignorant.[127] Another pamphlet author explicitly stated that he wrote his tract because so many faithful Catholics were aware of Ronge's ideas.[128] Although clerics in the Rhineland were alarmed that Ronge was trying to lure Catholics away from the church, their reaction was overblown and not proportionate to the minimal threat Ronge's German-Catholics ultimately posed.[129] Anti-Ronge writers were uncertain about the future of their confession under Prussian rule.

Catholic clergy in the Rhineland were anxious about their place in society. They feared that a new radical reformer, like Ronge, could upset their position and lead to an unravelling of the Peace of Westphalia. They worried that Ronge extended Christian reform even beyond Protestantism and threatened to plunge Central Europe into religious relativism. Clergy struggled to demonstrate how established Catholic practices, such as pilgrimage and physical healing through relics, complemented German culture. Priests used scripture and the church fathers to show that they were loyal potential citizens; clergy imagined a Catholic civics.[130] In order to assert their "Germanness" and to counter Ronge, Catholic authors called for Protestant cooperation and asserted that Catholicism laid the foundation for German culture.

Confusing Confessions: Protestants and Ronge

Clerics were careful not to associate Ronge too strongly with Protestantism in their correspondence. Meisenheim priests noted that part of the Ronge problem was that Protestants were buying Ronge's pamphlet "by the thousands." Church officials emphasized the need for swift state-sponsored action.[131] Commentators and participants in the Ronge episode mobilized terms like "Protestant" and "Protestantism" to their own ends, but failed to give these labels much texture. Instead, "Protestant" stood in for evidence, or as the punch line of an argument: Ronge was an enemy because his ideas reflected *Protestant* theology; or Ronge was a *secret Protestant*, planted to hurt the Catholic Church by attacking relics. In November 1844, Father Kirchhoff wrote Professor Marx in Trier and asked if he was familiar with the "author of … leprosy," Johannes Ronge. Kirchhoff hoped Marx would present a well-reasoned response to Ronge because the suspended priest had embittered Kirchhoff's parish. The Hügsburg pastor also confided that he suspected Ronge was a Protestant plant because he could not be a "good son" of Catholicism.[132] Kirchhoff imagined that "Protestants" bought Ronge's pamphlet and his popularity was rooted in Protestant support and the Reformation.

Although "Protestantism" often appeared as an undifferentiated faith – with authors conflating Lutheranism and Calvinism – Catholics projected their historical insecurities about schism onto the Ronge debate. During the Ronge episode there was no consensus among the confessions about how to deal with Ronge. Protestant authors – or more accurately, those pamphlets claiming a Protestant author – both supported and opposed Ronge. The same can be said about their comments regarding Johann Czerski. Ronge's attack went beyond a criticism of Catholic pilgrimage. It struck at Catholic and Protestant state-sponsored clergy and socio-religious structures. Catholics warned that Ronge threatened both Christian confessions with a loss of state recognition and with potential religious anarchy.

Protestants, both real and imagined, were divided on how to best respond to the Silesian ex-priest. For his part, Ronge expected that Trier participants would have to present a certificate of creed to gain access to the Holy Coat. He was surprised to learn that the pilgrimage was at times a bi-confessional affair. Protestants had "the fullest opportunity of seeing what was to be seen."[133] Ronge, wary of the church, assumed that Protestants would be kept away from the relic because they were drawn by curiosity, not piety.

Protestants did not attend just out of curiosity. Indeed, several publicly wrote in support of Bishop Arnoldi. In December 1844, for example, the *Katholische Sonntagsblätter* published an anonymous letter titled "Judgment of a Highly Respectable Protestant about Johannes Ronge."[134] The "Protestant" author contended that Ronge was a sign of the times, a part of the weakening position of religion in German society. "Well, we live in the nineteenth century, where everything that is good and holy is to be eradicated" and "the Communists wanted to establish a thieving proletariat, so we should not be surprised if robbery, also in our nineteenth century, is something glorious to be praised."[135] In essence, Ronge was doing only what was expected of him as an upright citizen (*Biedermann*): "crying out for light and Enlightenment, raging against the clergy and nobility" and attacking the "dumbing down of the mind and conscience."[136] Thus the author would not denounce Ronge outright, even though "he is undeniably a fanatic, a revolutionary demon."[137] Ronge, like other Biedermeier men, was suffering from a mental disease. A passion of the mind that was difficult to heal had overtaken him.[138] As a devoted Protestant, the author could only point out that Ronge was "surely not in his heart Catholic" and "unworthy of the title 'priest.'"[139] Ronge was a warning to Christians, a new threat to religion that stood outside the Protestant Reformation and Protestant tradition. The anonymous author was highly concerned that if Ronge gained a following he would set off a cascading descent into relativism.

Another self-identified Protestant, Dr. Wilhelm Böhmer, echoed the *Katholische Sonntagsblätter* sentiments in his 1845 tract. Böhmer systematically evaluated many of Ronge's boldest claims in order to assess their veracity. Böhmer sought to find a balance between the pro- and anti-Ronge extremes reflected in the pamphlet discussion since October 1844.[140] In his work, he restated one of Ronge's positions and then pronounced judgment. He noted that Ronge criticized Bishop Arnoldi for showing a piece of cloth for worship and found this position "correct," because Arnoldi would not guarantee its historical authenticity. More often than not, however, Böhmer ruled against Ronge, most notably regarding Ronge's statements about the beginnings of Christendom. Böhmer also rejected Ronge's statement that venerating images and relics was forbidden in the Gospels.[141] He sarcastically dismissed Ronge's appeal to early church tradition and Ronge's position that there were no images or relics in the early churches. Naturally not, noted Böhmer, "but of course, because they were not in possession of real churches."[142] Finally, Böhmer took Ronge to task for drawing false parallels between Roman-era paganism and the veneration of the Trier Coat. Böhmer discarded Ronge's analysis of the church fathers because they had in mind not the Trier Coat, but actual worship of classical idols, when they wrote their treatises.[143] The major point here is that Böhmer, as a Protestant, found neither Ronge's appeals to history nor his scriptural exegesis convincing.

Hilarius Jocosus Geron, "a Roman Catholic man from the Pfalz," argued that Ronge used Protestantism to protest Catholic practices without understanding Protestant thinkers.[144] If Ronge read Protestant theology, he would know that even Protestants maintained central tenets of Catholicism. Melanchthon supported church discipline, and Luther, in 1546, even affirmed the usefulness of confession.[145] Geron promised that he could give more quotes from David Hume, Gottfried Wilhelm Leibnitz, Johann Christian Senckenberg, and Johann Gottfried Herder that confirmed the Protestant belief in a church hierarchy.[146]

Geron's approach also appeared in pro-Trier newspapers. The *Luxemburger Zeitung*, for example, quoted Johann Kaspar Lavater as saying, "Nothing is more natural – however unnaturally it may also be abused – than the love of relics of good and pious people."[147] The editor also looked to Feßler and Döderlein as defenders of relics because they approved of "worship in spirit and truth."[148] Finally, Mauritius Moritz cited Gotthold Ephraim Lessing, Leibnitz, and Wolfgang Menzel as defenders of the Catholic Mass as "religious art."[149] These authors maintained that Ronge should not look to Protestants or declare himself the "Luther of the nineteenth century," because Protestantism was not synonymous with a carte blanche condemnation of Catholic practices.[150]

Ronge not only failed to understand Protestantism, but Protestants also found Ronge's "clerical revolution" unappealing. Moritz contended that Ronge often mimicked Protestant anti-Catholic arguments, such as attacking Latin as the language of the Mass and questioning the authority of the pope in Rome.[151] Ronge's parroting did not attract followers, because German-Catholics went too far and threatened to undermine Christian morality. Moritz also included in his pamphlet a section titled "Apology for the Confession [Catholicism] Composed by Protestant Writers." Protestants would not want to live in Ronge's "German nation" because there would not be sufficient clerical authority. Ronge wanted to destroy the priesthood, to "purify the religion, and to reconcile the high and low, the educated and illiterate, rich and poor part of mankind."[152] Still, Moritz was careful not to go too far with this Protestant-Catholic solidarity argument. He concluded his pamphlet by declaring, "We say before the entire world openly and freely that we are nothing but priests of the Roman Catholic Church. God will not leave his church, will not overturn the rock on which he himself built [the church]."[153]

Joseph Hillebrand, Vicarius in Dortmund, extended the thrust of Moritz's argument in 1845 by calling on Protestants to join Catholic clergy in repudiating Ronge. Hillebrand declared that Catholics had no problem at all with Protestants honouring Luther's ashes or images of the reformer, just as Protestants now left Catholics alone to honour their holy martyrs and relics. To preserve the religious peace, Protestants and Catholics needed to stand together: "Catholics and Protestants must together fight the enemy of Christian enthusiasm represented by Johannes Ronge."[154] Ultimately, for Hillebrand, Ronge was a menace beyond Christian confessional perspectives, a man who misrepresented Christendom in the past and present because he was given to counterfactual rants. Hillebrand demanded a pre-emptory strike from his readers: "German brothers! Catholics and Protestants! Let us not conjure up hostility, hatred, and bitterness for the furies of fanaticism! … It is supposed to be our first duty to tolerate each other, [do not allow] lies, slander, coarse ridicule to widen the crack [between Confessions] making the union almost impossible."[155] Without Christian ecumenical cooperation, Germany risked losing everything to a "revolution against the church."

The very foundation of society threatened to crumble if Protestants and Catholics took Ronge's bait and resumed open hostilities.[156] Böhmer agreed with Hillebrand that Ronge conjured up enthusiasm and cheap confessional division. Confessional baiting, such as the bickering about the church fathers, profited no one: not the state, and certainly not Protestants or Catholics.[157] Catholic pamphleteers appealed to Protestants because they feared Protestants would take advantage of the Rongean "moment" and join his attack against public Catholic religiosity.

For C.F.B. Franksmann, Ronge was a Protestant who worked to undermine Catholicism. He declared that Ronge was "in Protestant armies – with Protestant weapons in Protestant uniform" and cautioned his readers that they must consider Ronge "an authentic Protestant

believer."[158] Whereas Hillebrand dismissed Ronge's self-appointed titles, including his claim to be in Luther's line ("he calls himself Catholic
priest and Luther … he scoffs with the scoffers"), the author of *Lyser und
Ronge* placed Ronge in a long tradition of Protestant opposition to Catholic teachings.[159] For this pamphleteer, "the so-called German-Catholics,
which began in Schneidemühl, are no longer Catholic, because they re-
ject the essential dogmas of the church and give unmistakable homage
to Protestantism in their main features."[160] Ronge was a cranky child,
who did nothing but parrot Protestant polemics against Catholic practices.[161] Ronge's words were the "mother's milk" of Protestant theology. Ronge was a standard-bearer for Protestantism. He worked with
Protestants to combat the Jesuits and the sacraments. Ronge channelled
Voltaire and Luther but was even more dangerous because of his claim
to want a "clean Catholicism." "What," asked the author, "does Ronge
mean by 'clean Catholicism' that is different from Protestantism? Is
this not what Luther wanted?"[162] The author, "a Catholic layman," saw
Ronge as part of a drift towards unbelief and atheism.[163]

The logical conclusion of Ronge's criticisms was a war of all against
all, a world without God, and a politically divided Germany.[164] Even
worse, Ronge jeopardized the souls of the nation because the consequence of following his teachings was damnation to Hell.[165] Ronge
would break religion and throw out morality, and this would undermine the Christian foundation of society. Without a Christian moral
compass, self-interest would take the lead and unleash anarchy. In this
view, Ronge was a radical Protestant who took the Reformation to its
ultimate conclusion – Godless atheism and moral anarchy. There could
be no quarter for the German-Catholics who polluted the "Catholic"
title by undermining the church's sacraments and traditions.

Many pamphlets reminded their readers that Catholicism survived Luther and would easily weather Ronge's watered-down version of Lutheran
arguments. Johann Peter Lyser, an author and painter, sarcastically noted
that Ronge faced a monumental task in his fight for "light and truth,"
considering how many people were "stupid" enough to be "fooled" by
the clergy and go to Trier.[166] Lyser associated Ronge with a broader Enlightenment attack on nineteenth-century Catholicism. In his dichotomy
of religion versus Enlightenment Catholicism, he had just landed a sting-
ing blow in the form of a well-coordinated and successful pilgrimage.[167]
Ronge deposed himself as a Catholic priest. He broke his own staff when
he tried to rally the German nation via Luther and Jan Hus.[168] Lyser likened Ronge to a short tempest passing over German theology.

Even so, Lyser cautioned, Ronge's short-lived movement did not
mean that Ronge was innocuous. He reminded readers that "[Ronge's]

light is the wisp of reason, which toppled a great and mighty nation into blood and tears half a century ago!"[169] Other authors cautioned that Ronge could instigate a new Thirty Years' War, but for Lyser the danger was much more recent – the religious indifference and anticlericalism that fuelled the French Revolution. Ronge claimed that millions were like him, bitter and tired of clerical control. Perhaps Ronge had found a million followers, Lyser conceded, but they had never been real Catholics.[170] True Catholics stood together in a shared spirit of communal religion. Here the example of collective pilgrimage is all but stated. Only false believers could follow Ronge's individualism and shun Trier.

Catholic pamphleteers sought to dissuade Protestants from joining Ronge's German-Catholics. In an anonymous pamphlet, "for Catholics and Protestants," one author asked his readers to closely examine what Ronge actually wrote.[171] Because the ex-priest claimed to speak "in the name of millions of every station," he represented a threat to all of Christianity.[172] Although many of the author's arguments were directed towards a Catholic readership, he maintained that Ronge was a heretic, because he elevated the Holy Spirit above the Father and Son and thereby rejected the doctrine of the Trinity.[173] He cautioned Protestants about the articles coming from Silesia. Ronge sought to manipulate popular Protestant beliefs to his favour, for example, with statements like "Jesus left us his spirit, not his Coat" and "the Coat went to Jesus's executioners."[174] Protestants should see beyond Ronge's pithy statements and realize the actual threat he posed to the stability of German Christian civilization.

As Ronge's message spread outside of Germany, including to France and the Low Countries, Rhineland clerics felt trapped and gripped with a sense of urgency to find understanding with Protestant Christians and the Prussian regime. They worked to drown out pro-Ronge pamphlets directed towards Protestants. In an anonymous pamphlet, one author exclaimed that Ronge's "words echo loudly in the hearts of all Protestants, and the overwhelming majority of Catholic Christendom."[175] This writer took denunciation by the Catholic press as a badge of honour, evidence that he was doing something right when newspapers attacked his "Protestant views."[176] From this perspective, Ronge remained a priest and a proto-martyr. He was a man who followed the Bible and would receive a heavenly blessing for his sacrifice.

Catholic leaders worried about their political situation and about the possibility of open violence, of an anticlerical outbreak along the lines of Thomas Müntzer and the sixteenth-century Peasants' War.[177] The pro-Ronge rhetoric did nothing to calm their concerns. Treumund upheld Ronge and Czerski as two men who "broke the dam" and unleashed "the unstoppable flow of truth" into the world.[178] Protestants had to understand that Ronge was not actually Catholic and they needed to realize that Ronge's message went beyond Protestantism and brought Germany to the brink of nihilism and ruin. In their open letters to Germany, Catholics did not assert their faith as the only true form of Christianity; instead they appealed for calm. Ronge called the Peace of Westphalia into question and unsettled the confessional balance of Central Europe. Catholics and Protestants had to come together to stop his sect.

Conclusion

As Bishop Franz Rudolf Bornewasser prepared for the 1933 pilgrimage and sent out invitations to German bishops, his office typed up reports about foreign and diocesan participation in the 1844 and 1891 pilgrimages. The Breslau summary included an October 1844 article by the Weihbischof and Domkapitular that condemned the Ronge scandal.[179] In the summary, the Breslau clergy described Ronge as proud, hardened, and blasphemous. They hoped that with the close of the 1844 Holy Coat display, the critics and Ronge supporters would be silent. The Weihbischof and Domkapitular believed that the German Reich, like the Holy Coat, would not be divided.

This report drew the *Deutsche Allgemeine Zeitung*'s attention. The newspaper editors thought it particularly daring of the Catholics to draw parallels between a relic and the nation. They dismissed the Breslau report as "a sign of the times in which everyone can make a commentary."[180] The paper further noted that Catholic attempts to censor Ronge's letter had failed. In fact, Prussian Cultural Minister Karl Friedrich Eichhorn (1781–1854) informed a cathedral canon in Münster that Prussia could not protect Catholics from every criticism.[181] Ronge's opinions continued to spread through the *Sächsische Vaterlandsblätter* and were available in bookstores in pamphlet form. Although his writings remained widely available in the years before 1848, Ronge's message faded, remembered by 1933 clergy as only an anecdotal part of Breslau's 1844 participation. Clergy downplayed Ronge in 1933, but the memory of schism and public criticism continued to influence Rhineland religious practices through the nineteenth century.

The clerical response to Ronge was symptomatic of larger shifts among Catholic leadership that would unfold in the decades after 1844. These included increasing theological training and professionalization as a result of Franz Friedrich Wilhelm von Fürstenberg's (1729–1810) efforts to mandate seminary attendance for clergy in Münster, and Heinrich Ignaz von Wessenberg's (1774–1860) work to create "enlightened, well-educated and worldly priests" in Meersburg.[182] Accompanying more standardized seminary education, beginning in the 1840s bishops were more likely to be trained at the Collegium Germanicum in Rome. Eventually the church leaders in Mainz, Cologne, and Munich all attended the Collegium Germanicum.[183] This education was designed to orient clergy towards the Vatican rather than towards Europe's national capitals.

Ronge's critique thus arrived in a period of transition for the German episcopate. Clergy adapted to the reality of potential schisms by distancing themselves from pilgrim understandings of relics. Pilgrims continued to write about the sacred garments in Aachen and Trier as vessels of the divine and as sites where the eternal and temporal collided. Clergy, wary of facing further criticism, constructed new narratives about the origins of Rhineland relics. The Coat and Marienschrein became plausible historical and Christian artefacts, verified by primary sources rather than scriptural proof texts. Clergy worked to make Catholicism part of wider German society by curtailing the mysteries of pilgrimage miracle claims and by historicizing sacred objects. Ink and paper took precedence over the blood of pilgrims and the clothes of the Holy Family.

After 1844, Catholic clergy were reluctant to rely only on biblical proofs and the church fathers as stand-alone evidence that pilgrimage and relics were inherently Christian. In the next two chapters, I examine how Trier and Aachen church officials co-opted scientific experimentation to corroborate relic authenticity. Clergy sought external proofs, including fibre analysis, archaeology, and historical records to explain their appreciation of the Trier Coat and four Aachen Marian Shrine relics. Similarly, clergy focused on Constantine, in the case of Trier, and Charlemagne in Aachen, as founders of their cities and discoverers of their true relics. In other words, they found sources of authenticity beyond the rhetoric they used to counter Ronge's arguments. This ancient lineage stretching back to the earliest days of Germania indicated that Catholics were not only full members of the German community, but also laid the foundations for a future united Germany. Laity, as discussed in part 1, had their own understandings of pilgrimage and relic authority. Ronge's open letter, though a historical oddity by 1933, acted as a catalyst for changes in clerical presentations of relics, even as pilgrims continued to attend events in Trier and Aachen with the hope of encountering the sacred in the world through the four Aachen relics and the Holy Coat.

5 Clerical Crossroads: Medical Verifiability of the Sacred

> Oh! that holy coat has indeed wrought miracles, far more wonderful than the cure of a few hysterical women and rickety children! It has emancipated a nation! It has broken the chains of superstition and scattered them to the winds.[1]

Between 1832 and 1937 clerical attitudes towards the possibility of miracles grew increasingly pragmatic and bureaucratic. Trier and Aachen were focal points of debate on the efficacy of relics as healing objects in the nineteenth century. Unlike Lourdes, which, because of its scale, was able to support permanent medical personnel, Aachen and Trier relied on regional physicians and priests to corroborate pilgrim cures. Germany was not like France, with the principal miracle battle lines drawn up between Republicanism and Clericalism.[2] In the Rhineland, the struggle for authority regarding miracles took place along religious lines: between Catholics and Protestants, and between Catholics and Catholic dissenters like Johannes Ronge. Pilgrimage Committees responded to external and internal pressure by regulating what cure-seekers said about their own corporeal and spiritual selves. Committees instituted rigorous standards for who could stand as witness to sickness. They required pilgrims to visit doctors with elaborate forms that verified their pre-existing conditions. As clergy turned towards medical practitioners, cure-seekers remained steadfast in their conviction that relics could improve their health. Pilgrims lost unfettered and direct access to sacred objects over the course of the nineteenth century. Their ability to influence the Catholic Church's reports on their lived encounters with Rhenish relics diminished as clergy placed new obstacles between pilgrims and sacred relics.

Catholic clergy came to a theological crossroads in the late nineteenth century. Rhenish priests and bishops had to choose whether or not to support and affirm lay notions of divine presence or to respond to Ronge and to mounting criticism of the practice of pilgrimage. Ultimately, church authorities drifted away from pilgrim concepts of proof of divine intervention and instead sought to verify God's acts and sacred presence through medical statements and physician testimonials. But this clerical desire for positivist, or natural scientific, affirmations of miracles opened a rift between the clergy and cure-seekers.[3] By the 1890s, clergy suppressed "unofficial cures" that did not sufficiently satisfy Trier and Aachen clerical verification parameters.

As part of this professionalization, Pilgrimage Committees increasingly looked to male experts, physicians, and priests to confirm the physical and spiritual status of cure-seekers. The mid-nineteenth century saw the emergence of new medical institutions run by the state, including Bayreuth, Siegurg, and Illenau, and private medical centres such as in Bonn.[4] Care for the disabled also improved as the state moved away from chains and prisons and towards psychological treatment from physicians.

Rhenish clergy capitalized on the growing authority of professional medicine to corroborate miracle claims, so that after 1844 women were edged out as reliable "truth speakers" about their own bodies and religious experiences.[5] Following the public debate with Ronge's "German-Catholics," clergy first worked to contain lay testimony and verify their claims at the 1846 Aachen pilgrimage. In Trier, during the subsequent 1891 event, Michael Felix Korum (1840–1921), bishop of Trier since 1881, forbade cure reports until his office investigated and approved alleged healings. By the end of the nineteenth century, women's testimony was accepted only after they had taken vows to live in Christian community, or when a man (relative, doctor, or cleric) corroborated what they stated. This masculinization of truth was a consequence of formalizing the application process for cure-seekers keen to spend time with Rhineland relics. New clerical protocols for sick pilgrims developed alongside the naturalization of clerical understandings of demonstrability, further characterized by a decline in biblical proof texting as satisfactory justification for a rupture in the natural world. Formal testimony from trained medical professionals superseded biblical precedence for affirming the possibility that God cured through relics.[6]

The favouring of male voices in discussions of sacred presence accompanied new developments in medical practices during the nineteenth century. As medical practitioners professionalized, they transitioned from "bedside" practices to "laboratory" treatments between 1770 and 1870.[7] Physicians saw the body as a sum of parts that could be healed individually. German Catholic clerics' medical authority, like that of midwives and herbalists, eroded in the latter half of the nineteenth century. In order to respond to critics, Rhenish clergy mobilized "modern" medical knowledge by asking its professional practitioners to evaluate the merit of pilgrim healing claims. Yet throughout this chapter it is important not to think of "science" (*Wissenschaft*) on one side and "pilgrim" on the other – there was substantial overlap.[8] Some Catholic physicians argued passionately that their patient's only hope was a miracle, while others were annoyed that they had to fill out cleric-requested *Fragebogen*, or medical history forms (literally "questionnaire" or "questionary") in the first place.[9]

As German Catholic Church leadership developed a formalized method to verify alleged cures, they moved away from informal observation by laity, clerics, and physicians towards a rigorous examination that excluded non-medical sources of information. Wary of being mocked or embarrassed, the clergy clamped down on access to relics. They hindered publications about miracles by withholding imprimatur or waiting until years after an event to verify that a cure claimant had not relapsed. In addition, Catholic leaders expanded acceptable sources of truth: biblical arguments no longer stood on an equal footing with medical knowledge; male physician testimony, regardless of confession, triumphed and dominated in the corroboration of the divine. Finally, the pilgrims, especially cure-seekers, tended not to respect established clerical boundaries around the relics. Instead, as we saw in chapter 3, they enthusiastically reported their own encounters that were at odds with the hierarchical position, creating a rift between leaders and practitioners.

1844: The Dam Breaks

Trier officials had a dynamic and flexible system for verifying divine intervention in the 1840s. In 1844, clergy assembled a wide range of letters. Evidence for a miraculous cure varied from two to seventeen statements. The authors of corroboratory correspondence tended to be men, which was a product of two factors. First, men in the 1840s occupied official medical posts, such as the district physician and local physician. Trier officials sent inquiries about the cured to these offices. Women were full participants in local medical spheres but often in "unofficial" capacities, as midwives and herbalists.[10] Women still had opportunities to testify because local priests organized responses, submitted witness reports, and collected statements.[11] Second, those claiming a cure assumed that Rhineland clergy placed a higher value on men's perspectives, even when the cured was a woman. For example, in the case of eighteen-year-old Anna Josephine Wagner, out of the seventeen letters sent to Trier to attest to her previous condition, just three were from women, two of which were included in a group statement, and one was from Wagner herself.[12] Even with the clerical enquiry preference, women were given a voice in determining divine presence. In 1844, because Trier clergy acted informally and retroactively, there was space for lay women to testify to divine intervention in the world, and when available this testimony was filed alongside that of physicians.

Trier clergy worked to retroactively confirm miracles already made public after the 1844 pilgrimage. For example, Trier officials struggled to come up with witnesses to Josephina Wagner's cured epilepsy after she claimed healing. Even in January 1845, months after the pilgrimage closed, clergy sought to verify Wagner's story and find individuals who could speak to her moral reliability. Father Letsch, of Hambach, regretted to inform the district physician that he knew only a little of Wagner, having just met her in 1843. During that time she had some epileptic episodes, and he heard from other people that she previously suffered from fits in 1838–9.[13]

Clerics feared that the cured would embarrass the church by feigning illness, thus forging a divine act, or by having a scandalized past. The Wagner correspondence helps illuminate what the Trier officials sought in potential witnesses in the early nineteenth century. They first queried men of high public standing: mayors, doctors, priests, and chaplains. Father Letsch, for instance, also noted that he was not sure about the rumours that Wagner was previously pregnant. Clerics looked not just to doctors to assess their parishioners, but also weighed the opinions of local notables.

Margaretha Plein, from Speicher, had reached a point of emotional distress and instability that required the observation and intervention of the local mayor. The mayor wrote to Trier officials and explained that she was recently engaged to Joseph Becker. The two hoped to wed, but Becker lacked the means to fund the union and eventually called off the engagement. The break-up put Plein in an unhealthy state of mind that deteriorated until she eventually struck her father and tried to throw herself out of a window.[14] After visiting the Coat of Trier, Plein was cured of her emotional distress. At their darkest hour, German Catholics turned to the relics of Aachen and Trier, because they offered healing, hope, and physical restoration.

Clergy tentatively sought to verify cures like Plein's in 1844, but only in response to the reports of miracles appearing in the regional press, such as the *Luxemburger Zeitung*, during the actual display of the Coat. Following published reports, Trier officials began gathering evidence of the veracity of alleged healings. Most often this proof came in the form of correspondence with the cured. Claimants penned elaborate statements about their relic encounters. Further evidence came from persons familiar with cure-seekers: those who could corroborate their moral credibility and the physical or emotional issue that the Coat alleviated. Johann Michels, from Speicher, fifty-seven years old, was cured on 9 September 1844 in Trier of a shoulder malady and gout that had recently left him bedridden. His dossier includes correspondence with the local physician, the district physician, the "wound doctor" (who also helped with births), the mayor, several locals, a lawyer, and a sailor. Jacob Heinz, eleven years old, from Berncastel, was cured of speechlessness in 1844. The testimonials related to Heinz's divine encounter include his physician and a local man.[15]

However, Rhenish clergy did not consider medical statements essential for ascertaining whether or not a health-based cure occurred.[16] The Trierweiler pastor, for example, gave his word that Anna Elisabeth Pantenberg was healed and Catharina Hoelzer's arm remained fully functional after her visit. He also noted that Philipp Meth's testicular disease remained uncured after Trier. Meth, the pastor's "not-so-lucky" parishioner, believed the swelling in his scrotum had subsided after visiting the Coat in 1844. After fourteen days, it was clear to Meth that his condition had worsened. His right testicle was now thicker and harder than before. The Triererweiler priest confessed that he had only talked with Meth and the schoolteacher Johann Adam Hoffman about the sickness. A medical testimony was too impractical to include "[a] certificate from an unknown doctor about the current state of the tumour, etc. [of] Meth is probably impossible"[17] because to visit a doctor would require a three-to-four-hour walk in the snow.

In regards to Anna Elisabeth, the cleric further dismissed inquiries about alternative or natural possibilities for her recovery. "Whether or not this recovery was impossible in a natural way, without the help of medical services, I do not know," he wrote.[18] Father Koeppel, in December 1844, similarly testified that his parishioner Katharina Huppert was healed but was conspicuously evasive about offering medical evidence: "Also the woman consulted a doctor Cath[olic] I believe, in Münchwalde (in Doorwalde), he told her that her condition was incurable. Since the path through the forest is now impractical, I could not send the same testimony. The woman is not lying."[19] In this instance, Trier officials had to trust the word of the cleric, without medical testimony. The pilgrimage officials did not protest the lack of a physician's corroboration.

In the 1840s reports on cure-seekers' bodies and mental states were highly inconsistent. Trier clergy received corroborating, at times competing, information from a variety of individuals. Thus, in Wagner's case, Trier had a report from Father J. Steph Braemig, confirmed by a deacon and chaplain, that they were certain Wagner was epileptic before going to Trier. Deacon Schnitzler once found Wagner in a ditch on the side of the road suffering from an attack. He was only able to bring Wagner back to herself with strong wine.[20] After her pilgrimage to Trier, when Braemig again saw Wagner, the "wild, epileptic appearance was completely gone."[21] Braemig's testimony was supplemented by Father Wallerath's letter to the Trier district physician, which noted that Wagner first became epileptic in her twelfth or thirteenth year. Wallerath, however, remained sceptical of her healing and did not want to give a definite opinion. He acknowledged, though, that the mayor seemed convinced of a physical change.

Local priests also were not afraid to attack medical or clerical opinions contrary to their own. Father Kaess from Lutzerath began his letter to the Trier physician compiling data on alleged cures that he had heard "from all sides only bad things" about Wagner.[22] Kaess himself was not sure about Wagner. He had heard only that she was epileptic and that the local mayor would not corroborate her story. Kaess was ashamed to hear Wagner's name.[23] Against the sceptical reports, Braemig asserted he was able to come up with 1800 signatures that would attest to Wagner's former sickness.

While clerics did not require a medical evaluation in the 1840s, they still hoped for some form of medical testimony. They wanted to know, for example, whether the cure-seeker had previously sought professional medical assistance. On 23 August 1844 Jakob Heinz's parents took him to Dr. Schmitz in Berncastel for treatment because he had suffered from a renewed bout of vomiting and convulsions, and was from that time on incapable of speaking. Dr. Schmitz wrote to Trier about how he treated Heinz since the onset of his speechlessness. Schmitz described Heinz's symptoms as including abdominal pain, a bitter taste in his mouth, a swollen belly, and weak limbs.[24] Schmitz watched Heinz closely the last week of August and observed that pain spread to Jakob's knees and chest. The doctor concluded his report by noting that when he last saw Heinz, the boy could not speak and had not yet left for Trier. As a side-note, Schmitz added that he believed the speechlessness was genuine, because he had heard of Heinz being beaten up by a couple of other young men and he did not cry out. Schmitz's testimony served as a "before" snapshot, acquired to clash with the "after" letter from Caplay in February 1845 that Heinz now spoke "fluently, loud[ly], and understandably."[25]

Priests were not always convinced their parishioners were healed. Father Pauls, from Hettenis, wrote to Trier about Anna Maria Hammes.

Hammes was in her early forties and claimed to be cured of lameness after visiting the Holy Coat. Pauls was uncertain whether a miracle occurred because Hammes had experienced a recovery in the 1830s and was not now perfectly healed. In addition, he continued, Hammes continued to walk hunched over.[26] Similarly, Father Boll of Bruttig urged caution regarding the healing of nine-year-old Catharina Barthel: "Before she could not walk without crutches, after getting back from Trier she does not need crutches, but now can only go hunched over, and if she wants to go a longer distance must be led by the hand."[27] Boll could only say the child's health was "satisfactory." He speculated that she may improve over time but would not assert that a miracle (*Wunder*) had taken place before the Holy Coat. In both instances, the priests sought to temper the testimony of their parishioners and to walk back the cure-seekers' claims to absolute healing.

In 1844, some of the staunchest supporters of miracle claims used scripture to explain Rhineland miracles. This textual approach echoed clerical arguments that were also used to counter Johannes Ronge's assault against pilgrimage. The Trier district physician received a note from an anonymous supporter of Catharina Petsch's miraculous stroke healing. In his defence of the cure, the author used logic, scripture, and Petsch's medical history to defend her against detractors who claimed she was a fake cure, a dummy set up by the church, or an actor in a staged event designed to fool the laity into believing in the efficacy of the Coat. To begin, the supporter quoted the deuterocanonical book of Tobit 12:7: "It is good to conceal the secret of a king, but to acknowledge and reveal the works of God, and with fitting honour to acknowledge him. Do good and evil will not overtake you." Petsch was right to point out her recovery because it glorified God. Detractors argued that Petsch had in reality been better since 1842 and was able to get around, despite the stroke. If that was the case, she would have hidden her full recovery for two years. For the author, even the dullest mind must see that this was improbable and that claims of fraud were completely false.[28] Furthermore, the anonymous author continued, the critics were failing to distinguish a "cure" from "recovery."

A recovery left open the possibility of a relapse: one could recover from a sickness and fall back "2, 3, 4, 5, 6 times."[29] Conversely, a miracle was a permanent transformation, as Jesus healed in the Gospels. Lastly, the author took aim at those who claimed God could not have shown favour on Petsch because her son misbehaved and was not faithful. In response the author pointed to Ezekiel 18:20, "The person who sins shall die. A child shall not suffer for the iniquity of a parent, nor a parent suffer for the iniquity of a child; the righteousness of the righteous shall be his own, and the wickedness of the wicked shall be his own." Her cure was all the greater because God still heard her plea, despite her son's sinful behaviour. Petsch was healed to give others hope. She was not faking it, and she was fully cured of her ailment. By the next pilgrimage, however, scripture alone was inadequate to demonstrate that God had acted in the world.

1844–1891: Demonstrating Divine Presence

Taking a cue from the 1844 Trier troubles, the clergy in Aachen clarified who could and could not have access to their relics in 1846. Accordingly, after the church closed at 6:00 p.m., individual pilgrims who "first must have a note from a doctor that they suffer from bodily pain, or a chronic condition, and, second, must have a testament from their minister" could enter the cathedral for one-on-one time with Mary's Tunic. The pilgrimage organizers asked priests to speak to whether or not the pilgrim was a moral Catholic and had recently received the sacrament of Eucharist. Cure-seekers had to submit these documents to the clerical secretary (*Probst*) in the morning and were issued a "sick admission card." Once the church was empty, these petitioners were allowed briefly to touch the relic.[30] Trier officials adopted Aachen's certification system and created increasingly thorough forms in the 1890s and into the 1930s.

Rhineland clerics brought about two notable shifts within miracle testimony after 1844. First, because Pilgrimage Committees demanded specialized documentation from cure-seekers, medical testimony underwent professionalization. Second, female pilgrims, after the 1840s, required male corroborators of their alleged healings. In the 1840s, women, when available, evidently stood equal to men in offering evidence. Trier officials collected letters from men, women, acquaintances, physicians, clergy, and lawyers. In February 1845 officials collated twenty-two testimonies related to Peter Hohnemann's trip to Trier in September 1844 (see table 5.1). Peter, an adolescent at the time, travelled in order to recover the use of his left arm and leg. Both had become stiff, slow, and unresponsive after a bout of smallpox. Hohnemann asserted that after encountering the Coat he began to recover strength in his left limbs and reported that he could now move chairs around, carry water, and cut his own meat without assistance – he was cured.[31] No fewer than half of the testimonies gathered to corroborate this recovery came from laywomen.[32]

Table 5.1. Peter Hohnemann testimonials

Name	Age
Female	
Eva Kamp	19
Margaretha Immerschitt	19
Eva Eckes	26
Anna Frosch	33
Anna Hitzel	35
Franziska Schurgens	39
Catharina Hohnemann	41
Eleonora Elfen	42
Katharina Sewig	46
Anna Erf	46
Appolonia Immerschitt	49
Male	
Peter Jakob Hohnemann	14
Jacob Eckes	31
Peter Erf	36
Jakob Eck	38
Adam Heil	42
Wilhelm Hohnemann	43
Anton Bretz	44
Caspar Erf	48
Jakob Klein	60
Franz Jonas	60
Georg Eckes	65

Sources: Data from BATr, Abt. 91, Nr. 229, 248–68.

Similarly, in February 1845 Father Schneider and Protocol Leader Bräder, of Bingen, submitted the testimonials of residents willing to state that Theresia Bernette recovered from the lameness of her right side, caused by a stroke in May 1840 (see table 5.2). In this case, nine of the fourteen witnesses were women, or 62 per cent.[33] Women thus made up a notable percentage of corroboration testimony. Furthermore, the male witnesses here had no particular qualification or occupation. Catholic authorities relied on all Catholics – witnesses specified that they were a member of the "Catholic religion" – to verify the presence of a disease or physical limitation prior to pilgrimage and a notable change afterwards.

Conversely, by the late nineteenth century, the cult of Rhenish miracles fully incorporated the expertise from the burgeoning medical profession. One consequence of this shift was that Trier clergy favoured male attestation of the divine when publicly affirming a miracle. In his 1894 publication of approved cures from the 1891 pilgrimage, Bishop

Table 5.2. Theresia Bernette testimonials

Name	Age
Male	
Philipp Bernette	26
Karl Kruzius	32
Joseph Ohler	36
Adam Kirch	52
Peter Nix	60
Female	
Elise Bernet	15
Anna Bernett	18
Katharina Bender	43
Margaretha Frosch	45
Susanna Tapperich	46
Agnes Bischof	47
Anna Maria Müller	51
Franziska Schiffmann	53
Anna Maria Wolf	66

Sources: Data for this chart from BATr, Abt. 91, Nr. 229, 272–88.

Korum included the correspondence that led him and his committee to determine that either a miracle had occurred or that the pilgrim had been blessed with a "divine mercy." Korum proclaimed eleven cures and twenty-seven graces or mercies in 1891. The corroborative testimony included forty-one male clerics (pastors, priests, deacons, Jesuits), thirty-eight male physicians, and thirty-seven "other" witnesses (thirteen female, twenty-four male).

Figure 5.1 lays out Korum's four categories of witnesses in his 1894 pamphlet of approved, official cures. Women constituted 11 per cent, while men, either laity, clergy, or physicians, made up 89 per cent of the included testimony. Within the "male" and "female" categories there is substantial diversity. Importantly, female testimony that Trier officials counted was not independent. These statements tended to come from family members and were corroborated by a male witness or male official. In the case of Emil Herb, Frau Karoline Kistner confirmed that Herb suffered from arthritis and heart trouble and had a large, swollen knee. However, Kistner did not sign her statement alone, but issued her letter with the declaration of Johann Ernst Mülshörster.[34] Of the thirteen female witnesses, only four (31 per cent) were "bystanders," the rest (69 per cent) were family: five mothers, two daughters, one cousin, one sister-in-law. Conversely, only seven (29 per cent) of the twenty-four male witnesses were related to the cure claimant (five

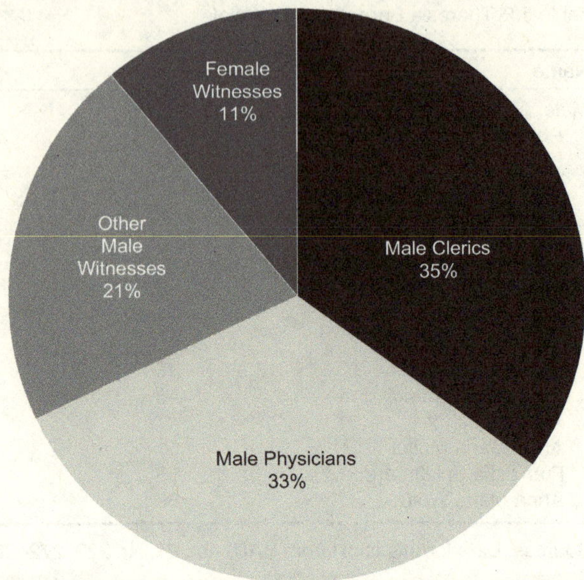

Figure 5.1. Testimony approved by Bishop Korum of Trier, 1891.
Source: Data from Korum, *Wunder und Göttliche Gnadenerweise*, 97.

fathers, one husband, one brother). By the end of the nineteenth century, Rhineland clerics sought confirmation of alleged cures systematically and from members of the curia and medical experts.

These developing systems of verification, or order of authenticity, allowed for one exception to the trend towards this masculinization of truth: women living in religious communities. In the testimonials, nuns stand equal to priests or deacons. Sister Ursula, a Franciscan sister from Waldbreitbach in Neuwied, was declared cured of her contorted elbow on the strength of her word and that of an anonymous doctor.[35] In a similar case, Sister Stephanie, from Trier, was approved with only her account and the evidence from Dr. H. Staub. After resting an *Andenken* on a growing nodule in her armpit in 1892, Stephanie's pain and swelling subsided.[36] Women who had not chosen to live in dedicated Christian communities received more scrutiny. These outsiders turned to local priests, physicians, and family members to affirm "before and after" physical conditions.

Nuns were also allowed to bypass the increased regulation of access to relics. Sister Angelica wrote in 1902 to clarify the rules in Aachen about accessing Jesus's Loincloth. She stated that there were several sick sisters and students, and that she would not be surprised if one of them was miraculously cured by the relic. Sister Angelica wanted to prevent a repeat of her 1895 experience when she brought a sick sister to the Aachen event but was denied access to the relic on the grounds that only the very sick, with proper certification, could touch the relics. Angelica bluntly reported, "She was really sick, and died shortly afterwards." In response, the Pilgrimage Committee sent the Order ten *Krankenkarten*, which afforded the sisters access to the relics when they visited.[37]

Growing clerical caution in the wake of the attacks on pilgrimage and relic authenticity filtered into the late nineteenth-century press. Local reporters now hesitated to proclaim miracles as the *Luxemburger Zeitung* had in 1844. In 1888, *Echo der Gegenwart* stressed that, despite all the rumours, talk, and energy surrounding claims, the alleged cures at the Heiligthumsfahrt Aachen and Cornelimünster were best left to clerical authorities. The editors had no doubt that such things were possible; after all, God's grace was endless. But now, with a greater concern over fraudulent accounts, the paper decided to respond negatively to all claims until the church verified them. Even with this disclaimer, *Echo der Gegenwart* further reported three potential healings: of a sick girl from Burtscheid who was healed after touching Jesus's Loincloth, of another young girl from Aachen who was cured of speechlessness after touching the Loincloth, and of a priest in Belgium who recovered after touching John the Baptist's Beheading Cloth.[38]

Popular interest in divine acts had not waned at the end of the nineteenth century. Despite clerical attempts to verify divine presence and thereby regulate the claims of cure-seekers, the press was decidedly more interested in selling stories about *potential* miracles than it was in completely yielding to church trends towards the professionalization of witness testimony. Even so, by the 1890s Rhenish clergy constricted the types of individuals who could reliably comment on a possible miracle. Korum and his committee favoured male testimony and insisted on external corroboration. Pilgrims could no longer rely solely on their own lived experience and the confirmation of friends and family.

1891: Bishop Korum Defines Miracles

In both 1844 and 1891, Trier clergy assembled testimonies about cures. However, the important difference between these two nineteenth-century events is that in 1891 Bishop Korum would not allow Catholics to claim they had been cured until their evidence underwent rigorous review. Although observer Richard Clarke drew parallels between the two pilgrimages, writing that "the same extraordinary conversions of hardened sinners, the same miracles worked on the bodies of the sick; the same impulse given to the faith in all the country round,"[39] he included no accounts of 1891 miracles. Clarke noted that "in this year of our Lord 1891, there have been cures not a few, undeniably miraculous. We will select one of two from a long list of those that happened in 1844."[40] Bishop Korum had not yet signed off on the authenticity of 1891 miracle claims.

Edward Plater, who wrote an English pamphlet about his travels through the Rhineland in the 1890s, noted that a sick woman was healed at the touch of the Coat, which church leadership explained by referencing the Gospel of Mark 6:55–6: "touch the hem of his garment: and as many as touched him were made whole."[41] As Plater explained the efficacy of relics, one way a relic can be verified is whether or not it has the power to heal the body. He quoted Aquinas: "God Himself has been pleased to honour such relics by working miracles in their presence."[42] Yet, like Clarke, Plater remained evasive about miracles actually happening in 1891. He felt compelled to address this issue, but provided a cursory answer: "What about miracles? And it is not yet the time to give the answer. That many and various miracles have been wrought during this Exposition is known to the favoured individuals, to their friends and relatives, and to the medical men and others on whom the task of verification devolves."[43]

The reluctance in these two 1891 pamphlets is somewhat surprising because it would be in the pilgrims' interest to convince their audience of the continued power of the relic in Trier. At the end of his account Plater reported, "The Bishop of Trier and his chapter have everywhere discouraged the publication of details [of miracles]; but so soon as the process of investigation has been closed, and the authority of science has confirmed, then, and not till then, will their complete history be made public."[44] Both Clarke and Plater complied with Korum's decree that no news of 1891 miracles was to be published prior to his verification in his 1894 pamphlet.

Catholic standing in Germany remained contentious and ambiguous after 1844. Bishop Korum's committee reviewed miracle evidence in the wake of the Ronge controversies, German unification, and the Kulturkampf. German statesman Otto von Bismarck (1815–98) challenged the role of the Catholic Church in German society throughout the 1870s and 1880s. Korum did not want to do anything to make the church vulnerable to criticism.[45] German Catholics had also weathered a wave of repression and public ridicule when the church promulgated Papal Infallibility in 1870. Following the pronouncement, Paul Hinschius, a National-Liberal deputy, proclaimed it a death sentence against the German state.[46] Liberal opposition to the doctrine centred on the claim that such a Catholic conviction was a threat to German loyalty. In 1871, the Reichstag passed the Pulpit Law, which prevented priests from discussing political affairs. Following a wave of laws designed to restrict Catholicism, priests responded by urging German Catholics to politically organize.[47] Korum himself took over the Trier bishopric in 1881 after it had been vacant for five years as the result of strained relations between Berlin and the Vatican over the right to appoint bishops.[48] Papal Infallibility laid the foundation for the Kulturkampf, after which Korum did not want a Trier miracle to incite new persecution or to ignite smouldering Liberal anti-Catholic prejudice.[49]

Bishop Korum sought to lay out the grounds for a miracle in his 1894 pamphlet on "approved" or "confirmed" 1891 cures. Korum followed Aquinas's conception of a miracle as "an obvious fact or effect, which is produced and established by God, and is brought forth in the order of nature."[50] Korum further explained to the faithful that there are three necessary arguments to establish a divine act: (1) that miracles are possible, (2) that there are ways of recognizing such deeds established in tradition and scripture, and (3) that divine assistance leaves behind tangible evidence or testimony. To the first condition, Korum explained that miracles can be classified into two tiers: first, acts that are impossible in nature, such as an individual being raised from the dead, and second, events that nature could produce, but not in the specific way it was brought about, such as a sick person who is suddenly healed from a disease that time and modern medicine could have cured.[51] Thus, the miraculous included the rapidity and abruptness of the physical transformation. Korum sought only to approve cures he viewed as beyond contradiction. His drive to verify miracles meant that he prevented clerics from reporting cures prematurely. Korum set out guidelines that defined what sort of information he wanted. Local clergy, under his strictures, could not make a case for cured pilgrims simply by sending in large numbers of corroborative statements; now they were required to secure the word of physicians, who were overwhelmingly male.

As he laid out the grounds for a miraculous cure, Korum established a new benchmark for reliable evidence in order to show that the Catholic Church approved only true divine interventions. A strong proponent of the two-point argument, he contended that there were two steps in recognizing a miracle: acknowledging that something supernatural has transpired, and accepting the inexplicable nature of the process.[52] To illustrate his point, Korum noted that a certain shepherd with dropsy from Herschwiesen, whose body had become so visibly distended that he could no longer button his clothes, and one hour after touching the Coat, was cleared of all symptoms, qualified as an instantly identifiable divine marvel. Miracles, for Korum, left no room for refutation. A wound that physicians diagnosed as requiring a certain amount of time to heal, but that cleared up well ahead of this schedule after a pilgrimage, did not qualify.[53] Korum also favoured cases like that of Helena Daniel, who was cured of blindness. There was nothing doctors could have done to help Daniel, and no medicine was used on her eyes before she came to Trier. Therefore, Korum maintained, God had restored her sight.[54]

For Korum, miracles left a trail of evidence for the faithful to follow. God pointed to the possibility of miracles in the scriptures, which offered the reader proof of divine miracle from Moses to Jesus to the apostles of the early church. The scriptures also answered questions that remained pertinent in the late nineteenth century: Why is not everyone who believes healed? Pointing to the Gospel of John, Korum noted that Jesus did not heal every ill individual at the pools in Bethesda (John 5). Korum similarly relied on Acts to show that it was possible for miracles to occur after Jesus ascended to Heaven. Beyond the scriptures, Catholics could rely on church tradition on the miraculous. St. Gregory the Great explained that miracles were less and less frequent because the church was no longer in its infancy and therefore required fewer proofs to win converts.[55] Furthermore, St. Thomas argued that miracles occurred to remind the faithful of God's grace and power over the natural world.[56]

Catholic clerics created new tools for establishing a miracle in the nineteenth century. Physicians now verified cures by examining patients before and after visiting Trier. Korum thanked German physicians for their cooperation in refuting and confirming healing, the latter at great risk to their practice, especially if their names appeared in Catholic newspapers.[57] Another clerical implement was negation, ruling out other possible sources for physical transformation. Here the *physical* was truly central because Korum disavowed mental or emotional "miracles." These claims could not be satisfactorily observed and made up a separate, lower category in his schema.

By eliminating unobservable changes, or at least demoting them, Korum deliberately struck at several nineteenth-century theories of the body. Miracles could not be brought on by auto-suggestion, hypnosis, energy of the will, trance, magnetism, clairvoyance, or hallucination.[58] Furthermore, Korum declared, "Our cases have absolutely no resemblance to experiments."[59] The bishop was willing to concede that the above methods might have some positive influence on mental strain or hysteria, but hypnosis could not make a blind child see, clear lupus, or heal dropsy.[60] Korum accepted only organic transformations, claims that none could gainsay. By the time of Korum's pamphlet, church officials engaged with the scientific and pseudo-scientific processes around them and offered the divine as a supplement to German Catholics. God could rupture the natural order at will and leave traces of divine work to strengthen the faithful.

The bishop waited until the pilgrimage had ended, on 3 October 1891, before he sent out the first requests for information about potential cases of cure, on 24 November. In this initial enquiry to deacons, Korum asked whether or not they knew of anyone who had been healed, and not just individuals who had touched the Coat but "also those cured as a result of venerating the relic (pilgrimage to Trier, devotions, etc.) or by those cured from an object that had been touched to the Coat."[61] Korum instructed clergy to gather pertinent information on anyone they thought healed, including:

1 Name, age, day they visited the Coat
2 Whether or not they had been treated by a physician
3 Whether the cure was gradual or sudden
4 If any natural remedies were used just before visiting the Coat that would have influenced healing
5 Whether they thought the cure-seeker deserved full faith, Korum hoped the cured could write out a statement chronicling a history of the experience
6 Whether or not reliable witnesses could be found, individuals who would be willing to give an oath, especially where the cure-seeker had no medical testimony *or* was healed indirectly by an object, without directly touching the relic
7 If possible, the cured should also send a medical testimony. As doctors often refused to say a miracle happened, the bishop did not require it but did want the doctor to state clearly that the individual under investigation was now in good health.[62]

All of these data were to be collated and sent back to Trier by the end of January 1892 for review.

As the bishop prepared his pamphlet for publication, he again sought the assistance of clergy in March 1893. In a new questionnaire, Korum was concerned primarily with the duration of the healing, whether or not the cure-seeker's condition had reversed:

1 Has the person remained healthy since visiting Trier? Has "the illness/evil [*Uebel*] not been reinstated?"[63]
2 If there was a healing from the Holy Coat, is there a medical explanation or means for the recovery? If so, what?[64]
3 Please send, where possible, a medical testimony regarding the pilgrim.
4 Ask the cured themselves and their families about the procedure and process of their recovery and send a simple, truthful report back, perhaps written by hand.[65]

Korum maintained an ambiguous opinion of medical practices and physicians. He affirmed their authority by asking for medical testimonies and yet also wanted to be sure that it was the divine and not a doctor who intervened to bring on a physical change. Korum kept himself at a distance, using intermediaries to gather data on his behalf. He looked to deacons and clergy to interview cure claimants and to relay the information in a coherent and timely manner. Afterwards, a panel of physicians, clerics, and scientists evaluated the thirty-eight miracles before Korum confirmed them as divine.[66] The miraculous healings included "nervous and hysterical affections, chorea or St. Vitus's dance, and a few cases of certain milder forms of lupus and tabes."[67]

Because of his plan to delay public declaration of cure, Bishop Korum was ambiguous about miracles in his final homily of the 1891 Exposition. He challenged science, but only to the extent that it could replace Catholicism or master the natural world. He declared the limits of natural explanations, saying, "Facts such as these [that bodily miracles had been wrought], which science is powerless to explain ... compel us to acknowledge that there exists a world beyond this material, visible, and finite world."[68] When the bishop mentioned miracles, he emphasized spiritual renewal and downplayed bodily cures: "Though many who were sick did not recover bodily-health, yet they received a great consolation of soul."[69] Although many came for physical cures, Korum explained that the greater cure was spiritual.

Similarly, the bishop discussed a specific case in which a young man received a bodily cure. Here again the spirit was more important than the body: "When he knelt before the Holy Coat he experienced such joy and consolation that he could not say whether his sufferings were not more precious to him than his health could have been if he had regained it."[70] The faithful were directed to understand their physical ailments as gifts from God. God gave corporeal challenges only if the laity could withstand them. True miracles occurred when pilgrims were internally renewed, not externally restored.

Despite Korum's best efforts to present the miracle claimants as confirmed, reviewed, and reasonable, he still faced detractors at home and abroad. Linguist Edward Payson Evans, in his 1895 article published in the *Popular Science Monthly*, attacked Korum for arguing that the miracles were scientifically sound. Evans contended, "Dr. Korum seeks to give his brochure a quasi-scientific character by a so-called 'documentary representation' of the miracles wrought by the 'holy coat,' consisting of certificates issued by obscure curates and country doctors and endorsed by an Episcopal commission of theologians and physicians, who have very discreetly forgotten to sign their names to their reports and thus relieved themselves of personal responsibility for their opinions."[71]

Korum was further criticized by Friedrich Jaskowski, a cleric in the Trier diocese. In 1894, Jaskowski published his own pamphlet and argued that the Trier Coat had not been considered miraculous until 1844 when Bishop Arnoldi emphasized the ability of the Coat to work bodily cures. Any cures from the Coat, argued Jaskowski, were the product of hetero- or auto-suggestion. The cured somehow willed themselves into healing after they encountered the Coat. As evidence he noted that Jesus said the faith of his followers cured them. These New Testament passages suggested that Jesus did not physically cure, but individuals healed themselves through their individual faith.

The Korum-Jaskowski confrontation betrayed the contested meaning of pilgrimage among clergy. For Korum, it could be empirically demonstrated that the Coat operated above the laws of nature for certain devout individuals. For Jaskowski, the Coat was symbolic, and any cures that came from a pilgrimage to Trier were the result of suggestion and an individual's will to be better.[72] As clerics in the early nineteenth century defended miracles with biblical proofs, in the late nineteenth century, clerical opponents of miracles turned to the Bible to undermine empirical evidence of bodily transformation before the Coat. Korum's system for confirming divine acts ushered in new bases of evidence and elevated physicians to the level of clergy as corroborators of the miraculous. Pilgrims required notes from both their parish priest and their local physician.

The Professionalization of the Miraculous

Physicians played an ambiguous role in confirming miracle claims but were not necessarily enemies of the pilgrimage experience. There was a wide range of medical responses to the supernatural possibility of

Catholic relics. These included embarrassment or shame, as in the case of Schwester Ursula's doctor who refused Korum permission to publish his name, to Dr. Thomé, a house physician, who sought to touch the Coat in 1891 for his own benefit.[73] In the case of Trier and Aachen it is too simplistic to state that pilgrims went looking for a miracle because they were impoverished and could not afford medical care or because there was a shortage of doctors after German unification.[74] The 1844 clerical excuse that a doctor was too inconvenient or far away became untenable after Pilgrimage Committees began requiring physicians' statements in 1846.[75] Once mobilized to help clarify cures, Rhenish physicians developed a position similar to that of their French colleagues: somewhere between being sympathetic towards the possibility of miracles and asserting "the coldness of scientific rationalism."[76]

The contested discussion of cure-seeker bodies led episcopal committees to impose restrictions on access to the relics with each successive pilgrimage to Trier and Aachen. Clerics sought to merge two types of evidence – clinical and spiritual – to confirm that their parishioners were *actually* healed. If doctors verified that one of their patients experienced an inexplicable physical or mental transformation, then miracles and cure-seekers moved beyond the reproach of a reformer like Johannes Ronge. Such Catholic critics would be silenced in the face of overwhelming third-party evidence.

At the same time, doctors were threatening because they could debunk, challenge, and undermine priestly claims of the divine breaking into the world. This ambiguity was further compounded by the fact that clerics hoped to prove the limits of contemporary physicians. There could not be a miracle if a doctor could cure or relieve pilgrim suffering. In 1895, Joh. Caster wrote after his cure, "Since then I have been completely healthy and no longer required any doctor."[77]

In essence, Aachen and Trier clergy sought statements from medical men that demonstrated their learning via precise diagnoses and conceded their limitations, because physican statements had to acknowledge that the pilgrim's illness was beyond their ability or that the patient had recovered faster than modern medicine could have predicted. German clerics created their own version of science that simultaneously allowed for divine miracle and demonstrability. Catholics were willing to partner with contemporary medicine and science in certain situations, such as miracle verification, in order to root out false claims and to illuminate further the instances when God chose to act through a relic.

Doctors and physicians were central to creating this clerical miracle system throughout the nineteenth century. Doctor Clemens wrote to the bishop of Trier in 1844 on behalf of Herr Michels, his patient.

Clemens stated that Michels had been sick with conditions "only God could heal" for sixteen years but was miraculously relieved after his September visit to Trier. Clemens added, "The man, whom I understood to be incurable, stands before me healthy."[78]

At the same time, doctors also had the power to problematize healing narratives. Already in 1844, clerical tempers occasionally ran hot on verifying miracles. On 21 December 1844, Pastor Breitz wrote to the doctor in Halsenbach to assure him that Philip Bersch's wounded head had been healed. Breitz complained that if one waited long enough the doctor could discount any cure because people eventually got sick again. Breitz concluded his note by threatening, "We should often read 2. Thessal[onians],"[79] in which Paul promises judgment to those who harass the faithful: "God is just: He will pay back trouble to those who trouble you and give relief to you who are troubled, and to us as well. This will happen when the Lord Jesus is revealed from heaven in blazing fire with his powerful angels. He will punish those who do not know God and do not obey the gospel of our Lord Jesus" (2 Thessalonians 1:6–8).

Not all pastors shared Breitz's fervour to proclaim their parishioners cured. Pastor Adams from Reifferscheid delayed responding to inquiries from Trier about the cure of Joh. Michael Dreser's eight-year-old son until February 1845. In his report Adams could only report inconclusive results: the child was born weak but had been getting steadily stronger. After visiting Trier, Dreser no longer needed crutches to get around, but his legs were still crooked.[80] Adams's caution was likely related to his low opinion of the boy's father, to whom he referred as a "tyrant." Even so, Adams was not convinced by the fact that the child could now walk without assistance because his improvement was unaccompanied by an observable change in his legs.

Physicians often took the time in their medical appraisals of patients about to embark on, or recently returned from, pilgrimage to offer their opinions on the Aesculapian potential of relics. Also in 1844, in his report on the recovery of Johann Michels from Speicher, Dr. Clemens conceded, "I had visited Herr Michels at his sickbed in early April of this year and left him with an odd consolation, I told him, 'There are sicknesses that only God can heal.'"[81] Clemens gave up on Speicher, noting that his consolation came from years of experience, and he saw in Speicher a man beyond the intervention of human hands.[82] The report wraps up cleanly with Speicher revisiting the doctor after going to Trier, physically restored and fit. Other physicians left special notes to show their doubts.

For some medical professionals, the excitement of the pilgrimage occasion explained physical improvements among their patients.

Dr. Suker in Gürzenich noted, for example, that his patient was often in pain, but that visiting Aachen only cured her of hysteria, which he did not consider an actual disease.[83] Similarly, when the *Neue Augsburger Zeitung* interviewed Frl. Hepting's physician, he was surprised that Hepting was able to move around but doubted there was a full cure, because she still could not do everything she could prior to her illness.[84] Hepting's doctor stated that she could have been "emotionally aroused" by the pilgrimage setting. Such an experience might have led Hepting to temporary relief. Furthermore, he wrote, it was not his job to declare or determine miracles.

In his report on the condition of Joseph Kripperath's wife after her 1925 Aachen pilgrimage, Dr. Suker stressed the placebo potential of a relic: "On the clinical change of her infected, swollen knee there was no objective change in the swelling or the form of the bones. In contrast, the psychological behaviour of Mrs. K[ripperath] underwent a change, which we summarize under the term 'hysteria.'" Suker went on to argue that the entire problem with Kripperath's knee had been auto-induced, so the emotional encounter with the relic was a "quite natural" explanation for her quick recovery.[85]

In his follow-up evaluation of Schwester M. Ethelvides from Neunkirchen-Saar in 1936, Dr. Jung initially only reported her leg measurements, as she was cured of hip joint tuberculosis. Yet, at the end of his report he added, "Comment. The sister was suffering from May 1930 to May 1931, bedridden from hip joint tuberculosis. She was then prescribed a leg prosthesis to correct the hip joint. This prosthesis fell away on 20 August 1933. The hip was organically improved according to the rules of general healing through the prosthesis, which had the sole purpose of [healing the leg]. [The prosthesis] fell away at a given time, [and] did not suddenly require a special moment."[86] Again, doctors' opinions of cure possibility varied, with some physicians interested in asserting a miracle while others went out of their way to offer natural explanations.

Throughout this century, Catholic clergy regarded Protestant doctors' testimony as especially powerful. Bishop Arnoldi received word from Kreuznach in 1844 that Sanitätsrath Prieger looked over his granddaughter, Countess Droste zu Vischering, and found her healthy. This was especially good news, as evidence "by a Protestant doctor cannot be regarded as entirely typical for healing from the Holy Coat."[87] Confessional division on relic healing potential continued to influence doctors into the 1930s. In 1937, Aachen officials reached out to Dr. Baurmann, office leader of the German Association of Statutory Health Insurance Physicians (*Kassenärztliche Vereinigung Deutschlands*), for help finding enough physicians to work the First Aid office. Baurmann wished the Aachen pilgrimage good luck in finding physicians to be on call during the event. For Dr. Baurmann, it was impractical to ask physicians, especially Protestants in the German Association of Statutory Health Insurance Physicians, to attend "the pilgrimage, which is a purely Catholic religious affair." Baurmann was certain that if the Pilgrimage Committee put out their call to Catholic doctors in the region, there would be adequate medical care for "your pilgrims."[88] Despite Baurmann's rebuff, there is no mention in the 1937 correspondence of a physician shortfall. Some Catholic doctors conceded the real need for a divine act. The Köln-Lindenthal physician who recommended Frau Wilhelmine Mohlberg did so in part because "the doctor who writes this testimony, Herr Doctor Sebastiany, is a devout Catholic." For good measure, Dr. Sebastiany added, "I personally know Frau Mohlberg ... as a devout Catholic woman."[89]

At the local level, clerics and physicians cooperated to keep cure-seekers safe.[90] Eventually physicians became part of Rhineland events, no longer participating solely as cure-seeker assessors. At the 1925 Aachen pilgrimage, the Committee established a Volunteer Ambulance Column (*Freiwillige Sanitäts-Kolonne*) to assist with the care and transport of sick pilgrims. This group worked with the First Aid stations (*Sanitätswache*) erected for the duration of the event. The *Sanitätswache* had several objectives in July 1925: they coordinated stretcher bearers, established patrols of their office and into the streets every fifteen minutes, ensured that members had balms and sufficient bandages, and, importantly, deferred to doctors. The volunteers were told, "The orders of doctors are to be executed."[91] The true rift was often not between doctors and priests, but between church leadership and pilgrims over identifying a cure.

Generally, doctors did not think visiting the relics would do any harm, so long as the patient was fit for extended travel.[92] Indeed, some Rhineland physicians were adamant supporters of pilgrimage. Dr. Maria Pütz, in 1937, not only recommended patients visit the Aachen relics but used her position as a physician to secure five tickets to the cathedral treasury for herself.[93] Furthermore, for Pütz, Aachen offered a chance for relief from physical and spiritual ailments. For instance, she issued Frau Wwe. Josef Capellmann a note so Capellmann could touch an Aachen relic. Capellmann suffered from hardened arteries and dizziness.[94] Pütz also recommended thirty-five-year-old Frl. Clara Müller as a candidate for time with Jesus's Loincloth, stating that Müller "is indeed bodily, that is, organically healthy, but has a difficult spiritual suffering."[95] Pütz thus continued a five-hundred-year-old tradition of local healers sending patients to shrines and relics for spiritual renewal or when disease was beyond their ability to heal.

In Aachen, clergy did not always strictly enforce medical certificate requirements in the late nineteenth and early twentieth century. House doctor Kleinseidtz, for instance, found the process annoying and wrote a blank statement for all of sisters of the Josephinisches Institut in 1881 because it was impractical to issue every nun an individual certificate, as "it would require days [of consultations] to satisfy those who want to touch [the relic]."[96] The pastor, Real H., of the Josephinisches Institut forwarded the Kleinseidtz note to Canon Spee, who, after consultation with colleagues, agreed that one note for all the sick of the Institute would be sufficient.[97] Kleinseidtz further asked that the Aachen officials let in the sick to touch the Loincloth regardless of what they brought with them so that they did not travel for nothing.[98] This complaining was not in vain.

The shifting corroborating document demands in Aachen continued to cause confusion among German and foreign clergy, as well as sick pilgrims, into the twentieth century. By the 1925 pilgrimage, sick travellers to Aachen required only a note from their pastor for admission into the cathedral between 9:00 and 9:45 a.m.[99] With only about a month before the 1937 pilgrimage, Father Bieger, from Opladen-Lützenkirchen, wrote to the Aachen Pilgrimage Office, enquiring whether or not his ill parishioners must also submit a physician's note before leaving.[100]

Meanwhile the 1933 Trier Pilgrimage Committee continued Korum's 1891 approach of delaying the approval of miracle claims. They only sent out follow-up inquiries to nineteen cure-claimants in January 1936, and they relied exclusively on the word of physicians and the formalized *Fragebogen* forms.[101] As discussed in chapter 3, *Fragebogen* required physicians to give patients a diagnosis, which included assessing personal and family medical history, whether they considered the applicant hysterical or psychologically imbalanced, whether they thought the disease "imagined," whether the patient had visited a natural healer, and, perhaps most important, whether the disease originated from spiritual troubles.[102] These soul-sicknesses included "tendency to drunkenness," "chain smoking," and "drugs."[103] Such "anti-social practices" could not expect to find miraculous relief before the Coat of Jesus.

Acquiring medical slips and doctors' services for the *Fragebogen* was not gratis and frustrated cure-seekers. Albert Lehnertz complained that he heard from his brother and a trusted Protestant source that doctors filling out the *Fragebogen* were charging ten Reichsmarks – the equivalent of more than a week of labour – keeping six for themselves and sending four on to the Trier Pilgrimage Committee.[104] Lehnertz knew the rumour to be false because his sister-in-law had already had her form filled out and it did not cost that much. However, Lehnertz urged the Pilgrimage Committee to issue a press release that made their financial policy on *Fragebogen* clear to the public and so that the Protestants could not criticize. The Pilgrimage Committee replied that they had instituted a flat, low fee for the doctors affiliated with the parish hospital, but regretted that they had no power to force other doctors to charge less than ten Reichsmarks, since "that is their own affair."[105] Ten Reichsmarks or not, at least 19,000 individuals applied for time with the Coat in 1933.

Pilgrims found the Trier *Fragebogen* process cumbersome and worried about being denied access to the Holy Coat. A group of Silesian pilgrims, for example, brought not only their sick, but also physicians who could attest that the ill required time with the relic. This led to a shortage of housing and office space, because the Pilgrimage Committee had to find rooms for the doctors to examine patients and to fill out the required medical form.[106] Father Steinmetz, from Kirchberg, expressed his frustration in 1933: "Twice I have already asked the Pilgrimage Committee to send me doctor's *Fragebogen* forms. The forms have not yet arrived."[107] Steinmetz explained that he needed only fifteen for his sick and suffering, and that he wanted his blind parishioner, Jacob Kreb, to have access to the Coat on 8 October 1933 when they visited as a group. Three days later Domkapitular Fuchs fulfilled Steinmetz's third request. Persistence was sometimes necessary during the chaotic weeks of the pilgrimage.[108] Fuchs also confirmed appointments for five of Steinmetz's parishioners prior to receiving their *Fragebogen*. In another instance of flexibility, Domkapitular Fuchs waived the form for the 200–300 deaf pilgrims who visited the Trier Coat at 4:30 a.m. on 26 July 1933 with the Reichsverband der katholischen Taubstummen Deutschlands e.V.[109]

Stonewalled and frustrated, Frau Wilh. Rosche complained to Trier officials about her inability to get a *Fragebogen* from her priest in Seibersbach: "I have already gone to see Pastor Minter twice [for a *Fragebogen*], whether Herr Pastor has forgotten it or what I do not know." Rosche planned to be in Trier in six days and needed assurance that her nine-year-old son, who was blind in his left eye and had poor vision in the right, would be allowed to touch the relic. The mother further noted that she had taken the boy to Lourdes two years prior, to no avail, but she now "believed with all her hope" that they would find relief in Trier.[110] This letter, like the Irish Catholics seeking medals and *Andenken* in the 1930s, again suggests a shared international European Catholic culture that sought healing and divine presence from a variety of European Catholic pilgrimage sites.[111]

When sick and distraught pilgrims arrived in Trier and Aachen in the twentieth century, they generally knew that conventional medicine would not resolve their suffering. The specificity of medical analyses reveals that pilgrims first sought medical intervention by the post–First World War I period. In Aachen, even without prompting from complex, detailed medical forms, doctors in the 1930s volunteered extensive, developed, and precise diagnoses of their patients. For example, Dr. Sasse, in a note for Christine Schwinges during the 1937 pilgrimage, wrote of Schwinges's throat difficulties:

> Swallowing difficulties for 2 years. 10 kg weight loss. The thick soft mass [*Kontrastbrei*] hangs level with the upper thoracic aperture. Here is a great mass as ovalbumin accumulation, which is to the rear and to the right of the esophagus in the lateral rotation. The outline of the shading is entirely sharp, one can recognize even a few peristaltic waves. Then the soft mass slides freely down to the cardia. The remaining portion of the esophagus is narrow and does not show any changes. Fold reliefs and intact peristalsis. In sagittal path can be seen that the shading is to the left of the esophagus.… The cardia is conically pointed, a sure failure is not visible here. X-ray of the chest is no evidence for coarser changes. Normal sized heart with sharp contours. The entire aortic arch is widened.[112]

Accompanying this trend, imprecise or vague notions of illness were unacceptable diagnoses (e.g., "pain," "suffering," "sickness") as legitimate physical grievances. Now cure-seekers looking to Jesus's Loincloth or Coat suffered from specific, complex medical conditions and had exhausted medicinal treatments. This is not to diminish their desire. Indeed, this subtle change points to a greater expectation of the liminal encounter with the relics.

Doctor's notes in the mid-nineteenth century, and later *Fragebogen* forms, codified physicians as intermediaries between the Coat and the pilgrim. By the 1930s, church officials found doctors willing to give their time and energy to prevent healthy pilgrims from touching the Coat and to ensure that *Fragebogen* were accurate.[113] In 1933, the Pilgrimage Committee established the Health Care Ministry to assist with expected cure-seekers. Physicians were available throughout the event and helped to facilitate the encounter between relic and ill pilgrim. There were also doctors on hand in Trier for those who forgot their form or who failed to realize they needed a specific document.[114] At the end of the pilgrimage these medical specialists were honoured and marched in the closing procession ahead of the *Frauenordnungdienst* (Women Steward Service). One *Frauenordnungdienst* participant,

Cäcilie, who called herself the "pilgrim mother," recognized her former physician in the parade, Dr. H., who was pleased to see her healed of Basedow's disease.

Numerically the number of cure-seekers continued to expand into the 1930s as modern transportation and church organization made it possible for more individuals to visit the relics. Already on 24 August 1933, Fuchs sent out a memo that the Pilgrimage Committee should not send out any more *Fragebogen* because there would not be enough time for all the sick to see the relic before the pilgrimage closed on 10 September.[115] Two days later, Trier organizers asked newspapers to inform the public that they could issue no more *Fragebogen* as the result of demand. In a letter to Dr. P. Louis, the head of the St. Sebastian Confraternity, Fuchs apologized that the sick wives of *Schützen* (shooting club) members would not be allowed to touch the Coat. Even so, he sent Louis a *Fragebogen* so that he would not miss this opportunity. But the form came with a warning that Fuchs would not allow individuals time with the Coat after 5:00 a.m. on 9 September.[116] In 1937 Aachen, clergy continued to campaign for access to Jesus's Loincloth and offered additional details to pilgrims' testimony where possible. The Mannheim-based priest at St. Peter's noted of his parishioner Frl. Margareta Lawo that she was at risk of losing her job as a result of her nerve troubles. He was concerned for her because she had no parents, and losing her sole source of income would be exceptionally difficult.[117] Belief in and hopes of miracles persisted into the twentieth century and remained an integral part of pilgrimage practices.

Conclusion

The clerical and medical debates about miracles ignored the opinions and hopes of cure-seekers, the cured, and pilgrims themselves. Pilgrims had great expectations of their physical encounter with the relics. They journeyed in anticipation of a life-changing event. Even though she was not cured herself, E. Wurzer believed if all Germans had heard the message of Trier, many non-Catholics would be forced to rethink their religious opinions. For Wurzer, the obvious evidence of healing left individuals no alternative but to draw close to the Catholic Church.[118] While the priestly and Aesculapian authorities debated Catholic bodies, pilgrims were oriented away from authorities and towards the divine. Pilgrims continued to have liminal and out-of-body experiences, and their healing narratives remained largely unaltered into the 1930s.

As clergy made use of physicians to verify divine presence, their parishioners continued to stress that science and medicine had failed to restore their health. Catholic pilgrims saw the limits of medical knowledge as the ideal place for God to show his power and to offer definitive proof that He had dominion over the natural world. Otto Hanck of Münster expressed his desire for a *Krankenkarte* "because I have suffered for twenty years from indescribably severe nerve pain in the face ... which, until now, no doctor has been able to eliminate or relieve."[119] Similarly, Father Adolf Lennartz noted of his parishioner, Frau Adene Schnitzler, that "she has consulted eight doctors [including] Sanitätsrat Dr. Lansenberg, and the famous Stemmler in Cologne."[120] Despite these consultations, Schnitzler continued to suffer from "a bad leg" for four years.[121]

Clerics enlisted the aid of physicians as ostensibly unbiased experts whose testimony would outweigh that of any future schismatic leader. Clergy relied on medical corroboration as a new source of truth about God acting in the world. Physicians helped to reinforce clerical practices and provided evidence that God revealed Himself through the relics. Thus in 1909, when the Prioress of the San Francisco Carmelites requested confirmation that Countess Droste zu Vischering had been healed of lameness in 1844, one important detail she wanted the Trier bishop to verify was that "she [Droste zu Vischering] presented herself to the bishop, Dr. Arnoldi, and the next day, for the first time, and afterwards at Kreuznach and Munster, was examined by some highly celebrated medical experts, such as Dr. Hansen at Treves [Trier], Dr. Prieger at Kreuznach, and Dr. Busch at Munster."[122] Importantly, physicians, though "highly celebrated," remained secondary to the initial revelation to Bishop Arnoldi. Even so, the doctor's somatic knowledge was intended to provide a buffer against the secular world. The Prioress herself might have been satisfied with just Arnoldi's word, but the physicians alleviated any potential doubt or uncertainty.

Priests in the Pilgrimage Committees alienated pilgrims with medical questionnaires and formal forms. Pilgrims worried about the cost of having a physician fill out the form and about the new procedures blocking their access to the physical presence of the relics. Still, Catholic clergy turned to medical knowledge, historical sources, archaeology, and fibre analyses to argue that the Rhineland pilgrimage was a legitimate practice. Priests eventually learned that even these new research techniques could not prove beyond doubt that their relics were authentic.

6 Historical Authenticity as Presence

In September 2012, Dr. Karen King, a Harvard divinity professor of history, unveiled a small piece of papyrus at a conference in Rome. The papyrus included the words "Jesus said, 'My wife.'" For King, the small artefact could spark debate over clerical celibacy and the role of women in Christianity.[1] The discovery led to a documentary, which was to air on the Smithsonian Channel on 30 September. However, persistent doubts about the authenticity of the papyrus led to a delay of the broadcast and to a round of scientific testing. After months of examination, in April 2014, scientists at the University of Arizona confirmed that the papyrus dated from eighth-century Egypt. Experts also studied the chemical composition of the ink and found it to be consistent with ancient Egyptian inks. Not all were convinced, though. Egyptologist Leo Depuydt at Brown University said of the papyrus, "It could be done in an afternoon by an undergraduate student," and the inscription was so fake as to be "ripe for a Monty Python sketch."[2] *Harvard Theological Review* published both King's article and a rebuttal by Depuydt.[3] This discussion about celibacy, Jesus's marital status, and women in the church pivoted on carbon dating, the University of Arizona's Mass Spectrometry Laboratory, historians, and micro-Raman spectroscopy.[4] Although the Vatican newspaper dismissed the papyrus as a forgery in September 2012, the media surrounding the document looked to experts, including Ariel Sabar's 2016 investigative journalism. In response to Sabar's provenance research, Dr. King acknowledged that the papyrus fragment could be a forgery. In the quest to ascertain whether Jesus ever said "My wife," authenticity was a question for professors, not for the Catholic Church.[5]

In Germany, the transition to scientifically based analyses of relics began in the nineteenth century. Rhineland clergy struggled to determine the relationship of science and history to their relics.[6] On 22 July

1891, C.J. Libertz, a priest from Olzheim, wrote to Trier officials to explain that the Holy Coat was authentic (*echt*), an actual garment worn by Jesus during his lifetime. In a sprawling treatise, Libertz combined analyses of scripture, Greek texts, Thomas Aquinas's theology, and recent works on the ancient world. He presented information on ancient Egyptian, Greek, Persian, and Hebrew garments. He traced biblical garments through the early Hebrew priesthood and into the Book of Judges, in order to show that Jesus's Coat marked him as a teacher and a member of the priesthood. He further explained that it made sense that Jesus would have worn his finest garments at his last dinner with his disciples. For Libertz, "the seamless Coat shows that he [Jesus] was not dressed as the poor; he died not as beggars, but as a priest and king."[7] He maintained that the colouring and form of the garment were consistent with tradition. Libertz did not, however, point to the 1844 miracles as evidence of the Coat's legitimacy. Indeed, after 1844, clerics sought temporal, historical explanations for relic origins to complement their established scripture-based arguments.

Beginning in the late nineteenth century, Aachen and Trier church officials co-opted scientific methods to corroborate relic authenticity. They thereby broadened the base of acceptable truth and evidence regarding the historical origins of cathedral treasures. This chapter considers clerical attitudes towards relics and further illuminates the divergent pilgrimage expectations of German Catholic clergy and laity. Clerics reacted to the 1844 attacks on relics by scientifically scrutinizing the Coat of Trier and the Aachen cathedral relics. Their goal was to show both the laity and detractors that it was reasonable to believe their items were linked to the earliest days of German Christianity, to Constantine, and to Charlemagne.[8] Most importantly, these examinations reveal a clerical willingness to broaden their acceptable sources of knowledge to explain Catholicism's devotion to certain Rhenish relics. Increasingly pilgrimage organizers stressed the symbolic nature of relics rather than their indisputable divine origins. This clerical turn outward – towards laboratories, fibre analysis, and archaeology – also indicates how clergy remained uneasy about popular religious practices in the later nineteenth century.

Relics and Respectability

Clergy wanted to rally Catholics to the relics while simultaneously appearing *bürgerlich*, or respectable.[9] As they advocated for new understandings of relics as symbols, clergy worked to undercut criticism that popular religiosity was unreasonable or superstitious.[10] Clerics had different measurements for the genuineness of relics from their laity both before and after the Kulturkampf, though Rhineland church authorities seriously pursued scientific arguments only following the 1844 Trier pilgrimage.[11] While the Kulturkampf was an important factor in shaping clerical presentation of religiosity, it was not a turning point. Instead, the ongoing confrontation with Bismarck intensified trends within German Catholicism. For example, Aachen first began investigating Charlemagne's bones in 1861 but did not consult experts in Berlin until 1907, after the Kulturkampf had subsided.

In pursuing their increasingly secular arguments, Catholic clergy risked leaving the laity behind and alienating pilgrim expectations of their pilgrimage. Catholics came together in associations and in politics over the nineteenth century but diverged in their understanding of divine presence.[12] For pilgrims, divine presence came in the form of spiritual and sometimes physical restoration. They wanted an intangible experience, the impossible made possible, a divine breaking into the world. Relics could heal bodies and physically connect pilgrims to God's *presence*. It was less clear what archaeological artefacts that contained fibres from the Near East had to do with whether the relics helped improve their bodies and spirits.

Rhenish clergy engaged new academic fields and research methods in their quest to affirm relic authenticity. In determining the veracity of relic origin myths, Catholic clerics pursued two interrelated goals. First, priests wanted to demonstrate the reasonableness of their belief. Thus, if the Coat of Trier was from the first century, then venerating Jesus in the Coat was a legitimate practice. Second, by proving that their relics were indeed ancient, Rhenish church leaders showed that Catholicism was modern and scientific – in other words, not arcane, outmoded, or superstitious, as detractors like Ronge and Czerski had suggested. German Catholic clergy worked to find an accommodation with science, to use new methods of research to further their own cause of showing the historical origins of Rhineland relics. Church leaders looked to new approaches to *Wissenschaft* (science) to explain relics, their origins, their chemical makeup, and their *potential* authenticity. Accordingly, they conceived of "authentic," or *echt/Echtheit* in German, as meaning the historical origins of the Coat in Trier and the four Aachen relics. For clerics, authentic included the reasonable historical possibility of legitimacy.

Authority: Sacred and Profane

In the nineteenth century, European intellectuals looked to "science" as an alternative to religious explanations of humanity's place in the natural world. J.W. Burrow notes that during this century, science became unassailable and science was the goddess who would not betray her worshippers.[13] In 1845 Alexander von Humboldt (1769–1859) published the first volume of his *Kosmos*, an attempt to write a narrative of the entire universe. By the 1850s, German academics described undemonstrated belief as a sin against reason.[14] Hermann von Helmholtz (1821–94) worked to represent human experience in mathematical terms and helped distinguish scientific disciplines, including physics, psychology, mathematics, biology, and physiology. Helmholtz sought to create a unified scientific system to describe the world.[15]

Some European thinkers declared science redemptive as German universities expanded science and medical faculties.[16] For example, Comte strove "not merely to eradicate Catholicism but to replace it with literally a new religion of science, progress and humanity, for religion human beings must have."[17] In 1887, Darwin's "bulldog" Thomas Henry Huxley reflected on the rise of science since 1850 and proclaimed science "the foundation of our wealth and the condition of our safety from submergence by another flood of barbarous hordes; it is the bond which unites into a solid political whole, regions larger than any empire of antiquity; it secures us from recurrence of the pestilences and famines of former times; it is the source of endless comforts and conveniences, which are not mere luxuries, but conduce to physical and moral well-being."[18]

For Huxley, science, not Christianity, explained how best to organize society, because science allowed humanity to make their own fate, free from the divine.[19] Faced with new intellectual discussions about the validity and veracity of Christian teachings, German Catholic leaders attempted to find a non-antagonistic relationship with scientific research by using scientific methods to confirm relic authenticity.

Rhineland clergy were not alone in Europe as they worked to integrate new research methodologies into established religious practices. In France, two divergent groups sought to define the place of science in French society. Positivists argued that new research methods displaced religion – humanity could find its morality via natural enquiry. Opposite the positivists, a diverse group of Catholic intellectuals and idealists, including French philosopher and novelist George Fonsegrive, contended that science was bankrupt. "Science" could not increase happiness nor serve as a moral compass. Between these opposing groups, French-Catholic scientists opposed attempts to use science as "an antireligious Juggernaut" and sought to reconcile a new scientific worldview with the tenets of Catholicism.[20] Across the Rhine, by the 1890s German Catholics had settled into an uneasy détente with the state. At the same time, German clergy were still working out how to respond to attacks on relic authenticity that originated in the mid-nineteenth century.

German Catholic clerics undertook an explanatory shift regarding relic authenticity in Trier between 1844 and 1891. In 1844, clerics found their version of the history of the Trier Holy Coat under siege as detractors denounced the relic as inauthentic on new grounds: that it was the wrong colour, or that competing relics rendered the Coat invalid. In 1890, the bishop of Trier, Michael Felix Korum, had the Coat scrutinized by a committee of experts – including the mayor, an architect, and fellow clergy – in order to assert that the Coat was indeed a genuine artefact. How did the Coat and Aachen relics become symbols instead of the actual garments of Jesus Christ? The Coat was always a rhetorical representation of unity, as previously discussed in the anti-Ronge arguments, but as scientific evidence remained inconclusive, *Symbol* increasingly dominated *Echtheit* after the 1844 authenticity debate.

Established Verification Procedures

In the early modern period, clergy discussed the origins of relics and reassured pilgrims that relics had not been tampered with since the last exhibition.[21] In 1959, Roman Catholic Church historian Erwin Iserloh argued that Christians in Trier debated the authenticity of the Coat before the Reformation began in Wittenberg. For example, in a 1514 pamphlet, Bishop Johann Enen (d. 1591) discussed whether or not the Coat could have come from the Holy Land to Trier in the first centuries of Christianity.[22]

To assuage fears of forgery, clergy demonstrated that relics were inaccessible between pilgrimages. The two most common forms of demonstrating relic integrity included clerics splitting up the reliquary key between two officials and publicly verifying that seals placed on the relic during the previous exhibition had not been broken. For example, in 1725, Trier officials broke the reliquary key in half and gave the bishop and the cathedral chapter each a piece.[23]

This tradition continued into the nineteenth century, when Aachen officials split the reliquary key and gave half to the bishop and half to the mayor. So too did the procedure of wrapping relics in silk with wax seals affixed to the seams. After opening the Marian Shrine, Aachen clergy held up the wrapped relics to their peers to assure them that the seals remained unbroken from the previous pilgrimage. Following the final display, clerics rewrapped the four Aachen relics in new silk and sealed them with wax that corresponded to the silk of each relic.[24] Seals of authenticity were not limited to the stored relics. Later, in 1925, one

Figure 6.1. Sealed *Andenken*, 1925.
Source: DAA, PA 67 a, Gottesdienst, Heiligtumsfahrt, 1925.

of the featured *Andenken* was a postcard with four pieces of silk that
had been used to wrap the relics for sixteen years. On the bottom left-
hand corner, church officials included an orange wax seal that attested
to the genuine origins of the attached cloth.

Secular authorities played a central role in evaluating sacred relics
during each unveiling and resealing of the shrines. Clerics had long
assembled bystander testimony to corroborate pre-existing sicknesses
during cases of alleged cures, and also invited witnesses to participate
in inspections between pilgrimages. In 1890, as Korum prepared to
have the Coat examined by a committee of experts, he invited not only
his fellow Trier clerics, but also the mayor, a canon from Cologne, and
Stephen Beissel, a Jesuit who wrote extensively on the topic of Rhineland relics.[25] Those present for the opening signed a protocol that stated
they found the sixteen 1844 seals still intact, that the 1844 silk wrap-
pings were still present, and that they found the Coat covered with a
considerable amount of mould.[26] After deciding that nuns would help

clean the relic, and that potential researchers needed actual cloth samples to determine the origin and consistency of the Coat, the assembled politicians, priests, and experts resealed the Coat. The major point here is that Korum and the cathedral canons did not tamper with the Coat alone; they called in collaborators who would be able to testify to the origins of the fibre samples and that the Coat had not been opened since 1844 – authentication demanded extra-church cooperation.

Clergy asked secular authorities to corroborate the integrity of relic seals. Thus, in 1930, Bernhard Witte, the apostolic goldsmith charged with opening the Marian Shrine, appeared before the Aachen mayor, Dr. Wilhelm Rombach. Witte swore before "God Almighty" to carry out his duties at the opening and closing ceremonies. The goldsmith was traditionally the first and the last to view the relics after breaking the lock on the Marian Shrine, so an oath of honesty was essential to prove the relics were authentic and undisturbed.[27] The oath of Witte, a non-cleric, before God and secular authorities was insurance against potential foul play.[28] After the 1930 opening ceremony, thirty-nine witnesses signed a protocol that summarized the events and confirmed that "it was found that the seals of the silk wrapped to seal the relics were unharmed."[29] The witnesses included clergy, the mayor, the city inspector, and the city councillors.[30]

Contesting Relic Origins

In 1844, at the previous unveiling of the Coat, Johannes Ronge had criticized Bishop Arnoldi and the pilgrims on theological grounds. In addition to Ronge's previously analysed popular critiques, pilgrims in 1844 were exposed to historical arguments against the veracity of St. Helena's relic. Orientalist Johann Gildemeister (1812–90) and historian Heinrich von Sybel (1817–95), both professors at Bonn, sought to critically examine the evidence for and against the Coat in a pamphlet titled *The Holy Coat of Trier and the Twenty Other Holy Seamless Coats: A Historical Inspection.*[31] These two Bonn professors presented a unique anti-pilgrimage critique that was not based on theology or scripture. Because the Coat was not an aspect of dogma, it was fair to subject the relic to a historical enquiry.[32] They hoped that their study would help to discredit the Coat, and cited historical precedents for the abandonment of relics, most famously the two heads of John the Baptist that required adjudication.[33] Furthermore, the Bonn professors stressed their appreciation of truth and thus demanded that Catholic pilgrims have access to all the historical facts of the Trier Coat. They vowed only to relate what was known, which included a rejection of the traditions that Mary had sewn the Coat, or that the Coat miraculously grew as Jesus got older and was therefore constantly present with him from childhood to execution.[34]

The authors' chief objective was to undermine Jakob Marx's version of the history of the Coat. Gildemeister and Sybel complained that the Trier bishop approved Marx's highly biased history, which led to a false confidence in the Coat's authenticity. For Sybel and Gildemeister, Marx labelled hearsay, legends, and sagas as "fact." How, they asked, could Helena bring the Coat to Trier in 330, when she died in 327?[35] Helena did visit Palestine to give thanks for Constantine converting, but did not find the True Cross or the Coat during that trip. If she had, Gildemeister and Sybel stressed, Eusebius would have written that down.[36] Or, if not Eusebius, then certainly Pope Sylvester would have recorded the Coat in his list of authentic items Helena found in Palestine.[37]

The professors did not limit their criticisms to the fourth-century tradition of the Coat. Gildemeister and Sybel sarcastically dismissed Marx's speculation that John the Apostle or Mary Magdalene could have purchased the Coat back from the Roman soldier at the foot of Jesus's cross: "Obviously it must be, as Mr. Marx presupposes about the unsewn Coat, that the early Christians had nothing more urgent to do than bring the Coat and keep it as a precautionary measure. Of all [the] things related to Christ ... but especially of so many things that [Christ could have] given his relatives and companions without the trouble and danger of buying [back] items his enemies possessed."[38] For Gildemeister and Sybel, truth meant the most logical explanation.

The Bonn professors mocked Marx's speculative approach to history in order to further discredit the Trier origins story. They sarcastically applied guesswork to the Coat said to be in Georgia in the Caucuses. Georgian tradition held that the soldier at the foot of the cross was from the Georgia region and that after he fought in Syria he returned home with the garment. That myth, they contended, sounded more plausible than Marx's version of events.[39] In fact, they explained, the idea that the Coat was even in Trier surfaced only in the eleventh century, when the Trier bishop undertook a search for the Coat but failed to find it.[40] The Coat was likely placed in the *Nikolausaltar* in 1121, without any canonical evidence attesting to its merit. In 1196, Bishop Johann opened the altar and found the Coat within, but it had been there for a mere seventy years, and certainly not since the fourth century.[41] Later, in 1512, when the Coat was again exhibited, its fame grew because of two historical contingencies. First, Central Europe was already religiously agitated with miracles and visions in the early sixteenth century, and this made the people vulnerable to a legend about a garment of Jesus. And second, once the Reformation began five years later, Catholics in the Trier area turned to the Coat as a sign of unity and affirmation of their universal religiosity.[42]

Gildemeister and Sybel concluded that the relic was an old piece of clothing being passed off as the Coat of Jesus. They weighed the Coat's potential legitimacy on four factors: form, colour, material, and conception.[43] Jesus, as a wandering teacher, would have worn a Coat that was similar to that of the Pharisees, a *Stola*. His garment would also follow Greek and Roman customs and not be so long that he could not walk and work freely. However, the Trier Coat was too long to fit these requirements.[44] Gildemeister and Sybel must have had a notion of how tall Jesus was to judge the form question, but they make no mention of average heights from the period. Colour, for the professors, was straightforward. The Trier Coat appears brown-reddish and must have previously been purple. However, Jesus, again as an impoverished teacher, could not have afforded a dyed garment, so the Trier Coat was a forgery. The authors analysed Greek, Roman, and Hebrew cultures to determine the consistency of ancient cloth, how garments were made, and how they aged. They guessed that the actual fabric was likely cotton or linen. Jesus would have worn clothing sewn from wool because, in antiquity, women and priests wore linen garments, not men. Unless Marx was saying Jesus was effeminate, Jesus the carpenter would have worn wool.[45]

One of the most recurring criticisms against the relic in Trier was that many other churches in Europe claimed to have the Holy Coat of Jesus. Certainly Jesus could not have owned all of them. Gildemeister and Sybel maintained that the Catholic Church had peddled false relics in earnest since the twelfth century. The Roman Church continued to allow superstition and false belief to spread among the laity in the nineteenth century, they contended. They thought that if they succinctly summarized the history of all the "competing" Coats in the world, Catholics would finally concede that the Trier Coat was inauthentic. Accordingly, they identified twenty of Jesus's coats, including those of Galatia, Safed, Santiago, Frankfurt, Westminster, Rome, Jerusalem, Mainz, Bremen, Loccum, Cologne, Moscow, Georgia, Turkey, Ghent, Constantinople, and Argenteuil. The historical Jesus was poor and did not possess multiple changes of clothing. And even if Jesus had several garments, they certainly would not have survived the nearly two thousand years since his crucifixion. For the Bonn professors, these duplicate relics revealed that Trier was no less absurd than those churches claiming to have Mary's breast milk or hair from Noah's beard.[46] Of the twenty alleged garments, the authors directed their ire towards Argenteuil, near

Paris, as the best example of how Catholic clergy peddled counterfeit objects.[47]

According to Argenteuil tradition, this garment came to Europe by way of Galatia, Safed, Jerusalem, and Constantinople. From Constantinople, the Byzantine royal family gave it as a gift to Charlemagne, who in turn donated the relic to a monastery in Argenteuil. When Normans attacked in the ninth century, the Argenteuil residents sealed the relic in a wall to protect it from looting.[48] After systematically ruling out the possibility of the Coat being in Safed, Jerusalem, or Galatia in the sixth century, Gildemeister and Sybel critiqued the idea that the Coat could have survived in a wall. Argenteuil was rebuilt, not remodelled in the twelfth century, suggesting that the Coat, were it in a wall, would have been lost.[49] Furthermore, had the Coat survived the Normans, Gildemeister doubted it would have survived the Huguenots, who plundered and sacked the town on 12 October 1567. The Argenteuil garment became a symbol for the French church only after the French Revolution. Thus in 1804 the bishop of Versailles, despite the seeming unlikelihood that the Argenteuil garment could have endured through the Normans, Huguenots, and Revolutionaries, affirmed the reliability of the relic. This declaration paved the way for Gildemeister and Sybel's disgust with Europe's multiple coat traditions. In 1843, Pope Gregory XVI declared the Argenteuil item authentic, seemingly contradicting Pope Leo X's 1 February 1514 affirmation that the Trier Coat was authentic and that Helena had brought it to Trier.[50] Faced with these theological and historical challenges to the Holy Coat's authenticity, 1840s German clerics began formulating new justifications, in conjunction with existing explanations, for the place of relics in religious practices.

(Re)reading the Sources

Clergy countered critiques like those of Gildemeister and Sybel by emphasizing historical evidence and Catholic Church tradition to argue for the Coat's authenticity. In Trier, the episcopate reissued Bishop Joseph von Hommer's (1760–1836) history of the Holy Coat in 1844.[51] In his overview, Hommer conceded that there were four potential coats, all of which Gildemeister and Sybel presented in their work: those in Rome, Cologne, Argenteuil, and Trier.[52] For Hommer, however, the Trier Coat was authentic for two reasons. First, medieval and early modern documents corroborated the oral tradition of the Coat. Second, the main Coat competitor, the relic in Argenteuil, was a different garment entirely and was also genuine. Two sources – Gregory of Tours (d. 587) and Abbot Theofrid von Echternach (d. 1110) – indicated that Jesus's

Coat moved through Galatia and Zapha, and was thus near Constantinople and Jerusalem respectively.[53] For Marx and Hommer, Tours and Echternach proved that the Coat was known and existed as early as the sixth century.

In order to put the Coat in St. Helena's hands, Hommer pointed to the reasonableness of tradition. St. Helena definitely visited Palestine and was friends with the bishop of Jerusalem, Marcarius.[54] Furthermore, Constantine, her son, ruled from Trier, so it was logical that she would bring one of the most precious relics she discovered during her Holy Land travels back to this key city on the Mosel River.[55] Unhelpfully, Tours and Echternach potentially referred to two separate relics. Tours wrote of a "seamless Coat" (*ungenähten Rock*) while Echternach described his relic as *"eine Tunica."*[56] Hommer used this distinction to argue that the Trier and Argenteuil garments were not mutually exclusive. In Argenteuil, it was entirely possible that Chalemagne got the relic from the Byzantine Emperor and donated it to a monastery outside of Paris. Jesus's second garment was possibly a "tunic," or *"Mantel"* (jacket) but not the seamless Coat.[57]

Like Hommer, Jakob Marx worked to demonstrate how Argenteuil did not compete with Trier. Marx drew parallels between Trier and Argenteuil, and the competing narratives about the Coat penned by Gregory of Tours and Fredegaire, a Frankish historian. Accordingly, both Tours and Fredegaire contended that the relic was rediscovered in 590: Tours in Galatia, near Constantinople, and Fredegaire in Jaffa, near Jerusalem. Marx decided that readers had two options: they could either discount both accounts, which would not be unreasonable, as Tours only reported rumour, and Fredegaire wrote about events far removed from him, both temporally and geographically.[58] Alternatively, following his attempt to parallel the narratives and the two relics, the reader could safely believe both accounts because Jesus certainly owned more than one garment. Marx also noted that even the outer garment, which was divided into four parts by the Roman soldiers in John 19, could have survived: "Although it had been divided into four parts, it might still have been purchased again from the hands of the soldiers, have been pieced together, and thus a precious memorial of the Saviour might have been formed from it."[59] It was therefore possible that Argenteuil possessed this other garment of Jesus, his outer cloak, while Trier had preserved the seamless Coat of their Saviour.

Marx pushed the coexistence of garments argument further than Hommer. "I ask," he wrote, "can these claims impair the tradition of the church of Trier respecting the seamless robe? We reply absolutely that they cannot; the authenticity of the garment at Argenteuil, even taken for granted, would not cast the shadow of a doubt on the tradition of Trier, and whoever will examine the matter without prejudice, will have no trouble to convince himself of it." Further, the medieval monk and abbot Robert de Monte, the first scholar to report the relic in Argenteuil, called it a cappa, or cloak, an outer garment.[60] The important authors of the sixteenth, seventeenth, and eighteenth centuries "unanimously maintain that the holy robe is in the cathedral of Trier, and it never came into the mind of any of them to take the garment of Argenteuil for the tunic."[61]

For Marx, when the Coat actually surfaced in the records, it was linked to Trier, not Argenteuil, giving more weight to the relic on the Mosel. Since the beginning of Christianity and into the medieval period, "the church and ecclesiastical writers nearly all regard the seamless robe as an emblem of the church."[62] Here Marx pointed to varied theologians who all alluded to the John 19 garment as a metaphor for the undivided church, including John Calvin; St. Augustine; St. Cyprian; Pacien, the bishop of Barcelona in the fourth century; Alexander, the bishop of Alexandria who confronted the Arian heresy in the fourth century; and St. Bernard.[63] For Marx, the aggregate of such diverse Christian theologians affirmed the seamlessness of the Coat.

After distinguishing the Argenteuil and Trier relics, Hommer contended that the post-Helena Catholic traditions about the relic were, in fact, reliable history. In this chronology, after Helena brought the relic north of the Alps, the Coat entered a period of obscurity during which it was likely hidden in one of the Trier altars. In 1196, Bishop Johann I sought to improve the Trier cathedral and remodelled large portions of the church.[64] During the construction, he found the Coat in the *Nikolausaltar* (Nicholas altar). The Trier citizens celebrated its reappearance with an improvised pilgrimage on the Philippus and Jacobs feast day, 1 May 1196.

Marx explained that because the relic was walled into an altar and not shown, there was no reason for scholars to leave behind written records on its presence. Following the 1196 display, clerics placed the Coat back into an altar until 1512, when Kaiser Maximilian visited Trier and pressured the bishop, Richard von Greifenklau, to show him the Coat. Greifenklau warned Maximilian that he might go blind after looking upon the relic, but Maximilian remained undeterred. They broke open the cathedral altar and pulled out the Coat on 14 April 1512, the Wednesday following Easter.[65] Maximilian did not go blind. The ensuing pilgrimage attracted over 100,000 pilgrims and was blessed by Pope Leo X. Now that the Coat was back in the public eye, pilgrimages were held more frequently, initially every seven years, but becoming less regular over time.

Jakob Marx concurred with Hommer's Coat narrative from the fourth century to the 1810 exhibition. Marx maintained that "St. Helena being once in possession of the Holy Coat [Robe], would naturally present it to the Church at Trier [Treves].... [S]he would have bestowed no mark of her attachment on Trier, where she had resided for so long a time?"[66] Marx also affirmed the miraculous traditions of the relic. Mary herself wove the Coat because, for Marx, this story was "based upon strong probabilities, especially when it is also remembered that a garment made by a mother's own hand was regarded as a token of love and tenderness for her son."[67] Marx hypothesized that the Roman soldiers at the foot of the cross would want to sell the Coat to one of Jesus's followers. Doing so would have been better than holding onto the possession of a criminal, someone the Roman soldier despised.[68]

Supporters and detractors of the Trier Coat continued to cite the Argenteuil robe into the 1891 pilgrimage. However, where Gildemeister and Sybel saw similarity and mutual exclusion, Edward Plater, author of an English-language history of the Coat, emphasized the differences between Trier and Argenteuil. Even if the garments shared an analogous tradition, they were substantively different artefacts: "[The coat of Argenteuil] is shown to have been of a totally different character to the Tunic of Trier, than which it is much smaller, and of wholly different material – a kind of woven camel's hair, still found in the East."[69] Furthermore, Plater, like Marx before him, maintained that the authenticity question was not an either/or issue – both coats could be legitimate. The Argenteuil garment was genuine, but it was not a coat like Trier's Coat. Rather it was an undergarment "intended to be worn beneath the more ample Coat [Robe] preserved at Trier."[70] Richard Clarke, another 1890s pamphleteer, reinforced Plater's argument and wrote that Trier did not claim to be the only garment of Christ extant, but asserted that they possessed the garment described in John 19.[71]

Ultimately there could not be a compromise between Gildemeister/Sybel and Marx/Hommer. For Gildemeister and Sybel, Marx was wildly off target when he considered the mentalities of saints or relied on the descriptions of New Testament individuals to speculate on how they would have responded to Jesus's execution. History, and by extension the truth about the Trier Coat, argued Gildemeister, could be found only in the surviving written records, and there were too few of those to make a convincing case for authenticity. Furthermore, the plethora of alternative relics undermined any possibility that the Trier relic survived from the first century to the nineteenth.

Against Gildemeister, Marx and Hommer's writings emphasized church tradition, exegesis, and the sermons of the church fathers to uphold their belief that the Trier Coat was authentic, that it held the actual drops of blood from the crucifixion. These mid-nineteenth-century arguments for the authenticity of the Coat hung on plausibility; it was probable that Helena brought the relic from Jerusalem and it lay in Trier undiscovered until 1196 and 1512.

Detractors of the relic stressed the unlikelihood that a garment could survive nearly two thousand years undetected. For critics, the documents did not reveal enough definitive information. Gildemeister and Sybel might have scoffed when Marx guessed at Kaiser Maximilian's motivations in 1512. Marx reported that Maximilian wanted to show the Trier Coat to "not only arouse the ancient piety of Christians, which slumbered and was dying in many hearts, but would also increase the honour of God among men."[72]

Marx did not limit his sources to historical monographs, letters, or other documents, but turned to the Holy Spirit as an agent in history that guarded the Coat. For Marx, only divine intervention and protection spared Church relics during unsettled times. Marx's history of the Coat is also a history of the Rhineland, told from the perspective of a sacred object. The Coat, at the centre, survived successive assaults on Trier. Trier was sacked in 410 by the Vandals and then by the Franks in 411 and 415.[73] The destruction was total, and the relic was safe because it was hidden within stone. Salvien wrote of the fifth-century Frankish attacks:

> There is not a single corner of the city in which the wrecks of the conflagration may not be found heaped pell mell upon one another with bones and the remains of victims; not a spot which is not stained with blood, strewed with dead bodies and mangled limbs; every thing presents the spectacle of a conquered city; terror and the image of death are every where. Those who have survived this disaster weep over the tombs of their unfortunate fellow-citizens, on all sides nothing is to be heard but the sound of lamentations.[74]

Subsequent centuries were not much kinder to the city. In 451, the Huns took the town and then in 880 the Normans attacked Aachen and Trier.[75] After the outbreak of the Reformation, Trier was again attacked by foreign armies.

For Marx, God not only chaperoned relics through this violent history but also facilitated each Trier pilgrimage. Following its discovery in 1196 and rediscovery in 1512, Pope Leo X affirmed the Coat as authentic and called for pilgrimages every seven years. These events were to coincide with the Aachen festivals, because both Rhenish towns possessed precious garments from Jesus. The Coat was shown to the faithful in 1545 and perhaps 1553, but that same year Albert Margrave of Brandenburg marched against Trier and burned the churches and convents.[76] Trier continued to stumble through the Wars of Religion (1562–98), and the region endured another conflict in 1592 as the Lord of Befort, Gaspard Buy, took Lusenburg.

During the Thirty Years' War (1618–48), the Trier region was attacked by Swedes and French in 1631–2, and even after the Peace of Westphalia it took time before Trier residents had total relief from the fighting.[77] In 1657 and in 1734, the Coat was moved to the Ehrenbreitstein fortress because of warfare in the Trier area. In 1759 the Coat was again moved because soldiers from Hannover marched against Ehrenbreitstein. The Trier Coat first went to Bamberg, until 1803, and then to Augsburg, until 1810.[78] During July 1810, French-appointed Trier Bishop Charles Mannay had the Coat brought back to Trier. To celebrate, the relic was displayed from 9 to 27 September, and more than 227,000 pilgrims came to the city.[79] Through these travails, the Coat, and Trier, and by extension Christendom endured. Marx wrote, "The history of the robe is a faithful picture of that of the Church!"[80]

In Marx's view, God providentially acted in history on multiple occasions to protect Trier and the relic. The Coat was meant to survive to strengthen Catholics. When returning from its exile, the Holy Coat re-entered its ancient cathedral. It found there the same pontifical power that Jesus Christ had established – "the same faith, the same sacrifice and the same sacraments."[81] Furthermore, the Coat was still extant to comfort the faithful.[82] The Coat was a historical actor – its divine origin ensured its survival through centuries of uncertainty and warfare in the Rhineland. Marx dismissed the Gildemeister and Sybel analysis as missing the entire sacred point of the Holy Coat of Jesus. However, after 1844, Rhineland clergy sought new arguments and new methodologies more immediate than the Holy Spirit to demonstrate that their relics were authentic.

Vivisecting Relics

By the 1891 Trier pilgrimage, the clergy had abandoned Marx and Hommer's document and Jesus-centred authenticity arguments. Clergy strove to bring contemporary, powerful arguments against potential critics by blending new scientific analyses with historical evidence that the Coat was the garment from John 19. Richard Clarke summarized the importance of accuracy about the Coat: "It is only on this ground [independent corroboration of the authenticity of the Coat] that we have any right to ask of those outside the Church to accept our belief in it."[83] Catholics could not expect respect from non-Catholics unless they demonstrated that the Coat was authentic, a relic worn by Jesus in the Gospels.[84]

In the run-up to the 1891 Trier display, Catholic authorities worked to resolve the authenticity question once and for all. In 1890, between 7 and 10 July, twelve individuals examined the Coat. The assembled included Bishop Korum, Mayor de Rys, the Jesuit Stephan Beissel, an architect, members of the cathedral chapter, and the Cologne Domkapitular Alexander Schnütgen. They found the garment in a bad state.[85] Following the 1810 and 1844 pilgrimages, the Coat was walled into the cathedral's stone altar, a damp and dark environment, and consequently the garment was covered in mould.[86] On the back of the Coat they found red and purple silk cloth that was not original to the Coat. The committee's report on the origins of the Coat relied heavily on an analysis of this previously unstudied silk cloth that lined part of the relic.

Korum, who was preparing for the 1891 pilgrimage, wanted to restore the garment. For help, he turned to the Arme Kinde Jesu sisters in Simpelveld. Dr. Franz Bock, from Aachen, recommended the restoration work of the Simpelveld nuns, especially Sister Francisca (Anna Maria Lauffs), because he was impressed with their work on the Aachen and Cornelimünster relics.[87] The sisters previously restored medieval vestments and also had experience improving antique garments. Korum, and members of the Domkapitel, oversaw the restoration between 6 and 13 August 1891. The Simpelveld sisters used alcohol to slowly clear away the mould.[88] All encounters with the Coat were recorded, even when there was no apparent change to the relic. Thus when cathedral architect Wirtz traced the silk bird pattern onto glass for analysis, Korum and company acknowledged and approved the procedure.[89]

Restoration proceeded with caution. The sisters used glue to stabilize the fabric, but only tested a little bit at first and left it overnight. After it was found to work well, they continued with the application to the whole Coat. The 1891 preservation hardened the textile surface and dulled the colour of the relic, giving it a brown appearance.[90] The leading sisters, Francisca and Maria Athanasia (Clara Pick), noted large cracks in the fabric, which they thought came from how the Coat was folded and stored. They used brown string to repair this damage.[91] Sister Francisca warned Korum that if they did not come up with a better way to store the garment, the next time they opened the altar they would find only dust.[92] Accordingly, the bishop hired Stuttgart-based Epple und Egge to design a wooden shrine to help preserve the relic.

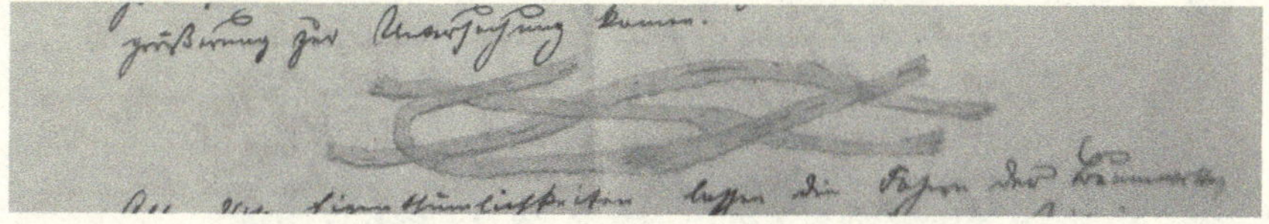

Figure 6.2. Drawing of the cotton fibres included in Schaffhansen's report.
Source: BATr, Abt. 91, Nr. 244, 11.

The new case was sufficiently large to let the Coat lie flat while being shown to pilgrims.[93]

That same year, Bishop Korum commissioned experts to analyse the garment, including Wilmowsky, an antiquities expert; Fischbach, a "connoisseur" of ancient fabric; Dr. Bock, who studied the cloth in an attempt to date the fabric; and a chemist from Mülheim, who used a microscope and chemical analysis to ascertain the material of the relic.[94] In addition, the bishop had seven particles of cloth removed and sent to Dr. J. Herzfeld for analysis, including parts from the relic itself, the inserted fabric on the back of the relic, the shoulder of the undergarment on the left arm, the upper shroud, the gauze on the back, patterned fabric from the front containing images of birds, and a bead from the front of the relic.[95] While the Coat was theologically a symbol of church unity, the garment itself was subjected to clerical dissection in order to verify its merit as a theological symbol.[96]

The test and examination results were inconclusive. Wilmowsky simply stated that the "design makes it clear that it belongs to an early date."[97] On 5 October 1891, Professor Dr. Hermann Schaffhansen, a physician from Honnef am Rhein, examined two pieces of fabric from the right shoulder of the Coat with a microscope.[98] He measured the two pieces of fabric and attempted to determine what material the Coat was made from and whether or not the spots on the relic were human blood. In his report to Trier, he concluded that the fibres from this part of the relic were cotton, thereby ruling out silk and wool. He also wrote, "After earlier experience in the investigation of old, dried blood, I must declare that the cotton fibers were most probably stained with human blood. Only if the study was repeated perhaps [would I] be able to argue this judgment more certainly."[99] Repeated analyses here took the place of scripture and tradition as the basis for determining authenticity.

Clerics turned to professors and physicians, Catholic and non-Catholic, as potential corroborators in the enquiry into authenticity. One month after Wilmowsky's examination, on 19 November 1891, Dr. Grisar, also a physician, submitted his report on silk and cotton fibres

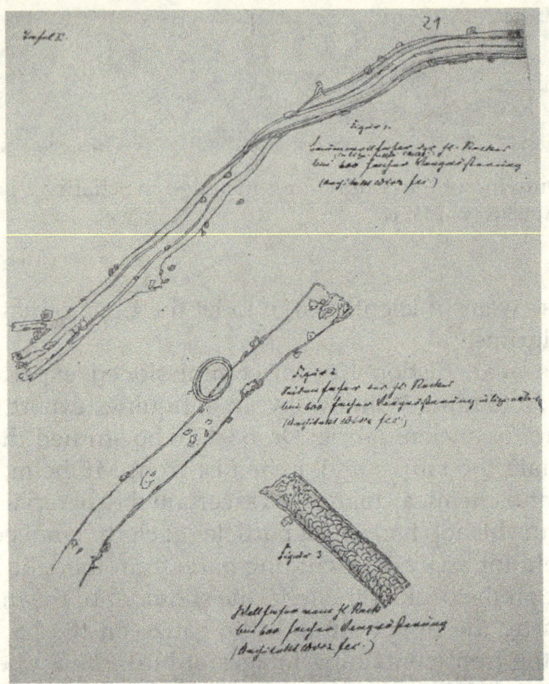

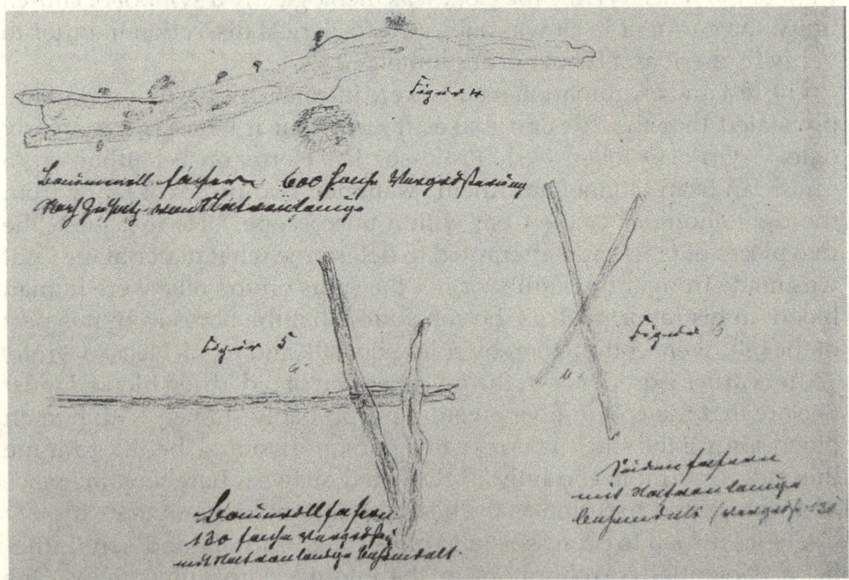

Figures 6.3 and 6.4. Drawing of fibres included in Grisar's report.
Source: BATr, Abt. 91, Nr. 244, 21–2.

from the Coat. These threads also came from the back of the Coat, from the same area of the garment that Schaffhansen drew his samples.[100] Grisar used a microscope and worked from 6 to 15 November on analysing the Coat's material. He noted that after scrutinizing the magnified cloth, he immediately recognized the brown material as cotton.[101] However, he was not willing to hazard a definitive conclusion about the origins of the garment. He made no comment about the possibility of bloodstains.

There were several other experiments and inquiries about the Coat. Father Dressel boiled Holy Coat fibres and exposed them to a zinc-chloride solution after looking at them under magnification.[102] Korum sought further assistance from academics. For example, he wrote to Professor Neumann in Vienna to enquire about Jewish clothing in the first century. Neumann, in turn, referred Korum to an "Orient expert" in Budapest.[103] The Trier bishop also consulted a Talmud scholar in Metz about Hebrew references to silk and cloth in the Mishnah and Talmud.[104] The significance of these investigations lies not in the findings, but in the great effort Trier church authorities expended to scientifically demonstrate the origins and consistency of the Coat.

Together, Korum, with Dompropst Scheuffgen, Domdechant de Lorenzi, and those present at the opening of the reliquary – Mayor Wirtz, and Meurer, H. Feiten, Ditscheid, Lager, Schnütgen, Nys, and Beissel, all experts or clerics – issued an analysis of the relic. Even with the mould it was possible for them to draw some conclusions from the garment "with absolute certainty."[105] The Coat, they noted, consisted of three layers: an outer fabric, silk, and gauze. The patterned silk, containing images of birds in yellow and purple, originated in the Orient sometime between the sixth and ninth centuries, though they did not explain how they arrived at this range of dates. But they confidently stated that during the physical examination they found nothing to contradict the traditions of the Trier church regarding the relic and its history: "The investigation has revealed nothing at variance with the time-honoured traditions of the Church of Trier."[106]

Richard Clarke interpreted the findings of the Bishop's Committee as firm evidence that the garment was indeed the Holy Coat of Jesus. Clarke was not concerned about the specific date; the antiquity of the cloth was sufficient evidence that the Coat was esteemed in ancient times and that it had to be protected from being cut up for relics.[107] Yet, unlike 1844 pamphleteers, 1890s commentators were wary of stating absolute surety. Clarke wrote, "It is quite obvious we cannot expect mathematical certainty."[108] Still there was a "practical certainty" he found convincing, because "the Holy Coat was treated as a relic of very special value as early as the fifth or sixth century, and was even at that time in danger of falling to pieces from its age."[109] In other words, the Bishop's Committee had dated the Coat back far enough for Clarke to consider the relic authentic.

Father C.J. Libertz in Olzheim in 1891 undertook a "biblical-archaeological investigation of the material and colour of the John 19:23 garment."[110] Libertz concentrated on biblical lexicons and commentaries to contend that Jesus's garment, as it appeared in scripture, was likely the Trier relic. Libertz outlined a number of tentative parallels throughout texts, but his argument rested primarily on two pillars: the transfiguration and Jesus's garment in the book of Revelation. Clergy must remember that, for all his other titles, Jesus was the new Adam, a king who established a new kingdom and religion. Jesus, though poor, did not dress as a pauper. His clothes were priestly garments, demonstrated by the fact that Jesus was anointed with oil.

Libertz next turned to the transfiguration in Matthew and Mark. He cited both passages. First, Matthew 17:1–3: "After six days Jesus took with him Peter, James and John the brother of James, and led them up a high mountain by themselves. There he was transfigured before them. His face shone like the sun, and his clothes became as white as the light. Just then there appeared before them Moses and Elijah, talking with Jesus." Then further emphasized in Mark 9:2–4: "After six days Jesus took Peter, James and John with him and led them up a high mountain, where they were all alone. There he was transfigured before them. His clothes became dazzling white, whiter than anyone in the world could bleach them. And there appeared before them Elijah and Moses, who were talking with Jesus." This encounter, during which Jesus's clothes are especially named as part of the transfiguration, revealed the extraordinary role of the Coat during Jesus's ministry.

As further evidence of the relic's special role in the Gospel, Libertz pointed to the baptism of Jesus by John, during which Jesus would have worn his Coat. Furthermore, Libertz continued, Jesus appeared in John's apocalypse with the Coat from his crucifixion. He also cited Revelation 19:13: "He [Jesus] is dressed in a robe dipped in blood, and his name is the Word of God." The reference to Jesus's blood-soaked garment in the apocalypse suggested that the Coat possessed a significance outside of time and would remain important to Christ's followers until the eschaton, the end of history.[111] Bishop Korum and the Domkapitel approved of Libertz's writings. Indeed, the bishop read Libertz's report with joy.[112] Yet even here, where Libertz turned back to scripture-based arguments like 1844 pamphleteers, he couched it in the language of a "biblical-archaeological" analysis.

Figure 6.5. St. Helena bringing the Trier Coat into the city, ivory tablet.[113]
Source: BATr, Abt. 100 Nr. 0004, Bd 3.

Edward Plater openly addressed the authenticity question by emphasizing the archaeological evidence for the Coat. For Plater, authenticity was centred on two arguments: the archaeological origins of an ivory tablet, and the now-familiar position that other garments that claimed to be the Holy Coat were not the same as the Coat located in Trier. Plater argued that an ivory tablet was the missing piece of evidence needed to assert the genuineness of the Coat. In 1836, Plater's tablet appeared in a private collection in Antwerp. Archaeologists in Frankfurt analysed the object ten years later, in 1846, and concluded that it was carved no earlier than the fourth century and no later than the ninth. The tablet measured 10.25 by 5.5 inches, and Plater concluded that it was part of a larger piece of ivory mentioned in an account of the 1512 pilgrimage. Unfortunately, the Trier church lost the reliquary at some point in the early modern period and Plater could not test his theory.[114]

Plater maintained that the bas-relief of a procession linked the Holy Coat to the fourth century. The female figure depicted at the entrance of the temple and holding a cross was the Empress Helena. The empress extended her hand to welcome the oncoming pilgrimage, which ends with a large horse-drawn cart. Behind Helena, Catholics were building the cathedral of Trier to house the faithful and their new relics. Above Saints Sylvester and Agritius, Jesus's head is depicted; his presence indicated that the relics being brought to Trier were truly his former possessions. Finally, Plater stated that the architecture of the scene implied that it was Trier. The building in the background "with arches, columns, and cornice (much in the style and proportions of the Porta Nigra at Trier, which indeed it strikingly suggests)."[115]

For Plater, the tablet filled in the scant documentary evidence of the history and origins of the Coat. This ivory carving now resides in the Trier Cathedral Museum, and the church no longer considers it to be related to the Trier Coat.[116] Recently, Prof. Dr. Wolfgang Schmid concluded that the relief came from Byzantium, not from Trier. "Although the building is reminiscent of the Porta Nigra and you think the Empress with the cross is Helena, mother of Constantine, who according to legend has given several relics to Trier, the ivory tablet makes no reference to Trier."[117]

Following the official 1890 investigation and restoration of the Holy Coat, Trier clergy adopted a flexible position on authenticity: since the Council of Trent, relic veneration had not been an article of Catholic faith. This vague approach left considerable room for interpretation. Plater made no appeal to fate, destiny, God's will, or divine intervention in relating the story of the tablet. He laid out his argument, but, like the other 1890s scientific reports, he did not conclude that it alone proved the Coat was authentic. Rather, the tablet was only one piece of the puzzle. It helped to establish that the Helena legend had precedence, possibly as early as the fourth century. Plater's ivory tablet argument, Leibertz's "biblical-archaeological investigation," and Korum's consultation of European experts on antiquity reveal how clergy looked beyond traditional sources for verification of the sacred.

Speaking Past Pilgrims: A Question of Reception

In late April 1925, parents complained to the Aachen canons that the religious instruction teacher, Neuss, told their children that the Aachen relics were not authentic.[118] The parents grumbled that there was already enough confusion in the world and that Neuss was undermining the religious lives of their sons. They further noted that telling children they did not have to believe in the relics was un-pedagogical. They called on the bishop to force Neuss to recant his tactless speech.

In his defence, Neuss asked the bishop whether or not religious instruction was supposed to enlighten students. He protested that he only confirmed church teaching and had not answered completely negatively. The student had specifically asked about the relics after school, and in that context Neuss felt he could speak freely.[119] Although the authenticity of the relics was not an official part of church dogma, Aachen residents took pride in the treasures of Charlemagne and viewed the objects as an important part of Catholic belief.

Nationalistic Catholics understood pilgrimage as part of an ancient German tradition, whether or not the object at the end of the journey was authentic. The *Rheinisch Westfäl. Volksfreund* reported that the Aachen pilgrimage was tied not only to Charlemagne, but also to the legacy of St. Bonifacius and the establishment of Central Europe as the Holy Roman Empire.[120] Futhermore, Pope Leo III consecrated the Aachen cathedral in 804, and Pope Leo X approved the Aachen pilgrimage in 1530, making the journey as important as travelling to Rome or Jerusalem. Here the central figures are not Jesus, Mary, or John the Baptist, but the Christian founders of "Germany." In 1925, Dr. Felix Brüll also saw pilgrimage to Aachen as part of early German history: "We see already the ancient Germans on the trek … in their future and current home country, in Gaul, Italy, and Hispania."[121] Brüll thus equated pilgrimage with German military expansion into the rest of Western Europe.

The pilgrims to Aachen and Trier had their own rubrics for authenticity and resisted qualifications for relic origins and credibility after the 1890s analyses.[122] In an anonymous prayer three weeks before the start of the 1925 pilgrimage, one Catholic linked the veracity of the Aachen relics to German ascendancy. The prayer asked God to strengthen the city; to show His power by healing pilgrims; and to give the poor security, the sinner new life, and the bereaved consolation. Here authenticity was guaranteed by results: comfort, increase in attendance, and healing. Similarly, Catholic pamphleteers pointed to the results of the pilgrimage as evidence for the authenticity of the relics. If thousands of people took to the roads and numerous bodies had been transformed, then obviously the items in Aachen or Trier had a link with the divine. Even after the 1890s investigations, these "fruits of the pilgrimage" arguments perpetuated Marx and Hommer's use of historical common sense to explain relic origins.

In his *Pilgrim Guide*, W.v.d. Fuhr included a chapter on the authenticity of the Aachen relics. For Fuhr, two interdependent arguments support the origin of the Aachen relics in the first century. First, Charlemagne was highly intelligent and would not have been fooled into acquiring a fake relic. Fuhr asked the 1895 pilgrims, "Would King Charlemagne, this deliberate monarch, call upon a relic, without confirming the authenticity with the popes, bishops, and princes from whom he received it?"[123] Clearly not. As further evidence for this point, Fuhr looked to the 813 Council of Mainz, which affirmed Charlemagne's practice of allowing only the laity to honour those relics that ecclesiastical authorities affirmed as worthy of veneration.[124]

In addition, historical contingencies had destroyed definitive paper evidence of the origins of the four Aachen relics. Instead pilgrims had to trust in Charlemagne's good judgment. Following Charlemagne's death, the Carolingians and their successors failed to protect Aachen's documents. In 881, the Normans turned Charlemagne's cathedral into a stable and burned the palace and churches. Later, Aachen suffered fires in 1146, 1224, and a cathedral fire in 1236. However, these were not nearly as bad as the 1656 fire that once again burned the churches, 4,660 houses, and the council and alderman archives.[125] War and violence in the past meant that it was unreasonable of critics to expect an unbroken documentary genealogy of Rhineland relics. Authors like Fuhr and Brüll emphasized a continuity of practice as a partial explanation of relic legitimacy.

Between 1895 and 1925 the Catholic press increasingly linked pilgrimage to German identity. In 1925, much like Brüll's Gauls of the past, Germans continued to make pilgrimages across Europe – to Kevelaer, southern France, Spain, Switzerland, Rome, and even Jerusalem.[126] That same year, the Aachen clergy sent out a flurry of press releases to German newspapers that included potential articles for publication. In "Die Aachener Heiligtümer!" clerics addressed the question of authenticity by stressing Charlemagne's relations to the Byzantine Empire and his desire to set up Aachen as a holy city on par with Rome and Constantinople.[127] Charlemagne had good connections for relics; he was close ("dear friends") with Pope Hadrian (772–95) and Leo III (795–816).[128] Charlemagne received gifts from the rulers of Persia and Baghdad, helped the Patriarch of Jerusalem, and had connections in the east.

Because of his prestige, world leaders sent the Aachen emperor Christian relics. Both Charles the Bald and Charles the Fat reported that Charlemagne collected relics, although these official Aachen press releases again pointed to the fires and sackings of the city that destroyed definitive records of the emperor's holdings. Here, importantly, the point of the article was not to offer incontrovertible proof, but to explain the possibility of historical authenticity to the public: "So long as one is not able to bring in evidence to the contrary, [they] should not and must not revile and despise the faith of pious Catholics."[129]

Also in 1925, Cardinal Schulte, from Cologne, addressed the merit of the relics during the opening ceremony of the Aachen pilgrimage.

Schulte adopted a cautious position on authenticity. The cardinal stressed that no one could completely discount the relics, even though reliable historical sources went back only to the eighth and ninth centuries.[130] Like interpersonal relationships, commerce, and civic life, relics required faith, "especially with our relics, which do not first originate from the uncritical period of the crusades, for our relics, which we have inherited from our spiritually and morally healthy German ancestors of the earliest time."[131] For Schulte, turning to relics required no more trust than what was required to overpay for an item and then to expect correct change in return.

Schulte advised that Catholics should look to the thousand years of Germans venerating the Aachen relics and depend on the reliability of their German forefathers. After all, experts had not demonstrated that the four cloth items were illegitimate, so pilgrims should carry on as they had in the past. Though Schulte mentioned Paul's garment healing in the Acts of the Apostles, Catholic history should be enough to settle the authenticity debate.

In Saxony, in 1930, the authenticity of the Aachen relics remained a point of contention between Protestants and Catholics. Aachen clergy supported harangued Catholic teachers by promising to send more information about the relics. Teachers were also told to consult Cardinal Schulte's opening homily from 1925, the 1925 *Pilgrim Book*, and Dr. Schiffer's work on the cultural history of the Marian Shrine.[132] Aachen clergy further offered the encouragement that "Viennese academics" were making a pilgrimage to Aachen, ostensibly to show that the journey was respectable among the *Bürgertum*. Finally, for a quick counter-offensive, teachers could remind Protestants that they held Luther's personal items in the Wartburg as venerable, so why should the Aachen shrine be different?

The question of relic authenticity did not wane between 1832 and 1937 but resurfaced with each successive pilgrimage. By 1937, articles like "Are the Relics authentic?" and "What the Carolingian Period Reports on the Aachen Relics" continued to appear in the Catholic press.[133] The *Ketteler-Feuer*, based in Munich, reported, "The authenticity [of the relics] was based on human, but credible, evidence."[134] For the *Ketteler-Feuer* author, the evidence in favour of authentic relics was overwhelming. Although the original Charlemagne documents had been lost to time, there was the fact that Alcuin, one of Charlemagne's counsellors, suggested that the emperor was interested in assembling relics. The writer noted Angilbert's 799 report that Aachen was gathering relics from around the world. Charlemagne had personal relationships with Popes Hadrian I and Leo III; thus "we can conclude that these two popes gave Charlemagne valuable, authentic relics as gifts."[135] There was also the Georg Rauschen legend of Charlemagne from the eleventh or twelfth century and the Albrici Chronicle of 1238 that suggested Charlemagne had acquired one or more of the Aachen relics. Even with this array of evidence, the author hesitated to draw definitive conclusions: "One can make of the authenticity of the relics what one wants."[136] However, the author suggests that to say the objects were forgeries was to countermand the beliefs of bishops, saints, cardinals, and thousands of pilgrims.[137]

For 1930s church leaders, authenticity meant a link to German forefathers, which was more historically secure than demonstrating that the relics originated in the first century. Clergy continued to respond to their circumstances with new justifications for pilgrimage. In 1937, the Aachen general press release announcing the upcoming pilgrimage referred newspaper readers interested in the authenticity of the Aachen relics to the work of Dr. Schiffers on the topic.[138] As additional evidence, though, the release reminded readers that, since 1239, the relics had been on display every seven years and had rested in Aachen since Charlemagne's lifetime.[139] *Der Johannesbote* in Schneidemühl printed the official release, which relied on Schiffers and Klinkenberg to offer tentative explanations for the origins of the relics, but conceded, "Our generation has become more critical, due to the intellectual development of the last centuries, than the strong belief [of the] Middle Ages."[140] The *Der Johannesbote* authors further highlighted even older sources to argue that Emperor Leo I moved Mary's relic from Galilee to Constantinople in the fifth century.[141]

Yet there was an important distinction made in 1937: "We venerate these relics because they are the sacred inheritance of our fathers, and saw the most important part of German history over a thousand years. Our generation is not ashamed of the past: by holding high the religious legacy of their fathers and forefathers it only fulfills a loving duty of high respect and gratitude."[142] The relics were certainly old, but, more importantly, were part of ancient German religious practices and therefore deserved respect and honour. In other words, to venerate the Aachen relics aligned with new National Socialist emphases on Germanic tradition and rootedness.

Also in the 1930s, the Nazis challenged Rhenish clerics' version of German pre-history. Nazis appealed to *Urgeschichte* and the ancient origins of Germanic tribes as a new foundational myth for German society. Catholic leaders claimed primacy to ancient Germania by aligning their relics with the first German king, Charlemagne. Rhenish pilgrims worked to firmly anchor Charlemagne to themselves, even as National

Socialists strove to parallel their own policies with Charlemagne.[143] Gauleiter Staatsrat Grohé explained in the *Westdeutscher Beobachter* in 1937 that every German citizen has religious freedom, so long as it is not anti-German. However, Grohé protested the Catholic Church co-opting Charlemagne for its own purposes. Charlemagne wanted a large German Reich and achieved his goal via warfare; without conflict his Reich would have been untenable. Like Hitler, Charlemagne had lifted the Germanic race out of selfishness and particularism.[144]

Grohé reminded Catholics that Catholic bishops had to humble themselves before Charlemagne and walk underneath his throne. Similarly, the 1937 church should accept the new regime and not worry about "concerned papal encyclicals."[145] Charlemagne was German, not Catholic. He gave the months German names, assembled Germanic hero songs, and created the laws of a German Reich. To counter this Nazi claim to Charlemagne's legacy, clergy fell back on 1840s arguments on the historical origins of their relics. They returned to common sense historical explanations to contend that Catholics, not Nazis, had the only legitimate claim to the founder of the first Reich.

Conclusion

Relic authenticity continued to fascinate Germans after the Third Reich. Following the 1959 Trier pilgrimage, Erwin Iserloh weighed the surviving written evidence and concluded that the Coat could not be a garment that Jesus actually wore. Nevertheless, he urged Catholics to view the cloth as a symbol of unity and of Jesus. Pilgrimage allowed Catholics to realize their "historical existence." The Coat made it possible for the faithful to seek "the unity of love in communion with our [Christian] brothers."[146]

In 1995, as part of preparation for the 1996 pilgrimage, textile conservationist Mechthild Flury-Lemberg wrote about her encounter with the Coat in the 1970s, when the cathedral was being renovated, and offered an analysis of the Coat's fabrics. Flury-Lemberg described a textile "sandwich" composed of seven different material layers on the backside of the Coat:[147] red-brown silk (1891); brownish fabric (1890); fine silk gauze; a felt layer; greenish taffeta; a felt layer; and silk gauze.

Flury-Lemberg hypothesized three unique stages in the life of the Coat: an original garment, which was later reinforced with a liturgical tunic from the sixteenth century, and a final layer of brown fabric. All layers were coated with a preservative in 1890–1. Ultimately, though, Flury-Lemberg conceded that "an analysis from the Coat's present conditions can do little more than guess."[148]

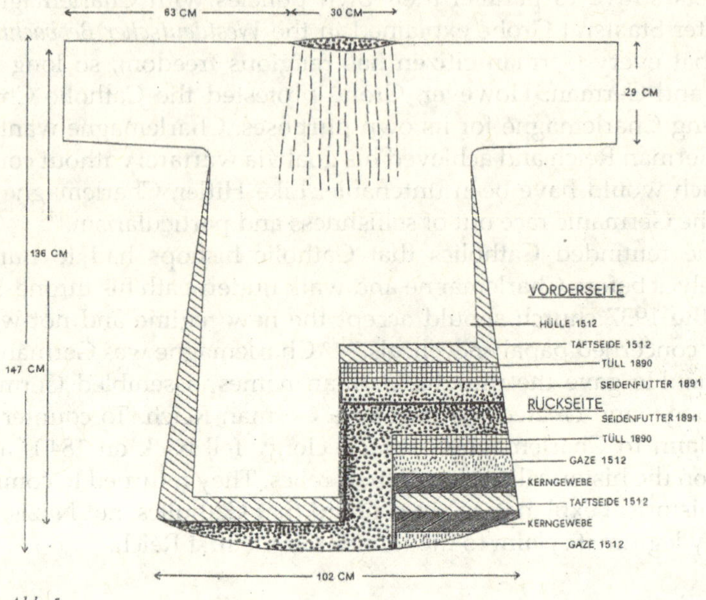

Abb. 5
Die Gewebeschichten des Heiligen Rockes.

Figure 6.6. Mechthild Flury-Lemberg's Coat layers diagram.
Source: Mechthild Flury-Lemberg, "Das Reliquiar," 696. Reprint courtesy of Paulinus Verlag.

Finally, during the 2012 Trier pilgrimage, one of Flury-Lemburg's students, textile archaeologist Regula Schorta, gave an interview with *Paulinus*, the daily pilgrimage newspaper. Dr. Schorta explained that she felt very privileged to view the Coat in the 1980s when Flury-Lemburg participated in an inspection of the relic.[149] In the course of the interview, the closest Schorta came to an evaluation of the genuineness of the garment was a rhetorical comment: "We must carefully distinguish findings and interpretation. Often the latter is obvious, seems clearer, but caution is appropriate. The Holy Robe is a robe, sure. But was the robe ever worn by a human? Is that what we have before us today? Perhaps, more likely, the image of a garment? Sometimes textile technology can give factual answers to even very basic questions. Ideally, we can give a 'biography to an object.'"[150] Even after the 1890–1 investigations, definitive answers regarding the Trier Coat's textile composition remain contentious.

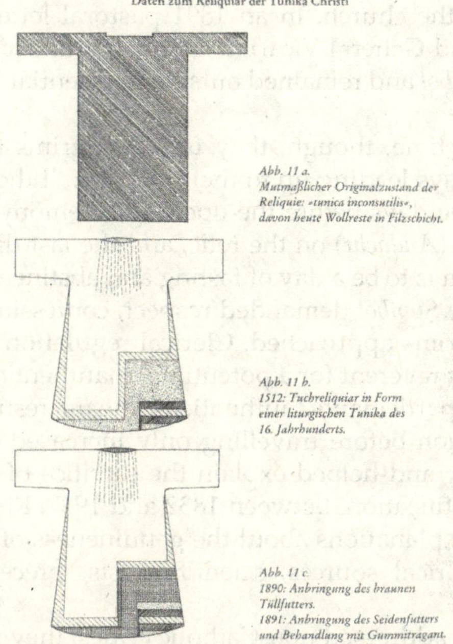

Figure 6.7. Mechthild Flury-Lemberg's three-stage theory.
Source: Mechthild Flury-Lemberg, "Das Reliquiar," 708. Reprint courtesy of Paulinus Verlag.

By the mid-twentieth century, pilgrims to Trier and Aachen encountered a cacophony of opinions about the origins and composition of relics. In a draft article for the pilgrims travelling from Basel in 1933, Ernst Wimmers, who worked with the Trier Pilgrimage Committee to coordinate trips out of Switzerland, stated, "The garment is … as worn by the inhabitants of Palestine during the time of Christ, unadorned, 1.48 [metres] long, below 1.09 wide, above 0.70, a simple design with short wide sleeves. The Holy Coat hangs on a rod in a specially created purpose box, which is stored in a cabinet in a fixed iron vault."[151] Not only were the measurements and style historically accurate, but the relic was stored in a space beyond tampering, suggesting that it could not be switched out or stolen. The early modern forms of establishing authenticity continued among the laity were not subsumed by historical contingency, fibre analyses, and microscopes.

Over and over, priests reminded pilgrims that relics were not part of Catholic orthodoxy. Pilgrims need not subscribe to the belief that the Trier Coat and Marian Shrine relics were authentic to be in good standing with the church. In an 1891 pastoral letter, Bishop Korum, Dr. Willems, and General Vicariate Henke reminded pilgrims that the Coat was a *Symbol* and remained outside of essential Catholic teachings and beliefs.

At the same time, though, they urged pilgrims to discipline their bodies in the days leading up to their journey: "I therefore decree that during the three days before the opening ceremony Catholics should pray and think (*Andacht*) on the relic, and the last day before the start of the exhibition is to be a day of fasting and abstinence throughout the diocese."[152] The *Symbol* demanded respect, confession, and the Eucharist before pilgrims approached. Clerical regulation of the pilgrimage sacraments was reverent for a potentially inauthentic relic.

For pilgrim participants, authenticity meant results: healing, help, relief. Purification before travelling only increased the import of the pilgrim journey and helped explain the sacrifice of the pilgrimage as a spiritual sanctification. Between 1832 and 1937, Rhineland clerics offered myriad explanations about the genuineness of Aachen and Trier treasures: historical sources, scientific tests, precedent, national or Catholic pride.

When clerics addressed non-Catholic critics, they ran the risk of losing touch with the religious aspirations of actual pilgrims. Thus, by the 1930s, faced with the Nazi conquest of the past and newspapers perpetuating the early nineteenth-century narratives that linked the Aachen Marian Shrine to Charlemagne and the Trier Coat to Helena and Constantine, the officials backed off. Rather than risking decoupling the laity from pilgrimage, officials once again embraced the *Zeitgeist* and linked pilgrimage to ancient Germanic practices, thereby once more expanding the base of acceptable truth to include an old argument with new significance.

Conclusion: Verifying Presence

When Frau Anna Maria Wagner arrived in Trier, she had been sick for four years. Her troubles began when she was thirty-three years old and first noticed a growing discomfort in her left lower jaw. The pain developed into a large, red, and inflamed tumour that stretched from her throat to her left eye. She could not sleep because of the constant pain. The people around Wagner tried to help her and offered a number of home remedies, but these brought no relief. One morning her tumour ruptured and a "bloody material flowed unceasingly out of her mouth and even in her throat."[1] Afterwards, Wagner stopped bleeding in her mouth, but the exterior wound refused to close. Nearly every hour she had to change the bandages on her face, which were soaked with alternatively white, then yellowish fluid flecked with blood. The open tumour continued to expand until finally she visited the district physician, Dr. Wieler from Lützerath. Dr. Wieler, however, was unable to help her with the wound.

So on 20 August 1844, Anna Maria and her husband began their pilgrimage to Trier. They hoped that the Holy Coat would restore what Dr. Wieler could not heal. When they neared the bridge over the Mosel River, Anna Maria drew to the back of the procession because she did not want to bring undue attention to her face. In the Trier cathedral she removed her facial veil and used her handkerchief to keep the wound dry. When Anna Maria came before the Coat, she angled the tumour so that it faced the relic. She also touched an *Andenken* to the Coat before exiting the church. She did not know that Bishop Arnoldi allowed the sick to directly touch the Holy Coat. Outside she was disappointed to find that the tumour persisted.

She covered the open wound once again, but before she did so she placed the *Andenken* against her mangled cheek. When Anna Maria got home, her bandages were dry and her face was restored. She was healed. Anna Maria was healed by her proximity to the relic, by the *direct* contact of sacred presence – contained within the Holy Coat *Andenken* – with the open tumour on the side of her face. For four unsuccessful years Anna Maria Wagner sought a remedy in both homemade medicine and with the district physician. Only the sacred centre of Trier restored her face to its former health.

By the time of the next Trier pilgrimage in 1891, Wagner's corroborating evidence would have been insufficient to confirm a miraculous healing. Her story appeared in an anonymous pamphlet as one of twenty-three miraculous cases of healing. The author did not have an imprimatur indicating church approval for the publication. But the writer did offer readers two witnesses to Wagner's recovery. The first was Anna Maria's husband, Mathias Steffens; the second was listed as the "wife of Caspar Benz," Margaretha Benz. Neither Margaretha nor Mathias would have qualified as members of Bishop Korum's 1891 panel of experts who reviewed miracle claims over the course of three years. They did not have the requisite expertise or standing in society to pronounce judgment on whether Wagner's cure was authentic.

In 1894, Korum shielded the church from pilgrimage criticism by adopting a conservative definition of the miraculous. Previously pilgrims like Anna Maria had to account only for the pains in their bodies. This difference in orientation – Anna Maria looking to the Coat for internal help with her tumour and pus-ridden throat as Korum looked outward to potential critics and backward to Gildemeister and Ronge – laid the foundation for two diverging discourses about the divine presence within the Rhineland sacred objects.

After the internal and external critiques of pilgrimage in 1844, German Catholics developed distinct rubrics for assessing the authenticity of Rhineland relics. In this book, I have linked these two standards to the attendees (pilgrims) and coordinators (clergy) of Rhineland pilgrimages. Following Ronge's call to sever spiritual and financial ties with Rome, and his criticisms of pilgrimage and Trier Bishop Arnoldi – the "blind tool" of the papacy – clergy worked to reframe what pilgrims said about relics and restricted their access to sacred objects.[2] After 1844, clerics described relics as symbols of German unity or Catholic religious practice, or as physical reminders of how Catholicism formed European civilization through Constantine and Charlemagne.

Instead of publicly proclaiming miracles as they occurred, the clergy urged caution in claims about the divine presence within relics.[3] In official pamphlets, newspaper articles, and their homilies, clerics offered Rhineland relics as important traditions, regardless of their authenticity. Yet the scientific examinations, medical forms, and textual analyses never satisfied staunch opponents. Critics continued to disparage Catholic claims about the sacred and relics well into the 1930s. Church leaders did succeed, however, in placing obstacles between pilgrims and relics. Pilgrims sought unmediated access to divine presence, but pilgrimage coordinators scheduled time with the relic and in the cathedral and they ensured that no pilgrim paused for too long in front of relics.

While clergy focused on the methods of pilgrimage and relic detractors, pilgrim participants continued to pursue divine presence, especially in the realms of *Andenken* and miracle culture.[4] Pilgrims saw their bodies and their landscapes as porous, open to the possibility of God intervening in the world by changing their corporeal composition or earthly condition.[5] After 1844, pilgrims continued to dwell on the four Aachen relics and the Holy Coat of Trier as sacred sites. In the relics, pilgrims found a place where heaven and earth met.[6] They resisted restrictions placed on access to relics by church authorities.

Pilgrims travelled for many different reasons. In their correspondence they emphasized the highly personal nature of their expectations in Aachen and Trier. They addressed their personal lives and immediate concerns in their correspondence.[7] Pilgrim correspondents saw their bodies and lives in terms of these sacred encounters, not as political or symbolic acts. Aachen and Trier pilgrims created and crossed sacred places, dwelled at the relics, then travelled back home. They demarcated the boundaries between holy and profane with their actions, in singing, praying, and processing.

As they sought a connection to the first-century Holy Family, pilgrims incorporated elements of modernity in approaching the sacred centre. They filled out medical questionnaires (*Fragebogen*) in order to visit relics while infirm, wrote songs, and prayed for divine intervention through the relics. Pilgrims to Aachen and Trier adapted to changes in medical care and included increasingly sophisticated descriptions of their ailments. But they did not see advances in science as undermining their sacred practices. Trains and automobiles meant more pilgrims could get to the cities; pilgrims trekked to these foci of presence in increasing numbers between 1832 and 1937; they travelled circular paths in pursuit of the transcendent.

Rhineland clergy looked for a path between orthodoxy and accommodation with new understandings of history and nature. They fixated on questions of relic authenticity (*Echtheit*) after 1844, when Johannes Ronge declared the Trier Coat a representation of clerical greed, and Gildemeister and Sybel labelled the Coat a fraudulent object. In response to claims that venerating relics was superstitious, medieval, and backward, the clergy sought accommodation with their critics.[8] By expanding the evidence for relics and miracles to include rationalistic explanations, they cut their own path into the nineteenth century. Clerics strove to fuse the methodology of their opponents with sacred practices. They turned outward, away from pilgrims, and developed new defences of both relics and popular pilgrimage practices. These included using naturalistic scientific tests, consulting experts in history and archaeology to verify the origins of their sacred objects, and working closely with medical practitioners on elaborate certificates to demonstrate the incurability of sick pilgrims.

Rhineland pilgrims traversed the border of secularization in German and European society before the Second World War. While the Rhenish pilgrimages of the nineteenth century have often been linked to the growth and organization of political Catholicism, this was only one part of the story. Historians have shown that weekly attendance in both Protestant and Catholic services declined over the nineteenth century, but this statistical presentation does not encompass the full range of European religious practices. In Aachen and Trier, Catholic men came for healing, wanted their clubs (*Vereine*) publicly represented in processions, and volunteered to guard sacred objects.

Pilgrim practices persisted and show remarkable continuity between 1832 and 1937, as participants at both ends of the century relied on tradition and established sacred events to orient themselves in the world.[9] German regimes could not provide all letter-writers with work, the military could not protect their sons, and textile factories could not manufacture authentic relic silk for Rhinelanders. Physicians and pharmacists could not cure the diverse ailments of pilgrims. In response to these perceived failings of science, the state, and society, pilgrims drew close to sites of sacred presence. Relics prompted Rhinelanders to move and act: to touch them, to write about them, to visit them, to sing and pray towards them, to cross landscapes, to create sacred place. By leaving their homes in pursuit of a relic encounter, pilgrims moved against assumptions about their agency, their gender, and their social class.

Together the pilgrim travellers and the pilgrimage organizers offer new insights into the role of German Catholic leadership through the nineteenth and into the twentieth centuries. Here clergy courted new research methodologies to better explain their faith to a sceptical audience. They acted as taste-makers, agents of modernization, and arbiters of divine presence. *Wissenschaft* was a sword that could cut two ways. Certainly, sceptics like Sybel and Gildemeister could deploy research to mock Trier and the "twenty other coats." But clerical supporters of the

Trier relic could also consult experts to show that the very fibres of the Holy Coat originated in the first century.

As an aggregate, the Aachen and Trier travellers and correspondents indicate that those engaged in public Catholicism were less feminized, less lower class, and less controlled by the episcopate than we might assume when examining weekly Mass attendance and the development of political Catholicism. Throughout this book I have sought to let the voices of Aachen and Trier explain their practices and beliefs. The cure-seekers described their bodies as sites where God might, through the physical relics retained by the church, enact rapid change. Even as *Andenken* were mass-produced, travellers and non-travellers infused them with existential meaning and hope. And *Andenken* correspondents from Brazil, the United States, and beyond pointed to exactly why they needed an object that was in close proximity to the Marian Shrine and the Holy Coat. Commercialization did not cheapen the value of objects that might cure blindness – or remove a haricot bean – or convert a family member, or provide economic stability. The Holy Coat of Trier and Marian Shrines offered shelter for a wide range of German Catholics through the uncertainties of a volatile century.

Coda

Pilgrim practices and Rhineland relics survived numerous wars and moments of violence since the French Revolution. Aachen and Trier relics were often under threat from foreign armies. In 1792, Trier officials moved the Holy Coat to a fortress, Ehrenbreitstein, to preserve it from French Revolutionary armies. In response to French incursions into the Rhineland, they moved the Coat again in 1795, first to Aschaffenburg, then to Bamberg, and finally on to Augsburg. The Coat did not return to Trier until 1810, when the Duke of Nassau, Frederik William, returned the relic to Trier Bishop Charles Mannay.[10] The popular response to the Coat's return prompted Bishop Mannay to declare the first pilgrimage to Trier of the nineteenth century. It took place from 9 to 27 September 1810. An estimated 227,000 people went to see the Coat.[11]

A century later the French army again entered the Rhineland. On 31 October 1918, Edmund Renard, the Provincial Conservator of the Rhine Province in Bonn, wrote to Trier and Aachen church authorities with a warning.[12] Renard anticipated that Entente soldiers would occupy both Aachen and Trier as part of the Versailles Treaty.[13] Renard wanted to "calm his conscience" by making sure the Aachen and Trier church authorities were not caught unawares.[14] He urged both cities to pack their relics and cathedral treasures immediately so they would be able to respond swiftly.

Even before Renard sent his warning, Aachen officials had implemented plans to move their relics to Paderborn, 250 kilometres northeast. An architect, Professor Buchkremer, worked with the head of the Aachen cathedral treasury, J. Crumbach, and Provost Kaufmann to inventory and pack the Aachen relics. They placed the sacred objects in twenty-nine wooden crates.[15] Charlemagne's bones rested in case twelve and the four Aachen relics went into case thirteen. On the morning of 28 October 1918, Aachen clergy, six workers, and Professor Buchkremer loaded the wooden cases and made an unofficial procession at 8:00 a.m.[16]

To avoid detection, Buchkremer's parade traversed different streets from those of the closing ceremony processions: Ritter-Chorusstraße, Klostergaße, Annastraße, Mörgensgaße, Kasernenstraße, Boxgraben, and Burtscheiderstraße to the train station. Buchkremer and his assistants transported the relics to Paderborn in two train cars and stored them there on the cathedral property.

In the wake of German defeat and occupation, local officials evacuated sacred centres from the Rhineland. Yet Rhineland pilgrimage survived the trauma of the First World War and emerged even more popular. At least a million pilgrims travelled to Aachen's 1925 event and over two million pilgrims went to Trier's 1933 display of the Holy Coat.

Aachen successfully hid and protected their relics through the French Revolution, Napoleon's occupation, the Franco-Prussian War, and the First World War. But the city was not so fortunate during the Second World War. Two months before the outbreak of war, on a Wednesday evening on 5 July 1939, Aachen clergy opened up the Marian Shrine to pray over and inspect the relics.[17] The assembled priests and Professor Buchkremer removed the four relics and then prayed three Our Fathers and an Ave Maria. They wrapped the relics in white and set them back in the thirteenth-century reliquary.[18] The assembled men petitioned Charlemagne, Mary, John the Baptist, and Jesus for protection from possible harm.[19]

Two years after the Marian Shrine prayer meeting, the Allies bombed the Aachen cathedral on 11 July 1941. Through the Second World War, the Aachen cathedral clergy counted six major moments of cathedral destruction. Stained glass, mosaics, and sculptures sat open to the elements. In November 1942 Professor Buchkremer and Msgr. Crumbach again inspected the relics.[20] They found them to be intact but could not reseal the Marian Shrine. Unable to find a new lock for the reliquary, they tied the shrine closed and sealed the knot. The protocol that had ensured the authenticity of the relics for the preceding century was set aside in the face of the unparalleled destruction of the Second World War.

Following this rushed examination, Aachen officials stored the relics in Siegen, Westphalia, alongside other regional treasures.[21] During the Second World War clergy moved the relics underground rather than evacuating them to the east as they had in 1918. The U.S. army eventually found them in a copper mine in 1945 and brought them back to Aachen. When the Aachen cathedral canons opened the reliquary in 1945, they found not only the four relics, but also the 1937 broken padlock, a note reporting the 1939 prayer, and the minutes from the 1942 opening.[22]

For three days, 19–22 July 1945, Aachen clergy displayed the relics, with American Colonel Thomas Alexander Parrot in attendance during the closing ceremony.[23] This brief post-war pilgrimage was called to thank God that the four cathedral relics survived the conflict. Clergy prayed that God would lead them back to an age of freedom "for church and people."[24] But there was no concluding ceremony during which the relics were paraded through the streets. Instead, a choir sang "Ave Maria" and the bishop sealed the relics once more in the Marian Shrine. In 1945, the relics were not shown from the exterior of the cathedral. Bishops from across Germany could not attend. Because they did not have access to fresh silk, they could not produce and distribute *Andenken* with the relic silk to German pilgrims. Aachen Bishop Johannes Joseph van der Velden, Aachen Mayor Dr. Wilhelm Rombach, and the cathedral canons reused the same silk from 1937 to wrap the relics.[25]

Since the rushed 1945 Aachen event, pilgrimages to the Holy Coat and Marian Shrine have continued through today. Pilgrim numbers to Aachen declined after 1945, hitting their lowest point in 1993 with roughly 80,000 attendees.[26] Trier waited until 1959 to again unveil the Holy Coat, drawing a crowd of 1.8 million pilgrims.[27] The following exhibition, in 1996, drew roughly 700,000 pilgrims.[28] In the two most recent exhibitions, in 2012 Trier brought half of a million pilgrims, and in 2014 Aachen drew 125,000 participants. Because of the COVID-19 global pandemic, the 2021 Aachen pilgrimage was rescheduled for 2023. The Rhenish relics continue to draw hundreds of thousands of pilgrims and point to the ongoing allure of pilgrimage, yet the overall postwar Rhineland story is a history of slow but steadily declining pilgrim attendance. Even so, the relics continue to fascinate and to attract people from throughout Germany and the world. Pilgrims and clergy still discuss and debate what these sacred items ultimately represent.

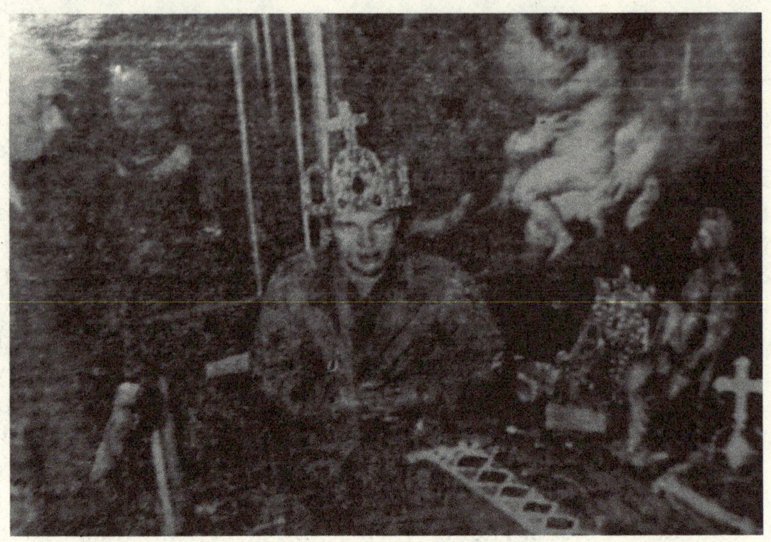

Figure 7.1. American T/5 (technician fifth grade) Edward Fisher wearing a copy of the Vienna imperial crown. The *Mule* reported inaccurately that he was wearing Charlemagne's crown. Today, the crown is with other copies of the imperial insignia in the Krönungssaal of the Aachen Town Hall.
Source: DAA, Domkapitel C 1.7.15 Fotokasten 15, *Mule* 1, no. 10 (18 May 1945).

Figure 7.2. Interior of the Aachen cathedral after the Second World War.
Source: DAA, Domkapitel C 1.7.15 Fotokasten 15.

Figure 7.3. Aachen in ruins after the war. Cathedral in the background.
Source: DAA, Domkapitel C 1.7.15 Fotokasten 15.

Figure 7.4. Soldiers standing outside the Siegen Copper Mine, where the
American Army discovered the Aachen relics.
Source: DAA, Domkapitel C 1.7.15 Fotokasten 15.

Figure 7.5. The Trier and Aachen relics continue to fascinate. Opening ceremony (*Eröffnungsfeier*), Trier, 13 April 2012.
Source: H. Thewalt/Bistum Trier.

Appendix 1. Selected Pilgrim Songs in Translation, 1839–1933

1839

"Begrüssung des Aachener Heiligthums"[1]	"Greeting the Aachen Relics"
Sey, o Heiligthum, gegrüßt,	Be, O Heiligthum, greeted,
Da du jenes Kleinod bist,	Since you are that treasure,
Das aus rein bewährten Quellen	That from pure, established sources
Und von Gott geweihten Stellen	And from God's consecrated places
Glaubensvoll für uns're Stadt	In faith for our city
Kaiser Karl gesammelt hat.	That Charlemagne has collected.
Was nach alter Sagen Spruch	What Mary according to ancient saying
Einst Maria leidend trug,	Once carried in suffering,
Als den Heiland sie geboren,	As she bore the Saviour,
Der vom Vater auserkoren,	Chosen by the Father,
Jenes Kleid bewahrst Du treu,	That garment you keep faithfully,
Jenes Kleid bleibt ewig neu.	That garment remains eternally new.
Sieh, es kam aus fernem Land	Look, it came from a far country
Uns ein anderes Liebespfand,	For us another pledge of love,
Jene dunkelgelbe Binde,	That dark yellow band,
Die dem lieben Jesus-Kinde	Which the lovely Jesus-child
Gegen Sturm und Windsgefahr	Against storm and winds
Einst die erste Rettung war.	Once was the first rescue.

(Continued)

"Begrüssung des Aachener Heiligthums"[1]	"Greeting the Aachen Relics"
Seht Joannes blut'ges Tuch,	Look at John's bloody cloth,
Worin man ihn damals trug,	In which one carried him at the time
Als er für sein treues Streben	As he in his faithful pursuit
hat das Leben hingegeben,	had given up his life,
Und sein Haupt als Preis im Spiel	And his head fell as the prize in the game
Eines schnöden Tanzes fiel.	Of a filthy dance.
Stadt, du hegst noch unversehrt	City, you hold still intact
Jenes Tuch, so hoch verehrt,	That cloth, so highly revered,
Das des Heilands Leib umhüllte,	That enveloped the body of the Saviour
Als er ganz die Schrift erfüllte;	When he completely fulfilled all the scriptures;
Als er leidend für uns starb,	As he died painfully for us,
Und uns ew'ges Heil erwarb.	And we acquired eternal salvation.
Heiligthum, dein Werth ist groß!	Heiligthum, your worth is great!
Dich bewahrt der Kircheschoos	You preserve the bosom of the church
Seit viel Hunderten von Jahren,	Since many hundreds of years,
Was für Schmach sie auch erfahren;	In indignity they also experienced;
Deiner Wunder Wirksamkeit	Your wonderful properties
Bot oft Schutz der Christenheit.	Often offered protection for Christendom.
Darum schauen wir auf Dich	We therefore look at you
Im Vertrauen inniglich,	In intimate trust,
Mit dem frommen Liebesflehen:	With pious, loving entreaty:
Laß uns Deine Gnade sehen,	Let us see your grace,
Und uns rein von bösem ahn	And purify us from evil man
Wandeln auf der Tugendbahn.	Transform our path to virtue.

1844

"Lied auf den heiligen Rock,"[2] Nach der Melodie "Alles meinem Gott zu Ehren"	"Song to the Holy Coat," to the Melody "All My Honour to God"

1. Eilt beflügelt fromme Christen!
Eilt begeistert hoch erfreut
Voll vom wärmsten Dankgefühl
Zu dem Schatz der Heiligkeit,
Den die Hand der Vorsicht wieder
Unsrer Stadt zurückgestellt,
Den der wahre Christ noch immer
Heilig und höchst schätzbar hält.

Hasten inspired, pious Christians!
Hasten enthusiastically thrilled
Full of the warmest gratitude
To the treasure of holiness,
Our city postponed,
That the true Christian still
Holds sacred and highly treasurable.

2. Kommt von Liebe ganz
    durchdrungen,
Stimmt ein Lob- und Danklied an!
Singt mit Ehrfurcht vollen Zungen
Dem, Der uns hat wohl gethan.
Laßt uns dieses Heilthum achten
Würdig, wie es sich gebührt,
Es im Geist der Buß betrachten,
Tief von Gottes Huld gerührt.

Come completely imbued with love,

Voice a song of love and thanks!
Sing with full, reverent tongues
To Him who to us has done well.
Let us make this Heilthum
Worthy, as we ought,
View it in the spirit of penance,
Deeply stirred by God's grace.

3. Würdigstes der Alterthümer!
Das uns je die Welt gezeugt;

Dir sei nach dem Allerhöchsten
Ehre auch von uns erzeigt.
Denn du bist das heil'ge Kleinod,
Welches Jesus lange Zeit
Als ein Kleid am Leib getragen
Hier in Seiner Sterblichkeit.

Most worthy of antiquities!
That we and the world ever
    witnessed;
To you be after the Most High
Honour bestowed upon by us,
For you are the sacred garment,
Which Jesus for a long time
Wore as a garment on his body
Here in his death.

4. Wer kann all'die Wunder zählen,
Die in diesem heil'gen Kleid
Der Erlöser hat gewirket
So viel Tausenden zur Freud!
Nur den Saum von diesem Kleide
hat ein krankes Weib berührt
Gleich gesund an Leib und Seele
Ward sie Jesu vorgeführt.

Who can count all the miracles,
In his sacred Coat
The Saviour had worked
So many joy for thousands!
Only the hem of His Coat
Had touched a sick woman
Equally healthy in body and soul
She was presented to Jesus.

(Continued)

"Lied auf den heiligen Rock,"[2] Nach der Melodie "Alles meinem Gott zu Ehren"	"Song to the Holy Coat," to the Melody "All My Honour to God"
5. Dieses Kleid auf Thabor glänzte Wie der Schnee beim Sonnenschein, Nahm die Herzen der Apostel Jesu mit Verwundrung ein. Da war es ein klares Vorbild Jener hohen Reinigkeit, Die die Himmelsbürger kleidet In dem Reich der Herrlichkeit.	This Coat shone at Tabor As [bright as] the snow in sunshine, It took the hearts of the apostles Of Jesus with wonderment. As it was a clear example That high purity, [In which] the citizens of heaven dress In the kingdom of glory.
6. Dieses Kleid trug er am Oelberg, Wo Er Blut wie Schweiß vergoß, Als Er ging zur Schädelstätte, Wo Sein letzter Tropfen floß. Da ward es die Beut der Kriegsknecht, Die mit wilder Grausamkeit An das Kreuz genagelt haben Ihn, den Herrn der Ewigkeit.	He wore this Coat on the Mount of Olives, Where he shed his blood like sweat, When he went to Calvary, Where his last blood flowed. Since it was the booty of a soldier With the direst cruelty Nailed to the cross Him, the Lord of Eternity.
7. Heil'ges Kleid! du warest Zeuge Da, wo Jesus stark und matt, Stark in Thaten, matt durch Leiden, Uns zum Heil gewirket hat. Werd auch Zeuge unsres Dankes, Unsrer Ehrfurcht, unsrer Lieb, Die wir dir dahier geloben, Stärk in uns den heil'gen Trieb.	Holy Coat! You who were witness There, where Jesus strong and feeble, Strong in deeds, through feeble suffering, For us has wrought salvation. You are also witness of our gratitude, Our respect, our love, Which we here promise you, Strengthening in us the sacred instinct.

(Continued)

"Lied auf den heiligen Rock,"[2] Nach der Melodie "Alles meinem Gott zu Ehren"	"Song to the Holy Coat," to the Melody "All My Honour to God"

8. Du, der du dies Kleid anschauest,
Sei auch wohl auf das bedacht,
Was ein Gottmensch dir zum Nutzen,
Zur Erlösung hat vollbracht.
Weinen sollen Aller Augen,
Jeder, der den Heiland kennt,
Und vertrauen auf Seine Güte
Weil Er ist, was Er Sich nennt.

You, who look on this Coat,
Be well also mindful of this,
What a God-man for your benefit,
To salvation has accomplished.
All eyes should weep,
Anyone who knows the Saviour,
And trusts in His goodness
Because He is, what He calls Himself.

9. Heiland! Du Hast hier auf Erden
Blinde, Lahme oft geheilt,
Und den Todten und den Sündern
Neues Leben mitgetheilt.
mach auch ißt, wir bitten flehend

Durch der Liebe Wunderkraft,

Die in diesem Kleid gewirket,
Uns gerecht und tugendhaft.

Saviour! You have here on Earth
Blind, lame often healed,
And the dead and the sinners
Communicated new life.
Make also sustenance, we ask
    pleadingly
Through the miraculous power of
    love,
That was wrought in this Coat,
Us righteous and virtuous.

10. Christen! Trierer! macht euch
    würdig
Dieser hohen Vorzugs Gnad,
Jesus Rock hier zu besitzen:
Wandelt auf dem Tugendpfad!
Denkt, was ehmal, was noch heute
Er zu unserm Heil gethan.
Freut euch, Fromme! zittert, Sünder!
Fangt ein neues Leben an.

Christians! Trier citizens! Make
    yourselves worthy
This high, preferential grace,
The Coat of Jesus to here have:
Walking on the path of virtue!
Think, what was, what even today
He has done for our salvation.
Rejoice, pious! Tremble, sinner!
Begin a new life.

1867

"Grußlied. h. Lendentuch"[3]	"Greeting Song for the Holy Loincloth"
Die Ihn entblößet hatten,	When bare, he was
Beschenkt mit einem Gewand	Presented with a robe
Der Heiland, als Ihn Schatten	The Saviour, as he was shadowed by
Der Finsterniß umwand.	The eclipse transformation.
Die Wunden die Ihn begossen,	The wounds poured upon Him,
Die Striemen die Ihn entstellt,	The welts disfigured Him,
Dies Tuch von Blut durchflossen	The cloth soaked with blood
Das Kleid sind so Er behält.	Which the garment retains.
Als in dem Kleid der Schmerzen	As in the garment of sorrows
Ihn seine Mutter sah,	He saw His mother,
Wie bohrte ihr im Herzen	Like her, pierced in the heart
Das Schwert des Mitleids da.	There the sword of compassion
Er hieß sie auf uns Sünder,	He called on us sinners,
Uns auf sie Mutter seh'n,	On us, to see [His] mother,
Die uns dem Ueberwinder	The conqueror of death
Des Tods gebar in Weh'n.	Given to us in birth pangs.

1881

8. "Den Gästen," Nach der Melodie "Strömt herbei etc."[4]	"The Guests," to the Melody "Flock Here, Etc."
Offen steh'n des Domes Hallen	The cathedral halls stand open
In der heil'gen Gnadenzeit,	In the holy period of grace,
Und zum Heiligthum zu wallen	And go up to the Heiligthum
Sehnet sich die Christenheit.	Long for the Christianity.
Strömt herbei aus allen Landen,	Flowing forth from every land,
Kommt mit gläubig-frommen Sinn;	Comes with pious-faith sense;
Bei den Heiligthümern fanden	Found in the Heiligthümern
Fromme Gnad' stets und Gewinn.	Pious grace and profit.

(Continued)

8. "Den Gästen," Nach der Melodie "Strömt herbei etc."[4]	"The Guests," to the Melody "Flock Here, Etc."
Wer da trägt der Krankheit Schmerzen	Whoever carries the pain of disease
Hoffend zu dem Heiligthum,	Hoping to the Heiligthum
Und wer auch mit trübem Herzen	And who also has a sad heart
Gläubig schaut nach Tröstung um:	Believers looking for consolation to:
Den durchbebt "der Zeichen" Segen	By the trembling of "the signs" blessing
Geisterhaft, so er sich naht,	Phantasmal, he will come near,
O er fühlt, dass Gott zugegen,	Oh he feels that God is present,
Und bei Gott ist Hilf und Gnad'.	And through God is help and grace.
Heil dem, der mit freier Stirne	Blessed is he who with a clear brow
Sich zum Heiligthum bekennt,	Confesses to the Heiligthum,
Ob der Feind mit blödem Hirne	Whether the enemy with idiotic brains
Es auch Tand und Trug benennt.	Names it [the Coat] baubles and deceit
Ob der Unglaub' höhnt und eifert,	Whether the unbeliever jeers and disclaims,
Wahre Du die Einfalt Dir.	Truly the simplemindedness is yours.
Wie's im Bösen brennt und geifert	Such as burns and drools for evil
Singt es froh im Herzen Dir.	Sing it gladly in your heart.
Die Ihr kommt, mit uns zu ehren	That you come, with us to honour
Unser hehres Heiligthum,	Our noble relics,
Ihr, die Priester, die uns lehren, -	You, the priests who teach us,
Und Ihr, Deutschlands Stolz und Ruhm,	And you, Germany's pride and glory,
Die für's Recht der Kirche streiten, -	You who fight for church law,
All' Ihr, die um uns geschaart:	All you who rallied around us:
Seid willkommen! Mög' begleiten	You are welcome! May you be accompanied with
Gottes Segen Eure Fahrt	God's blessing on your journey

(Continued)

1881

10. "Zur Heiligthumsfahrt," Nach der Melodie "Was schimmert dort auf dem Berge so schön"[5]	"To the Aachen Pilgrimage," to the Melody "What Light There so Beautiful on the Mountains"
Was schwebet dort oben in luftiger Höh', -	What soars there in airy heights,
Was tönen die Glocken so mild? -	That sound the bells so mild?
"Das ist der reinsten Jungfrau Kleid!" -	"This is the purest Virgin's dress!"
O Pilger verehre die Mutter dein!	O pilgrims adore your mother!
O Pilger verehre die Mutter dein!	O pilgrims adore your mother!
Was kündet des würdigen Priesters Wort	What heralds the holy priest proclaims word
Vom hohen und heiligen Dom? -	From the high and holy cathedral?
"Das sind die Windeln unsers Herrn!" -	"These are the swaddling clothes of our Lord!"
O knieet ihr Pilger von Nah und Fern!	O kneel you pilgrims from near and far!
O knieet ihr Pilger von Nah und Fern!	O kneel you pilgrims from near and far!
Was schall'n die Posaunen vom hohen Thurm	What do the trumpets from the high tower sound
Wie ein Lied aus vergangener Zeit? -	Like a song from the forgotten past?
"Sie grüssen das Lendentuch des Herrn!" -	"They greet the loincloth of the Lord!"
O betet ihr Pilger von Nah und Fern!	O pray you pilgrims from near and far!
O betet ihr Pilger von Nah und Fern!	O pray you pilgrims from near and far!
Was singt so melodisch der Sänger Chor,	What does the choir sing so melodiously,
Wie Engelstimmen so rein? -	Like angelic voices so pure?
"Das ist des Täufers geheiligtes Tuch!" -	"This is the [beheading] cloth of the Baptist!"
O Pilger beweinet die Sündenschuld!	O pilgrims lament the guilt of sin!
O Pilger beweinet die Sündenschuld!	O pilgrims lament the guilt of sin!

1891

"Lied 4"[6]	"Song 4"
1. Nun, Christen kommet, laßt uns gehen,	Well, Christians come ye, let us go,
Der Liebe Wunderwerk zu sehen,	To see the lovely miracle,
Das man uns jetzt vor Augen stellt.	This one is now before our eyes.
Gedenkt an den und dessen Thaten,	Consider him and his deeds,
Der unsre Schuld auf sich geladen,	He who took our guilt on Himself,
Und blutend starb für's Heil der Welt.	And bleeding He died for the world's salvation.
2. Die Gottes Sohn, der Engel Freude,	The Son of God, the joy of angels,
Dir Menschen Sohn, und Deinem Kleide,	You Son of Man, and Your Coat,
Sei Ruhm und Lob von uns gebracht.	Let praise and love from us be brought.
Du zogest uns aus dem Verderben;	You draw us out of perdition;
Du schufst uns um zu Himmelserben,	You make us heirs to Heaven,
Du hast uns heil und froh gemacht.	You make us whole and happy.
3. Was können wir wohl Dir vergelten?	How can we repay you?
Beherrscher, König aller Welten!	Ruler, king of the whole world!
Was ist, was liebt, was schwebt, ist Dein,	What is, what loves, what hovers, is Yours,
Nimm unser Herz, nimm unsern Willen;	Take our heart, take our will;
Wir wollen Dein Gebot erfüllen:	We want to fulfill your bidding:
Dich lieben, Dir gehorsam sein.	Love You, be obedient to you.
4. Nun bitten wir um diesen Segen,	Now we ask for this blessing,
Daß Fürst und Volk auf Deinen Wegen	That prince and people to your paths
So wand'le ohne still zu stehen,	So stroll without standing still,
Daß sämmtliche am End der Zeiten	That all at the end of time
Gelangen zu des Himmelsfreuden.	Go to the joys of heaven
Sprich hierauf: ja! Es soll geschehen.	Say thereto: yes! It shall be done.

1895

"Gemeinsamer Schlußgesang der Pilger."[7]	"Common Final Song of the Pilgrims"

I. Wir sind im wahren Christenthum,
O Gott, wir danken dir
Dein Wort, dein Evangelium,
An dieses glauben wir.
Die Kirche, deren Haupt du bist,
Lehrt einig, heilig, wahr;
Für diese Wahrheit giebt der Christ
Sein Blut und Leben dar

We are in the true Christianity,
Oh God, we thank you
Your word, your Gospel,
In this we believe.
The church, whose head you are,
Teaches one, holy, true;
For this the Christian gives
His blood and life

II. Großer Gott! wir loben dich,
Herr! wir preisen deine Stärke;
Vor dir neigt die Erde sich,
Und bewundert deine Werke;
Wie du warst vor aller Zeit,
So bleibst du in Ewigkeit!
Alles, was dich preisen kann,
Cherubim und Seraphinen
Stimmen dir ein Loblied an;
Alle Engel die dir dienen,
Rufen dir stets ohne Ruh';
Heilig, Heilig, Heilig zu!

Great God! we praise you,
Lord! we praise your strength;
Before you, the earth bows down,
And admires your works;
As you were before all time,
So you stay forever!
All that can praises you,
Cherubim and seraphim
Sing to you a song of praise;
All the angels serve you,
Call you always, without rest;
Holy, holy, holy!

III. O du heilige,
Du jungfräuliche,
Süße Jungfrau Maria!
Selig Gepries'ne,
Herrliche erwies'ne!
Ave, ave Maria!

Oh thou holy,
You virginal,
Sweet Virgin Mary!
Blessed praised,
Proven magnificent!
Ave, ave Mary!

Dir begnadigte,
Dir Gesegnete,
Jachzen Himmel und Erde;
Himmlische Lieder,
Tönen hernieder.
Ave, ave Maria!

You are pardoned,
You are blessed,
Heaven and Earth rejoice;
Heavenly songs,
Tones descend.
Ave, ave Mary!

1895

"Grußlied"[8]	"Greeting Song"
Gott in der Höh sei Ehre,	Glory to God on high,
Den Menschen auf Erden Fried',	Peace to the people on earth,
Des Höchsten Ruhm sich mehre	Glory to the Most High who is multiple
Mit seines Reichs Gebiet!	With his kingdom territory!
Der Geist sich hoch entzücke	The spirit enraptures highly
Und mach den Schöpfer groß,	And makes the creator great,
Das Herz sich tiefer bücke	The heart reaches deeper
Zum Heiland aus Jungfrauschooß!	The Saviour from the Virgin's bosom
O öffnet weit die Pforten	Oh open wide the gates
Der Jungfrau-Mutter Kind,	The Virgin Mother's child,
Das Zuflucht aller Orten	That refuge of all places
Es in den Herzen find'!	Find it in the hearts!
O könnt' ich Dich umschmiegen	Oh that I could embrace you
Gleichwie die Windelein,	Just as the swaddling clothes,
So nah wie sie Dir liegen,	As close as they are to you
Du göttlich Kindelein!	You divine child!

1933

"Reiselieder 1"[9]	"Untitled Travel Song 1"
1 Laßt uns froh zum Dome wallen,	Let us joyfully sojourn to the cathedral,
wo das heilge Kleinod ruft;	where the holy cloth calls;
Jubel-Lieder laßt erschallen,	let cheering songs resound
dem unschätzbar hohen Gut.	the inestimable good.
Christen eilt mit demuts sinn,	Christians hurry with appropriate humility
zu dem heilgen Kleide hin.	towards the Holy Coat.
2 Laßt den Glauben uns bekennen,	Let us confess our faith,
dem der dieses Kleid einst trug,	the faith that once wore this garment,
mag die Welt uns thöricht nennen,	let the world call us foolish,
ihr ist alles Heilige Lug.	for them all that is holy lies.

(Continued)

"Reiselieder 1"[9]	"Untitled Travel Song 1"
3 Laßt der Hoffnung Kranzergrünen,	Let the hope of the chaplet/wreath blossom,
der gewandelt in dem Kleid,	which transformed into the Coat,
wollt auch unsre Schulden sühnen,	[you] also want to atone for our sins
führen uns zur Seligkeit.	and lead us to salvation.
4 Laßt vor allem unsre Herzen-lodern	Let our hearts above all blaze
auf in Liebesglut ihm,	in His ardour,
der unter tausend Schmerzen	he who under a thousand wounds
gab aus Lieb sein letztes Blut.	gave us his last blood out of love.
5 Herr! wir nahen mit Vertrauen, dir,	God! we confidently draw near to you,
du Heil der Christenheit,	you salvation of Christendom,
mach uns würdig einst zu schauen,	make us worthy to see once,
dich im Kleid der Herrlichkeit.	you in the Coat of glory.

1933

"Reiselied 2"	"Untitled Travel Song 2"
1 Nun laßt die Fahnen wehen den Pilgerstab zur Hand	Now take the pilgrim staff to hand, the flags are flying
Wir wollen betend gehend ins heilge Trier Land	We go prayerfully into holy Trier land
Wir wollen lobend wallen zum sehen Gottes-Kleid,	We want to go up to praise and to see God's Coat,
dem Heiland wirds gefallen, drum eilt von weit und breit.	the Saviour will be pleased that we hurry from far and wide.
2 Es zieht mit mächt'gen Banden, zum Gottes Kleid uns hin,	It attracts us with a powerful push to God's Coat,
Vor dem die Väter standen, In gläubig frommen Sinn.	Before it stood the fathers, in devout meditative appreciation.
Was uns in jungen Tagen Erzählt der Mutter Mund,	What our mothers narrated in earlier days,
Bekennen ohne Zagen Auch wir zu jeder Stund.	We confess without trepidation at every hour.

(Continued)

"Reiselied 2"	"Untitled Travel Song 2"
3 Mag auch die Welt sich streiten, Uns höhnen stets aufs neu,	The world also likes to quarrel, to mock us always again anew,
Wir stehe zu allen Zeiten, Zu unserm Bischof treu.	We stand at all times, true to our bishop.
Und mag die Höll uns wehren, In blinder, wilder Wut,	We defend ourselves against Hell in a blind, wild rage,
Wir werden stets dich ehren Mit glaubensfrohem Mut.	We will always honour God with a joyful, courageous faith.
4 Herr segne unsre Pfade, Halt von uns Unheil fern,	God bless our paths, keep evil away from us,
Leih uns das Last der Gnade, Laß leuchten deinen Stern,	lend us the weight of grace, let your star shine
damit wir heimwärts Kehren, Mit reichlichem Gewinn,	so we return home, with ample profits,
Und deinen Ruhm vermehren, Erneut an Herz und Sinn	And propagate your glory, once again in heart and mind.

Appendix 2. Daily Pilgrim Totals, Trier 1891

Date	No. of pilgrims
20 August	24,600
21 August	41,252
22 August	37,849
23 August	44,300
24 August	45,000
25 August	42,000
26 August	30,344
27 August	31,042
28 August	36,452
29 August	41,179
30 August	47,286
31 August	36,348
1 September	45,000
2 September	45,625
3 September	33,000
4 September	36,452
5 September	24,274
6 September	33,500
7 September	38,830
8 September	40,282
9 September	31,646
10 September	30,051
11 September	28,646
12 September	33,964
13 September	39,312
14 September	39,820
15 September	44,950
16 September	40,750
17 September	46,994
18 September	35,045

(*Continued*)

Date	No. of pilgrims
19 September	35,521
20 September	53,381
21 September	44,688
22 September	56,128
23 September	44,998
24 September	53,133
25 September	45,241
26 September	59,223
27 September	74,093
28 September	58,678
29 September	55,023
30 September	49,316
1 October	54,697
2 October	63,149
3 October	52,042
Total	1,925,130
Daily average	42,781

Source: Hulley, *Kurze Geschichte*, 57–8.

Appendix 3. Daily Pilgrim Totals, Trier 1933

Date	Day	No. of pilgrims
Week 1		
23 July	Sunday	37,950
24 July	Monday	27,893
25 July	Tuesday	25,726
26 July	Wednesday	30,347
27 July	Thursday	31,722
28 July	Friday	25,698
29 July	Saturday	19,069
Subtotal		198,396
Week 2		
30 July	Sunday	42,417
31 July	Monday	35,954
1 August	Tuesday	36,490
2 August	Wednesday	45,356
3 August	Thursday	42,844
4 August	Friday	39,591
5 August	Saturday	29,414
Subtotal		272,066
Week 3		
6 August	Sunday	42,092
7 August	Monday	43,844
8 August	Tuesday	40,466
9 August	Wednesday	37,041
10 August	Thursday	35,956
11 August	Friday	25,446
12 August	Saturday	26,615
Subtotal		251,460
Week 4		
13 August	Sunday	57,759
14 August	Monday	41,219

(Continued)

Date	Day	No. of pilgrims
15 August	Tuesday	49,052
16 August	Wednesday	40,382
17 August	Thursday	43,451
18 August	Friday	34,606
19 August	Saturday	38,386
Subtotal		304,855
Week 5		
20 August	Sunday	46,542
21 August	Monday	47,785
22 August	Tuesday	40,023
23 August	Wednesday	43,873
24 August	Thursday	42,623
25 August	Friday	36,081
26 August	Saturday	50,546
Subtotal		307,473
Week 6		
27 August	Sunday	54,882
28 August	Monday	52,944
29 August	Tuesday	45,476
30 August	Wednesday	52,248
31 August	Thursday	45,203
1 September	Friday	47,000
2 September	Saturday	51,554
Subtotal		349,307
Week 7		
3 September	Sunday	97,202
4 September	Monday	63,111
5 September	Tuesday	64,557
6 September	Wednesday	92,407
7 September	Thursday	78,591
8 September	Friday	70,626
9 September	Saturday	40,070
Subtotal		506,564
Total		2,190,121
Daily average		44,700

Source: BATr, Abt. 90, Nr. 173, 610.

Appendix 4. Holy Coat Songs in Trier Hymnal, 1846–1955

1846

1. Sei gegrüßet, liebster Jesu! (Fünf-Wunden-Lied)	1. Hail, dearest Jesus! (five-wound-song)
2. Spende Lob, erlöste Seele (Tunika, Nägel, Lanze)	2. Bounty praise, redeemed soul (tunic, nails, lance)
3. O ungenähetes Gewand. (Tunika)	3. O seamless robe (tunic)
4. Eil't mit flammender Begierde (Tunika)	4. Hasten with flaming eagerness (tunic)
5. Sieh, hier das Kleid, mein armer Christ! (Tunika)	5. See, here the gown, my poor Christ! (tunic)

1871

1. Sei gegrüßet, liebster Jesu! (Fünf-Wunden-Lied)	1. Hail, dearest Jesus! (five-wound-song)
2. Sieh, hier das Kleid, mein armer Christ! (Tunika)	2. See, here the gown, my poor Christ! (tunic)
3. Eil't mit flammender Begierde. (Tunika)	3. Hasten with flaming eagerness (tunic)

(Continued)

1892

1. Kommt zu grüßen, kommt zu preisen! (Tunika und Leidenswerkzeuge)	1. Come to greet, come to praise! (tunic and suffering tools)
2. Sieh, hier das Kleid, mein armer Christ! (Tunika)	2. See, here the gown, my poor Christ! (tunic)
3. Eil't mit flammender Begierde (Tunika)	3. Hasten with flaming eagerness (tunic)

1955

1. O ungenähtes Heilandskleid (Tunika)[1]	1. O seamless Saviour garment (tunic)

Appendix 5. Pilgrimage Dates

Aachen	Dates
1825	9–24 July
1832	10–24 July
1839	10–24 July
1846	10–31 July
1850	1 July, opened for King of Bavaria, Max II
	10–24 July
1853	9–24 July
1860	9–24 July
1867	9–24 July
1874	10–24 July
1881	9–24 July
1888	9–24 July
1895	9–24 July
1902	10–24 July
1909	9–28 July
1916	First World War: no pilgrimage
1923	Rhineland occupied: no pilgrimage
1925	10–26 July
1930	10–27 July
1937	10–25 July
1945	19–22 July
1951	8–22 July
1958	10–27 July
1972	10–21 August
1979	10–20 August

Trier	Dates
1810	9–27 September
1844	18 August–6 October
1891	10 August–3 October
1933	23 July–10 September

Appendix 6. Sick Pilgrim Complaints, Trier, 1933

Disease	Complaint in German	No.
Accident	Anfall	7
Alopecia	Alopecia	2
Anus	After	2
Arm	Arm	38
Arthritis	Arthritis	99
Asthma	Asthma	99
Back	Rücken	57
Basedow's	Based	1
Bladder	Blase	4
Blind	Blind	84
Blood	Blut	63
Body	Körper	15
Bones	Knochen	36
Breast	Brust	20
Cancer	Krebs	35
Cervix	Muttermund	14
Child lameness	Kinderlähmung	44
Cramps	Krämpfe	40
Cretinism	Kretinismus	1
Deaf	Taubheit	69
Deformity	Deform	3
Dementia	Demenz	3
Depression	Depression	12
Diabetes	Diabetes	65
Ears	Ohren	81
Epilepsy	Epilepsie	163
Eyes	Augen	143
Face	Gesicht	12
Fever	Fieber	7
Flu	Grippe	11
Foot	Fuß	15

(Continued)

Disease	Complaint in German	No.
Gall bladder	Gallen	29
Genetic defect	Erbfehler	2
Genitals	Genitalien	6
Giantism	Akromegalie	2
Goiter	Kropf	6
Gout	Gicht	27
Head	Kopf	73
Heart	Herz	198
Herpes	Herpes	1
Hypochondriac	Hypochonder	1
Hysteria	Hysterie	32
Idiocy	Idiotie	31
Imbecility	Imbicilität	10
Joint	Gelenk	141
Kidneys	Nieren	33
Lameness	Lähmung	181
Legs	Beine	171
Liver	Leber	10
Lungs	Lungen	218
Lupus	Lupus	24
Lymphoma	Lymphoma	3
Megakolon	Hirschsprung'sche	1
Mental health: paranoid, psychopathic, senile, schizophrenic	Paranoia, Psychopathisch, Senil, Schizophrenie	13
Mouth	Mund	2
Multiple sclerosis	Multiple Sklerose	45
Muscle	Muskel	26
Mute	Stumm	4
Nerves/nervous	Nerven/Nervöse	150
Nose	Nase	5
Operation	Operation	7
Ovaries	Ovarien	6
Pain	Schmerzen	21
Palsy	Schuttellähmung	4
Paralysis	Paralyse	18
Parkinson's	Parkinson	15
Polio	Polio	8
Rheumatism	Rheumatismus	69
Ribs	Rippen	7
Rickets	Richitis	1
Sciatica	Ischias	19
Sick	Krank	132
Skin	Haut	50
Sleep disorder	Schlafkrankheit	6

(Continued)

Disease	Complaint in German	No.
Spasms	Spastische	4
Speech impediment	Sprachfehler	8
Spinal injuries: spina bifida, spinal child lameness, curvature of the spine	Spina Bifida, Spinale Kinderlähmung, Wirbelsäulenkrummung	71
Spiritual illness	Geist	14
St. Vitus disease	St. Vitus	14
Stomach	Magen	105
Stroke	Schlaganfall	11
Suffering	Leidend	15
Syphilis	Syphilis	4
Throat	Hals	6
Thyroid	Hyperthyreose	4
Thyroid sarkoma	Schilddrüsen Sarkom	1
Tuberculosis	Tuberkulose	120
Typhus	Typhus	1
Urinary tract	Urin	1
War wound	Krieg	6
Weakness	Schwäche	9
Total		3,447

Appendix 7. Aachen Closing Ceremony Procession, 1867

1. Male congregations
2. Sodality [guild or brotherhood]
3. Sisters of the Poor Child Jesus, with their pupils
4. Poor Sisters of St. Francis
5. Sisters of Charity for the Poor and Orphans
6. Christenserinnen
7. Franciscan Brothers, with their pupils
8. Alexian Brothers
9. Men of the parish brotherhoods with their torches
10. Holy orders clergy in their choir robes
    a. Franciscans
    b. Redemptorists
    c. Jesuits
11. Parish clergy
    a. Entire chorale, with crosses of St. Foilans church at the front
    b. All chaplains, but those who carry relics from their churches [wear] dalmatics
    c. All parish priests, in choir robes
12. Clergy with relics of the collegiate church
    a. Collegiate choir, singers next to the music choir, with the chapter crosses between two candles at the front
    b. Collegiate vicars, augmented by other clerics in dalmatics, who carry the relics and the large reliquary on a stretcher adorned with carpeting
    c. On either side of the reliquary, silver censers and lanterns of the collegiate and the other churches of the city
    d. Honour guard of ordained canons in choir robes

13. Rev. Mr. Archbishop and the other bishops attending, with staff, mitre and vestments, each between two chaplains, who hold the tip of the [bishops'] caps;
14. The Magistrate
15. Dignitaries with torches
16. Society (*Gesellverein*)

Notes

Introduction

1 The following is taken from *Für den Sonntag*, "Die Heilung einer Wall-
fahrerin: Ein Besuch bei der anläßlich der Berührung des Heiligen Rockes
in Trier geheilten Frau Willmann aus Mutterstadt," Nr. 170 (Samstag 5
August 1933), 5.

2 Smith, *To Take Place*; Porter, "The Patient's View."

3 The hyphenated German-Catholic indicates Ronge's new church, as op-
posed to German Catholics, Germans who followed Roman Catholicism.
Ronge's group adopted the name *Deutschkatholiken*, but rendering this as
Germancatholics is too clunky.

4 Depending on the source, authors use Trier, Trèves, or Treves to refer to
this city on the Moselle River. In the interest of uniformity, I have rendered any alternate spelling or use of Treves as Trier throughout.

5 The German term for the relic of Trier is *Der Heilige Rock*. Most English
translations on the topic use the term "robe," "coat," "shirt," or "tunic,"
but this book will use Coat because it best captures the nature of the
garment. The terms "shirt" and "tunic" imply that this item of clothing
could be worn alone and do not capture the length of the Coat. Both
"robe" and "coat" describe the fact that the garment was worn externally
and likely held around the waist with a belt. I favour "Coat" over "robe"
because the King James Version, American King James Version, American
Standard Version, and Bible in Basic English translations all render the
item in John 19:23 as a "coat."

6 Anon., *Pilgerheft: Aachener Heiligtumsfahrt 9. bis 18. Juni 2000*, 33. In 2000,
pilgrims to Aachen learned that the John the Baptist relic could have been
a tablecloth or a burial cloth. Their *Pilgrim Guide* also taught them that
"decapitation" was a misnomer, because the church originally honoured
this garment as the burial cloth of John the Baptist. Throughout this century, though, German Catholics did not make these distinctions.

7   Gumbrecht, *Making Sense*, 92. Gumbrecht attributes this point to Reinhart Koselleck in Bergeron, Furet, and Koselleck, *Das Zeitalter*, 296.

8   See chap. 3, "Auguste Comte and Positivisms," 62–84 and chap. 7, "The Rise of Materialisms and the Reshaping of Religion and Politics," 122–63 in Olson, *Science and Scientism*.

9   Feldhay, "Religion," 746.

10   See table 1.2 for list of Aachen pilgrimage dates and estimated attendance.

11   On the important intersections of politics, society, and religion see Schneider, "Vergessene Welt?"

12   Großbölting, *Losing Heaven*, 23; Brodie, *German Catholicism at War*.

13   In addition to Großbölting on post-1937 religious life, see Mitchell, *The Origins*; Ruff, *The Battle*.

14   In James Donnelly's "The Marian Shrine of Knock," he relied on Irish clerical newspapers and periodicals in his analysis of Marian apparitions in Knock. And David Blackbourn, in a study of the Marian apparition at Marpingen, examined the political and economic consequences of that 1876 event. Blackbourn, *Marpingen*, 373. This approach helps situate the event in the national political and cultural context, but tends to leave out the perspective of the pilgrims. See also Oded Heilbronner's article pointing out the fact that Catholics still inhabit the "marginal position of the historiography." Heilbronner, "From Ghetto to Ghetto," 454; Ziemann, "Der deutsche Katholizismus."

15   See Margaret Lavinia Anderson's thesis on the political realignment of Catholics towards the confessional Zentrum after 1870 in national elections: Anderson, "The Kulturkampf"; Anderson and Barkin, "The Myth"; Anderson, "Interdenominationalism, Clericalism, Pluralism." See also Sperber, *Popular Catholicism*, which discusses shifts in Rhenish Catholic politics beginning earlier as part of church organization after the confused responses to secularization from 1830 to 1850.

16   Healy, *The Jesuit Specter*; Drury, "Anti-Catholicism."

17   Gross, "The Strange Case," 70, 79. See also Steinhoff's review of "Michael B. Gross, The War against Catholicism: Liberalism and the Anti-Catholic Imagination in Nineteenth-Century Germany"; Róisín Healy, "The Jesuit Specter in Imperial Germany."

18   Schieder, *Religion und Revolution*, 11, 28. The title of the book points to the main argument: 1844 as a chance for clergy to minimize growing revolutionary sentiment among the laity. Sperber, *Popular Catholicism*, 70.

19   Sperber, 70.

20   Jeffrey Zalar's *Reading and Rebellion* recently laid bare the limits of clerical attempts to control what Catholics read. But whereas Zalar identified Catholic readers eager to ignore conservative clerical instruction on

appropriate literature, the pilgrims to Aachen and Trier act as the preservers of tradition against shifts within clerical teachings about relics.

21 On the Catholic milieu theory, see Repgen, "Christ und Geschichte"; Arbeitskreis für kirchliche Zeitgeschichte (AKKZG), Münster, "Katholiken zwischen Tradition und Moderne"; Metzger, "Konstruktionsmechanismen."

22 Olenhusen, "Die Feminisierung von Religion und Kirche."

23 Welter, "The Feminization of American Religion."

24 But as Bernhard Schneider has shown in "Feminisierung der Religion," close analysis of lived religion puts the lie to generalized gender assumptions in the case of German Catholicism.

25 On the feminization thesis, see also McLeod, "Weibliche Frömmigkeit – männlicher Unglaube?; Hastings, "Fears of a Feminized Church"; Steinhoff, "A Feminized Church?"; Van Osselaer, "Feminization Thesis"; Van Osselaer, "Sensitive but Sane."

26 A reverse phenomenon occurred in nursing in Wilhelmine Germany, what Aeleah Soine has called the "feminization of nursing," in "The 'Gender Problem' in Nursing."

27 Hiort, "Constructing."

28 Gumbrecht, *The Production of Presence*, 124; Graf, "Euro-Gott im starken Plural?"

29 Applegate, "Metaphors of Continuity."

30 Connolly, "Imagined Pilgrimage."

31 BATr, Abt. 90, Nr. 173, 188.

32 BATr, Abt. 90, Nr. 173, 188–9. This story appears in Matthew 8:5–13. Unfortunately, only Figulla's request is in the BATr and not the Pilgrimage Committee's response. However, it is highly likely her ring was returned; see similar requests and responses in chapter 3, "The Sacred Economy."

33 Dahlberg, "The Body," 48. In the historiography, Ruth Harris has been most sympathetic towards cure-seekers. Aachen and Trier are distinct from Lourdes because neither town had a permanent bureau to investigate miracle claims. I also analyse miracle claims in the context of the body, what Catholics believed could happen to them if they drew close enough to the divine in the relics, whereas Harris considers cure-seekers in terms of the "self."

34 No relation to Karl Marx (1818–83), who was also born in Trier. Dr. Anton Joseph Binterim signed the letter "Dr. Binterim," whose full name is cited in another publication: Gratz and Binterim, *Drei öffenliche Stimmen*, 11.

35 BATr, Abt. 91, Nr. 255, 12–13, 1 November 1844.

36 Schneider, "Wilhelm Arnoldi (1842–1864)."

37 Schieder, "Church and Revolution," 80.

38 In the view of Rebecca Ayako Bennette, "Catholics became defensive, turned inward, and separated themselves from the rest of German society." See Bennette, "Threatened Protestants," 169.

39 Gregory, "The Other Confessional History."

40 Marx, *History of the Robe*, 91–3. See Flury-Lemberg, "Das Reliquiar," 696.

41 The Aachen measurements often appear in pamphlet literature, see especially works by Franz Bock and Johann Hubert Kessel: Bock, *Das Heiligthum zu Aachen*; Kessel, *Geschichtliche Mittheilungen*, 13. The metric system measurements come from Anon., *Pilgerheft*, 29.

42 Anon., *Pilgerheft*, 31.

43 Anon., *Pilgerheft*, 35.

1 What They Practised: Prayer, Songs, and Processions

1 Michael Merten, "Monumentales Mahnmal gegen Arbeitslosigkeit," *Paulinus: Die Tageszeitung zur Wallfahrt*, 20 April 2012, 8–9.

2 Bruno Sonnen, "Ein Schaff-Rock wird Teil der Wallfahrt," *Paulinus: Die Tageszeitung zur Wallfahrt*, 18 April 2012, 14.

3 Zeljko Jakobvac, "Er beeindruckt schon liegend," *Paulinus: Die Tageszeitung zur Wallfahrt*, 18 April 2012, 2.

4 BATr, Abt. 90, Nr. 125, 83.

5 BATr, Abt. 90, Nr. 125, 83.

6 BATr, Abt. 90, Nr. 100, 94.

7 See Domarchiv Aachen, PA – Propstarchiv (DAA, PA) 59, "Ordnung der Frohnleichnams-Prozession" documents.

8 DAA, PA 59, "Aachen, den 10 September 1915."

9 Zimmer, *Remaking the Rhythms of Life*; see chap. 7, "Corpus Christi."

10 Walking is also an integral part of the history of European pilgrimage; see Chaucer's *Canterbury Tales*; Christian Jr., *Apparitions*, 84.

11 Anthon, *A Pilgrimage to Treves*, 98.

12 Anthon, 98–9.

13 DAA, PA 58, Aachen den 14 April 1846.

14 DAA, PA 62, Joseph Bonneritz. In the correspondence Bonneritz spells the city as "Niederlantenbach."

15 DAA, PA 62, "Aachen, den 10 April 1902."

16 DAA, PA 62, "Aachen, den 10 April 1902."

17 DAA, PA 62, "Aachen, den 15 April 1902."

18 DAA, PA 58, "Publicandum bezüglich der Heiligthumsfahrt, welche vom 9. bis 24. Juli 1860 im Münster zu Aachen stattfinden wird."

19 DAA, PA 59, "Reihenfolge der Processionen nach den Einzelnen Tagen."

20 DAA, PA 65, "Köln den 8 Juli 1909."

21 DAA, PA 65, "Aachen 9 Juli 1909."

22 DAA, PA 58, "Erzbischofliches Gen Vik d.d. 8 Juni 1846," 41.

23 BATr, Abt. 90, Nr. 117, 48.

24 Lambertz, *Aachener Heiligtumsfahrt*, 13.

25 DAA, PA 58, Düsseldorf 3 June 1860.

26 DAA, PA 61, Köln den 15 June 1881.

27 "Zur Heiligtumsfahrt," *Aachener Zeitung*, Montag, 16 July 1860.

28 BATr, Abt. 90, Nr. 173, 650.

29 BATr, Abt. 90, Nr. 173, 651.

30 BATr, Abt. 90, Nr. 173, 212.

31 BATr, Abt. 90, Nr. 173, 214.

32 BATr, Abt. 90, Nr. 124, "15 Juli 1933, Fräulein Lucie Ruffert."

33 See Allcock, "Tourism as a Sacred Journey"; Rinschede, "Forms of Religious Tourism." Rinschede notes that the car and bus became the most important modes of transport for religious travel in the late nineteenth and early twentieth centuries.

34 See Koshar, "History of the Automobile."

35 BATr, Abt. 90, Nr. 199-70, 30.

36 BATr, Abt. 90, Nr. 199-70, 32.

37 BATr, Abt. 90, Nr. 101, 87: "Es wird von der Trierer Wallfahrtsleitung dringend gewünscht, daß die Wallfahrer sich nur in geschlossenen, von Geistlichen geführten Prozessionen, nicht aber in kleineren Reisegesellschaften nach Trier begeben."

38 BATr, Abt. 90, Nr. 101, 87: "und unter Leitung von Generalsekretär Schroeder steht. Alle auf die Wallfahrt bezüglichen Anfragen ersuchen wir an dieses Büro zu richten."

39 BATr Abt. 90, Nr. 173, 618. The *Einzelpilger* arrived via the national trains, Reichs Bahn Direktion.

40 BATr, Abt. 90, Nr. 110, 138.

41 BATr, Abt. 90, Nr. 100, 26 (p. 10 of their report).

42 BATr, Abt. 90, Nr. 100, 96.

43 BATr, Abt. 90, Nr. 106, 54: "Ich merkte bald, daß es sich um wilde Pilger handeln müsse," and "Warum greift die Wallfahrtsleitung nicht mit aller Schärfe gegen die wilden Pilger ein. Das ist doch keine Wallfahrt."

44 BATr, Abt. 90, Nr. 106, 55.

45 BATr, Abt. 90, Nr. 110, 110.

46 BATr, Abt. 90, Nr. 110, 128.

47 BATr, Abt. 90, Nr. 110, 113.

48 BATr, Abt. 90, Nr. 106, 26. For another instance of this type of complaint, see Beuer's letter at BATr, Abt. 90, Nr. 106, 54.

49 BATr, Abt. 90, Nr. 106, 29.

50 BATr, Abt. 90, Nr. 100, 103.

51 BATr, Abt. 90, Nr. 100, 105.

52 BATr, Abt. 90, Nr. 106, 87–8.

53 BATr, Abt. 90, Nr. 106, 87.

54 BATr, Abt. 90, Nr. 106, 90.

55 BATr, Abt. 90, Nr. 100, 92.

56 BATr, Abt. 90, Nr. 100, 96.

57 BATr, Abt. 90, Nr. 100, 101.

58 BATr, Abt. 90, Nr. 100, 92–3.

59 BATr, Abt. 90, Nr. 100, 108.

60 BATr, Abt. 90, Nr. 100, 154.

61 BATr, Abt. 90, Nr. 100, 98.

62 BATr, Abt. 90, Nr. 110, 111–12; Jackowski and Smith, "Polish Pilgrim-Tourists."

63 DAA, PA 59, "Circular für die Mitglieder des Arbeiter-Vereins zum h. Paulus für Aachen und Burtscheid."

64 *Echo der Gegenwart*, Mittwoch, 8 July, *Erstes Blatt*, "Programm für den Festzug, welcher am Donnerstag den 8. Juli zur Vorfeier der Heiligthumsfahrt stattfinden soll."

65 DAA, PA 61, "Heiligthumsfahrt zu Aachen im Jahre 1888. Am Eröffnungstage, den 9. Juli, Abends 7 Uhr."

66 DAA, PA 61, "Heiligthumsfahrt zu Aachen / im Jahre 1895 / Am Eröffnungstage, den 9. Juli, Abends 7½ Uhr."

67 DAA, PA 62, "Am Eröffnungstage den 9. Juli, Abends 7¾ Uhr: Grosser Festzug der nachgenannten Vereine Aachens und Burtscheids," "Ochsen- und Schweinemetzger, Bäcker, Maler und Anstreicher."

68 DAA, PA 65, "Heiligthumsfahrt zu Aachen im Jahre 1909 / Am Eröffnungstage, den 9. Juli, Abends 7½ Uhr."

69 For the origins of Rhenish Catholic associations in the first half of the nineteenth century, see Brophy, *Popular Culture*.

70 DAA, PA 65, "J No. 6835." "Münsterkirche aus über Annastraße, Löhergraben, Jakobstraße, Markt, Großkölnstraße, Comphausbadstraße, Peterstraße, Friedrich Wilhelmplatz, Kapuzinergraben, Kleinmarschierstraße, Schmiedstraße und Fischmarkt zieht und von dort zur Münsterkirche."

71 DAA, Domkapitel 4.1.1.4, "Heiligtumsfahrt 1937, Kommando der Schutzpolizei." The route they followed was almost unchanged from previous pilgrimages: "Vom Münster, Domhof, Fischmarkt, Annastrasse, Löhergraben, Jakobstrasse, Markt, Groß-Kölnstrasse, Comphausbadstrasse, Petersstr., Friedrich-Wilhelm-Platz, Kapuzinergraben, Kleinmarschierstr, Jesuitenstr., Annastr., Fischmarkt, und zurück zum Münster"; "die große Reliquienprozession in der ein Kardinal, 4. Bischöfe und 20 000 Männer mitgingen. 120 000 Gläubige umsäumten mitbetend und = singend die Prozessionsstraßen. Die Gesamtpilgerzahl während der Heiligtumsfahrt wird amtlich mit rund 800 000 Pilgern ausgegeben."

72 DAA, Domkapitel 4.1.1.4, "Heiligtumsfahrt 1937, Kommando der Schutzpolizei," "Prozessions Ordnung."

73 DAA, Domkapitel 4.1.1.11, *Bistumsblatt, Passau*, "Eines der größten deutschen Kirchenfeste: Gewaltiger Abschluß der Aachener Heiligtumsfahrt, 8.8.1937."

74 For this correspondence, see DAA, PA 59.

75 DAA, PA 62, "5 Juli 1902," "Mocken, 5/7 1902."

76 See BATr, Abt. 90, Nr. 128, 295–365. On the Nazi presence in 1933 Trier, see Doney, "Brown and Black Boundaries." On Nazi trials against Catholics for currency violations, see Martina Cucchiara, "The Bonds That Shame." On Catholicism and Nazism, see Hastings, *Catholicism and the Roots of Nazism*.

77 See appendix 7 for the ordering of the 1867 Aachen closing ceremony procession, for example.

78 DAA, PA 61, "Heiligthumsfahrt. Zur Schlußfeier am 24 Juli 1888."

79 DAA, Domkapitel 4.1.1.4, "Anmeldungen Reliq. Proz."

80 DAA, PA 61, "Heiligthumsfahrt. Zur Schlußfeier am 24 Juli 1888."

81 DAA, PA 61, "Heiligthumsfahrt. Zur Schlußfeier am 24 Juli 1888," "a. Stiftsvikare, soviel nöthig durch andere Geistliche vermehrt, in Dalmaticen und Reliquien tragend."

82 "Kaiserin Josefine und die Aachener Heiligtümer," *Aachener Pius-Blatt, Festnummer: Das Anlaß der Aachener Heiligtumsfahrt 1909* 28 (1909): 222. This issue of the *Pius-Blatt* is undated, but is most likely from July 1909. A librarian wrote on the newspaper that it was no. 28.

83 BATr, Abt. 90, Nr. 128, 367.

84 BATr, Abt. 91, Nr. 214, 90. Brodstraße [*sic*].

85 BATr, Abt. 91, Nr. 244, 1.

86 BATr, Abt. 91, Nr. 244, 4.

87 BATr, Abt. 90, Nr. 128, 290.

88 BATr, Abt. 90, Nr. 128, 290.

89 BATr, Abt. 90, Nr. 128, 285.

90 DAA, PA 58, "Programm b. für den Schlußtag der Heiligthumsfahrt, Dienstag, den 24. Juli 1860." See also DAA, PA 58, "Programm für den Schlußtag der Heiligthumsfahrt, Sonntag den 24 Juli 1853."

91 DAA, PA 58, "Programm b. für den Schlußtag der Heiligthumsfahrt, Dienstag, den 24. Juli 1860."

92 DAA, PA 59, "Programm für den Tag der Eröffnung der Heiligthumsfahrt, Donnerstag, den 9. Juli 1874."

93 DAA, PA 58, "Programm b. für den Schlußtag der Heiligthumsfahrt, Dienstag, den 24. Juli 1860."

94 BATr, Abt. 90, Nr. 102, 24.

95 DAA, PA 58, "Aachen, 21 Mai 1860." The indulgence was still in place in 1860.

96   DAA, PA 59, "Publicandum, Aachen den 9 April 1874."

97   "Die Eröffnung des Karlsschreins im Aachener Münster," *Echo der Gegenwart*, 1906, no. 162.

98   "Die Wiedereinschließung der Gewebestoffe des Karlsschreins," *Echo der Gegenwart*, 19 November 1906, Nr. 268.

99   See especially this circular: "Merkblatt für die Wallfahrt zum hl. Rock in Trier (Beilage zum Kirchlichen Anzeiger für die Erzdiözese Köln)," in BATr, Abt. 90, Nr. 106, 125.

100   DAA, PA 58, "Ordnung bei der Krankenberührung mit dem h. Lendenthuche."

101   DAA, PA 57, "Aachen 3 August 1914."

102   DAA, PA 57, "Aachen, den 11. Mai 1915 abends 8 Uhr."

103   BATr, Abt. 90, Nr. 102, 120.

104   BATr, Abt. 90, Nr. 106, 48.

105   BATr, Abt. 90, Nr. 106, 49.

106   BATr, Abt. 90, Nr. 106, 49.

107   "Deutschland," *Sonntagsblatt f.d. kath. Familien*, München, 22 August 1937. "Sturm" has many resonances in wider German culture and history, such as Goethe and the "Sturm und Drang" Romantic movement of the late eighteenth century. On this movement, see Nipperdey, *Germany from Napoleon to Bismarck*, 389–95; Reardon, *Religion*. In the 1930s the Nazis adopted the term, for instance, the "Sturmabteilung," or SA, the Nazi Party paramilitary unit.

108   BATr, Abt. 90, Nr. 148, 132.

109   DAA, Domkapitel 4.1.1.30, "5.6.1937," "der Aachener Heiligtumsfahrt heute eine wertvolle Gelegenheit sein, einen Gebetssturm von Hunderttausenden zum Himmel für Kirche, Volk und Vaterland zu senden."

110   BATr, Abt. 90, Nr. 111, 180.

111   DAA, Domkapitel 4.1.1.32, "Predigtskizze zur Aachener Heiligtumsfahrt 1937."

112   DAA, Domkapitel 4.1.1.32, "Predigtskizze zur Aachener Heiligtumsfahrt 1937."

113   Herbermann et al., *The Catholic Encyclopedia*, 345, 608.

114   BATr, Abt. 90, Nr. 126, 47.

115   DAA, PA 66, "Gebet am Tag der Einziehung der Tücher."

116   DAA, PA 66, "Wir haben gebetet, und du hast vom Himmel unser Flehen erhört."

117   BATr, Abt. 90, Nr. 125, 291–2.

118   DAA, PA 66, "B. Kühlen Kunst und Verlagsanstalt M. Gladbach."

119   BATr, Abt. 91, Nr. 230, 29.

120   DAA, PA 68, "Pilgerbuch zur Aachener Heiligtumsfahrt!"

121   DAA, Domkapitel 4.1.1.31.

122 BATr, Abt. 90, Nr. 148, 89. Clergy had a similar problem in 1891, when socialist workers accosted pilgrims with political literature; see Korff, "Heiligenverehrung und soziale Frage"; Korff, "Formierung der Frömmigkeit."

123 BATr, Abt. 91, Nr. 228, 3.

124 BATr, Abt. 91, Nr. 250, 5.

125 BATr, Abt. 90, Nr. 173, 637.

126 BATr, Abt. 90, Nr. 173, 640.

127 On "mental pilgrimage," see Leclercq, *The Love of Learning*. See also Connolly, "Imagined Pilgrimage." Connolly considers pilgrimages of the mind to Jerusalem by thirteenth-century monks. On "throwing prayers" as a way of blessing, see Corr's study of religious practices in the Andes: Corr, "To Throw the Blessing."

128 BATr, Abt. 91, Nr. 231, 57–8.

129 BATr, Abt. 91, Nr. 231, 57.

130 BATr, Abt. 91, Nr. 58, "wie jeder andern Mensch, ganz gut."

131 BATr, Abt. 91, Nr. 230a, 24.

132 DAA, PA 58, "30 Juni 1860, Bishop of Speyer."

133 DAA, PA 61, "Fulda, den 22 Juni 1895."

134 BATr, Abt. 91, Nr. 249a, 75.

135 DAA, PA 62, "28 Mai 1902, Bischof von Osnabrück," "31 Mai 1902 Bischof von Münster."

136 BATr, Abt. 90, Nr. 199-70, 32.

137 BATr, Abt. 90 Nr. 128, 69.

138 BATr, Abt. 90, Nr. 128, 96, "Verleihe uns die Gnade"; BATr, Abt. 90, Nr. 128, 96, "Gewähre uns die Gesinnung des getreuen Knechtes der nicht besser gekleidet sein will als sein Herr."

139 BATr, Abt. 90, Nr. 128, 94, "Ihre Übertragung der Festhymne hatte ja inzwischen durch die Vertonung des Herrn Domkapellmeisters weiteste Verbreitung gefunden." See also, "Andacht zu Ehren des heiligen Rockes," in BATr, Abt. 90, Nr. 128, 95.

140 BATr, Abt. 90, Nr. 128, 95, "Du trugst das Kleid Deines Landes und Deines Volkes."

141 BATr, Abt. 90, Nr. 128, 97.

142 BATr, Abt. 90, Nr. 128, 97.

143 BATr, Abt. 90, Nr. 128, 98.

144 BATr, Abt. 90, Nr. 128, 99.

145 BATr, Abt. 90, Nr. 101, 62–3.

146 BATr, Abt. 90, Nr. 101, 67.

147 Herbermann et al., *The Catholic Encyclopedia*, 85: "Pilgrimages were set down as adequate punishments inflicted for certain crimes. The hardships of the journey, the penitential garb worn, the mendicity it entailed made a pilgrimage a real and efficient penance."

148 BATr, Abt. 90, Nr. 199-70, 29.

149 Johannes Ronge, "Zur Geschichte der Anfänge einer deutsch-kathol. Kirche: Ein Wort an die Römlinge Deutschlands und nur an diese, zum Neujahr 1845," *Allgemeine Kirchen Zeitung*, 2 February 1845, Nr. 19. See also BATr, Abt. 91, Nr. 231, 164, "Wenn die Trier'schen Wallfahrer rufen: 'Heiliger Rock, bitte für uns'; so ist und bleibt dieß ein Götzendienst."

150 BATr, Abt. 91, Nr. 231a, 26.

151 Thanks to Katie Jarvis for reminding me of this quote from St. Augustine during a writing session on 2 August 2013.

152 BATr, Abt. 91, Nr. 241, 352. On confessional conflict in the Rhineland, see Bennette, "Threatened Protestants."

153 BATr, Abt. 91, Nr. 241, 356–8.

154 BATr, Abt. 91, Nr. 241, 360.

155 BATr, Abt. 91, Nr. 241, 361.

156 BATr, Abt. 91, Nr. 241, 362.

157 BATr, Abt. 91, Nr. 241, 364–6.

158 BATr, Abt. 91, Nr. 241, 363–7.

159 BATr, Abt. 91, Nr. 231, 24.

160 These local Holy Coat songs disappeared completely in 1975 with the introduction of the national Catholic hymnal. Heinz, "Die Lieder vom Heiligen Rock," 526.

161 BATr, Abt. 91, Nr. 230.

162 BATr, Abt. 91, Nr. 230, 6.

163 BATr, Abt. 91, Nr. 230, 12.

164 BATr, Abt. 91, Nr. 230, 15.

165 BATr, Abt. 91, Nr. 230, 44.

166 BATr, Abt. 91, Nr. 230, 50.

167 BATr, Abt 91, Nr. 230a, 18.

168 BATr, Abt. 91, Nr. 214, 7.

169 BATr, Abt. 90, Nr. 112, 128.

170 BATr, Abt. 91, Nr. 220, 33.

171 BATr, Abt. 91, Nr. 220, 34. Petsch had trouble recalling exactly what she exclaimed, but it was either "Ach mein Gott" or "Ach mein Heiland."

172 DAA, PA 58, "Programm für die Heiligthumsfahrt zu Aachen im Jahre 1853"; "Von den Pilgern wird bei dem Anziehen durch die Kirche abwechselnd und laut gebetet oder gesungen."

173 DAA, PA 58, "Entwurf des Programms für die Heiligthumsfahrt pro 1853"; "laut gebetet und gesungen."

174 Anon., *Lieder zur Heiligthumsfahrt*, 10.

175 BATr, Abt. 90, Nr. 128, 79–80.

176 Anon., *Andachtsübungen bei der feierlichen Aussetzung des heil*, 4–5.

177 BATr, Abt. 90, Nr. 128, 79–80.

178 BATr, Abt. 90, Nr. 102, 106. For full lyrics of many of the songs here discussed, see appendix 1: "Selected Pilgrim Songs in Translation, 1839–1933."
179 BATr, Abt. 90, Nr. 144, 59.
180 BATr, Abt. 91, Nr. 230, 61.
181 BATr, Abt. 91, Nr. 230, 61.
182 Clifford Geertz, *The Interpretation of Cultures*, 17. See also Geertz, "'The Pinch of Destiny.'" For recent work on the usefulness of Geertz in the study of religion, see studies by Schilbrack, "Religions, Models of, and Reality"; and Springs, "What Cultural Theorists."
183 Subdiakons: BATr, Abt. 90, Nr. 128, 291; Presbyter: BATr, Abt. 90, Nr. 128, 292; Ehrendiakone: BATr, Abt. 90, Nr. 128, 293.
184 Fuhr, *Die Heiligthümer Aachens*, 29.
185 BATr, Abt. 90, Nr. 128, 79–80.

2 Modern Miracles

1 Anon., *Der heilige Rock und seine Wunderkraft*.
2 Anon., *Bericht über die wunderbaren Heilungen*, 8: "ein so lautes Weinen aus, daß alle Anwesenden auf das Heftigste erschüttert wurden und sich der Thränen nicht erwehren konnten."
3 Anon., 8. See also Marx, *History of the Robe*.
4 Gross, "The Strange Case." See also Blackbourn, *Marpingen*, 159: "Catholic poor, supported by priests and Catholic newspapers, against the state authorities, supported by doctors and the liberal press." Mallmann, "'Maria hilf, vernichte unsere Feinde.'"
5 Schieder, "Church and Revolution."
6 Blackbourn, *Marpingen*, 161. See also Kselman, *Miracles*. Kselman argues that alienation may have caused the sicknesses that plagued those seeking cure (59).
7 Blackbourn, 163.
8 Blackbourn, 151.
9 See William Egginton's discussion of "pockets of presence" in the modern period in *How the World Became a Stage*, 7.
10 Ruth Harris has observed that there are "limitations of historical understanding," in *Lourdes*, 345.
11 Anthropologists have developed a range of analytic tools for looking at the miraculous religious experience. For an example of recent sociolinguistic analysis of religion, see Robbins, "God Is Nothing but Talk." See also Jon P. Mitchell's criticism of his colleagues for relying on semiotic and practical forms of knowledge without developing an adequate theory for the emotional component of cognition, in "A Moment with Christ," 81.

12 This application of rite of passage to the nineteenth century requires rejecting Turner's thesis that the liminal rite of passage is more prevalent in so-called "primitive" or "pre-literate" societies. See Turner, "Comments and Conclusions."

13 There are many examples in the correspondence: see BATr, Abt. 91, Nr. 220, 98–100 (#10. Magdalena Steff).

14 Luhrmann, Nusbaum, Thisted, "The Absorption Hypothesis," 74–5.

15 Shoaps, "'Pray Earnestly.'"

16 Turner, *Dramas, Fields, and Metaphors*, 197; Jonas, "Restoring a Sacred Center."

17 Tweed, *Crossing and Dwelling*, 157. For Tweed the body is "the actual Here that surveys other spaces, both close and distant; it is the actual Now from which humans narrate the past and imagine the future."

18 Orsi, "The Cult of the Saints," 65.

19 Blackbourn, *Marpingen*, 148.

20 Harris, *Lourdes*, 306.

21 Anon., *Bericht über die wunderbaren Heilungen*.

22 Anon., *Drei und zwanzig wunderbare Heilungen*.

23 Hansen, *Achtzehn Wunderbare Heilungen*.

24 From Korum, *Wunder und Göttliche Gnadenerweise*.

25 Ninety-nine *Akten* in the BATr are devoted to doctor's notes confirming that pilgrims were sick. Trier officials required these testaments for the ill to gain access to the cathedral. I have taken detailed notes on nineteen of these *Akten*, which are arranged in alphabetical order, and found 3,625 applications within. Taking this as the average, there are 190.79 applications per *Akta* times eighty *Akten* I have not included, as well as the 3,625, equals 18,888 applications. Of course, the actual number of people is likely much higher, as there will be an increased number of applications with more common first letters in last names; for example, *T* and *S*. See BATr, Abt. 90, Nr. 175–Abt. 90, Nr. 199-70. In the charts that follow I am working out of BATr, Abt. 90, Nr. 175-Nr. 191. The hope is that these 3,625 applications are representative, as they are taken as they appear in the records. BATr, Abt. 90, Nr. 173, 489. This page is also the source for table 2.9.

26 BATr, Abt. 90, Nr. 134a–134b. Kranken Attest, Krankenausweis. Even more than gender, these data are particularly useful in showing where pilgrims originated, and how far they travelled to get to Trier.

27 This fact problematizes any assumption that women filled pews while men retired to saloons on Sundays. There is a large literature on this topic to be addressed elsewhere. For example, see McLeod, "Weibliche Frömmigkeit – männliche Unglaube?" On this process in the United States, see Welter, "The Feminization of American Religion."

28 BATr, Abt. 90, Nr. 131.

29 Age is included for only 143 of 672 petitioners, or 21 per cent. This percentage is too low to draw meaningful conclusions from this data set.

30 I here follow Thomas Childers's work on German voting patterns during the Weimar Republic and early Third Reich. Childers relied on the 1925 German census and voting information from 500 German locales to establish his *Stände*, or class, categories. See Childers, *Nazi Voter*, esp. introduction and chap. 2.

31 Classifying the "working class" is highly challenging, but on the *Fragebogen* this group consists of foreign workers, construction workers, roofers, painters, daily workers, mechanics, gardeners, quarrymen, and laundresses.

32 For example, the new middle class includes bankers, businessmen, engineers, office assistants, typists, mayors, and national train employees (Bahn Oberschaffner, Bahnbeamter, etc.).

33 *Kaplan, Klosterbruder, Klostermeister, Missionspater, Bruder, geistl. Regen, Augusterin, Vinzenskloster, Sauglingsschwester, Franziskanerin, Klosterfrau, Klosterschwester.*

34 Childers, *Nazi Voter*, 202, 242.

35 Blackbourn, *Marpingen*, 138.

36 Lambertz, *Aachener Heiligtumsfahrt*, 95.

37 Lambertz, 105.

38 The data for this analysis come from DAA, 4.1.1.18, Krankenkarten A–C, 4.1.1.19, Krankenkarten D–G, 4.1.1.20, Krankenkarten H–K, 4.1.1.21, Krankenkarten L–P, 4.1.1.22, Krankenkarten Q–Z. Assigning the M and F is hardly scientific and requires inference, but I have tried to minimize error. For example, an individual named "Hub.," "Christ.," or "Jos." is excluded from the analysis because this could be the beginning of a male or female name.

39 This total is attained by adding the group totals to the categorical totals (removing the thirty-three groups from the equation).

40 Blackbourn, *Marpingen*, 149.

41 Evans, *Third Reich in Power*, 328–36.

42 Mosse, *The Image of Man*, esp. chap. 8, "The New Fascist Man."

43 Evans, *Third Reich in Power*, 520.

44 On the intersection of suffering and Catholic piety, see Kane, "'She Offered Herself Up.'" On gender and the cult of suffering, see O'Sullivan, *Disruptive Power*, esp. chap. 4.

45 See van Osselaer's discussion of male and female religious identities: van Osselaer, "Feminization Thesis." On masculinity and Marian apparitions, see van Osselaer, "Sensitive but Sane."

46 BATr, Abt. 91, Nr. 221, 150.

47 BATr, Abt. 91, Nr. 220, 154–6.

48 For a treatment of religious transformation as a multi-step process, see Rebbeca J. Lester's work on the Siervas convent in Mexico: Lester, *Jesus in Our Wombs*.

49 BATr, Abt. 91, Nr. 220. They reported eighteen cured and only one of them male.

50 BATr, Abt. 91, Nr. 220, 1. Peter Marx, Schiffer aus St. Barbele; Thomas Varain, Rothgarber; Andreas Kauth, Gastwirth; Jakob Seeberger, Baumeister; Christian Trempert, Metzger; Jakob Bentz, Privat Sekretär.

51 BATr, Abt. 91, Nr. 220, 4. Testimony from Peter Marx.

52 Hermand, *Der deutsche Vormärz*, 157–8. The song is originally titled "Freifrau von Droste-Fischering." Throughout this book, I have standardized the spelling of the countess's name as Countess Droste zu Vischering.

53 BATr, Abt. 91, Nr. 220, 21–5.

54 Anon., *Bericht über die wunderbaren Heilungen*, 9–10.

55 BATr, Abt. 91, Nr. 220, 42–5.

56 Quoted in Myerhoff, "Return to Wirikuta," 233. See also Smith, "Acknowledgements,"; Studstill, "Eliade."

57 DAA, PA 58, "Zum Andenken and das Große Wunder welches bei der siebenjährigen Vorzeigung der Aachener Heiligthümer geschehen ist."

58 DAA, PA 58, "Sohn Dawitz (Davids) erbarme dich meiner."

59 Here one can think of the relics in terms of Eliade's talismans and paradisial states. Through the Coat, pilgrims gained access to divine favour and contacted an otherworldly state. See Eliade, "Yearning for Paradise."

60 "Die Heilung einer Wallfahren: Ein Besuch bei der anläßlich der Berührung des Heiligen Rockes in Trier geheilten Frau Willmann aus Mutterstadt," *Für den Sonntag*, Samstag, 5 August 1933, Seite 5, Nr. 170.

61 The 1933 cures were often widely publicized. Frau Willmann of Mutterstadt went home after her cure and did not seek any media attention, but was later interviewed by reporters from *Für den Sonntag*. "Die Heilung einer Wallfahren: Ein Besuch bei der anläßlich der Berührung des Heiligen Rockes in Trier geheilten Frau Willmann aus Mutterstadt," *Für den Sonntag*, Samstag, 5 August 1933, Seite 5, Nr. 170.

62 BATr, Abt. 91, Nr. 230, 42.

63 BATr, Abt. 91, Nr. 229, 187–90.

64 BATr, Abt. 90, Nr. 129, 210.

65 BATr, Abt. 90, Nr. 129, 110. "Schwerkrank nach Trier – genesend zurück," *Neue Augsburger Zeitung*, 12 September 1933, Nr. 204.

66 BATr, Abt. 91, Nr. 220, 75–81.

67 BATr, Abt. 91, Nr. 230; Schneider, "Feminisierung der Religion."

68 BATr, Abt. 91, Nr. 220, 50–60.

69 BATr, Abt. 91, Nr. 220, 143–5. Keiss came to Trier from Senheim.

70 BATr, Abt 91, Nr. 250, 2–6.

71 BATr, Abt. 91, Nr. 250, 6. I will consider the the turn towards verifiability and necessity for scientific soundness in the next chapter.

72 BATr, Abt. 91, Nr. 241, 86–90. Trier den 21 Juli 1830, Rosalia.

73 BATr, Abt. 91, Nr. 228, 51, Halsenbach, d. 19. October 1844, Breitz, Pfr. In chap. 5, "Clerical Crossroads," I will address how clergy worked to verify claims like that of Johann Müller II.

74 BATr, Abt. 91, Nr. 230, 50.

75 BATr, Abt. 91, Nr. 231, 59–60.

76 See Math. Fischer's testimony: BATr, Abt. 91, Nr. 229, 199–218.

77 BATr, Abt. 91, Nr. 228, 21–3.

78 BATr, Abt. 90, Nr. 173, 654.

79 BATr, Abt. 91, Nr. 228, 59.

80 Heinz was popular in the 1844 pamphlets, but is also in the correspondence; see BATr, Abt. 91, Nr. 229, 91–4.

81 BATr, Abt. 90, Nr. 124, 219.

82 BATr, Abt. 90, Nr. 124, 217–19.

83 BATr, Abt. 91, Nr. 220, 148–9.

84 DAA, PA 67 a. 65 Gottesdienst. Heiligtumsfahrt 1925, "Esch. der 16 Sept. 1925."

85 DAA, PA 72, "Prüm, den 12 Juli 1895."

86 BATr, Abt. 90, Nr. 130, 79–82.

87 BATr, Abt. 90, Nr. 130, 11–12.

88 BATr, Abt. 90, Nr. 131, 146.

89 Egginton, *How the World Became a Stage*, 123.

90 BATr, Abt. 90, Nr. 101, 65.

3 The Sacred Economy

1 Kaufman, "Selling Lourdes"; Eade, "Pilgrimage and Tourism"; Gross, "The Souvenir and Sacrifice."

2 See Cohen, "Authenticity and Commoditization."

3 See Hans-Joachim Kann's work for lists of postcards and medals: "Heiligrock-Postkarten-Probleme" and "Unedierte Metallene Heiligrock-Andenken."

4 On presentification, see Gumbrecht, *The Production of Presence*, 123–5.

5 See Gumbrecht, 49; see also Runia, "Presence"; and Strathausen, "A Rebel."

6 Erik Cohen has convincingly argued that commodification does not necessarily change the meaning of cultural products because "tourists" (here I would add modern pilgrims) "entertain concepts of 'authenticity' which are much looser than those entertained by intellectuals and experts." See Cohen, "Authenticity and Commoditization," 383.

7 I am indebted in part to Surinder Mohan Bhardwaj's notion of "pilgrim flows," which made me think of circular motion. See Bhardwaj, *Hindu Places*; Williams and Zelinsky, "On Some Patterns."

8 Again, the Rhineland pilgrimages here are different from those of Lourdes, as they are periodic and not perpetual, invariably influencing pilgrim perception and the scale of what can be bought. See Fleischer, "The Tourist"; Rinschede, "The Pilgrimage Center of Fatima/Portugal," 90–3.

9 Much of the work in German catalogues various objects; see Kann, "Heiligrock-Postkarten-Probleme" and "Unedierte Metallene Heiligrock-Andenken" and Kevin Köster, "Wallfahrtsmedaillen und Pilgerandenken." See also Hagen, *Die Wallfahrtsmedaillen des Rheinlandes*. Hagen describes the development of pilgrimage medals and how their appearance changed over time.

10 See Cohen, "Pilgrimage and Tourism; Cohen, "A Phenomenology of Tourist Experiences."

11 Kaufman, "Selling Lourdes," 70.

12 See Gesler, "Lourdes," 104.

13 See Blackbourn, *Marpingen*, 163–72. Blackbourn is too quick to write off the potential uniqueness of pilgrim remembrances, stating that they "were much the same at all the apparition sites, with suitable alterations to fit local circumstances," (169).

14 Kaufman, "Selling Lourdes," ff. 27, 87.

15 Dühr and Groß-Morgen, *Zwischen Andacht und Andenken*, 479.

16 Stephany, "Der Zusammenhang." For a concise history of the Aachen pilgrimage before the fifteenth century, see Wynands, *Zur Geschichte der Aachener Heiligtumsfahrt*.

17 In *The Canterbury Tales*, Geoffrey Chaucer describes pilgrims wearing jewelled and pewter badges and carrying rosaries to mark their travels in fifteenth-century England. See also Christian Jr., *Apparitions*; and Constable, "Opposition to Pilgrimage."

18 On the German middle class marking their homes, see Tebbe, "Landscapes of Remembrance."

19 Dühr and Groß-Morgen, *Zwischen Andacht und Andenken*, 268–306.

20 There is a similar increase in medals between 1810 and 1844. In Dühr's compilation of *Andenken* she found one Wallfahrtsmedaille for 1810 and five for 1844.

21 DAA, PA 58, Iven in Cologne to Grosman in Aachen, 2 June 1846.

22 Part of a larger trend of Aachen taking lessons from the 1844 pilgrimage, for example, Aachen wanted to model the security around the cathedral on what was done in 1844 Trier; see Article 3 in "Akten betreffend die im Jahre 1846 hierselbst in Aachen Stadt findende Heiligthumsfahrt. 1. Bericht an den Herrn Erzbischof d.d. 31 März 1846," DAA, PA 58.

23 Dühr and Groß-Morgen, *Zwischen Andacht und Andenken*, 249.

24 Dühr and Groß-Morgen, 249. Dühr also notes (p. 250) that critics of Trier produced their own set of literature and remembrances about the pilgrimage.

25 ZBA, Heiligtumswallfahrt, 1902 envelope.

26 Two examples, one to France and one to Belgium, can be found at DAA, PA 64. These postcards are both from the 1909 pilgrimage.

27 DAA, PA 82c. 1902 Postcard An Frl. Gretchen Stephany in Trier.

28 DAA, PA 56. Letter to Dr. Alphons Bellesheim, 15 May 1902.

29 DAA, PA 64. Emil Grözinger, Gen Repräsident erster Engos und Export Handelsfirma to Stiftskapitel Aachen, 15 June 1909.

30 Below I will address the significance pilgrims assigned to objects that were in close contact with the Aachen and Trier artefacts.

31 Poll, *Geschichte Aachen in Daten*, 268–9. In 1920 the population of Aachen was 148,993; see Poll, 273.

32 DAA, PA Nr. 67 a.

33 DAA, PA Nr. 67 a.

34 DAA, Domkapitel 4.1.1.30, Ausweis-Karte, Pilgerbücher.

35 Isabel Gebhardt, "Von Jesus kann man nie genug haben," *Paulinus: Die Tageszeitung zur Wallfahrt*, 11 May 2012, 13.

36 There is also evidence into the twentieth century of pilgrims designing pipes for their journeys. See Kann, "Trierer Wallfahrtspfeifen." Kann points out that there were two types of pipe on sale in 1891 Trier, but church authorities suppressed the sale of pipes in 1933 as kitsch. For an image of a pipe that is shaped like Mary's head, see Dühr and Groß-Morgen, *Zwischen Andacht und Andenken*, 403.

37 Michael Merten, *Paulinus: Die Tageszeitung zur Wallfahrt*, "Tief im Herzen schöne Erinnerungen, 5 May 2012, 11.

38 DAA, PA, Nr. 66, "Ordnung für den Pilgerzug des Dekanates Hochneukirch am 13. Juli 1925."

39 BATr, Abt. 90, Nr. 115, 10.

40 BATr, Abt. 90, Nr. 148, 65, "In allen Pfarreien gibt es genug Leute, die gerne für einen Armen die 30 Pfg. aufbringen können."

41 BATr, Abt. 90, Nr. 163.

42 BATr, Abt. 91, Nr. 257 a. "Paulinus Druckerei, Trier, den 10. Juni 1891."

43 Irsch (1872–1956) was an art historian and leveraged this knowledge to help set the aesthetics for 1933 *Andenken*. See his *Die Wallfahrt zum Hl. Rock im Dome zu Trier 1933*.

44 BATr, Abt. 90, Nr. 136, 110, Irsch letter to Gesellschaft für Christliche Kunst, München.

45 BATr, Abt. 90, Nr. 136, 46.

46 BATr, Abt. 90, Nr. 136, 236.

47 BATr, Abt. 90, Nr. 136, 50.

48 BATr, Abt. 90, Nr. 59.

49 BATr, Abt. 90, Nr. 136, 259.

50 BATr, Abt. 90, Nr. 136, 352.

51 Based on index at the front of: BATr, Abt. 90, Nr. 136, 1–11.

52 BATr, Abt. 90, Nr. 136, 110.

53 BATr, Abt. 90, Nr. 136, 109.

54 BATr, Abt. 90, Nr. 136, 132, "Wir setzen jedoch voraus, dass Sie den Gesichtsausdruck würdiger und klarer gestalten werden. Auch möchten wir raten, statt 'Heiligtumsfahrt' entsprechend trierischer Tradition zu schreiben: 'Ausstellung des Hl. Rockes Trier 1933.'" This modification of the text away from "Heiligtumsfahrt" is likely an attempt to distinguish the Trier event from its Aachen counterpart.

55 BATr, Abt. 90, Nr. 136, 318.

56 BATr, Abt. 90, Nr. 136, 61–2.

57 See Auslander, *Taste and Power*, on changing French tastes and style from Louis XVI to First World War.

58 W.J.T. Mitchell quoted in Neslon, *The Persistence of Presence*, 4 on an object as medium, or "a space or pathway or messenger that connects two things – a sender to a receiver, a writer to a reader, an artist to a beholder, or (in the case of the spiritualist medium) this world to the next."

59 Here one can also think of MacCannell's notion of authenticity within tourism as occurring when tourists gain access to "back areas." In pilgrimage this is decidedly not the case. Authenticity came from those "front objects" that were embraced and approved by church officials. See MacCannell, "Staged Authenticity"; Goldberg, "Identity and Experience." See also Hagen's survey of the range of Rhineland *Andenken*. She shows an increase in Catholic commemorative medals after the Kulturkampf and after the First World War. Hagen, *Die Wallfahrtsmedaillen des Rheinlandes*.

60 BATr, Abt. 91, Nr. 230, 29. These were located on Simeonsstraße, Fleischstraße, at the market, on the Landstraße and Pallaststraße.

61 BATr, Abt. 91, Nr. 230, 29.

62 BATr, Abt. 91, Nr. 241, 293.

63 BATr, Abt. 91, Nr. 241, 293, #7.

64 DAA, PA 61, "Bei der diesjährigen Heiligthumsfahrt vom 9. bis zum 24. Juli d.J. sind folgende Vorschriften zu beobachten." There are only slight deviations in procession routes between the 1888 and 1895 Police Regulations.

65 DAA, PA 61, "Bei der diesjährigen Heiligthumsfahrt," #9.

66 DAA, PA 61, "Bei der diesjährigen Heiligthumsfahrt," #11.

67 DAA, PA 62, "Aachen 10/4 1902."

68 DAA, PA 62, "Aachen, 12 März 1902."

69 DAA, PA 62, "20 Juni 1902. Schneidermeister."

70 DAA, PA 64, "Aachen, 28 Mai 1909."

71 DAA, PA 64, "Aachen 1 Juni 1909." The rejection of Busch's request is made clear in a letter from Frau Wilh. von Agris, enquiring if she can set up stands, since Busch's proposal was declined. See DAA, PA Nr. 64, "Aachen 18 Juli 1909." By 1937 all residents of the *Altstadt* (old city) who intended to rent out benches or seats on their roof for the pilgrimage were asked to inform the Pilgrimage Committee. See DAA, Domkapitel 4.1.1.9, "katholische Kirchenzeitung Aachen, J.No. 5968."

72 DAA, PA 80, "3. Juli 1930":

1. Auf dem Katschhof, auf dem oberen Teile des Münsterplatzes, auf dem Domhof und dem Fischmarkt dürfen keine Verkaufsbuden aufgestellt werden. Die Erlaubnis zur Aufstellung von Buden an anderen als den oben beziechneten Plätzen erteilt die Polizei nach eigenem Ermessen.

2. Die Anwohner des Katschhofes, Münsterplatzes und Fischmarktes dürfen in ihren Fenstern Auslagen von Devotionalien anbringen."

73 "Bekanntmachungen der Stadt Trier," *Trier Landeszeitung*, 26 April 1933. There were eleven areas: Herz-Jesu-Kirche (Schulhof St. Barbara); Maximinkirche; Paulinuskirche; Pauluskirche (Paulusplatz); Südbahnhof; Abteiplatz und Matthiasstraße; Römerbrücke (Westseite); Jesuitenkirche (2 Stände); Hauptmarkt (soweit noch Platz vorhanden ist); Ecke Flanderstraße – Sie um Dich; Am Verkehrshäuschen (Adolf-Hitler-Straße).

74 *Trier Landeszeitung*, 26 April 1933: "Die Anträge sind bei der Polizeiverwaltung Trier spätestens bis 15.5.1933 einzureichen und müssen bestimmte Angaben über Platzgröße, Warenart und Platzgeldangebot enthalten. Anträge, in denen diese Angaben fehlen, bleiben unberücksichtigt. Zugelassen werden nur solche Gewerbetreibende, die in Trier ansässig sind." Article can also be found at BATr, Abt. 90, Nr. 111, 261.

75 BATr, Abt. 90, Nr. 106, 13–14.

76 DAA, Domkapitel 4.1.1.2, J.Nr. 21823.

77 BATr, Abt. 90, Nr. 111.

78 BATr, Abt. 90, Nr. 111, 260.

79 BATr, Abt. 90, Nr. 111, 251.

80 BATr, Abt. 90, Nr. 111, 252.

81 BATr, Abt. 90, Nr. 115, 29–30.

82 BATr, Abt. 90, Nr. 115, 29–30.

83 BATr, Abt. 90, Nr. 199-69, "Auszug aus dem Kirchl. Amtsanzeiger für die Diözese Trier. Ausgabe 14 vom 13. Juli 1933," "größte Vorsicht anzuraten."

84 BATr, Abt. 90, Nr. 199-69, "Auszug aus dem Kirchl. Amtsanzeiger für die Diözese Trier. Ausgabe 14 vom 13. Juli 1933."

85 BATr, Abt. 90, Nr. 105, 5.

86 BATr, Abt. 90, Nr. 105, 5, "Dann handeln Sie, wie ein kluger Beamter von wahrer Geistes – u. Herzensbildung handeln soll, damit das Volk nicht zur Selbsthülfe greifen muss."

87 BATr, Abt. 90, Nr. 100, 175.

88 DAA, PA 59, *Echo der Gegenwart*, Sonntag, 19 July 1874: "ihren Körbchen und Tüchern bei sich führen mustern noch rasch ihre Einkäufe, Erinnerungen an die Stadt Aachen und deren Heiligthümer, Bücher, Bilder, geweithe Kreuze und Rosenkränze u.s.w."

89 This 1874 rush on stands is also indicative of the decline in pilgrims creating their own remembrances. At least in the Trier and Aachen archives the number of surviving, non-mass-produced objects is strongest in the first half of the nineteenth century. Afterwards, *Andenken* are generally put out by either the Pilgrimage Committees or regional manufacturing firms.

90 As William Egginton has stated, presence should be taken "in its theological sense, as in the Real Presence of the body of God" because it signifies "that experience of space that subtends such diverse experiences as … the miracle of transubstantiation": *How the World Became a Stage*, 3.

91 Plater, *The Holy Coat of Treves*, 86–7.

92 "Trier, 7. October," *Trier'sche Zeitung*, 8 October 1844, Nr. 282, "Das Merkantile betreffend, hat sich herausgestellt, daß Abbildungen des h. Rockes, Medaillen, Wallfahrtsbüchlein und Rosenkränze die am meisten gesuchten und abgesetzten Artikel waren."

93 BATr, Abt. 90, Nr. 106, 17.

94 BATr, Abt. 91, Nr. 241, 170.

95 DAA, PA 60. Mar. Hospital Burtscheid. d. 27/7 1881.

96 BATr, Abt. 91, Nr. 249 a., 79.

97 Robert Orsi has studied mail-order devotion amongst U.S. Catholics in the twentieth century and linked this practice to a shift from space to time as devotional practice (from crossing distances to taking time to write letter or petition). Letters sent from the United States to Trier and Aachen help explain that letter writing was established amongst U.S. Catholics before Orsi's study begins. Yet Aachen and Trier diverge from the Chicago St. Jude shrine because petitions sent in were unbidden and the German church hierarchy did not encourage letters as a substitute for attending. See Orsi, "The Center Out There," 223.

98 DAA, PA 58, 22 July 1860.

99 DAA, PA 58. See thank you note, 3 September 1860, Erzbischof Johannes von Geissel von Köln.

100 DAA, PA 58. See Contzen, O. Bürgermeister, 30 July 1867.

101 On presence, see Runia, "Presence," 1. In this section I am attempting to make concrete Runia's theory that "the presence of the past thus does not reside primarily in the intended story or the manifest metaphorical content of the text, but in what story and text contain in spite of the intentions of the historian."

102 DAA, PA 59, 22 July 1874. Another 1874 example can be found at DAA, PA 82 c. In this case four pieces of silk are sent to a Catholic in Amsterdam.

103 DAA, PA 59, Aachen, 13 September 1874.

104 DAA, PA 59, Rensdorf, 5 August 1874.

105 BATr, Abt. 90, Nr. 128, 243–4. Fuchs sent her the small piece of silk for free.

106 DAA, PA 65, "Aachen, den 7 Juli 1909."

107 BATr, Abt. 90, Nr. 148, 205, "Ruttand, Dublin, Ireland 4th September."

108 BATr, Abt. 91, Nr. 249 a., 15.

109 BATr, Abt. 91, Abt. 91, Nr. 249 a., 23.

110 BATr, Abt. 90, Nr. 173, 190.

111 BATr, Abt. 91, Nr. 249 a., 71–3.

112 BATr, Abt. 91, Nr. 249 a., 14.

113 BATr, Abt. 91, Nr. 249 a., 75.

114 BATr, Abt. 90, Nr. 128, 255.

115 BATr, Abt. 90, Nr. 128, 256.

116 BATr, Abt. 90, Nr. 125, 553–4.

117 BATr, Abt. 91, Nr. 249 a., 45.

118 BATr, Abt. 90, Nr. 128, 272–3.

119 BATr, Abt. 90, Nr. 128, 274. Capitalization, spelling, and punctuation in original.

120 BATr, Abt. 90, Nr. 128, 275.

121 BATr, Abt. 90, Nr. 148, 221.

122 BATr, Abt. 91, Nr. 249 a., 29.

123 BATr, Abt. 90, Nr. 128, 262–5.

124 BATr, Abt. 91, Nr. 249 a., 50–1, "Ueber 100 Rückverschiedener (P51) Andenken habe ich bereits vertheilt."

125 BATr, Abt. 91, Nr. 249 a., 66–7.

126 DAA, PA 65, "Amsterdam, 22 Juli 1909."

127 BATr, Abt. 91, Nr. 128, 258.

128 BATr, Abt. 90, Nr. 128, 249.

129 BATr, Abt. 90, Nr. 128, 249.

130 BATr, Abt. 90, Nr. 128, 249. This suggests the individual in question faces either physical or spiritual death. If Pfluzer received a response, there is no record of it here.

131 BATr, Abt. 90, Nr. 128, 252.

132 BATr, Abt. 90, Nr. 128, 252.

133 BATr, Abt. 90, Nr. 102, 152.

134 BATr, Abt. 90, Nr. 148, 124.

135 BATr, Abt. 90, Nr. 125, 562.

136 BATr, Abt. 90, Nr. 125, 564.

137 BATr, Abt. 90, Nr. 125, 561, 565.

138 As Blackbourn has demonstrated, in the nineteenth century Catholics were under-represented in the propertied and educated middle classes. See *Marpingen*, 138.

139 In the theological sense that they reflected *sacramentalia*, "the object of which is to manifest the respect due to the sacrament and to secure the sanctification of the faithful" with the goal of "enhance[ing] the dignity of the Holy Sacrifice and arouse the piety of the faithful." Herbermann et al., *The Catholic Encyclopedia*, 292.

140 On presentification see Gumbrecht, *The Production of Presence*, 2004. He defines presentification as not being about assigning meaning but requiring that scholars ask "how we would have related, intellectually and with our bodies, to certain objects … if we had encountered them in their own historical everyday worlds" (124).

4 Rending Religiosity: Johannes Ronge and the 1840s Trier Controversy

1 Eschirn, *Johannes Ronges Brief*, 29.

2 Henning, *Der Heilige Rock*, 19.

3 By illuminating the muddiness of the Protestant/Catholic distinction during this moment of heated religious debate in the nineteenth century, this section cautions historians about the usefulness of "confession" as a demarcation of a particular theological milieu. The debates surrounding the term "confessionalization" are expansive and cannot be dealt with here. However, see Forster, *Catholic Germany*, 3. Recently, German historians have debated whether or not this term is useful for the modern period. See Blaschke, *Konfessionen im Konflikt*. For Blaschke's affirmation that there was a "second confessional age" between 1817 and 1960, see Blaschke, "Das 19. Jahrhundert"; Kretschmann and Pahl, "Ein 'Zweites Konfessionelles Zeitalter'?" See also most recently Zalar, *Reading and Rebellion*.

4 Andreas Daum situates Ronge's movement in the context of the Protestant Lichtfreunde ("Friends of Light"), an association of rationalistic Liberal Protestant clergy and laity in Saxony and Prussia organized in 1841. Daum, *Wissenschaftspopularisierung*, 195–209, focuses on German-Catholic biologist Emil Adolf Roßmäßler (1806–67) and argues that both groups

helped popularize science, revolution, and a pantheistic appreciation of nature: "Lichtfreunde, Deutschkatholiken und die Naturwissenschaften 1841–1859." See also Kojman, "Germanness and Religious Universalism," for a discussion of the interconnections between the German-Catholic movement and the Friends of Light.

5 Mueller, *Johannes Ronge.*

6 Pilick, *Johannes Ronge*, 29–35.

7 Ronge's writing first appeared as a newspaper article: *Säschsische Vaterlands-Blättern*, 4. Jhrg., Nr. 164, 1 October 1844. The article was reprinted in the *Frankfurter Journal*, Nr. 300. Ronge supporters also reprinted the pamphlet to spread Ronge's message; see for example Blum, *Johannes Ronge's offenes Sendschreiben*; Henning, *Der Heilige Rock*, 21–4. The article is also available in the Trier church archives; see BATr, Abt. 91, Nr. 241, Folie 1.

8 Ronge, *Urtheil eines katholischen Priesters*, 6.

9 Ronge, *Schreiben*, 4.

10 Ronge, *The Holy Coat of Treves*, 14.

11 For an examination of the political legacy of the German Catholics, especially vis-à-vis 1848, see Graf, *Die Politisierung*.

12 Ronge established this group in February 1845. See Weir, *Secularism and Religion*, 40.

13 See Kertesz, "Rationalist Heresy."

14 Pilick, *Johannes Ronge*, 35.

15 For another image of Ronge, see Weir, *Secularism and Religion*, 42.

16 Quoted in Kertesz, 360. The Leipzig Council left out the portions in brackets.

17 The hyphenated "German-Catholic" indicates Ronge's new church in this chapter, as opposed to "German Catholics," who were Germans who followed Roman Catholicism. In German, Ronge's group was titled either *"deutsch=Katholiken"* or *"Deutschkatholiken."*

18 Himioben, *Katholische Sonntagsblätter zur Belehrung*, 413.

19 Himioben, *Katholische Sonntagsblätter zur Belehrung*: "und er [Ronge] bleibt nur in so weit ein Priester, wie ein Christ den unverteilgbaren Charakter der Taufe behält, wenn er auch vom Christenthum abfällt und zum Judenthum oder Muhammedanismus übertritt."

20 Weir, *Secularism and Religion*, 44.

21 Weir, 44.

22 Eschirn, *Johannes Ronges Brief*, 16.

23 Eschirn, 16.

24 Himioben, *Katholische Sonntagsblätter zur Belehrung*: "Aber der Umstand, daß Ronge sich einen katholischen Priester nennt, seinen Artikel aus der

Mitte des katholischen Oberschlesiens datirt, daß andere Zeitungen ihn gar für einen katholischen Pfarrer ausgeben, der mit seinen Ansichten gewiß Anklang finden würde, und endlich, daß derselbe am Schlusse seinen Aufruf an seine Amtsgenossen (katholische Seelsorger?) richtet, dieß zwingt uns im Interesse der Wahrheit und um uns vor Schande zu schützen, Folgendes mitzutheilen."

25 Pilick, *Johannes Ronge*, 43. Treumund, *Die Geschichte des heiligen Rockes*, 31–5, reports the contents of the declaration. For more on New Catholics and their relationship to Roman Catholics, see Smith, *Protestants, Catholics, and Jews*.

26 Treumund, 31: "Wir sagen uns los vom römischen Bischof und seinem ganzen Anhange."

27 Treumund, 38: "der wir von ganzém Herzen das schnellste und dauerndste gedeihen wündschen, nehmen möge, wir, d.h. wir Lutheraner und Reformirte, mit einem Worte, wir Protestanten haben an ihnen jetzt Geistesverwandte, wer weiß ob in der Zukunft nicht vielleicht gar Brüder gewonnen."

28 In England, Ronge gained a reputation as an educator. He helped establish a kindergarten system. See Ronge and Ronge, *A Practical Guide*. On anti-Catholicism in England during this period, Paz, *Popular Anti-Catholicism*.

29 Ronge continued this work for years and beyond Germany. In December 1870, for instance, he worked to help establish a Hungarian kindergarten system. See his letter to Ludmilla Assing in Pilick, *Johannes Ronge*, 88–90.

30 See Ronge's pro-Garibaldi pamphlet, Ronge, *Brief von Johannes Ronge*. This pamphlet is also available in Landeshauptarchiv Koblenz (LHA Ko), Bestand 442, Nr. 10439.

31 LHA Ko, Bestand 442, Nr. 10439, "Saarbrücken den 21 Februar 1863."

32 LHA Ko, Bestand 442, Nr. 10439, "Ottweiler, 24. Februar 1863."

33 Ronge, *Urtheil eines katholischen Priesters*, 4.

34 Ronge, *Schreiben*, 4, "Die meisten dieser Tausende sind aus den niederen Volksklassen, ohnehin in großer Armuth, gedrückt, unwissend, stumpf, abergläubisch und zum Theil entartet." Wolfgang Schieder echoes this negative portrayal of the participants in "Church and Revolution," 72. Individual costs of the pilgrimage and how much the Trier Church made from the pilgrimage are difficult to gauge. Maria Fröhlich's experience, for example, likely paid more than a single Reichstaler (thirty Silbergroschen) for her trip from Neuwied to Trier, a journey of about 150 kilometres. For perspective, a day labourer in 1844 likely took home no more than seventy Reichstaler a year. This cost suggests that a trip to Trier was an investment for some pilgrims. However, many pilgrims walked and avoided the expense of a boat trip down the Mosel or Rhine River.

Richard Laufner estimates that each pilgrim donated about ten Silbergroschen in Trier, and that this allowed the church to make repairs to east chancel and Domkreuzgang after the pilgrimage. See Fröhlich, "Die Wallfahrt der Maria Fröhlich "; Laufner, "Logistische und Organisatorische."

35 Ronge, *Urtheil eines katholischen Priesters*, 6.

36 Ronge, *Urtheil eines katholischen Priesters*, 4.

37 Ronge, *Urtheil eines katholischen Priesters*, 6.

38 Ronge, *Schreiben*, 7.

39 Ronge, *Holy Coat of Treves*, 19.

40 Ronge, *Holy Coat of Treves*, 18.

41 Ronge, *Holy Coat of Treves*, 18–19. Charles Edward Anthon supported Ronge's position. He described the presence of the crutches in the cathedral as "an evidence – a dubious one, certainly – to the reality of the miracle!" See Anthon, *A Pilgrimage to Treves*, 111.

42 Ronge, *Holy Coat of Treves*, 27.

43 Ronge, 29.

44 Moritz, *Offene Antwort*, 6. Moritz wrote to Arnoldi directly on 11 January 1845 to thank the bishop for responding to Ronge. BATr, Abt. 91, Nr. 234, 5.

45 BATr, Abt. 91, Nr. 232, 30.

46 BATr, Abt. 91, Nr. 232, 30, "die Widerlegung des jungen Priesters Maritus Moritz in Aschaffenburg erscheint mir schmach, und unzeitig, doch jedenfalls wohlgemeint."

47 Regarding Marx's relationship to Bishop Arnoldi, see Sperber, *Rhineland Radicals*, 125. Sperber describes Marx as "the bishop's [Arnoldi's] right-hand man in political questions."

48 Ritter, *Ueber die Verehrung*, 5, "richtiger vernünftig, oder nicht."

49 Heide, *Der Rock des Herrn*, 20.

50 Heide, 20. See also Neumann, *Sendschreiben*, 11; Vecqueray, *Der Aufruf des Herrn Joh. Ronge*, 24; Hillebrand, *Neue Aergernisse*, 10. This was an important argument, and other authors beyond those above also pointed to Acts 19 to defend their anti-Ronge standpoint.

51 Moritz, *Die Verehrung heiliger Reliquien*, 44.

52 Three examples: Volk, *Die Berliner Gewerbeausstellung*, 22; Anon., *Der heilige Rock zu Trier und der katholische Priester Johannes Ronge*, 14; Moritz, *Offene Antwort*, 8. This episode also appears in Mark 5:25–35, and sometimes this version was cited; see Heide, *Der Rock des Herrn*, 20.

53 BATr, Abt. 91, Nr. 227, 115.

54 Moritz, *Offene Antwort*, 12.

55 Ritter, *Ueber die Verehrung*, 20.

56 Neumann, *Sendschreiben*, 5.

57 Neumann, 14.

58 Moritz, *Offene Antwort*, 29.

59 Vecqueray, *Aufruf des Herrn Joh. Ronge*, 32.

60 Heide, *Der Rock des Herrn*, 4.

61 Polycarp is still cited in Catholic teaching of the origins of pilgrimage. Herbert Thurston, "Relics"; Bitton-Ashkelony, *Encountering the Sacred*.

62 This story is retold in several pamphlets, four examples: Reinerding, *Glaubensbekenntniß von Johannes Ronge*, 31–2; Hillebrand, *Neue Aergernisse*, 14–16; Stolz, *Der neue Kometstern*, 4; Franksmann, *Beleuchtung*, 19–21.

63 On Reinerding's name and occupation, *Theologisches Literaturblatt zur Allgemeinen Kirchenzeitung*, 31 March 1845, Nr. 39, 322.

64 The annual procession argument is also made by Anon., *Die Wallfahrt nach Trier*, 6.

65 Heide, *Der Rock des Herrn*, 11, "hochschätzen." For another example, see Anon., *Die Wallfahrt nach Trier*, 5.

66 Franksmann, *Beleuchtung*, 47–8.

67 Hillebrand, *Neue Aergernisse*, 17.

68 Volk, *Die Berliner*, 20–1.

69 Geron, *Sternschnuppe*, 3.

70 Anon., *Herr Johannes Ronge mit Gründen widerlegt*, 40.

71 Anon., *heilige Rock zu Trier*, 13.

72 Franksmann, *Beleuchtung*, 22.

73 Anon., *heilige Rock zu Trier*, 7.

74 Anon., *Herr Johannes Ronge mit Gründen widerlegt*, 24. See also Lyser, *Sendschreiben an Johannes Ronge*, 9; Ritter, *Ueber die Verehrung*, 12.

75 Reinerding, *Glaubensbekenntniß von Johannes Ronge*, 21–3. See Eire, *War against the Idols*.

76 Reinerding, 21.

77 For a brief description of Jarcke's entanglement with tracts against Prussian censorship laws, see Grogan, *The Noblest Agitator*, 67–9.

78 BATr, Abt. 91, Nr. 235, 160–2.

79 BATr, Abt. 91, Nr. 237, 2.

80 BATr, Abt. 91, Nr. 237, 2, "kränkendste verletzer."

81 BATr, Abt. 91, Nr. 237, 4–5, "Mit tiefer Indignation haben wir besonders gewahrt, wie unsere h. Katholische Kirche von der Tagespresse mißhandelt wird, wie ihre Heiligthümer in der Koth herabgezogen, ihre uralten dogmen und ehrwürdiger Ceremonien angefeindet und entstellt werden."

82 BATr, Abt. 91, Nr. 237, 6–7.

83 BATr, Abt. 91, Nr. 237, 10.

84 BATr, Abt. 91, Nr. 237, 11.

85 BATr, Abt. 91, Nr. 237, 18–19.

86 BATr, Abt. 91, Nr. 237, 34.

87 BATr, Abt. 91, Nr. 237, 24–5.

88 Lüdtke, "The Role of State Violence," 188–9.

89 BATr, Abt. 91, Nr. 241, 158–60.

90 His article "Zur Geschichte der Anfänge einer deutsch-kathol. Kirche: Ein Wort an die Römlinge Deutschlands und nur an diese, zum Neujahr 1845" was reprinted and distributed: *Allgemeine Kirchen Zeitung*, 2 February 1845, No. 19. See also BATr, Abt. 91, Nr. 235, 164–8.

91 BATr, Abt. 91, Nr. 235, 164–8, "die Hohenpriester und das Pfaffenthum der Juden fraß bloß die jüdische Nation, ihr aber habt die unglückseligen Geschicke vieler Völker von Europa auf euch."

92 BATr, Abt. 91, Nr. 235, 164–8, "daß ein Bischof so viel Geld von der armen leichtgläubigen Menge hingenommen hat? Wie?"

93 BATr, Abt. 91, Nr. 235, 164–8.

94 BATr, Abt. 91, Nr. 235, 164–8, "Heiliger Rock, bitte für uns."

95 BATr, Abt. 91, Nr. 235, 164–8, "Ein ganz einfacher Mensch, ohne Reichthum, ohne Macht, ein Mensch, der keine andere Heimath hat, als die Herzen seiner Freunde und des größten Theils der Völker, die ihr mißhaldelt."

96 BATr, Abt. 91, Nr. 235, 164–8.

97 BATr, Abt. 91, Nr. 235, 164–8.

98 Steinruck, "Die Heilig-Rock-Wallfahrt von 1844," 315.

99 Kuhn, "Deutschkatholiken," 559.

100 See Grosse, "Adolf Glaßbrenner."

101 Robert Blum was the editor of *Sächsische Vaterlandsblätter*; see Schieder, "Church and Revolution," 72; Daum, *Wissenschaftspopularisierung*, 204. He was born in Cologne; for a contemporary biography, see Frey, *Robert Blum*.

102 Blum, *Johannes Ronge's offenes Sendschreiben*.

103 For a critical evaluation of Czerski and his teachings, see Sonst, *Der Priester-Apostat Johann Czerskil*. In some of the pamphlets Czerski appears as Czersky. For the sake of uniformity, I use the "Czerski" spelling. Another priest, Peter Alois Licht (1781–1847), also left the Catholic Church to join the German-Catholics. He also engaged in the pamphlet debate but was not as prolific as the Ronge-Czerski connection. See Embach, "Die Trierer Heilig-Rock-Wallfahrt von 1844," 809.

104 Steinruck, "Die Heilig-Rock-Wallfahrt von 1844," 312.

105 Treumund, *Die Geschichte des heiligen Rockes*, 16: "weil man immer noch Rücknahme seiner Irrlehren, wie man sie nannte, von ihm erwartete."

106 Treumund, 27.

107 Treumund, 27.

108 Treumund, 28–9.

109 Treumund, 30, "Wir bekennen fest, daß Christus allein das Oberhaupt seiner Kirche und sein Stellvertreter auf Erden der Heilige Geist ist." There are twelve total declarations of faith in the Schneidemühl confession.

110 This includes Witte, *Der Heilige*.

111 Anon., *Luther und Ronge*, 81.

112 Anon., 81.

113 Geron, *Sternschnuppe*, 16.

114 Pfaff, *Den neuen deutsch-katholischen Gemeinden*.

115 Eschirn, *Johannes Ronges Brief*, 24.

116 Frühwald, "Die Wallfahrt nach Trier," 367 ff. 3.

117 Steinruck, "Die Heilig-Rock-Wallfahrt von 1844," 311. Pilick, *Johannes Ronge*, 33. Historian Wolfgang Frühwald has argued that Ronge's writings were oriented towards an educated audience (gebildetes Publikum). This appears to be the case because of Ronge's theological orientation and emphasis on Church fathers and philosophers.

118 Steinruck, "Die Heilig-Rock-Wallfahrt von 1844," 312–13. See also Kuhn, "Deutschkatholiken," 561.

119 Daum, *Wissenschaftspopularisierung*, 197.

120 Daum, 204.

121 Marx used his summations to help him write his 1844 pamphlet (see below).

122 BATr, Abt. 91, Nr. 230, 69–70, #22–3.

123 See Eines katholischen Laien, *Lyser und Ronge*; Anon., *Luther und Ronge*; Schubach, *Der heilige Rock in Trier*.

124 Eduard Maria Oettinger, ed., "Die streitende Röcke Gedicht mit erklaerenden und sehr belehrenden, vom Verfasser gezeichneten Holzschnitten. Nebst einem historisch-kritischen Anhange von S. Zed," *Charivari* 116 (16 December 1844): 1845. In a separate chapter on authenticity I address the criticism that there were multiple coats and this pluralism negated Trier.

125 Stadtarchiv Aachen (SAT), "1844 Ronge."

126 SAT, "1844 Ronge."

127 Moritz, *Offenes Schreiben*, 6–7.

128 Vecqueray, *Der Aufruf des Herrn Joh. Ronge*, 5.

129 This book and this chapter are in part a response to Graf's call for more research on the varied topography of belief within European religion. See Graf, "Euro-Gott im starken Plural?," esp. 248–50.

130 For a Marxist interpretation of Ronge and his movement, see Kolbe, "Demokratische Opposition."

131 BATr, Abt. 91, Nr. 237, 36.

132 BATr, Abt. 91, Nr. 231, 52. Professor Jakob Marx did follow the Ronge events closely, in part because he tried to gather all the 1844-related

newspaper articles for analysis; see BATr, Abt. 91, Nr. 230, "Literatur über den hl. Rock Ausstellung 1844 Notizen des Prof. Marx, *Mannheimer Zeitung* usw," esp. 1–2, 48–9. Kirchhoff was not alone in looking for an official response; Father Moritz thanked Bishop Arnoldi for clarifying his position vis-a-vis Ronge, BATr, Abt. 91, Nr. 232, 5.

133 Ronge, *Holy Coat of Treves*, 12.

134 Himioben, *Katholische Sonntagsblätter zur Belehrung*, 416–17. Whether or not this letter was actually written by a Protestant is impossible to determine.

135 *Katholische Sonntagsblätter zur Belehrung*, 417, "wir leben ja im 19ten Jahrhunderte worin alles Gute und Heilige ausgerottet werden soll"; "Wollte ja doch Einer der Communisten ein stehlendes Proletariat gründen; und so wird's uns nicht wundern, wenn auch Raub in unserem 19ten Jahrhundert als etwas Ruhmvolles wird ausposaunt werden."

136 *Katholische Sonntagsblätter zur Belehrung und Erbauung*, 22 December 1844, Nr. 51, 413–420, 417.

137 *Katholische Sonntagsblätter zur Belehrung*, 417, "aber er ist unleugbar ein fanatischer, revolutionärer Ungeist."

138 The Biedermeier period in German-speaking Europe occurred between the fall of Napoleon (1815) and the 1848 Revolutions. On Biedermeier and Biedermann, see Hahn, *The 1848 Revolutions*, 27–40. See Thomas Nipperdey's discussion of Biedermeier literature and portraits in *Germany from Napoleon to Bismarck*, 495–519.

139 *Katholische Sonntagsblätter zur Belehrung*, 417, "Nur muß ich im Namen besonnener und ernster Protestanten das Bekenntniß aussprechen, daß jener Herr Ronge, der doch gewiß im Herzen kein Katholik, und des Namens eines Priesters unwürdig ist, auch für einen Protestanten zu schlecht ist."

140 Böhmer, *Der heilige Rock in Trier*, 4. Böhmer contends he is most interested in the truth: "Weder das eine, noch das andere Aeußerste dürfte die ganze Wahrheit in sich schließen."

141 Böhmer, 9.

142 Böhmer, 9–10. On the topic of early Christendom Böhmer tended to echo the major Catholic critiques against the suspended priest.

143 Böhmer, 11, "Ist dagegen die von Arnoldi für den trier'schen Rock in Anspruch genommene Verehrung keine Anbetung, besteht sie in der darauf gegründeten Achtung des Gewandes, daß es dem Betrachtenden Christum als Gegenstand frommer Verherrlichung in's Gedächtniß zurückruft: so ist keine Befugniß vorhanden, den Spott, welchen Kirchenväter über die heiden wegen ihrer (götzenhaften Verehrung von Bildnissen und Reliquien ausgegossen haben, als Grund gegen die Verehrung des Rockes geltend zu machen."

144 Geron, *Sternschnuppe*, 1.

145 Geron, 9.

146 Geron, 7.

147 *Offenes Schreiben an Herrn Johannes Ronge in Laurahütte*, "den in Trier aus-gestellte heiligen Rock betreffend," Verlag der "Luxemburger Zeitung" (14 November 1844), "Nichts natürlicher – wie unnatürlich es auch gemi-ßbraucht worden seyn mag – als die Liebe zu Reliquien von guten und frommen Menschen." Schieder argues that the *Luxemburger Zeitung* was one of Arnoldi's principal propaganda organs during the conflict. As Schieder explains, the Prussian government denied a request to move the newspaper to Trier. This argument makes sense, given that many of the miracle reports first appeared in the *Luxemburger Zeitung*. See Schieder, "Church and Revolution," 80.

148 Moritz, *Offenes Schreiben*: "Doch vielleicht wünschts der Herr Hauslehrer bei dem evangelischen Geistlichen zu Laurahütte lieber protestantische Stimmen zu hören. Vernehmen Sie also die Urtheile selbst unterrichteter und nicht in confessionnellen Vorurtheilen befangener Katholiken über die Bilder- und Reliquien verehrung der katholischen Kirche."

149 Moritz, *Die Verehrung heiliger Reliquien*, 58.

150 As Todd Weir has noted, as far away as New York, Ronge was described as "a second Luther, who has arisen to complete the deliverance of his country from the thralldom of Rome," by Baptist minister John Dowling. Weir, *Secularism and Religion*, 40.

151 Moritz, *Offene Antwort*, 21, 9.

152 Moritz, 28.

153 Moritz, 29.

154 Hillebrand, *Neue Aergernisse*, 17.

155 Hillebrand, 29.

156 Hillebrand, 29.

157 Böhmer, *Der heilige Rock in Trier*, 20.

158 Franksmann, *Beleuchtung*, 6: "in den protestantischen Schlachtreihen – mit protestantischen Waffen – in protestantischen Uniform," "ächt protes-tantischen Glaubensbruder."

159 Hillebrand, *Neue Aergernisse*, 3.

160 Eines katholischen Laien, *Lyser und Ronge*, 5.

161 Eines katholischen Laien, 6.

162 Eines katholischen Laien, 12.

163 Eines katholischen Laien, 14, 19.

164 Eines katholischen Laien, 20–2.

165 Eines katholischen Laien, 23.

166 Lyser, *Sendschreiben an Johannes Ronge*, 3–5.

167 Lyser, 5.

168 Lyser, 11.
169 Lyser, 13.
170 Lyser, 12.
171 Anon., *Herr Johannes Ronge mit Gründen widerlegt*, 3–4.
172 Anon., 13.
173 Anon., 16.
174 Anon., 60.
175 Anon., *Ueber den heiligen Rock*, 2.
176 Anon., 4.
177 This concern appears in several pamphlets, including Anon., *Der heilige Rock zu Trier*, 22; Anon., *Herr Johannes Ronge, der falsche*, 11; Anon., *Luther und Ronge*, 90. For secondary literature, see Stayer, *The German Peasants' War*; Ozment, *Mysticism and Dissent*.
178 Treumund, *Die Geschichte des heiligen Rockes*, 19.
179 BATr, Abt. 90, Nr. 101, 146–7.
180 BATr, Abt. 90, Nr. 101, 147, the *Deutsche Allgemeine Zeitung* is on the same page as the conclusion to the Breslau article and dated 15 November. Presumably this report came from the same year, and I am assuming it is 1844. "Dieses Schreiben ist gewiß ein merkwürdiges Actenstück, auch ein Zeichen der Zeit, zu dem sich jeder den Commentar machen kann. Die Verbindung des untheilbaren deutschen Reichs mit dem ungetheilten heiligen Rock ist mindestens etwas gewagt." These two articles also appear in BATr, Abt. 90, Nr. 141, 57–8.
181 Steinruck, "Die Heilig-Rock-Wallfahrt von 1844," 320.
182 Großbölting, *Losing Heaven*, 247–75; Nipperdey, *Germany from Napoleon to Bismarck*, 360.
183 Nipperdey, 363.

5 Clerical Crossroads: Medical Verifiability of the Sacred

1 Marx, *History of the Robe*, Translator's Preface, 4.
2 See Harris, *Lourdes*, 1999. In the scholarship on French nineteenth-century medicine, Jean-Martin Charcot's studies of hysteria in his hospital, Salpêtrière in Paris, feature prominently. For example, see Ruth Harris, *Murders and Madness*. On hysteria, see also Gilman et al., *Hysteria beyond Freud*; Goldstein, "The Hysteria Diagnosis"; Goldstein, "Moral Contagion"; Hunter, "Hysteria, Psychoanalysis, and Feminism."
3 Thomas A. Howard argues that as the nineteenth century progressed, positivism became more influential and was linked to the natural sciences. By the end of the nineteenth century, *Wissenschaft* in German thought was associated with neutrality. See Howard, *Protestant Theology*, 29–30. Thomas Nipperdey identifies a similar trend in legal thought, and

in historical writing after Ranke went out of fashion, in *Germany from Napoleon to Bismarck*, 454–8.

4 Nipperdey, 124. See also Purvis, *Theology and the University*.

5 See Shapin, *A Social History of Truth*, on how English gentlemen established boundaries of reliability and truth in order to corroborate the results of scientific experiments.

6 Rhenish clergy cut their own path towards a natural understanding of miracle, but the trend is reflected in the broader Catholic Church. Pope Pius XI (1922–39), for instance, established the Pontifical Academy of Sciences in 1936. At the opening session, "Cardinal Pacelli remembered Pius XI's wish 'to declare open this scientific senate conceived and created by him to foster the development of science an d research.'" Marini-Bettòlo, *Pontifical Academy of Sciences*, 3, 10.

7 Jewson, "The Disappearance of the Sick-Man"; Harrison and Roberts, *Science without God?*, 10: "Only in the nineteenth century was there a concerted attempt to articulate a version of scientific naturalism that opposed itself to 'supernaturalism' and sought to eliminate it."

8 Schaefer, "Program for a New Wissenschaft."

9 On the relationship between medical practice and religion, see Pickstone, "Establishment and Dissent"; see also Bynum, *Science and the Practice*.

10 In the case of mid- to late eighteenth-century France, see Gelbart, *The King's Midwife*.

11 In his analysis of miracles in early-modern Naples, David Gentilcore found that midwives and other "unofficial" healers were more likely than "official" doctors to insert themselves into medical narratives. See Gentilcore, "Contesting Illness."

12 BATr, Abt. 91, Nr. 229, 94–122.

13 BATr, Abt. 91, Nr. 229, 120.

14 BATr, Abt. 91, Nr. 228, 45.

15 BATr, Abt. 91, Nr. 229.

16 This was part of a European-wide attempt by Catholic clerics to confirm the presence of a miracle; see, for another example, Donnelly, "Marian Shrine of Knock." Donnelly looks at the 1879 apparition of Mary in Knock; in the 1880s Irish clerics introduced medical certificates.

17 BATr, Abt. 91, Nr. 228, 86–7.

18 BATr, Abt. 91, Nr. 228, 77–9.

19 BATr, Abt. 91, Nr. 226, 126.

20 BATr, Abt. 91, Nr. 229, 109–10.

21 BATr, Abt. 91, Nr. 229, 109–10, "Ich fand seiner Zustand ganz verändert, das wilde, epileptische Aussehen war ganz verschwunden."

22 BATr, Abt. 91, Nr. 229, 106.

23 BATr, Abt. 91, Nr. 229, 106, "Bürgermeister kann ihr kein Attest ausstellen; es wird überhaupt so wüstes von derselben erzählt, daß man sich schämen muß, auch nur ihren Namen zu hören."

24 BATr, Abt. 91, Nr. 229, 91.

25 BATr, Abt. 91, Nr. 229, 93, "daß der Knabe seit der Wiederer langung seiner Sprache zu Trier fortwährend fließend, laut und verständlich spricht."

26 BATr, Abt. 91, Nr. 229, 170–1.

27 BATr, Abt. 91, Nr. 229, 244.

28 BATr, Abt. 91, Nr. 229, 221–40.

29 BATr, Abt. 91, Nr. 229, 233, "So giebt es ja Leute welche die sitzige Krankheit, oder das Nervensieber, oder andere Krankheiten 2,3,4,5,6 mal hatten."

30 DAA, PA 58, Neues Programm für die Heiligtumsfahrt pro 1846, #11. Aachen den 31 März 1846.

31 BATr, Abt. 91, Nr. 229, 248–50.

32 The women were, on average, 35.91 years old and the men eight years older, with an average age of 43.73. In the Akta, the testimonials appear in the following order: Peter Jakob Hohnemann, Eleonora Elfen, Appolonia Immerschitt, Eva Eckes, Franziska Schurgens, Katharina Sewig, Adam Heil, Jakob Eck, Caspar Erf, Jakob Klein, Franz Jonas, Georg Eckes, Anna Frosch, Jacob Eckes, Peter Erf, Anton Bretz, Anna Hitzel, Catharina Hohnemann, Anna Erf, Eva Kamp, Margaretha Immerschitt, Wilhelm Hohnemann.

33 In this instance, the average female eyewitness was 42.67 years old, the average male, 41.2. In the Akta, the testimonials appear in the following order: Peter Nix, Philipp Bernette, Franziska Schiffen, Katharina Bender, Agnes Bischof, Anna Maria Müller, Susanna Tapperich, Margaretha Frosch, Anna Maria Wolf, Anna Bernette, Elise Bernet, Adam Kirch, Joseph Ohler, Karl Kursus.

34 Korum, *Wunder und Göttliche Gnadenerweise*, 97.

35 Korum, 37–9.

36 Korum, 69–70.

37 DAA, PA 74, "Aachen, Jacobstr 21 Herr Pralat."

38 *Echo der Gegenwart*, Donnerstag, 19 July, *Erstes Blatt*. "Von wunderbaren Heilungen."

39 Clarke, *Pilgrimage*, 36.

40 Clarke, 38.

41 Plater, *The Holy Coat of Treves*, 25. Clarke and Plater were thought of as twin publications. See *Month: A Catholic Magazine and Review* 74 (London: January–April, 1892): "The Holy Coat of Treves," 292–93. "They agree in general in their outline of facts, in their testimony to the devotion of the

pilgrims, and in their belief in the authenticity of the Holy Coat as at least highly probably, even if it be not morally certain," 293.

42 Quoted in Plater, *The Holy Coat of Treves*, 12. From S. Thom. *Aq. Pars.* iii *Qu.* xxv., Art 6.

43 Plater, 100.

44 Plater, 101. Italics added.

45 For a breakdown of the German Liberal thrust against Catholicism, see Gross, "Kulturkampf and Unification." Gross characterizes the attack as "the campaign [against the Church…] launched in the name of the modern state, science, *Bildung*, and freedom," 546. See also Blackbourn, "Progress and Piety."

46 Gross, "Kulturkampf and Unification," 546. Locally, Oliver Zimmer has found ample evidence of compromise between Catholicism and the Second Empire in "Beneath the 'Culture War'."

47 For a discussion of the laws passed against Catholics, see Borutta, "Enemies at the Gate," esp. 249–50.

48 Treitz, *Michael Felix Korum:*, 35–83.

49 Kitchen, *A History of Modern Germany*, 140–1. On the visual material printed against the church, see, e.g., Gross, *War against Catholicism*, esp. 128–84.

50 Korum, *Wunder*, 8.

51 Korum, 8.

52 Korum, 11.

53 Korum, 13.

54 Korum, 14.

55 Korum, 17.

56 As one example, see Aquinas's discussion of transubstantiation, quoted in McGrath, *The Christian Theology Reader*, 562–3.

57 Korum, *Wunder*, 20.

58 Korum, 14.

59 Korum, 14: "absolute keine Aehnlichkeit mit gewissen Experimenten."

60 On the occult and its relationship to German modernity, see Mosse, *The Crisis of German Ideology*; Treitel, *A Science for the Soul*; Staudenmaier, "Occultism, Race"; Kurlander, *Hitler's Monsters*; Wolffram, *The Stepchildren of Science*. Korum's attempt to verify miracles is different because it is rooted in Catholic insecurity following the Ronge scandals of the mid-nineteenth century and the Kulturkampf. Korum wanted to save face and show Germany that there was a thorough review process. Furthermore, unlike the occult, this was not an "alternative form of knowledge," but prioritized conventional science to show the possibility of the divine breaking into the temporal world.

61 At the outset of his pamphlet, Korum includes his requests to the deacons; see here Korum, *Wunder*, 21: "sondern auch um jene Heilungen, die durch bloße Verehrung des hl. Rockes (Wallfahrt nach Trier, Andachtsübungen etc.) oder durch Gebrauch eines an die hl. Reliquie angerührten Gegenstandes erfolgt sind."

62 Korum, 21–3.

63 Korum, 23: "hat sich das frühere Uebel nicht wieder eingestellt?"

64 Korum, 23: "Ist nach der durch Verehrung des hl. Rockes erfolgten Heilung noch ein ärztliches Mittel für die Genesung von den betreffenden Leiden angewandt worden und event. welches?"

65 Korum, 24: "Man bittet die Geheilten selbst oder deren Angehörigen, über den Vorgang und Verlauf der Genesung einen einfachen, wahrheitsgetreuen Bericht, womöglich eigenhändig geschrieben, einzusenden."

66 Evans, "Recent Recrudescence," 765. See the last chapter for a discussion of the constant presence of male cure-seekers between 1892 and 1937.

67 Evans, "Recent Recrudescence," 763.

68 Bishop Korum's final address, as quoted in Clarke, *Pilgrimage*, 137.

69 Clarke, 137.

70 Clarke, 137.

71 Evans, "Recent Recrudescence," 763. See Jaskowski, *Der heilige Rock von Trier*.

72 On the role of neuropathologists and auto-suggestion in the post-pilgrimage miracle debates, see Evans, 765–6. Autosuggestion has played a role in the historiography of religiosity since the early twentieth century. Marc Bloch concluded his study of scrofula and the Royal Touch with an autosuggestion argument: "What created faith in the miracle was the idea that there was bound to be a miracle." See Bloch, *The Royal Touch*, 243. In Ireland, Donnelly notes that the clergy were aware of autosuggestion and it made them uncertain what to think of miracle claims at Knock. See Donnelly, "Marian Shrine," 89.

73 BATr, Abt. 91, Nr. 249, 88.

74 See Blackbourn, *Marpingen*, 155–7.

75 Blackbourn, 157: "The perceived arrogance of doctors was undoubtedly one reason, together with non-availability and cost, why the sort of people who put their trust in Marpingen were often reluctant to consult a medical man."

76 Harris, *Lourdes*, 329.

77 DAA, PA 61, Prüm, 12 July 1895: "Seitdem bin ich vollständig gesund und bedurfte keines Arztes."

78 BATr, Abt. 91, Nr. 229, 2.

79 BATr, Abt. 91, Nr. 228, 56.

80 BATr, Abt. 91, Nr. 228.

81 BATr, Abt. 91, Nr. 229, 2: "den ich Anfangs April dieses Jahres an seinem kranken Bette zuletzt besuchte, der etwas sonderbaren Trost hinterließ, indem ich ihm sagte: Es gäbe kränkliche Zustände, die nur Gott allein heilen könne: er der Kranke möge sich diesem nur völlig überlassen."

82 BATr, Abt. 91, Nr. 229, 2.

83 DAA, PA 66, Gürzenich, den 29 August 1925.

84 BATr, Abt. 90, Nr. 129, 110. Hepting also suffered from heart troubles and joint rheumatism.

85 DAA, PA 66, Gottesdienst. Heiligtumsfahrt 1925, "Gürzenich, den 29 August 1925."

86 BATr, Abt. 91, Nr. 131, 83–4.

87 BATr, Abt. 91, Nr. 232, 54: "indem ein Evangelischer Arzt nicht als gartypisch für die Heilung beim Heil Rocke kann angesehen werden."

88 DAA, Domkapitel 4.1.1.7, J. No. 15650: "der Heiligtumsfahrt, welche eine rein katholisch konfessionelle Angelegenheit darstellt," "hinreichende ärztliche Betreuung Ihrer Pilger sicherzustellen."

89 DAA, Domkapitel 4.1.1.20, 3 July 1937: "Der Arzt, welcher das Zeugnis ausgestellt hat, Herr Dr. Sebastiany, ist ein strenggläubiger Katholik. Frau Mohlberg ist mir persönlich als erhebend, fromme katholische Frau bekannt."

90 Blackbourn sets up two opposing camps in *Marpingen*, 159: "Catholic poor, supported by priests and Catholic newspapers, against the state authorities, supported by doctors and the liberal press."

91 DAA, Domkapitel 4.1.1.7: "Vorschriften für die Sanitätswache bei der Heiligtumsfahrt."

92 In both the early modern and modern periods, healers referred patients to shrines for non-medical problems. One-fifth of early modern cure-seekers to Cubas, Spain, sought relief from non-medical issues. There is also a long tradition of pilgrimage to heal a range of ailments that William Christian Jr. has classified as "circulatory problems" beyond the ability of contemporary healers. Christian refers to a woman in the 1560s who suffered a heart attack in Serranillos: "The barber in the adjacent village advised her to turn to the shrine, since it was a heart problem." Christian Jr., *Apparitions in Late Medieval*, 82–3.

93 DAA, Domkapitel 4.1.1.19 Krankenkarten D–G, "Düsseldorf, den 11.7.37."

94 DAA, Domkapitel 4.1.1.19 Krankenkarten D–G, "Düsseldorf, den 8.7.1937."

95 DAA, Domkapitel 4.1.1.19 Krankenkarten D–G, "Düsseldorf, den 11.7.1937." "35 J. alt, ist zwar Körperlich, d.h. organisch gesund, hat aber ein schweres seelisches Leiden, weswegen ich herzlich bitte, sie zur Krankensegnung anläßlich der Aachener Heiligtumswallfahrt."

96 DAA, PA 60, "Aachen 12 Juli 1881"; "und es ist unmöglich, für die Einzelnen ein ärztliches Attest auszustellen, es würden Tage dazu gehören, alle zu befriedigen, die die Berührung wünschen."

97 DAA, PA 60, "Aachen den 13. Juli 1881."

98 DAA, PA 60, "Köln d. 13.7.1881."

99 DAA, PA 66, "Heiligtumsfahrt im Münster zu Aachen vom 10. bis 26. Juli 1925." "Kranke werden täglich vorm. 9 bis 9¾ Uhr im Münster mit den Heiligtümern berührt. Diese Kranken müssen im Besitze einer mit dem Pfarrsiebel versehenen kurzen Empfehlung ihrer Seelsorger sein und diese Empfehlung an der Wolfstüre vorzeigen, um Einlaß zu finden."

100 DAA, Domkapitel 4.1.1.21, Krankenkarten L–P, 6 Juni 1937 An das Büro. "ob die Kranken, welche mit unseres Herrn Lendentuch berührt werden, ein ärztliches Attest vorlegen müssen."

101 BATr, Abt. 90, Nr. 130.

102 BATr, Abt. 90, Nr. 130, 8–9, "Hat er (Kranken) sonstige seelische Alterationen?"

103 BATr, Abt. 90, Nr. 130, 8–9.

104 Labourer wages in 1938, before the war, ranged from "78.7 pfennigs (18.7 cents) for skilled male workers to 44.0 pfennigs (10.5 cents) for unskilled female workers." See "Labor Conditions in Germany," *Monthly Labor Review* 60, no. 3 (March 1945): 498–524, 498.

105 BATr, Abt. 90, Nr. 106, 103–4.

106 BATr, Abt. 90, Nr. 100, 165.

107 BATr, Abt. 90, Nr. 121, 301–2.

108 BATr, Abt. 90, Nr. 121, 303.

109 BATr, Abt. 90, Nr. 106, 114–15, "Ist für alle diese Taubstummen eine Berührung des hl. Rockes statthaft? (Ja) Sind auch für diese Taubstumme besondere Attest notwendig? (Nein)"

110 BATr, Abt. 90, Nr. 106, "dann ich war schon zweimal selbst zum Herrn Pastor Minter und unser Junge schon zweimal selbst, ob Herr Pastor es vergessen hat oder was da ist ich weiß es nicht." And "und jetzt glaube ich doch mit aller Hoffnung das unser lieber Heiland unserem Kinde helfen wird."

111 BATr, Abt. 90, Nr. 148, 205, "Ruttand, Dublin, Ireland 4th September."

112 DAA, Domkapitel 4.1.1.19 Krankenkarten D–G, "24. Mai 1937, Herrn Dr. Sasse."

113 BATr, Abt. 90, Nr. 199-70, 35–6.

114 BATr, Abt. 91, Nr. 260, 165. A group of Silesian pilgrims brought their own physicians and needed space for them to set up their consulations.

115 BATr, Abt. 90, Nr. 124, 24 August 1933, von Fuchs, An Beuthen Reisebüro.

116 BATr, Abt. 90, Nr. 123, 62.

117 DAA, Domkapitel 4.1.1.20, Mannheim, 22 July 1937, "die Besitzerin dieses Schreibens, ist laut ärztl. Zeugnis schon längere Zeit schwer

Nerven leiden und in Gefahr ihren Beruf ob dieser Krankheit zu ver-
lieren. Da sie keine Eltern mehr hat, wäre das sehr schwer."

118 BATr, Abt. 90, Nr. 173, 654.

119 DAA, PA 79, Münster i.W. den 16 July 1925, "da ich seit 20 Jahren all-
jährlich an unbeschreiblich heftigen Nervenschmerzen Neuralgie Arigen
leiden, und zwar im Gesicht, davon Beseitigung oder Linderung bisher
nach keinen Arzte gelungen ist."

120 DAA, PA 66, Esch. der 16 September 1925, "8 Ärzte hat sie in Anspruch
genommen und a. Sanitätsrat Dr. Lansenberg, den berühmten Hönör-
paten Stemmler in Köln."

121 DAA, PA 66, Esch. der 16 September 1925, "ein schlimmes Bein."

122 BATr, Abt. 91, Nr. 250, 6.

6 Historical Authenticity as Presence

1 "'Jesus Wife' Documentary Broadcast Delayed amid Doubts," BBC, 2
October 2012, http://www.bbc.com/news/world-us-canada-19796163;
"Scholar Karen King Finds Ancient Reference to 'Jesus Wife,'" BBC, 19
September 2012, http://www.bbc.com/news/world-europe-19648862.

2 Quoted in Laurie Goodstein, "Papyrus Referring to Jesus' Wife Is More
Likely Ancient Than Fake, Scientists Say," *New York Times*, 10 April 2014,
http://www.nytimes.com/2014/04/10/science/scrap-of-papyrus-refer-
ring-to-jesus-wife-is-likely-to-be-ancient-scientists-say.html?_r=0.

3 *Harvard Theological Review* published a volume containing King's article,
papers on the tests conducted to determine authenticity, Depuydt's criticisms, and a response to Depuydt by King. See *Harvard Theological Review*
107, no. 2 (April 2014): 131–93.

4 There was extensive press coverage on this event in April 2014; see Lisa
Wangsness, "No Evidence of Modern Forgery in Ancient Text Mention-
ing 'Jesus' Wife,'" *Boston Globe*, 10 April 2014, http://www.bostonglobe.
com/metro/2014/04/10/new-tests-show-evidence-forgery-gospel-jesus-
wife/IusII8b4eI86HgDTKipLhN/story.html; "'Wife of Jesus' Reference
in Coptic 4th Century Script," BBC, 19 September 2012, http://www.bbc.
com/news/world-europe-19645273; Scott Neuman, "'Gospel of Jesus's
Wife' Papyrus Not a Forgery, Harvard Says," NPR, 10 April 2014, http://
www.npr.org/blogs/thetwo-way/2014/04/10/301432378
/gospel-of-jesus-wife-papyrus-not-a-forgery-harvard-says; Ariel Sabar,
"The Unbelievable of Tale of Jesus's Wife," *Atlantic*, July/August 2016,
https://www.theatlantic.com/magazine/archive/2016/07/the
-unbelievable-tale-of-jesus-wife/485573/; Ariel Sabar, "Karen King Responds to 'The Unbelievable Tale of Jesus's Wife': The Harvard Scholar
Says Papyrus Is Probably a Forgery," *Atlantic*, 16 June 2016, https://

www.theatlantic.com/politics/archive/2016/06/karen
-king-responds-to-the-unbelievable-tale-of-jesus-wife/487484/.

5 See Elisabetta Povoledo, "Vatican Says Papyrus Referring to Jesus' Wife Is Probably Fake," *New York Times*, 28 September 2012.

6 In 2009, Ronald Numbers edited a volume specifically written to tackle popular misconceptions about this relationship: *Galileo Goes to Jail*. The relationship between Catholicism and science was revisited with the ascension of Francis I to the papacy. Francis, who was trained as a chemical technician, at the beginning of his papal term urged the church to help protect the environment. See Florence Davey-Attlee, "Vatican Seeks to Rebrand Its Relationship with Science," CNN, 11 April 2013, http:// edition.cnn.com/2013/04/11/world/pope-vatican-science/index.html?hpt=hp_c4. Davey-Attlee incorrectly states that Galileo was imprisoned, implies he was harshly interrogated, and contends that Galileo was lucky to get away so easy, especially compared to Giordano Bruno.

7 BATr, Abt. 91, Nr. 244, 78.

8 On Charlemagne as the quintessential memory of the Middle Ages in the Rhineland, see Stambolis, "In den Steinbrücken 'lokaler'." On Constantine, Barnes, *Constantine and Eusebius*.

9 Eric Yonke has pushed the Catholic milieu beyond the *Bürgertum* paradigm. See Eric Yonke, "The Problem." Yonke sees the middle class as being much broader than the *Bürgertum* within the Catholic milieu and including members of the *Mittelstand*, artisans, retailers, and the lower middle class (264).

10 See Sperber, "Bürger, Bürgertum, Bürgerlichkeit, Bürgerliche Gesellschaft"; Blackbourn and Evans, *The German Bourgeoisie*; Kocka, "The European Pattern."

11 Zalar's 2018 work *Reading and Rebellion* is essential in showing the varied intellectual origins of Catholic leaders.

12 See O'Sullivan also on the Catholic milieu. This chapter responds to his call for approaches to German Catholicism that move away from structural approaches of the 1990s and adopt cultural and social history approaches to religiosity. O'Sullivan, "From Catholic Milieu."

13 Burrow, *Crisis*, 55.

14 Burrow, 56. On materialism, see Gregory, *Scientific Materialism*, esp. "The Rise of Materialisms and the Reshaping of Religion and Politics," 122–63.

15 See the "Introduction" in Cahan, *From Natural Philosophy*. On Hermann von Helmholtz, see Cahan, *Hermann von Helmholtz*.

16 By the 1860s, Germany overtook France and Britain as the leading European country for medical research: Nipperdey, *Germany from Napoleon to Bismarck*, table 35c, 438.

17 Burrow, *Crisis*, 79.

18   Huxley, *The Advance of Science*, 17. This essay was originally published in 1887 by Thomas Humphry Ward in *The Reign of Queen Victoria: A Survey of Fifty Years of Progress*.

19   On the origins and dissemination of the "conflict thesis" between science and religion, see James C. Ungureanu's study of John William Draper and Andrew Dickson White in *Science, Religion, and the Protestant Tradition*.

20   Paul, "The Debate," 320. Paul situates this French debate in the 1890s because he sees the Catholic-scientific drive for reconciliation between the church and theories of the natural world as part of a French Catholic response to Leo XIII's 1892 order that Catholics make peace with the Republic, 304.

21   In 1959, Iserloh (above) argued that Christians in Trier debated the authenticity of the Coat before the Reformation began in Wittenberg.

22   Iserloh, "Der Heilige Rock," 163–7.

23   Seibrich, "Die Heilig-Rock-Ausstellungen."

24   This practice appears in numerous newspaper and archival reports. See "Schluß der Heiligtumsfahrt 1909. Aachen, 26. Juli," *Echo der Gegenwart*, Montag, 26 July 1909, Nr. 172, Abend-Ausgabe. And "Programm a. Für den Tag der Eröffnung der Heiligthumsfahrt," *Aachener Zeitung*, Montag, 9 July 1860.

25   BATr, Abt. 91, Nr. 244, 48–9.

26   BATr, Abt. 91, Nr. 244, 49.

27   "Von der Landesgrenze," *Fliegende Taube*, Samstag, 10 July 1909, Nr. 78. The author explains that the goldsmith oath was a centuries-old tradition: "Dieser Eid ist seit vielen Jahrhunderten für die gewissenhafte Wahrnehmung der dem erwählten Goldschmiede obliegenden bedeutungsvollen Handlung vorgeschrieben."

28   DAA, PA 69, "Verhandelt zu Aachen, im Rathause, den 9. Juli 1930."

29   Examples of the Aachen protocols abound in the archive; for example, see DAA, PA 58, "Programm für die Heiligthumsfahrt 1832"; and, DAA, PA 58, "Neues Programm für die Heiligthumsfahrt pro 1846." For an example in Trier, see BATr, Abt. 91, Nr. 241, 196–218. This account describes removing the Coat in 1844 for the pilgrimage. During the ceremony the witnesses verified the seals before opening up the relic display.

30   DAA, PA 69, "In der Anlage übersende ich Abschrift des Protokolls über die Öffnung des Marienschreines und die Erhebung der Heiligtümer am 9. Juli 1930."

31   Gildemeister and Sybel, *Der Heilige Rock*. See also Frühwald, "Die Wallfahrt nach Trier," 380.

32   Gildemeister and Sybel, vii: "Was nicht Sache des Glaubens ist, muß nothwendig Sache des historischen Beweises sein."

33 Gildemeister and Sybel, ix.
34 Gildemeister and Sybel, 53.
35 Gildemeister and Sybel, xiii: "daß die schon um 327 gestorbene Helena den Rock um 330 nach Trier geschickt habe, und so festes Vertrauen in den Trierer Rock setzt."
36 Gildemeister and Sybel, 19–20.
37 Gildemeister and Sybel, 24.
38 Gildemeister and Sybel, 9.
39 Gildemeister and Sybel, 12.
40 Gildemeister and Sybel, 30.
41 Gildemeister and Sybel, 47.
42 Gildemeister and Sybel, 55.
43 Gildemeister and Sybel, 1: "ob er nach Form, Farbe, Stoff und Arbeit der Vorstellung entspreche."
44 Gildemeister and Sybel, 4: "Es ist daher zu urtheilen, daß der Trierer Rock zu lang sei, um für das ächte ungenähte Kleid Christi gelten zu können."
45 Gildemeister and Sybel, 6.
46 Gildemeister and Sybel, 60.
47 Gildemeister and Sybel serve as a case study of questions of authenticity surrounding the Trier Coat. The correspondence on this topic becomes more prevalent later in the century as Trier clergy began to respond to the question of *Echtheit*. See also BATr, Abt. 91, Nr. 239b, Korrespondenzen über das Officium und die Echtheit des hl. Rocks.
48 Gildemeister and Sybel, 60–7.
49 Gildemeister and Sybel, 68.
50 Gildemeister and Sybel, 72.
51 See Kilian Harrer's University of Wisconsin-Madison dissertation (*Places of Power and Peril: Reinventing Pilgrimage in Europe's Age of Revolution*), which discusses the 1810 Trier pilgrimage; Hommer, "Geschichte des heiligen Rockes."
52 Hommer, *Geschichte des heiligen Rockes*, 2–3.
53 Hommer, 4–6.
54 Hommer, 13.
55 Hommer, 15.
56 Hommer, 6.
57 Hommer, 10–12.
58 Marx, *History of the Robe*, 31–2.
59 Marx, 31–2.
60 Marx, 36.
61 Marx, 36.
62 Marx, 37.

63 Marx, chap. 8, "What the Holy Fathers Have Said of the Garments and Especially of the Robe of Our Lord: Mystical Signification of the Seamless Robe," 39–43.

64 Hommer, *Geschichte des heiligen Rockes*, 17.

65 Hommer, 21.

66 Marx, *History of the Robe*, 19.

67 Marx, 15.

68 Marx, 16–17.

69 Plater, *The Holy Coat of Tréves*, 60.

70 Plater, 60.

71 Clarke, *Pilgrimage*, 4.

72 Marx, *History of the Robe*, 47.

73 Marx, 47.

74 Marx, 27.

75 Marx, 28.

76 Marx, 53.

77 Marx, 68.

78 Hommer, *Geschichte des heiligen Rockes*, 29–30.

79 Hommer, 33.

80 Marx, *History of the Robe*, 87.

81 Marx, 88.

82 Marx, 94.

83 Clarke, *Pilgrimage*, 57.

84 Science provided the church with a new vocabulary to describe the Coat's origins with evidence beyond tradition. Scientific argumentation also provided a response to the Kulturkampf for German Catholics. Michael Gross has convincingly argued that the German liberal attack on Catholicism was prompted by a belief in science, *Bildung*, and German unity. For Gross, German liberals viewed the fight against Catholics as a war over German identity. See Gross, "Kulturkampf and Unification."

85 Clarke, *Pilgrimage*, 119–22.

86 Hesse, "Die Restaurierung des Hl. Rockes."

87 BATr, Abt. 91, Nr. 244, 61–7. This order was established in Aachen in 1848, but because of the Kulturkampf they moved to Simpelveld in the Netherlands in 1878. See Hesse, 338.

88 BATr, Abt. 91, Nr. 244, 54, "III. Abschrift Trier, den 9. Juli 1890."

89 BATr, Abt. 91, Nr. 244, 55, "Trier, der 10. Juli 1890."

90 Flury-Lemberg, "Das Reliquiar," 691–2.

91 BATr, Abt. 91, Nr. 244, 54, "III. Abschrift Trier, den 9. Juli 1890."

92 BATr, Abt 91, Nr. 244, 68–9: "Nach neuen 40–50 Jahren in dem Verließ, worin einmal eine Sonnestrahl dringt wird sie wohl ganz zerfallen sein."

93 Hesse, "Die Restaurierung des Hl. Rockes," 341–3.

94 BATr, Abt. 91, Nr. 244, 1–3.

95 BATr, Abt. 91, Nr. 244, 2.

96 For an article that summarizes the importance of the Coat as a theological symbol of unity in the medieval period, see Ronig, "Die Tunika Christi," 67–79.

97 Clarke, *Pilgrimage*, 61.

98 BATr, Abt. 91, Nr. 244, 11: "Bericht über meine am 5. October 1891, Nachmittags 3 Uhr in Trier vorgenommen mikroskopische Untersuchung zweier Stückchen des Gewebes der Tunica des heiliger Rockes sowie des dieselbe bedeckender Byssus."

99 BATr, Abt. 91, Nr. 244, 12.

100 BATr, Abt. 91, Nr. 244, 17.

101 BATr, Abt. 91, Nr. 244, 18.

102 BATr, Abt. 91, Nr. 244, 33–4.

103 BATr, Abt. 91, Nr. 244, 36.

104 BATr, Abt. 91, Nr. 244, 38.

105 BATr, Abt. 91, Nr. 244, 51.

106 BATr, Abt. 91, Nr. 244, 52–3. Clarke, *Pilgrimage*, 121.

107 Clarke, 63.

108 Clarke, 64.

109 Clarke, 64.

110 BATr, Abt. 91, Nr. 244 (2), 75: "biblisch-archäologische Untersuchung über Stoff und Farbe des … aus Joh 19.23." This Akta is quite brief, and consists only of the Libertz correspondence.

111 On Catholic theology of the end of history, see Toner, "Eschatology."

112 BATr, Abt. 91, Nr. 244 (2), 83.

113 See also Plater, 42. The Ivory Tablet is now housed in the Trier Domschatz. For a colour image, visit "Domschatz," *Kirchliche Museen*, http://www.kirchliche-museen.org/museen/profil.php?museum=96.

114 Plater, *The Holy Coat of Tréves*, 41–7.

115 Plater, 44.

116 The tablet can be seen at "Domschatz," *Kirchliche Museen*, http://www.kirchliche-museen.org/museen/profil.php?museum=96.

117 See Wolfgang Schmid, "Reliquienprozession," *Der Trierer Dom St. Petrus*, https://www.dominformation.de/bauwerk/domschatz/reliquienprozession/: "Die Elfenbeinschnitzerei des 5. Jahrhunderts ist ein Hauptwerk der Kunst der Spätantike, sie zeigt uns ein detailliertes Bild einer Reliquienprozession und des byzantinischen Hofzeremoniells... Auch wenn das Gebäude an die Porta Nigra erinnert und man bei der Kaiserin mit dem Stabkreuz an Helena, die Mutter Kaiser Konstantins denkt, die der Trierer Kirche der Legende nach zahlreiche Reliquien geschenkt hat, dürfte die Elfenbeinschnitzerei keine Bezüge nach Trier aufweisen: Die

Tafel gelangte erst im 19. Jahrhundert aus einer Privatsammlung in den Domschatz."

118 DAA, PA 66, "Aachen 25. iv. 25."

119 DAA, PA 66, "Aachen, den 1. Mai 1925": "Auch da habe ich meine Antwort rein negativ nicht gehalten."

120 DAA, PA 58 (Beilage zum *Rheinisch Westfäl. Volksfrend*): "Wie aber seine Nachfolger, so bewahrte auch das deutsche Volk durch alle Zeiten hindurch treu und dankbar das Andenken an den großen Kaiser, und mit Recht: Karl und der h. Bonifacius waren ja die Gründer des heiligen römischen Reiches deutscher Nation."

121 DAA, PA 68: "Zur Aachener Heiligtumsfahrt von Dr. Felix Brüll."

122 Perhaps the clearest form of resisting clerical historical descriptions of the relics came in the form of pilgrims ascribing great worth to *Andenken* in proximity to the Rhenish sanctuaries. Another example not included in the "Economy of the Sacred" chapter: in 1925 Frau Anton Schumacher wrote to Aachen from Adenau to request silk and "several Andenken" (etliche *Andenken*) because she was too sick and impoverished to attend the festival. See DAA, PA 79, "Adenau bez. Koblenz, Frau Anton Schumacher."

123 Fuhr, *Die Heiligthümer Aachens*, 41: "Sollte nun Kaiser Karl d. Große, dieser umsichtsvolle Monarch, sich eine Reliquie haben zustellen lassen, ohne von den Päpsten, Bischöfen oder Fürsten, von denen er sie erhielt, über deren Echtheit sich Gewißheit zu verschaffen?"

124 Fuhr, 41.

125 Fuhr, 43.

126 DAA, PA 68: "Prozessionen nach heiligen Orten in der Nähe und in der Ferne zu veranstalten und Wallfahrten selbst über die Alpen und über die See, bis nach Rom und Jerusalem, bis zum südlichen Frankreich und nach Spanien zu unternehmen. Einsiedeln in der Schweiz und in der rheinischen Heimat Kevelar."

127 DAA, PA 68, "Die Aachener Heiligtümer!"

128 DAA, PA 68, "innigster Freund."

129 DAA, PA 68: "Solange man also nicht Beweise des Gegenteils bei-zu-bringen vermag soll und darf man den Glauben frommer Katholiken nicht schmähen und verachten."

130 "Der Beginn der Aachener Feierliche Oeffnung des Marienschreines und Erhebung der Heiligtümer. Aachen, den 10. Juli 1925," *Aachener Rundschau*, Aachen, Freitag, 10 July 1925.

131 "Besonders bei unseren Reliquien, die nicht erst aus der kritiklosen Periode der Kreuzzüge stammen, bei unsern Reliquien, die wir von unsern geistig und sittlich gesunden deutschen Vorfahren der frühesten Zeit überkommen haben?," *Aachener Rundschau*, Aachen, Freitag, 10 July 1925.

132 DAA, PA 80, "Mein lieber Landmesser!"

133 DAA, Domkapitel 4.1.1.9. DAA, Domkapitel 4.1.1.10, H. Schiffers, "Was die Karolingerzeit über die Aachener Reliquien berichtet," *Sanct Josephsblatt*, Bonn, Nr. 19, 9 May 1937.

134 DAA, Domkapitel 4.1.1.10, "Die Heiligtumsfahrt nach Aachen," *Ketteler-Feuer*, München, 3 June 1937.

135 DAA, Domkapitel 4.1.1.10: "können wir doch den Schluß ziehen, daß diese beiden Päpste Karl dem Großen wertvollste, echte Reliquien zum Geschenke machten."

136 DAA, Domkapitel 4.1.1.10: "Man kann sich zur Echtheit der Reliquien stellen wie man will."

137 DAA, Domkapitel 4.1.1.10: "Tatsache ist, daß tausende und abertausende Katholiken in den Jahrhunderten nach Aachen gepilgert sind. Kaiser und Könige, Fürsten und Adelige, heilige, von denen nur die hl. Brigitta, der sel. Heinrich Suso, die hl. Dorothea von Montau genannt seien, Bischöfe und Kardinäle. Sie alle haben an die Echtheit der Reliquien geglaubt."

138 Correspondence shows the pressing concern of establishing the link between Charlemagne and the relics as evidence of authenticity, for both domestic and foreign pilgrims. See DAA, Domkapitel 4.1.1.31, "15. Mai 1937, An Schriftwaltung."

139 DAA, Domkapitel 4.1.1.9, "Große Aachener Heiligtumsfahrt."

140 DAA, Domkapitel 4.1.1.11, *Der Johannesbote*, Schneidemühl, "Sind die Aachener Heiligtümer echt?," 4 July 1937, Nr. 27, 4–5.

141 For evidence that the Aachen clergy wrote and sent out press releases, including, "Sind die Aachener Heiligtümer echt?," see DAA, Domkapitel 4.1.1.32, "23.6.1937 An Schriftwaltung."

142 DAA, Domkapitel 4.1.1.11: "wir verehren diese Reliquien, weil sie heiliges Erbgut unserer Väter sind und den Hochteil deutscher Geschichte über ein Jahrtausend lang gesehen haben. Unsere Generation schämt sich der Vergangenheit nicht: dadurch, daß sie die fromme Hinterlassenschaft ihrer Väter und Ahnen hochhält, erfüllt sie nur eine liebe Pflicht der Hochachtung und Dankbarkeit."

143 DAA, Domkapitel 4.1.1.30, *Westdeutscher Beobachter*, Gauleiter Staatsrat Grohé, "Zur Aachener Heiligtumsfahrt," 24 July 1937.

144 DAA, Domkapitel 4.1.1.30, *Westdeutscher Beobachter*, Gauleiter Staatsrat Grohé, "Zur Aachener Heiligtumsfahrt," 24 July 1937: "so wenig wie wir heute ein einiges deutsches Volk hätten, wenn Adolf Hitler nicht die Eigensucht der Klassen und die Eigenwilligkeit partikularistischer und separatistischer Kreise gebrochen hätte."

145 DAA, Domkapitel 4.1.1.30, *Westdeutscher Beobachter*, Gauleiter Staatsrat Grohé, "Zur Aachener Heiligtumsfahrt," 24 July 1937: "das praktische Christentum in unseren Tagen im Nationalsozialismus enthalten ist, vom

nationalsozialistischen Staat allein gepflegt und vom nationalsozialistischen deutschen Volk trotz päpstlicher Sorge-Enzykliken betätigt wird."

146 Iserloh, "Der Heilige Rock," 172: "die Einheit der Liebe in der Gemeinschaft mit unseren Brüdern." For a detailed exposition on the sixteenth-century Trier Coat authenticity discussion, see Gildemeister and Sybel, *Der Heilige Rock*, xviii–xxi.

147 Flury-Lemberg, "Das Reliquiar," 696.

148 Flury-Lemberg, 707: "Darum kann eine Analyse, die von heutigen Gegebenheiten ausgeht, kaum über Vermutungen hinauskommen."

149 Eva-Maria Warner, "Geheimnisse der Vergangenheit lüften," *Paulinus Tageszeitung zur Wallfahrt*, 2 May 2012.

150 Warner, "Geheimnisse der Vergangenheit": "Dabei muss sorgfältig unterschieden werden zwischen Befund und Interpretation. Oft ist diese letztere sehr naheliegend, scheint mehr als nur eindeutig, Vorsicht ist aber immer angebracht. Der Heilige Rock ist ein Gewand, sicher. Aber wurde dieses Gewand je von einem Menschen getragen? Ist das, was wir heute vor uns haben vielleicht eher das Abbild eines Kleidungsstückes? Manchmal können textiltechnologische Fakten Antworten sogar auf solche, sehr grundsätzlichen Fragen geben. Im Idealfall können wir die Biographie eines Gegenstandes erarbeitet, seinen 'Lebensweg' nachzeichen."

151 BATr, Abt. 90, Nr. 125, 481: "Das Kleidungsstück ist ein ungenähter Leibrock, wie ihn die Einwohner Palästinas zur Zeit Christi trugen, unverziert, 1.48 lang, unten 1.09 breit, oben 0.70, einfacher Ausführung mit kurzen breiten Aermeln. Das hl. Gewand hängt an einem Stab in einem eigens dazu geschaffenen Kasten, der in einem eisernen Schrank in festen Gewölbe aufbewahrt wird."

152 BATr, Abt. 91, Nr. 246, 7: "Ich verordne daher, daß an den drei Tagen vor der Eröffnung der Feier eine Andacht vor dem ausgesetzten hochwürdigsten Gute stattfindet, und der letzte Tag vor Beginn der Ausstellung in der ganzen Diöcese als ein Fast- und Abstinenztag gehalten werde."

Conclusion: Verifying Presence

1 Anon., *Drei und zwanzig wunderbare Heilungen*, 11–14.

2 See Ronge, *Sendschreiben*. This pamphlet also appears in LHA Ko, Bestand 442, Nr. 10439.

3 On presence and incarnation, see Gumbrecht, "Incarnation, Now."

4 Throughout this book I have used individual voices to characterize a group, following Aziz, "Personal Dimensions."

5 On the distinction between "buffered and porous selves," see Charles Taylor, *A Secular Age*, 38–9. On Taylor's study and historical narrative, see Nash, "Reconnecting Religion"; Gordon, "The Place of the Sacred."

6 Peter Brown describes a similar process in early Christianity that took place at the sites of martyr graves. See Brown, *The Cult of the Saints*, esp. 1–22.

7 Much of the historiography on pilgrimage takes a political focus and this has permeated into popular literature. For example, see Carroll, *Constantine's Sword*, 493–4. For Carroll, the 1891 Trier pilgrimage was "nothing less than an ongoing political victory rally." This is an important part of the story, but Catholics did not attend solely because they were staunch Zentrum Party supporters.

8 See Frederick Gregory's survey of the limits of accommodation between theology and materialism: Gregory, "Intersections of Physical Science."

9 See Gumbrecht's questioning of the twentieth-century chronotype in "Incarnation, Now."

10 BATr, Abt. 91, Nr. 241, folie 2, 7–17.

11 This total comes from Jakob Marx's history of the Coat. See Marx, *History of the Robe*, 93. Kilian Harrer suggests this figure is as high as 244,000 in his University of Wisconsin-Madison dissertation: see "Appendix: Quantifying and Mapping Pilgrim Movement to Trier in September 1810."

12 DAA, PA 57, Der Provinzialkonservator der Rheinprovinz Bonn, 31 October 1918.

13 Renard wrote that there were three possible forms for this forthcoming French seizure: occupation of a twenty-kilometre strip of the border, which would include Aachen; occupation of bridges and bridgeheads on the Rhine; occupation of the entire left bank of the Rhine.

14 DAA, PA 57, Der Provinzialkonservator der Rheinprovinz Bonn, 31 October 1918, "möchte ich mein Gewissen wenigstens insoweit beruhigen."

15 DAA, PA 57, Inventar=Verzeichnis der Kisten.

16 See Buchkremer's retelling of stowing the Aachen relics in Paderborn: DAA, PA 57, Bericht über die Fortschaffung der Heiligtümer von Prof. Jos. Buchkremer, Münsterbaumeister.

17 DAA, Domkapitel 4.1.2.1 Heifa 1945, "Aachen, den 5. Juli 1939."

18 Herta Lepie, "600 Jahre Gotische Chorhalle des Aachener Domes," in Domkapitel, *Pilgerheft*, 24.

19 DAA, Domkapitel 4.1.2.1 Heifa 1945, "Aachen, den 5. Juli 1939," "vor Unheil beruhen."

20 DAA, Domkapitel 4.1.2.1 Heifa 1945, "Urkunde Aachen, den 5. Nov. 1942."

21 DAA, Domkapitel C 1.7.15 Fotokasten 15.

22 DAA, Domkapitel 4.1.2.1 Heifa 1945, "Aachen, den 5. Juli 1945."

23 DAA, Domkapitel 4.1.2.1 Heifa 1945, "Aachen, den 17. Juli 1945."

24 Anon., *Verehrung der Aachener Heiligtümer, 19. Juli-22. Juli 1945*: "soll uns dies in der Hoffnung stärken, daß der Herr uns wieder friedlichen Zeiten für Kirche und Volk entgegenführen möge."

25 DAA, Domkapitel 4.1.2.1 Heifa 1945: "Protokoll über die feierliche Ver-
    schließung der vier großen Heiligtümer in den Marienschrein am 22.
    Juli des Jahres 1945," "wurden diese wieder mit der Seide, in die sie am
    Schlusse der Heiligtumsfahrt 1937 eingewickelt worden waren, verhüllt."

26 Dieter P.J. Wynands, "Heiligtumsfahrt," in Domkapitel, Pilgerheft,
    20. After 1945, the next Aachen pilgrimage took place in 1951. At
    the most recent pilgrimage, 2014, more than 100,000 people visited
    the four Marian Shrine relics. See "Die Aachener Heiligtumsfahrt"
    in Franz Kretschmann, "Domkapitel gibt Termin für die Heilig-
    tumsfahrt 2021 bekannt," Kirche im Bistum Aachen, 26 June 2018,
    https://www.bistum-aachen.de/aktuell/nachrichten/nachricht/
    Domkapitel-gibt-Termin-fuer-die-Heiligtumsfahrt-2021-bekannt/.

27 Like Aachen, Trier was occupied early in the American offensive into
    Germany. See Carroll, *Constantine's Sword*, 259. General Patton crossed
    the Rhine River south of Mainz on 22 March 1945.

28 The 1959 and 1996 attendance figures come from Kurt Beck, "Grußwort
    von Ministerpräsident von Rheinland-Pfalz," in *Paulinus die Tageszeitung
    zur Wallfahrt*, 13 April 2012, 3.

Appendix 1: Selected Pilgrim Songs in Translation, 1839–1933

1 Anon., *Die Aachener Heiligthumsfahrt auf das Jahr 1839*, 9–10. This song was
   still used up to the 1860s, but by 1895, Aachen had a new welcome song
   for the relics. See Fuhr, *Die Heiligthümer Aachens*.

2 Anon., *Andachtsübungen bei der feierlichen Aussetzung des heil*, 4–5.

3 Bock, *Karl's des Großen Heiligthümer*.

4 Anon., *Lieder zur Heiligthumsfahrt*, 10.

5 Anon., *Lieder zur Heiligthumsfahrt*, 12.

6 Anon., *Pilgerfahrt nach Trier 1891*, 25–6.

7 Mießen, *Andachtsübungen*, 15–16.

8 Fuhr, *Die Heiligthümer Aachens*, 29.

9 BATr, Abt. 90, Nr. 128, 79–80. Both songs are designated as "Reiselieder."
   The second song here transcribed does not have page numbers, but appears in the same Akta after pp. 79–80.

Appendix 4: Holy Coat Songs in Trier Hymnal, 1846–1955

1 Heinz, "Die Lieder vom Heiligen Rock," 531.

Bibliography: Primary Works

Archives

AEK	Archiv des Erzbistums Köln
BATr	Bischöfliches Archiv Trier
BDA	Bischöfliches Diözesanarchiv Aachen
DAA	Domarchiv Aachen (PA – Propstarchiv)
GStA PK	Geheimnes Staatsarchiv Preußischer Kulturbesitz, Berlin
LHA Ko	Landeshauptarchiv Koblenz
SAA	Stadtarchiv Aachen
SAT	Stadtarchiv Trier
ZBA	Zentralbibliothek Aachen

Films

Die Grosse Wallfahrt zum Hl. Rock Trier 1933
Die Wallfahrt nach Trier zum Hl. Rock 1933
Eröffnungsgottesdienst der Heilig-Rock-Wallfahrt 2012, 13 April 2012
Heiligtumsfahrt Aachen, 1937
Lasset die Kinder zu mir kommen, 1934
Wallfahrt zum heiligen Rock nach Trier im Hl. Jahr 1933, 1934

Newspapers

Aachener Hausfreund
Aachener Heiligthumsfahrt Zeitung 1881
Aachener Illustrierte
Aachener Pius-Blatt
Aachener Post
Aachener Rundschau

Aachener Sonntagsblatt
Aachener Sonntagsblumen
Aachener Zeitung
Allgemeine Zeitung
Allgemeine Zeitung Augsburg
Augsburger Volkszeitung
Charivari
Der Volksfreund
Echo der Gegenwart (Aachen)
Festzeitung zur Ausstellung des hl. Rockes (Trier: Philippi u. Koch, 1891)
Fliegende Taube
Frankfurter Ober-Postamts-Zeitung
Für den Sonntag
Germania Berlin
Heimat und Welt
Hl. Rock Ausstellung Zeitungsschnitt (1891)
Kölnische Zeitung
Metzer Katholisches Volksblatt
Paulinus: Die Tageszeitung zur Wallfahrt (2012 Trier)
Politisches Tagesblatt
Rheinischer Figaro
Sonntagsblatt f.d. kath. Familien (Munich)
Trierer Nationalblatt Zeitung
Trierer Volksfreund
Trier Landeszeitung
Trier'sche Zeitung
Westdeutschland in Wort und Bild

Primary Publications, by City

Aachen

Anon. *Aachener Heiligtumsfahrt: Beschreibung der Reliquien und Kunstschätze mit Abbildungen*. Aachen: Joseph Kessels, 1930.
– *Aachener Heiligthumsfahrt. Passendes Festgeschenk*. Aachen: Friedrich Lagasse, 1895.
– *Aachen Heiligtumsfahrt 1925 vom 10–26 Juli*. Aachen: Xaverius-Verlagsbuchhandlung, 1925.
– *Aachen Heiligtumsfahrt 1930 vom 10–27 Juli*. Aachen: La Ruelle'sche Accidenzdruckerei, 1930.
– *Aachener Heiligthumsfahrt im Jahre 1881. Beschreibung der Heiligthümer nebst frommen Andachtsübungen*. Aachen: Och, 1881.

– *Andachtsübungen bei der Heiligthumsfahrt nach Aachen und Cornelimünster.*
Schleiden: J.F.E. Söchting, 1846.

– *Andachtsübungen bei der Heiligthumsfahrt zu Cornelymünster oder Anleitung
zur heilsamen Verehrung der Reliquien, welche unter Karl dem Großen und
seinen Söhnen in die dortige ehemalige Benedictiner-Abtei.* Cornelimünster:
Kirchenvorstande zu Cornelymünster, 1874.

– *Beschreibung der großen und kleinen Heiligthümer, die in der Dom-Kirche, in der
St. Adalberts- und Theresiäner-Kirche in Aachen, in Burtscheid auf St. Johann
Baptist und zu Cornelmünster aufbewahrt und alle sieben Jahre vom 10. bis 24.
Juli, öffentlich zur Verehrung vorgezeigt werden: nebst einer kurzen Geschichte
der Stadt Aachen und einer Andacht zur frommen Verehrung der h. Reliquien.*
Aachen: J. Hensen u. Comp., 1839.

– *Beschreibung der Heiligthümer, welche von dem erhabenen Kaiser Karl in die
Krönungskirche dahier versammelt worden, und alle sieben Jahre in der Heiligthumsfahrt
öffentlich zur Verehrung vorgezeigt werden.* Aachen: Leuchtenrath, 1846.

– *Beschreibung der Heiligthümer, welche von dem erhabenen Kaiser Karl in die
Krönungskirche dahier versammelt worden, und alle sieben Jahre in der Heiligthumsfahrt
öffentlich zur Verehrung vorgezeigt werden.* Aachen: Leuchtenrath, 1853.

– *Beschreibung der Heiligthümer, welche von Kaiser Karl dem Großen gesammelt, in
der Kollegiat Stiftskirche zu Aachen aufbewahrt sind und alle sieben Jahre während
der Heiligthumsfahrt den Gläubigen zur Verehrung gezeigt werden.* Köln: J.
Lumscher's Buchhandlung, 1853.

– *Das älteste national kirchenfest der Deutschen.* 1881.

– *Das Heiligtum zu Aachen.* Aachen: Urlichs, 1902.

– *Den 10. July 1804 (21. Messidor J. 12) neu eröffnete Schatzkammer des Aachner
Heiligthums oder kurze Beschreibung der hh. Reliquien, welche von dem glorwürdigsten
Kaiser Karl dem Großen in der Krönungs und Domkirche U.L.F. versammelt worden,
darin aufbehalten, und alle sieben Jahre in der Heiligthumsfahrt dem christlichen Volke
der Verehrung gezeigt werden.* Aachen: Müller, 1804.

– *Denkwürdige Erinnerungen aus der Geschichte der Aachener Heiligthumsfahrt.*
Aachen: Commissions-Verlag von Wehers-Kaatzer, 1881.

– *Die Aachener Heiligthumsfahrt. Beschreibungen und Abbildungen der
Heiligthümer Carl des Großen als Erinnerung an die Heiligthumsfahrt zu Aachen.*
Aachen: Math. Lemaire, 1874.

– *Die Aachener Heiligthumsfahrt auf das Jahr 1839: neueste Beschreibung der
Heiligthümer, welche alle sieben Jahre den Christgläubigen zur Verehrung vorgezeigt
werden, nebst genauer Bezeichnung der übrigen Reliquien und der in geschichtlicher
Beziehung merkwürdigen Ornate der hiesigen Münsterkirche.* Aachen: Vlieckx, 1839.

– *Die Aachener Heiligthumsfahrt eine Festgabe für die frommen Wallfahrer zu
derselben.* Aachen: Ulrichs, 1867.

– *Die Aachener Heiligthumsfahrt: eine Festgabe für die frommen Wallfahrer zu
derselben.* Aachen: Urlichs Sohn, 1881.

– *Die Aachener Heiligthumsfahrt und die Aachener Reliquien von einem Katholischen Laien.* Aachen: J. Hensen, 1846.

– *Die Aachener Heiligthumsfahrt und die Aachener Reliquien von einem Katholischen Laien.* Aachen: Vereins-Verlag von B. Boisserée, Cremersche Buchhandlung, J. Hensen und Comp., J.A. Mazer, E. Wengler, 1846.

– *Die Aachener und St. Korneli-Münsterer Heiligthumsfahrt: vorständige Beschreibung der Heiligthümer und Reliquien in Aachen, Burtscheid und in Korneli-Münster.* Aachen, 1846.

– *Die Heiligthümer zu Aachen, Burtscheid und Cornelimünster. Beschreibung der Heiligtümer nebst Betrachtungen und Gebeten bei der feierlichen Vorzeigung derselbem.* Aachen: Ferd. Och, n.d.

– *Die Heiligthümer zu Aachen, Burtscheid und Cornelimünster. Beschreibung der Heiligthümer nebst Betrachtungen und Gebeten bei der feierlichen Vorzeigung derselben.* Aachen: Verlag von Gottfr. Och, 1895.

– *Die Heiligthümer zu Aachen, Burtscheid und Cornelimünster. Eine Festgabe dem katholischen Volke bei Gelegenheit der Heiligthumsfahrt dargeboten.* Aachen: Jacob Nevels, 1902.

– *Die Heiligthümer zu Aachen, Burtscheid und Cornelimünster. Eine Festgabe dem katholischen Volke dargeboten bei Gelegenheit der Heiligthumsfahrt.* Aachen: Debey- Crolla, 1895.

– *Die Heiligthümer zu Aachen, Burtscheid und Cornelimünster: Mit Abbildungen, Beschreibungen und Ablassgebeten.* 1952?

– *Die Heiligthümer zu Aachen, Burtscheid und Cornelimünster: mit Abbildungen, Beschreibung und Ablaßgebeten.* 1895?

– *Die Heiligthümer zu Aachen, Burtscheid und Kornelymünster. Eine Festschrift den frommen Wallfahrern zu denselben gewidment.* Aachen: Urlichs, 1895.

– *Die Heiligtümer und Reliquien in Aachen, A-Burtscheid und Kornelimünster. Eine Festgabe mit Illustrationen für die Pilger der Heiligtumsfahrt 1909.* Aachen: Heinr. Baÿer, 1909.

– *Die Heiligthümer zu Aachen, Burtscheid und Cornelimünster. Eine Festgabe den frommen Wallfahrern zu denselben gewidmet.* Aachen: Urlichs, 1902.

– *Die Heiligthumsfahrt! Oder getreue Abbildung des Doms und der Heiligthümer zu Aachen (und seiner Umgebung nebst Beschreibung und Geschichte; Mit einem Vorworte über Heiligen Bilder- und Reliquen- Verehrung und das Wallfahrten.* Coblenz: J Hölscher, 1846.

– *Die Heiligthumsfahrt in Aachen: vollständige Beschreibung der größern und kleinern Heiligthümer un Kleinodien u.s.w., welche in der berühmten Münsterkirche zu Aachen aufbewahrt, und dem christlichen Volke öffentlich zur Verehrung vorgezeigt werden, nebst Beschreibung der h. Reliquien der übrigen Kirchen zu Aachen und der Umgegend, wie z.B. der vormaligen Abteikirchen zum h. Cornelius und Cyprianus in Cornelimünster und zum. h. Johann Baptist in Burtscheid.* Aachen: M. Urlichs Sohn, 1860.

– *Die Heiligthumsfahrt in der Kaiserstadt Aachen im Jahre 1853*. Aachen: Urlichs Sohn, 1853.

– *Die Heiligthumsfahrt zu Aachen, Burtscheid u. Cornelimünster*. Aachen: Leonard Keller, 1853.

– *Die Heiligthumsfahrt zu Aachen, Burtscheid und Cornelimünster: mit Beschreibung und Ablaßgebeten*. Aachen: Keller 1881.

– *Führer für die Heiligtumsfahrt 1925 Aachen und Cornelimünster*. Aachen: Josef Micheels, 1925.

– *Gedenkschrift zur Aachener Heiligthumsfahrt f. d. Jahr 1895 nebst e. Beschreibung der Reliquien von Burtscheid und Cornelimünster*. Aachen: Joseph Kessels, 1895.

– *Gedenkschrift zur Aachener Heiligthümsfahrt: Geschichte und Beschreibung der Aachener Heiligthümer, sowie der Reliquien der Kirchen zu Aachen-Burscheid und Cornelimünster*. Aachen: Jakob Lauffs Jr., 1909.

– *Gedenkschrift zur Aachener Heiligthümsfahrt: Geschichte und Beschreibung der Aachener Heiligthümer, sowie der Reliquien der Kirchen zu Aachen-Burscheid und Cornelimünster*. Aachen: Kessels, 1902.

– *Gedenkschrift zur Aachener Heiligtumsfahrt nebst einer Beschreibung der Reliquien von Burtscheid und Cornelimünster*. Aachen: Joseph Kessels, 1909.

– *Gedenkschrift zur Aachener Heiligtumsfahrt nebst einer Beschreibung der Reliquien von Burtscheid und Cornelimünster*. Aachen: Joseph Kessels, 1925.

– *Geleit-Büchlein für die Besucher der Aachener Heiligtumsfahrt im Jahre 1895: nebst kurzer Erläuterung der Reliquien-und Kunstschätze der Kirchen Aachens und Umgegend*. Köln: Heinrich Theissing, 1895.

– *Heiligtumsfahrt 1951*. Aachen: Wilhelm Metz, 1951.

– *Heiligtumsfahrt 1958*. Aachen: M. Brimberg, 1958.

– *Heiligtumsfahrt 1965*. Aachen: M. Brimberg, 1965.

– *Heiligtumsfahrt 1972*. Aachen: Arend und Ortmann, 1972.

– *Heiligtumsfahrt 1979 Aachen, Kornelimünster, Mönchengladbach: eine Handreichung für die Schule*. 1979.

– *Heiligtumsfahrt Kornelimünster "Erbarme Dich, Herr."* Aachen-Kornelimünster, Kath. Propsteipfarramt St. Kornelius, 1979.

– *Kurze Beschreibung der Heiligthümer, welche von dem erhabenen und großen Kaiser Karl in die Krönungskirche dahier versammelt worden, und alle sieben Jahre in der Heiligthumsfahrt öffentlich zur Verehrung vorgezeigt werden*. Aachen: Leuchtenrath, 1832.

– *Kurze Beschreibung der Heiligthümer, welche von dem erhabenen und großen Kaiser Karl in die Krönungskirche dahier versammelt worden, und alle sieben Jahre in der Heiligthumsfahrt öffentlich zur Verehrung vorgezeigt werden*. Aachen: Leuchtenrath, 1839.

– *Lieder für die festlichen Veranstaltungen bei Gelegenheit der Heiligthumsfahrt zu Aachen 1895*. Aachen: Dr. des "Volksfreunds," Oeterre, 1895.

– *Lieder zur Heiligthumsfahrt im Jahre 1881*. Aachen: Jacobi, 1881.

– *Mittheilungen über die Rosenkränze, welche durch Seine Heiligkeit den Papst Pius IX zu Rom am 24. April gesegnet und mit Ablässen versehen sind, sowie als andenken an die Aachener Heiligthumsfahrt des Jahres 1853 durch Herrn Bürgermeister Carl Nellessen- Kelleter in Aachen den Freunden der Restauration des Aachener Münsters geschenkt werden.* Aachen: 1853.

– *Pilgerbüchlein für die Aachener Heiligtumsfahrt im Jahre 1937.* Aachen: Van Heiss, 1937.

– *Pilger-Führer für die Heiligthumsfahrt zu Aachen 1909.* Aachen: Albert Jacobi, 1909.

– *Pilgerführer für die Aachener Heiligtumsfahrt 1925.* Aachen: L. Ollfisch, 1925.

– *Pilgerführer zur Aachener Heiligthumsfahrt Die Heiligthümer zu Burtscheid und Cornelimünster.* Aachen: J. Schweitzer, 1895.

– *Pilgerheft Aachener Heiligtumsfahrt 1. bis 10. Juni 2007.* Aachen: Domkapitel Aachen, 2007.

– *Pilgerheft: Aachener Heiligtumsfahrt 9. bis 18. Juni 2000.* Aachen: Domkapitel Aachen, 2000.

– *Schatzkammer des Aachner Heiligthums: oder kurze Beschreibung der hh. Reliquien, welche von dem glorwürdigsten Kaiser Karl dem Großen in der Krönungs und Domkirche U.L.F. versammelt worden, darin aufbehalten, und alle sieben Jahre in der Heiligthumsfahrt dem christlichen Volke zur Verehrung gezeigt werden.* Aachen: Vlieckx, 1818.

– *Schatzkammer des Aachner Heiligthums: oder kurze Beschreibung der hh. Reliquien, welche von dem glorwürdigsten Kaiser Karl dem Großen in der Krönungs und Domkirche U.L.F. versammelt worden, darin aufbehalten, und alle sieben Jahre in der Heiligthumsfahrt dem christlichen Volke zur Verehrung gezeigt werden.* Aachen: Vlieckx, 1825.

– *Schatzkammer des Aachner Heiligthums: oder kurze Beschreibung der hh. Reliquien, welche von dem glorwürdigsten Kaiser Karl dem Großen in der Krönungs und Domkirche U.L.F. versammelt worden, darin aufbehalten, und alle sieben Jahre in der Heiligthumsfahrt dem christlichen Volke zur Verehrung gezeigt werden.* Aachen: Vlieckx, 1832.

– *Schatzkammer des Aachener Heiligthums, oder kurze Beschreibung der hh. Reliquien, welche von dem glorwürdigsten Kaiser Karl dem Großen in der Krönungs und Domkirche U.L.F. gesammelt worden, darin aufbehalten, und alle sieben Jahre in der Heiligthumsfahrt dem christlichen Volke zur Verehrung gezeigt werden.* Aachen: Vliecks, 1836.

– *Schatzkästlein mit Perlen zur Verehrung von Heiligümern des Münsters zu Aachen und der Abteikirche Cornelimünster nebst Erläuterungen zu den lithographischen Darstellungen der Reliquien auf Postkartenformat.* Aachen: Ferd. Berck, 1902.

– *Unschätzbares Heiligthum des seien Kaiserlich- ehemaligen Reichs-Stifts zu St. Corneli- Münster auf der Inden, Ordens des h. Erz-Vaters Benedicti, welches bei Gelegenheit der in deisem jetzt laufenden 1818. Jahre vorwesenden so genannten Heiligthums-Fahrt.* Aachen: Th. Vlieckx, 1818.

– *Verehrung der Aachener Heiligtümer.* 1945.

– *Wahre Abbildung der h. Reliquien der Kathedral Kirche zu Aachen, wovon die 4 erst nur alle 7 Jahre vom 10 bis 24 Juli öffentlich und die Andere auf Begehren gezeigt werden.* Aachen, 1818.

– *Zur Erinnerung an die Aachener Heiligthumsfahrt. Beschreibung der grossen u. kleinen Heiligthümer der Münsterkirche zu Aachen, sowie bildliche Darstellung der grossen Reliquien.* Aachen: Verlag von Jos. La Ruelle, 1888.

– *Zur Erinnerung an die Aachener Heiligthumsfahrt: Einladung zur Verehrung der Heiligthümer, die nach altem Gebrauche in der Collegiat-Stiftskirche zu Aachen alle sieben Jahre öffentlich vorgezeigt werden.* Aachen: Och, 1881.

– *Zur Erinnerung an die heiligthumsfahrt zu Aachen im Jahre 1881: Kurze Beschreibung Karl's des Großen Heiligthümer zu Aachen, Mit dreizig erklärenden Holzschnitten und Betrachtungen und Gebeten bei der öffentliche Zeigung.* Düsseldorf: L. Schwann'schen Verlagshandlung, 1881.

Aqeunsis. *Die Reichskleinodien: ihre Bedeutung für Aachen als Krönungsstadt und ihre Schicksale im Laufe der Jahrhunderte.* Aachen: Creutzers Verlagshaus, 1925.

Beissel, Johann Peter Jos. *Aachener Heiligthumsfahrt.* Aachen: Strecken, 1860.

– *Die Heiligthumsfahrt: Gedanken über Reliquien-Verehrung überhaupt.* Aachen: Druck von J. Strecken, 1860.

Beissel, Stephan. *Kleines Heiligthums-Büchlein: Anleitung zu einer frommen Feier der Heiligthumsfahrt zu Aachen, Cornelimünster und Burtscheid.* Aachen: Barth, 1881.

– *Neues Heiligthumsbüchlein Anleitung zu einer verständigen und frommen Feier der Heiligthumsfahrt zu Aachen, Cornelimünster, und Burtscheid.* Aachen: Barth, 1881.

Bock, Franz. *Das Heiligthum zu Aachen: Kurzgefasste Angabe und Abbildung sämmtlicher "großen und kleinen Reliquien" des ehemaligen Krönungs-Münsters, sowie der vorzüglichsten Kunstschätze daselbst; … als Erinnerung an die "Heiligthumsfahrt des Jahres 1867".* Köln: Schwann, 1867.

– *Das Heiligthum zu Aachen: Kurzgefaßte Beschreibung und Abbildung sämmtlicher "großen und kleine Reliquien" des ehemaligen Krönungs-Münsters, sowie der vorzüglichsten Kunstschätze daselbst; allen Besuchern der Karolingischen Heiligthümer als Erinnerung an die "Heiligthumsfahrt des Jahres 1867" zu Nutz und Frommen gewidmet.* Aachen: Stadt, 1992.

– *Das Heiligthum zu Aachen: Kurzgefaßte Beschreibung und neuesdung sämmtlicher "großen und kleine Reliquien" des ehemaligen Krönungs-Münsters, sowie der vorzüglichsten Kunstschätze daselbst; allen Besuchern der Karolingischen Heiligthümer als Erinnerung an die "Heiligthumsfahrt des Jahres 1867" zu Nutz und Frommen gewidmet.* Köln: Schwann, 1867.

– *Die Reliquienschätze der ehemaligen gefürsteten Reichs-Abteien Burtscheid und Cornelimünster, nebst den Heiligthümern der früheren Stiftskirche St. Adalbert und der Theresianer-Kirche zu Aachen; zur Erinnerung an die Heiligthumsfahrt von 1867.* Köln: Schwann, 1867.

– *Die textilen Byssus-Reliquien des christlichen Abendlandes, aufbewahrt in den Kirchen zu Köln, Aachen, Cornelimünster, Mainz und Prag*. Aachen: La Ruelle, 1895.

– *Die textilen Byssus-Reliquien des christlichen Abendlandes, aufbewahrt in den Kirchen zu Köln, Aachen, Cornelimünster, Mainz und Prag*. Aachen: La Ruelle'sche, 1895.

– *Karl's des Großen Heiligthümer zu Aachen: Kurze Beschribung derselben nebst Betrachtungen und Gebeten bei der öffentlichen Zeigung*. Köln and Neuß: Verlag der L. Schwann'schen Verlagshandlung, 1867.

– *Karl's des Großen Heiligthümer zu Aachen. Kurze Beschreibung derselben nebst Betrachtungen und Gebeten bei der öffentlichen Zeigung*. Köln und Neuß: Verlag der L. Schwann'schen Verlagshandlung, 1874.

– *Kurze Beschreibung Karl's des Großen Heiligthümer zu Aachen: mit 30 erklärenden Holzschnitten und Betrachtungen und Gebeten bei der öffentlich Zeigung*. Düsseldorf: Schwann, 1888.

– *Zur Erinnerung an die Heiligtumsfahrt im Jahre 1909. Kurze Beschreibung Karls des Großen Heiligtümer zu Aachen*. Düsseldorf: Schwann, 1909.

Bock, Franz, and Johannes Theodor Laurent. *Der Reliquienschatz des Liebfrauenmünsters zu Aachen in seinen kunstreichen Behältern: zum Andenken an die Heiligthumsfahrt von 1860*. Aachen: Selbstverlag des Verfassers, 1860.

Crumbach, Johann. *Pilgerbüchlein für die Wallfahrt zum Gnadenbilde der lieben Mutter Gottes im Aachener Münster*. Aachen: La Ruelle'sche Accidenzdruckerei, 1915.

Domkapitel. *Pilgerheft: Heiligtumsfahrt Aachen 2014*. Aachen: Power + Radach, 2014.

Erasmus, Winand. *Heiligthums-Büchlein oder Einladung zur Verehrung der Heiligthümer, die nach altem Gebrauche in der Collegiats-Stiftskirche zu Aachen alle sieben Jahre öffentlich vorgezeigt werden: nebst frommen Andachtsübungen bei der feierlichen Vorzeigung der h. Reliquien im Jahre 1846 vom 10. bis 31. Juli einschließlich*. Aachen: Selbstverlag, 1846.

Evangelisches Bundes. *Vortrag des Herrn Pfarrer Thümmel über die Aachener Heiligthumsfahrt*. Duisburg: Verlag von Joh. Ewich, 1888.

Floss, Heinrich Joseph. *Geschichtliche Nachrichten über die Aachener Heiligthümer*. Bonn: Marcus, 1855.

Foesser, O. "Johannes Theodor Laurent, Titularbischof von Chersones, Apostolischer Vikar von Hamburg und Luxemburg und seine Verdienste um die katholische Kirche in Deutschland," in *Frankfurter zeitgemäße Broschüren*, edited by Johann Michael Raich. Frankfurt a.M.: Luzern, 1890.

Fuhr, W.v.d. *Die Heiligthümer Aachens, Burtscheids und der ehemaligen Abtei Cornelimünster. Festschrift zur Aachener Heiligthumsfahrt vom 10. bis 24. Juli 1895. Dem Hochwürdien Stiftskapitel zu Aachen gewidmet und den frommen Bewohnern und andächtigen Besuchern der alten Kaiserstadt dargereicht*. Aachen: "Volksfreunds", 1895.

Haagen, F. *Geschichte Achens*, 2. Bd. Aachen: Kaatzer, 1873–4.

Hermans, J. Christian von. *Erinnerung an die Stadt Aachen, insbesondere an ihr Münster und Rathaus*. Aachen: M. Ulrichs Sohn, 1867.

Kessel, Johann Hubert. *Das Gnadenbild Unserer Lieben Frau in der Stiftskirche zu Aachen*. Aachen: Ulrichs, 1878.

– *Geschichtliche Mittheilungen über die Heiligthümer der Stiftskirche zu Aachen nebst Abbildung und Beschreibung der sie bergenden Behälter und Einfassungen; Festschrift zur Heiligthumsfahrt von 1874*. Köln: Schwann, 1874.

Kleinermanns, Josef. *Die biblischen Heiligtümer in der früheren reichsabteilichen Benedictinerkirche, nunmehrigen Pfarrkirche zu Cornelimünster*. Aachen: Kaazer, 1907.

Krebs, Joseph. *Zur Geschichte der Heiligthumsfahrten. Als Erinnerung a.d. Aachener Heiligthumsfahrt i.J. 1881 hrsg.* Köln: Theissing, 1881.

Kreiten, Wilhelm. *Zur Aachenfahrt: dem frommen Pilger der Verehrung der Heiligthümer gewidmet*. Aachen: Rud. Barth, 1881.

Lelotte, Carl Joseph. *Der Reliquieschatz der Münsterkirche zu M. Gladbach*. M. Oberbach: Oberger, 1881.

Lennartz, Josef. *Festschrift zur Erinnerung an die Aachener Heiligthumsfahrt von 1895 nebst Beschreibg. d. Reliquienschätze von Aachen, Burtscheid und Kornelimünster*. Dülmen: A. Laumann, 1895.

Meyer, Karl Franz. *Historische Abhandlung über die großen Reliquien in der ehemaligen Kron- Stifts nun hohen Dom Kirche zu Aachen*. Aachen: Verlag bei Johann Joseph Plum, 1804.

Mießen, Matthias. *Andachtsübungen bei der Heiligthumsfahrt zu Cornelimünster*. Cornelimünster: Hsgr., 1895.

– *Andachtsübungen bei der Heiligtumsfahrt zu Cornelimünster*. Cornelimünster: Selbstverlag, 1909.

– *Andachtsübungen bei der Heiligtumsfahrt zu Cornelimünster*. Cornelimünster, Wilhelm Müller, 1925.

– *Andachtsübungen bei der Heiligtumsfahrt zu Kornelimünster*. Kornelimünster: Wwe. Wilh. Coir, 1937.

– *Cornelimünster und seine Heiligthümer: Geschichtliches über den Ort und kurze Beschreibung der Kirche und der in derselben aufbewahrten heil. Reliquien*. Aachen: Weyers-Kaatzer, 1888.

Mueller, Moritz. *Ausstellung von Andenken an die Aachener Heiligtumsfahrt 1909*. Aachen: Leo Speckheuer, 1909.

Pschmadt, Johannes. *Die Aachener Heiligthumsfahrt: das älteste nationale Kirchenfest der Deutschen*. Kaldenkirchen: Missionsdruckerei, 1881.

Quix, Christian. *Die Pfarre zum h. Kreuz und die ehemalige Kanonie der Kreuzherren in Aachen* Aachen: Math. Urlichs, 1829.

– *Historische Beschreibung der Münsterkirche und der Heiligthums-Fahrt in Aachen, nebst der Geschichte der Johannischerren: Mit 3 Abbildungen und 40 Urkunden*. Aachen: Urlich, 1825.

Reichsabtei, Burtscheid. *Die Reliqueinschätze der ehemaligen gefürsteten Reichs-Abteien Burtscheid und Cornelimünster nebst den Heiligthümern der früheren Stiftskirche St. Adalbert und der Theresianer-Kirche zu Aachen; zur Erinnerung an die Heiligthumsfahrt vom Jahre 1888.* Düsseldorf: Schwann, 1888.

Schervier, Carl Gerhard. *Die Münsterkirche zu Aachen und deren Reliquien: Bearbeitet auf Veranlassung des Karls-Vereins bei Gelegenheit der mit 500 jährigen Säkularfeier der Erbauung des Münsterchors zusammenfallenden Heiligthumsfahrt im Jahre des Heils 1853.* Aachen: C.G. Schervier, 1853.

Schmitz, Matthias. *Die Heiligtümer zu Aachen, Burtscheid und Cornelimünster mit Abbildungen und Geschichtlichen Nachrichten.* Aachen: Peter Urlichs Hofbuchdruckerei, 1925.

– *Die Heilgtümer zu Aachen, Burtscheid und Cornelimünster mit Abbildungen und Geschichtlichen Nachrichten.* Aachen: Peter Urlichs, 1930.

Schüren, Nikolaus. *Aachener Heiligthums-Legenden.* Aachen: Urlichs, 1881.

– *Anleitung zur Verehrung der Aachener Heiligthümer: nebst Angabe, Beschreibung und Abbildung derselben.* Aachen: J. Hensen u. Comp., 1846.

– *Die Aachener Heiligthumsfahrt und die in der hohen Münsterkirche daselbst befindlichen, alle sieben Jahre der Verehrung der Gläubigen ausgestellten heiligen Reliquien.* Aachen: Hensen, 1846.

– *Die Aachener Heiligthumsfahrt und die in der hohen Münsterkirche daselbst befindlichen, alle sieben Jahre der Verehrung der Gläubigen ausgestellten heiligen Reliquien. Historisch dargestellt von einem Katholischen Laien.* Aachen: B. Boisserée, Cremersche Buchhandlung, J. Hensenn u. Co., 1846.

Selung, B., ed. *Heiligtumsfahrt Aachen 1937.* M.-Gladbach: B. Kühlen Kunst, 1937.

Thisseny, A. *Heiligtumsfahrtbüchlein Seine Hochwürden.* Aachen, 1911.

Thümmel, Wilhelm. *Die Aachener Heiligthumsfahrt und die Reliquienverehrung überhaupt.* Barmen: Hugo Klein, 1888.

Thümmel-Remscheid, Wilhelm. *Die Aachener Heiligthumsfahrt.* Barmen: Druck und Verlag von D.B. Wiemann, 1888.

Vlieckx, J.W.Th. *Andachtsübungen bei der Heiligthumsfahrt zu Cornely-Münster oder Anleitung zur heilsamen Verehrung der Reliquien.* Aachen: Hrsg, 1853.

– *Die Aachener Heiligthumsfahrt auf das Jahr 1846.* Aachen: Vlieckx, 1846.

– ed. *I. Ordnungs-Vorschrift für die Heiligthumsfahrt. II. Zuspruch an die lieben Pilgersleute. III. Von der Verehrung der Heiligthümer. IV. Von den in der Münsterkirche zu Aachen aufbewahrten Heiligthümern. V. Vorzeigung und Verehrung der Heiligthümer. VI. Nachmittag-Andacht während der Heiligthumsfahrt auf Veranlassung des Collegiat-Capitels und mit Genehmigung der geistlichen und weltlichen Censurbehörde.* Aachen: Vlieckx, 1846.

— *Schatzkammer des Aachener Heiligthums oder kurze Beschreibung der hh. Reliquien, welche von dem glorwürdigsten Kaiser Karl dem Großen in der Krönungs und Domkirche U.L.F. versammelt worden, darin aufbehalten, und alle sieben Jahre in der Heilgthumsfahrt dem christlichen Volke zur Verehrung gezeigt werden.* Aachen: Joh. Müller, 1811.

Winand, Erasmus. *Heiligthums-Büchlein oder Einladung zur Verehrung der Heiligthümer, die nach altem Gebrauche in der Collegiats-Stiftskirche zu Aachen alle sieben Jahre öffentlich vorgezeigt werden: nebst frommen Andachtsübungen bei der feierlichen Vorzeigung der h. Reliquien im Jahre 1846 vom 10. bis 31. Juli einschließlich.* Aachen: Selbstverlag, 1846.

Kevelaer

Schützen, M. *Marianisches Pilger=Büchlein für die Wallfahrt nach Kevelaer.* Viersen: Gesellschaft für Druck u. Verlag GmbH, 1928.

1512 Trier

Sankt Wendel, Johann von. *Ein wahrhafftige und gewisse verkündung von dem closter zu sant Marien der alten by Trier gelegen unnd von dem Rock marie und anderem hochwirdigem Heiligthum da selbst enthalten.* Metz: Hochfeder, 1512.

1844 Trier

Anon (einem katholischen Freunde der Wahrheit). *Aller Streit hat nun ein Ende! Angabe des einzig untrüglichen Kennzeichens, durch welches die Aechtheit des ungenähten h. Rockes zu Trier, vor den zwanzig andern ungenähten h. Röcken nach dem Gebote der h. Synode zu Saragossa u.a.h. Synoden geprüft und bewährt werden soll.* Frankfurt a.M.: Carl Koerner, 1845.

— (von einem Alterthumsfreunde). *Kurzgefaßte Geschichte des heiligen Rockes unseres heilandes und Erlösers Jesus Christus.* Köln: Lumscher's Buchhandlung, 1844.

— (von einem Christen). *An die Christen und Deutschen: Ein fliegender Brief in Sachen der Kirchensehden.* Neuwied: G.A. van der Beeck, 1845.

— *Andachtsübungen bei der feierlichen Aussetzung des heil. Rockes unsers Herrn und Heilandes Jesu Christi in der Domkirche zu Trier, im Herbste des Jahres 1844.* Trier: Lintz'schen Buchhandlung, 1844.

— *Andachtsübungen bei der feierlichen Aussetzung des heiligen Rockes unseres Herrn und Heilandes Jesu Christi in der Domkirche zu Trier vom 18. August bis Ende September 1844.* Trier: Verlagsbuchdruckerei, 1844.

– *Ansichten und Betrachtungen über die Ausstellung des hl. Rockes zu Trier, über J. Ronge und über die jetztigen kirchlichen Bewegungen. Von e. Protestanten.* Regensburg: Georg Joseph Manz, 1845.

– *Ausführliche und getreue Lebensbeschreibung der heiligen Helena, Kaiserin und Wittwe, welche den heiligen ungenähten Rock unseres Heilandes Jesu Christi wieder aufgefunden und nach Trier geschenkt hat.* Saarlouis: Stein, 1844.

– *Beschriebung des heiligen Rockes zu Trier.* Trier: D. Niesen, 1844.

– *Der heilige Rock im Jahre 1512 und im Jahre 1844: Ein brüderlicher Glückwunsch an die deutsch-katholischen Gemeinden.* Berlin: Hermes, 1845.

– *Der heilige Rock und seine Wunderkraft. Oder ausführliche Berichte über die während der Ausstellung des heiligen Rockes geschehenen wunderbaren heilungen nebst einer kurzen Geschichte des heil. Kleinodes und einem vollständigen Gebet- und Erbauungsbuche worin die bei Verehrung der heiligen Reliquie gebräuchlichen Morgen-, Abend-, Meß-, Beicht-, und Communion-Andachten enthalten sind.* Borken: Emil Carl Brunn, 1844.

– *Der heilige Rock zu Trier. In zwei Gedichten. 1. Der Irrende. 2. Der Prophet.* Trier: Schillinger'schen Buchdruckerei, 1845.

– *Der heilige Rock zu Trier und der katholische Priester Johannes Ronge.* Mainz: Halenza, 1844.

– *Der Heilige Rock zu Trier und die Lästerer desselben.* Luxemburg: Conseil, 1844.

– *Der himmlischen Traum vor Ende des Jahres 1844; erzählt in vier Gesängen von einem Propheten wider Willen und dabei in schöne Verse gebracht für Jedermann, der's lesen und verstehen kann.* Leipzig: Gebrauer'sche Buchhandlung, 1845.

– *Der hl. Rock zu Trier: Eine Anklageschrift gegen Dr. C. Willems, bischöfl. Sekretär.* Bonn: Jos. Bach, 1844.

– *Die höhe Bedeutung des heiligen Rockes Jesu Christi zu Trier, zur Rechtfertigung der Verehrung desselben.* Würzburg: Voigt u. Mocker, 1845.

– *Die Wallfahrt nach Trier: Eine Stimme aus Nassau.* Siegen und Wiesbaden: Friedrichsche Verlagsbuchhandlung, 1844.

– *Drei und zwanzig wunderbare Heilungen die sich während der Ausstellung des h. Rockes in der Domkirche zu Trier vom 18. August bis 6 Oktober 1844 ereignet.* Coblenz: J. Hölscher, 1845.

– *Freimüthige Vertheidigung des Bischofs Arnoldi von Trier gegen die Angriffe des Priesters Ronge nach Beweisen aus dem Leben geführt von einem Nichtkatholiken.* Berlin: Plahn'schen Buchhandlung, 1844.

– *Geschichte des heil. ungenäheten Rockes unsers herrn und heilandes Jesu Christi.* Trier: F.A. Gall, 1844.

– *Geschichte und Bedeutung des Heiligen Rockes in der Domkirche zu Trier.* Königsberg: C.J. Dalkowski, 1844.

– *Geschichte und Begebenheiten des ungenähten h. Rockes Jesu Christi, vom Jahre 326 bis zum September 1844 in zwei Abtheilungen.* Trier: D. Niesen, 1844.

– *Gottes Urtheil über die Wallfahrt zum heiligen Rocke oder unumstößlicher Beweis für die Aechtheit des heiligen Rockes in Trier und die Rechtmäßigkeit seiner*

Verehrung aus den wunderbaren Heilungen, die sich während der Ausstellung desselben im Jahre 1844 bei demselben ereignet haben. Coblenz: Blum, 1845.

– *Heil-Rock-Album eine Zusammenstellung der wichtigsten Aktenstücke, Briefe, Adressen, Berichte und Zeitungsartikel über die Ausstellung des Heiligen Rockes in Trier.* Leipzig: Mayer und Wigand, 1845.

– *Herr Johannes Ronge, der falsche "Katholisches Priester". und die schlechte Presse.* Mainz: Schott und Theilmann, 1844.

– *Herr Johannes Ronge mit Gründen widerlegt, für Katholiken und Protestanten.* Mainz: Schott und Thielmann, 1844.

– *The Holy Coat of Treves and the New German Catholic Church.* New York: Harper & Brothers, 1845.

– *Johannes Ronge und der heilige Rock. Ein Beitrag zur Geschichte des 19. Jahrhunderts.* Arnstadt: Meinhardt'schen Buchhandlung, 1845.

– *Johannes Ronge und seine Irrthümer.* Münster: Theissingschen Buchhandlung, 1844.

– *Kurze Geschichte und Beschreibung des in der Domkirche zu Trier aufbewahrten ungenähten heiligen Rockes unseres Herrn und Heilandes Jesu Christi.* Borken: Emil Carl Brunn, 1844.

– *Luther und Ronge, oder Aufklärungen aus dem 16. Jahrhundert zum Verständniss des 19. Zugleich als Widerlegung der Schmähschrift: "Wunderthater und Ablaßkrämer im 19. Jahrhundert Wesel, bei Bagel."* Neuß: Jacob Hüsgen, 1845.

– *Offener Brief eines deutschen Katholiken an die deutschen Bischöfe.* Aus dem Vaterland, 1844.

– *Polizei-Reglement für die Zeit, während welcher der h. Rock Jesu Christi in Trier zur öffentlichen Verehrung ausgesetzt werden wird.* Trier: Königl. Preuß. Regierung, Abtheilung des Innern, 1844.

– *Selbstbiographie und Selbsterkenntnisse des heiligen Rockes zu Trier. Nebst dessen Urtheil über Johannes Ronge und Bischof W. Arnoldi. Niedergeleget in einem Schreiben des heil. Rockes an die katholische und protestantische Welt.* Hamburg: B.S. Berendsohn, 1845.

– *Statistische Uebersicht der während der Ausstellung des heil. Rockes im herbste 1844 zu Trier gewesenen Fremden und Beschreibung der Feierlichkeiten welche dabei stattgehabt.* Trier: J. Schillinger'schen Buchdruckerei, 1844.

– *Ueber den heiligen Rock zu Trier.* Aus der Berl. Vossischen Zeitung, 1844.

– *Ueber den Heiligen Rock zu Trier: erschienen in der Extra Beilage des Frankfurter Journals No. 300 v. 30 Oct. 1844 von dem katholischen Priester Johannes Ronge zu Laurahütte unterzeichneten.* Frankfurt: Die heilige Schrift, n.d.

– *Umtriebe der Sektirer unserer Zeit. Predigt, gehalten auf dem Kapitelslage.* Wittlich: J. Kuopp, 1845.

– *Urtheil eines Katholiken über Johann Ronge zu Laurahütte, über Fra Johann Baptist aus Karmel im heiligen Lande, üb er den Erzpriester Fiezeck in Oberschlesien und die Katholische Geistlichkeit.* Berlin: Eyssenhardt'schen i.Comm., 1844.

– *Worte der Verständigung über die Wallfahrt zum heil. Rock in Trier.* Speyer: Wappler, 1844.

Anthon, Edward Charles. *A Pilgrimage to Treves, through the Valley of the Meuse and the Forest of Ardennes, in the Year 1844.* New York: Harper & Brothers, 1845.

Arnoldi, Wilhelm. *Call for 1844 Pilgrimage.* Trier: Lintzsche Buchdruckerei und Buchhandlung, 1844.

– *Rede beim Schlusse der Trierer Feierlichkeit.* Borken: Brunn, 1844.

Baltzer, J.B. *Preßfreiheit und Censur mit Rücksicht auf die Trierer Wallfahrt und den doppelten Anklagezustand der schlesischen Tagespresse.* Breslau: Georg Philipp Aderholz, 1845.

Binterim, Anton Joseph. *Zeugnisse für die Aechtheit des heil. Röcke der Prof. D.D. Gildemeister und von Hebel.* Düsseldorf: P. Roschüß und Co., 1845.

Blum, Robert. *Johannes Ronge's (Katholischer Priester) offenes Sendschreiben an den Bischof Arnoldi zu Trier. Ferner: Der Kampf zwischen Licht u. Finsterniß.* Offenbach am Main: L. Ph. Wagner, 1845.

– *Rede am Grabe des Herrn Joseph Della Porta der ersten Leiche der deutsch-katholischen Gemeinde zu Leipzig.* Leipzig: Robert Friese, 1845.

Böhmer, Wilhelm. *Der heilige Rock in Trier und der katholische Priester Herr Johannes Ronge. Eine unbefangene Beurtheilung.* Breslau: J. Urban Kern, 1845.

Christhold, Lucilius Lucianus. *Nothwendige und gründliche Vertheidigung des H. Bischofs Arnoldi zu Trier wegen der ihm zum Vorwurfe gemachten Ausstellung des hl. Rockes.* Leipzig: Verlag von Otto Wigand, 1845.

Clarus, Ludwig. *Die Berliner Gewerbeausstellung und die Ausstellung des heiligen Rockes in Trier mit bes. Bezugnahme auf den Rongeschen Brief. E. Brief von einen Protestanten.* Münster: Friedr. Regensberg, 1845.

Clemens, Franz Jakob. *Der heilige Rock zu Trier und die protestantische Kritik.* Coblenz: W. Blum, 1845.

Czerski, Johannes. *Offenes Glaubensbekenntniss der christlich-apostolisch-katholischen Gemeinde zu Schneidemühl in ihren Unterscheidungslehren von der römisch-katholischen Kirche das heißt hierarchie.* Stuttgart: H.F. Köhler, 1844.

– *Rechtfertigung meines Abfalles von der römischen Hofkirche: Ein offenes Sendschreiben an Alle, die da hören, sehen, und prüfen wollen oder können.* Dromberg: Louis Levst, 1845.

Devora, Peter Joseph. *Die Pilgerfahrt zum heiligen Rock im Jahre 1844.* Koblenz: R.F. Hergt, 1844.

Eines katholischen Laien. *Lyser und Ronge und der Rationalismus in seinem Verhältnisse zu den neuesten Religionsfragen.* Würzburg: Verlag von Voigt & Mocker, 1845.

Engeln, J. *Warum ist dem katholischen Christen das Oberhaupt der Kirche so heilig und so theuer?* Münster: Theissingschen Buchhandlung, 1845.

Ernest, Grégoire. *Bericht über die wunderbaren Heilungen, welche sich, zur Zeit der öffentlichen Anstellung des heiligen Rockes unseres Herrn und Heilandes*

Jesu Christi in dem hohen Dom zu Trier vom 18. August bis 6 October 1844.
Luxemburg: Expedition der Luxemburger Zeitung, 1844.

Eschirn, Gustav. *Johannes Ronges Brief an Bischof Arnoldi von Trier: Mit einer Einleitung und Nachwort.* Frankfurt a.M.: Neuer Frankfurter Verlag, 1908.

Förster, Heinrich. *Der Feind kommt, wenn die Leute schlafen. Predigt, gehalten am Vierundzwanzigsten Sonntage nach Pfingsten.* Breslau: Ferdinand Hirt, 1844.

Franksmann, C.F.B. *Beleuchtung des Ronge'schen Schreibens an den Hochwürdigsten Herrn Bischof Arnoldi zu Trier, nebst einigen Bemerkungen über Zeitungscribenten, Dankadressen und die Nachschrift des Herrn Dr. Harms über den heil. Rock in seiner Reformationspredigt.* Kiel: Bünsow in Comm, 1845.

Fröhlich, Maria, *Die Wallfahrt der Maria Fröhlich aus Neuwied zum hl. Rock in Trier im Jahre 1844.* Edited by Eduard Lichter. Trier: Verein Kurtierisches Jahrbuch, 1978.

Geron, Hilarius Jacosus. *Die Sternschnuppe das ist Johannes Ronge.* Speyer: A. Wappler, 1845.

Gervinus, Georg Gottfried. *Die Mission der Deutsch-Katholiken.* Heidelberg: Verlagshandlung von C.F. Winter, 1845.

Gildemeister, Johann, and Heinrich von Sybel. *Der heilige Rock zu Trier und die zwanzig andern heiligen ungenähten Röcke: Zweiter Theil Die Advocaten des Trierer Rockes.* Düsseldorf: Julius Buddeus, 1845.

Goebel, K. *Der heilige Rock, ein evangelisches Zeugniß.* Neuwied: G.A. van der Beeck, 1844.

Goltz, Bogumil. *Der heilige Rock und der Brief des Herrn Johannes Ronge.* Leipzig: Leopold Michelsen, 1845.

Görres, Guido. *Vier Gedichte: Die Arme Pilgerin zum heiligen Rock, Der kritische Katzenjammer, die Gottesfahrt nach Trier, des Teufels Landsturm.* Coblenz: Blum, 1844.

Görres, Johann Joseph von. *Die Wallfahrt nach Trier.* Regensburg: Georg Joseph Manz, 1845.

– *Vorreden und Epilog zum Athanasius.* Regensburg: Georg Joseph Manz, 1838.

– *Zum Jahresgedächtniss des zwanzigsten Novembers 1837.* Regensburg: Montag und Weiss, 1840.

Gratz, Peter Alois, and Anton Joseph Binterim. *Drei öffenliche Stimmen gegen die Angriffe des Pastors Binterim auf den Kommentar des Proffessors Gratz, gesammelt nebst drei Beilagen.* Bonn: Adolph Marcus, 1825.

Hagen, Friedrich Heinrich von der. *Der ungenähte graue Rock Christi: wie König Orendel von Trier ihn erwirbt, darin Frau Breiden und das heilige Grab gewinnt, und ihn nach Trier bringt.* Berlin: Schultze, 1844.

Hansen, Valentin. *Aktenmäßige Darstellung wunderbarer Heilungen welche bei der Ausstellung des h. Rockes zu Trier im Jahre 1844 sich ereignet nach authentischen Urkunden, die von dem Verfasser theils selbst an Ort und Stelle aufgenommen, theils ihm direkt durch die H. Pfarrer, Aerzte u.s.w. eingeschickt, großentheils geordnet.* Trier: Verlag von F.A. Galls Buchhandlung, 1845.

Hecht, Laurenz. *Der heilige Leibrock Unsers Herrn Jesu Christi in der Pfarrkirche zu Argenteuil und die durch ihn gewirkten Wunder*. Einsideln: Benziger, 1845.

Heide, Franz. *Der Rock des Herrn zu Trier und Johannes Ronge, oder über die Reliquienverehrung der katholischen Kirche. Predigt gehalten in der Stadtpfarrkirche zu Ratibor am 1. Advent-Sonntage als wenige Tagevorher der Ronge'sche Brief an den Bischof von Trier verbreitet worden*. Kreuzburg: S. Landsber'she Buchhandlung, 1845.

Heinmann, Friedrich. *Wunderthäter und Ablaßkrämer in neunzehnten Jahrhundert: Eine Parallele des 16. Und 19. Jahrhunderts*. Wesel: J. Bagel, 1845.

Hillebrand, Joseph. *Alte und neue Vorurtheile, bei Gelegenheit des Ronge-Streites*. Münster: Theissing Buchhandlung, 1845.

– *Herodes und Pilatus oder Johannes Ronge und sein Advokat in der Trierer Sache*. Münster: Theissing'schen Buchhandlung, 1845.

– *Kampf und Sieg der katholischen Kirche. Predigt, gehalten am Pfingstmontage, den 12. Mai 1845*. Münster: Theissing Buchhandlung, 1845.

– *Neue Aergernisse oder Der sogen. Kath. Priester Johannes Ronge und Schmähartikel gegen den hl. Rock des Erlösers in Trier beleuchtet und zurechtgewiesen*. Münster: Theissing, 1844.

– *Reichthum, Würde und Seligkeit des christlichen Berufes. Predigt für fromme Eltern und deren Lieblinge in einer Zeit des Unglaubens und der Verführung*. Münster: Theissing Buchhandlung, 1845.

Himioben, Heinrich, ed. *Katholische Sonntagsblätter zur Belehrung und Erbauung. Zu Vereine mit der Geistlichkeit der Diöcesen Fulda, Limburg, Mainz und Speier*, no. 41. Mainz: 22 December 1844.

Hommer, Joseph von. *Geschichte des h. Rockes unsers Heilandes*. Trier: Verlag von F. Gall, 1844.

– *Geschichte des heiligen Rockes unsers Heilandes welcher in der Domkirche zu Trier aufbewahrt und vom 18. August d.J. ab, während eines Zeitraums von sechs Wochen öffentlich wird ausgestellt werden*. Bonn: T. Habicht, 1844.

Irenäus, Friedrich. *Der heilige Rock unseres Herrn und Heilandes Jesu Christi: ein offenes Antwortschreiben an einen Freund zur Berichtigung und Ausgleichung der verschiedenen Ansichten über die Geschichte des im Dome zu Trier aufbewahrten heiligen Rockes*. Saarlouis: Stein, 1844.

Karl, J.W. *Ueber den Glauben an das Wunderbare*. Münster: Theissing Buchhandlung, 1846.

Katholischer Geistlichen und Laien. *Die katholische Kirche vertheidigt gegen die Angriffe der Gegner. Eine Sammlung zeitgemässer Schriften*. Münster: Theissing'schen Buchhandlung, 1845.

Kemminghausen, Karl Schulte. *Die Briefe der Annette von Droste=Hülshoff, Bd. II*. Jena: Eugen Diederichs erlag, 1947.

Kraft, Johann Jakob. *Matthias Eberhard. Bischof von Trier. Ein Lebensbild*. Trier: St. Paulinus Druckerei, 1878.

Läncher, Karl August Ferdinand. *Die rechte Mitte zwischen dem Rocke und dem Leben Jesu, jenem zu Trier, diesem von Strauss*. Norhausen und Leipzig: Ferdinand Förstemann, 1844.

– *Die Rechte Mitte zwischen dem Rocke und dem Leben Jesu jenem zu Trier, diesem von Strauss*. Nordhausen und Leipzig: Ferdinand Förstemann, 1844.

Laven, Philipp. *Die Kirchliche Tradition vom h. Rocke, mit Rücksicht auf die historische Unteruschung der hh. Dr. Gildemeister und Dr. v. Sybel durch noch lebende Volkssagen und durch das altdeutsche Gedicht vom Grauen Rock in Schutß genommen*. Trier: Verlag der Fr. Linß'chen Buchhandlung, 1845.

– *König Orendel von Trier oder Der graue Rock*. Trier: Lintz, 1845.

Leitner, Ph. V. *Anhang zum Juliheft der Geschichte des Jahres 1844. Der ungenähte Rock Christi zu Trier*. Burg u. Berlin: Otto, 1844.

Licht, Peter Alois. *Katholische Stimmen gegen die Trierische Ausstellung im Jahr 1844*. Frankfurt a.M.: Carl Körner, 1845.

Lichter, Philipp. *Andachts-Büchlein zum Gebrauche bei der öffentlichen Verehrung des heiligen Rockes unsers Herrn Jesu Christi*. Wittlich: Knopp, 1844.

Liebetrut, Friedrich. *Ueber die Verehrung der Heiligen Reliquien und Bilder*. Berlin: L. Dehmigke, 1845.

Linde, Justin Timotheus Balthaser. *Betrachtung der neuesten kirchlichen Ereignisse aus dem Standpunkte des Rechts und der Politik. Von einem rechtsgelehrten Staatsmann*. Mainz: Florian Kupferber, 1845.

Lyser, Johann Peter. *Lyser und Ronge und der Rationalismus in seinem Verhältnisse zu den neuesten Religionsfrage*. Würzburg: Voigt u. Mocker, 1845.

– *Sendschreiben an Johannes Ronge in Laurahütte*. Würzburg: Voigt u. Mocker, 1844.

Marx, Jacob. *Die Ausstellung des h. Rockes in der Domkirche zu Trier im herbste des Jahres 1844*. Trier: Verlag der Fr. Linß'chen Buchhandlung, 1845.

– *Geschichte des heil. Rockes in der Domkirche zu Trier*. Trier: Fr. Linß'schen Buchhandlung, 1844.

– *History of the Robe of Jesus Christ: Preserved in the Cathedral of Tréves*. New York: Saxton & Miles, 1845.

– *Wallfahrten in der katholischen Kirche. Historische-kritisch dargestellt nach den Schriften der Kirchenväter und der Concilien von den ersten christlichen Jahrhunderten bis auf die neuere Zeit*. Trier: Linz, 1842.

Marx, Johann. *Einleitung in die Geschichte des heiligen Rockes in der Domkirche zu Trier*. Berlin: Eyssenhardt i.Comm., 1844.

Moritz, Mauritius. *Die Verehrung heiliger Reliquien und Bilder und das Wallfahrten nach der Lehre der katholischen Kirche*. Aschaffenburg: Theodor Pergay, 1845.

– *Offene Antwort auf das Schreiben des Herrn Johannes Ronge an die niedere katholische Geistlichkeit mit besonderer Rücksicht auf dessen Rechtfertigungschrift*. Frankfurt a.M.: Franz Barrentrapp Verlag, 1845.

– *Offenes Schreiben an Herrn Johannes Ronge in Larahütte, den in Trier aufgestellten heiligen Rock betreffend*. Köln: Welter, 1844.

Neumann, Johann Peter. *Sendschreiben eines katholischen Priesters an Johannes Ronge*. Mainz: Schott u. Thielmann, 1844.

Ney, Johann Baptist. *Erwiederung der "Katholischen Stimmen gegen die Trierische Ausstellung 1844"*. Trier: n.p., 1844.

– *Der h. ungenähte Rock Christi zu Trier, und außer diesem kein anderer*. Trier: Hrsg., 1845.

Pastor, Ludwig. *August Reichensperger. 1808–1895. Sein Leben und sein Wirken auf dem Gebiet der Politik, der Kunst und der Wissenschaft*. Freiburg im Breisgan: Herder'sche Verlagshandlung, 1899.

Pfaff, Johann Leonard. *Den neuen deutsch-katholischen Gemeinden und ihren Führern Czerski und Ronge*. Mainz: Schott u. Thielmann, 1845.

Reinerding, J.H. *Glaubensbekenntniß von Johannes Ronge*. Münster: Theissing'schen Buchhandlung, 1844.

Remlinger, Georg. *Betrachtungen über das Sendschreiben von Johannes Ronge. Von einem Pfarrer der Diözese Trier*. Koblenz: Aug Reiff, 1845.

Rhenanus, A. *Der hl. Rock in Trier: eine Beleuchtung der unter gleichem Titel erschienen Schrift des Domkapitulars Hrn. V. Wilmowsky*. Trier: Paulinus Druckerei, 1876.

Ritter, Joseph Ignaz. *Ueber die Verehrung der Reliquien und bes. des hl. Rockes in Trier. Eine Vorlesung, veranlasst durch ein Schreiben des Herrn Johannes Ronge*. Breslau: Georg Philipp Aderholz, 1845.

Ronge, Johannes. *An die niedere katholische Geistlichkeit*. Altenburg: Schnuphase'sche Buchhandlung, 1845.

– *An meine Glaubensgenossen und Mitbürger*. Altenburg: Schnuphase'sche Buchhandlung, 1845.

– *Brief von Johannes Ronge an Garibaldi, Frankfurt a.M. den 10 Januar 1863*. Saarbrücken: A. Hofer, 1863.

– *Die vierzehn Artikel des Badischen Ministeriums wider die Deutschkatholiken*. Deßau: H. Neubürger, 1846.

– *Schreiben des katholischen Pfarrers Johannes Ronge an den Bischof Arnoldi von Trier den heiligen Rock betreffend*. Braunschweig: Meinecke, 1844.

– *Sendschreiben an die Katholiken Deutschlands von Johannes Ronge*. Frankfurt am Main, o.d.: Selbstverlag, Reinhold Baist, 1862.

– *The Autobiography and Justification of Johannes Ronge (The German Reformer)*. Translated by John Lord. London: Chapman, Brothers, 1846.

– *Urtheil eines Katholischen Priesters über den heiligen Rock zu Trier*. Wesel: Bagel, 1844.

Ruges, Arnold. Paul Nerrlich, ed. *Arnold Ruges Briefwechsel und Tagesblätter aus den Jahren 1825–1880*. Berlin: Weidmannsche Buchhandlung, 1886.

Ruland, J.N. *Von der Verehrung der Reliquien im Allgemeinen und des heiligen Rockes zu Trier insbesondere. Predigt*. Berlin: Eyssenhardt i.Comm., 1844.

– *Was wird uns das neue Jahr bringen?* Berlin: Baumann u. Huhn, 1845.

S.B. *Worte der Verständigung über die Wallfahrt zum heil. Rocke in Trier an die Besonnenen in den deutschen Landen. Von B.S.* Speyer: Wappler, 1844.

Schmitz, Johann Hubert. *Die Katholiken als Verehrer der heiligen, ihrer Reliquien und Bilder vor dem Richterstuhl des Vernunft und des Christenthums.* Trier: Fr. Lintzs'schen Buchhandlung, 1843.

Schönhuth, Ottmar Friedrich Heinrich. *König Orendel von Trier oder der heilige Rock.* Neutlingen: Enßlin und Laiblin, 1847.

Schreiner, Joseph Balduin. *Predigt über die heil. Reliquie des Rockes unseres Herrn Jesu Christi, aufbewahrt in der Domkirche zu Trier.* Koblenz: R.F. hergt, 1844.

Schubach, Mathias. *Der heilige Rock in Trier und kein anderer, oder die kritischen Schneider in Bonn, d.i. Ungelehrte Widerlegung d. gelehrten Buches: Der hl. Rock zu Trier und die 20 anderen hl. Ungenähten Rocke von J. Gildemeister u. H.v. Sybel. Von eine Koblenzer Pilger.* Koblenz: Blum, 1844.

Schuselka, Franz. *Ronge in Weimar den 14., 15., und 16. November 1845.* Weimar: Wilhelm Hoffmann, 1845.

Siegel, Ludwig. *Was wir wollen! Gedicht, allen deutschen Katholiken und deren freisinnigen Vorfechtern Joh. Ronge und Rob. Blum.* Oschatz: Fr. Oldecop's Erben, 1845.

Sonst, Laurentius. *Der Priester-Apostat Johann Czerski und die apostolische Duodezkirche zu Schneidemühl vor dem Richterstuhle der heiligen Schrift, der kirchlichen Geschichts-Ueberlieferung und des gesunden Menschenverstandes; zugleich eine Vertheidigung und Rechtfertigung der katholischen Kirch.* Regensburg: Georg Joseph Manz, 1845.

Sotzmann, Johann Daniel Friedrich. *Der ungenähte Rock Christi in Trier.* Trier: Bibl. Publ., 1845.

Steinmann, Friedrich. *Wünderthäter und Ablasskrämer im 19. Jahrhundert Verlasst durch die Wallfahrt nach Trier: eine Parallele des 16. U. 19. Jahrhunderts zur Charakteristik unserer Tage.* Wesel: Bagel, 1845.

Sternberg, Peter Christoph. *Der heilige Rock zu Trier. Stimme der Sehnsucht. Seiner Hochwürden Gnaden Herrn Bischof Wilhelm Arnoldi, Ritter u.s.w. in tiefster Hochachtung gewidmet von S. Chr. P.* Trier: J. Schillinger'schen Buchdruckerei, 1844.

– *Vollständige Beschreibung des heiligen Rockes Jesu Christi zu Trier / Unseres Herrn Jesu Christi heiliger Rock zu Trier. Ein Büchlein für fromme Seelen und für alle diejenigen, welche gern an das Leben und Leiden des Heilandes denken.* Trier: Schillinger'schen Buchdruckerei, 1844.

Stolz, Alban. *Amulet gegen jungkatholische Sucht, zusammengesetzt v. Verf. D. Kalenders für Zeit u. Ewigkeit.* Freiburg i.Br.: Herder'sche Verlagsbuchhandlung, 1845.

– *Der neue Kometstern mit seinem Schweif oder Johannes Ronge und seine Briefträger.* Freiburg im Breisgau: Herder, 1845.

Strachwitz, A.G. Friedrich von. *Nicht der heil. Rock zu Trier, sondern nur der katholische Priester Herr Johannes Ronge.* Breslau: Georg Philipp Aderholz, 1845.

Tetzel, Johannes. *Der Ablaßkämer: ein Seitenstück zu d. Reliquienverehrung u. d. hl. Rock zu Trier.* Leipzig: Orthaus, 1845.

Treumund, F. *Die Geschichte des heiligen Rockes zu Trier. Ronge und Czersky, Wort und That, Gegenwort und Zukunft.* Leipzig: Pönicke und Sohn, 1845.

Varnhagen von Ense, Karl August. *Tagebücher, Bd. II.* Leipzig: Brockhaus, 1861.

Vecqueray, Franz Gerhard. *August oder die Wunderkraft des heiligen Rockes in der Domkirche zu Trier: Eine Erzählung als Festgeschenk für Jedermann.* Coblenz: J. Hölscher, 1845.

– *Der Triumph der Römisch-Katholischen Kirche! Eine Betrachtung über die öffentliche Ausstellung des heiligen Rockes in der Domkirche zu Trier, vom 18. August bis 6. October 1844.* Coblenz: J. Heinrich Müller, 1844.

Vecqueray, J. *Der Aufruf des Herrn Joh. Ronge und Würdigung desselben. Ein Sendschreiben für Jedermann. Von dem Verf. Mein Weg zu Gott!* Koblenz: J. Heinrich Müller, 1844.

Wagner, Friedrich Ludwig Wilhelm. *Der heilige Rock zu Trier: Katholischer Text mit protestantischen Noten.* Darmstadt: Leske, 1844.

Witte, Karl. *Der heilige Rock, Ronge und Czerski.* Breslau: Josef Max und Komp., 1845.

Zimmermann, Heinrich. *Worte eines Arztes gegen den Herrn Dr. B. Hansen: Reflexionen und Bemerkungen zum Werke des Herrn Dr. V. Hansen, königlich Preußischer Stadt-Kreis- Physikus zu Trier.* Saarbrücken: Arnoldsche Buchhandlung, 1845.

1891 Trier

Anon. *Der heilige Rock in neuer und vermehrter Auflage: Eine Streitschrift gegen die neumodischen römisch-papstischen Eiferer, die Feinde des Lichtes und der Freiheit, von einem Katholiken.* Leipzig: Verlag von Otto Wigand, 1868.

– *Der heilige Rock zu Trier. 2 durchgesehene Auflage. Sonder Abdr. Aus "Die Christliche Welt".* Barmen: Hugo Klein, 1891.

– *Die "Rockfahrt nach Trier" vor Gericht: Ein Stenographischer Bericht nebst Anhang.* Trier: Paulinus Druckerei, 1892.

– "Festschrift zum Andenken an die Ausstellung des hl. Rockes," in *Katholische Die Welt.* München-Gladbach, 1891, 770–84.

– *Pilgerfahrt nach Trier 1891. Der hl. Rock. Kurze Beschreibung und Geschichte des im Dom zu Trier aufbewahrten ungenähten Gewandes unseres Herrn und Heilandes Jesu Christi. Mit geschichtlichen Mittheilungen über den Dom und die übrigen Kirchen der Stadt sowie deren Haupt-Sehenswürdigkeiten.* Trier: Philippi u. Koch, 1891.

– *Prozess Verhandlungen vor der Strafkammer zu Trier am 19. September 1892 gegen stud. Theol. W. Reichard aus Trier als Verfasser und Buchdruckereibesitzer*

E. Sonnenburg aus Trier als Verleger der Broschüre: Die Rockfahrt nach Trier unter der Aera Korum. Trier: A. Sonnenburg, 1892.

– Schriften für das evangelische Volk: Der heilige Rock zu Trier. Barmen: Klein, 1890.

Auerbach, O. Das Prinzip in den Selbständigkeits-Bestrebungen der evangelischen Kirche. Barmen: Druck und Verlag von D.B. Wiemann, 1890.

Bach, Josef. "Der heilige Rock zu Trier." In Frankfurter zeitgemäße Broschüren, edited by Johann Michael Raich. Frankfurt a.M. und Luzern: Verlag von A. Foesser Nachfolger, 1891, 369–95.

– Die Trierer Heiligtumsfahrt im Jahre 1891: Ein Rückblick. Straßburg: E. Bauer, 1892.

Baur, Hermann Joseph. Zur Erinnerung an die Ausstellung des hl. Rockes in Trier. Köln: Fuhrmann, 1891.

Beissel, Stephan S.J. Geschichte der Trierer Kirchen ihrer Reliquien und Kustschaetse. Trier: Paulinus Druckerei, 1887, 1889.

– Geschichte des Heiligen Rockes. Trier: Paulinus Druckerei, 1891.

Benecke, Heinrich. Bischof Dr. Korum und die Wunderwirkung des Heil. Rockes. Berlin: Bibl. Bureau, 1891.

– Der heilige Rock zu Trier im Jahre 1891. Berlin: Verl des Bibliogr. Bureaus, 1891.

Beyschlag, Willibald D. Vaterländisch-kirchliche Erinnerungen aus Trier. Ein protestantisch- patriotisches Promemoria zur Trierer Rockausstellung von 1891. Halle a.S.: Strien, 1891.

Braasch, August Heinrich. Der Rock in Trier nach eigenen Eindrücken. Jena: Fr. Mauke's Verlag, 1892.

Cassel, D. Paulus. Arba Kanfos. Ein Sendschreiben an den Bischof Dr. Korum über den Heiligen Rock zu Trier. Berlin: Druck und Verlag von R. Boll, 1891.

Clarke, Richard F. A Pilgrimage to the Holy Coat of Treves: With an Account of Its History and Authenticity. London: Longmans Green, 1892.

Dasbach, Georg F. Festschrift zur Ausstellung des hl. Rockes mit Illustrationen. Trier: Paulinus, 1891.

Diel, Philipp. Die St. Mathias Kirche bei Trier und ihre Heiligthümer. Trier: Paulinus Druckerei, 1881.

Einem evangelischen Theologen. "Ein Wort zum Frieden in dem confessionellen Kampf der Gegenwart". In Frankfurter zeitgemäße Broschüren, edited by Johann Michael Raich. Frankfurt a.M.: Luzern, 1890.

Felten, Wilhelm. Wallfahrt zum heiligen Rock und zu den Kirchen und Heiligthümern in Trier. Bonn: Hanstein, 1891.

Flugschriften des Evangelischen Bundes. Wider den Priester Stöck und die Jesuiten: Gedanken ueber die geritchtliche Verhandlung vor der Strafkammer in Trier gegen den Katholischen Priester Stöck wegen Entführung eines evangelischen Kindes. Leipzig: Verlag der Buchhandlung des Evang. Bundes von C. Braun, 1892.

Förster, Theodor. Der hl. Rock von Trier im Jahre 1844 u. 1891. Frankfurt: Foesser, 1891.

310 Bibliography: Primary Works

Geile, Wilhelm. *Der hl. Rock in der Domkirche zu Trier*. Oberhausen: Witzler, 1891.

Goebel, Gerhard. *Sollen Wir den Rock unseres Heilandes verehren?* Halle: Mühlmann, 1891.

Grunau, Josef Elmar. *Der heilige ungenänte Rock zu Trier*. Neuss: Van Haag, 1891.

Hansen, Valentin. *Achtzehn wunderbare Heilungen welche bei der Ausstellung des h. Rockes zu Trier im Jahre 1844 sich ereignet*. Bonn: Hanstein, 1891.

Haupt, Antonie. *Der hl. Rock. Roman aus den Tagen der Kaiserin Helena*. Trier: Paulinus, 1891.

Henning, Ludwig. *Der Heilige Rock zu Trier im Jahre 1844 und 1891 mit einem Anhang: Offener Brief Johannes Ronge's an den Tetzel des 19. Jahrhunderts, Bischof Arnoldi von Trier, vom 1. Oktober 1844*. Berlin: Verlag von Rubenow, 1891.

Höhler, Matthias. *Ist der hl. Rock zu Trier echt? Eine kleine Hotelgeschichte*. Trier: Paulinus-Druckerei, 1891.

Hulley, Joseph. *Andenken an die Schatzkammer des Domes zu Trier*. Trier: Paulinus, 1891.

– *Kurze Geschichte der Wallfahrt zum Heilige Rock in Trier im Jahre 1891*. Trier: Druck und Verlag der Paulinus Drukerei, 1891.

Jaskowski, Friedrich. *Der Trierer Rock und seine Patienten vom Jahre 1891, eine Antwort auf Bischof Korum's "Wunder und göttliche Gnaderweise"*. Saarbrücken: Carl Schmidtke, 1894.

– *Der heilige Rock von Trier, gerichtet von seinen eigenen Freunden: nebst einem Anhang: Verzeichniss der unzähligen Reliquien der Stadt Trier*. Trier: Klingebeil, 1891.

– *Verlauf und Fiasko des Trierer Schauspiels im Jahre 1891*. Saarbrücken: Verlag H. Klingebeil, 1891.

Kastor-Hülf, E.J. *Der heilige Rock von Trier gerettet von seinen eigenen Feinden*. Barmen: Druck und Verlag von D.B. Wiemann, 1891.

Keil, Joseph. *Die Trierer Heiligtumsfahrt: Gratis-Beilage zur Trierischen Landeszeitung*. Trier: Paulinus, 1891.

Kempel, Franz. *Die Gottesfahrt nach Trier im Jahre 1891 oder Geschichte der diesjährigen Ausstellung des hl. Rockes in der Trierer Domkirche unter besonderer Berücksichtigung der Anfeindung des grossartigen Festes*. Mainz: Kupferberg, 1891.

Korum, Michael Felix. *Wunder und göttliche Gnadenerweise bei der Ausstellung des hl. Rockes zu Trier im Jahre 1891*. Trier: Verlag der Paulinus-Druckerei, 1894.

Kreutzkamp, J. *Auf nach Trier! Wallfahrtsbüchlein zum hl. Rock in Trier*. Dülmen: Lammann, 1891.

Kurtz, Hermann. *Trier und der hl. Rock*. Zürich: Verlags-Magazin, 1892.

Lindner, Max. *Der hl. Rock zu Trier und die Wunderheilungen*. Leipzig: Max Hesse's Verlag, 1891.

Melchisedech, Balthasar. *Eine Lanze für Den heiligen Rock in Trier 1891 Grunderste Sache in luftigen Reimen Ohne Bischöfliche Erlaubnis*. Düsseldorf: Verlag der Ruchdruckerie C. Kraus, 1891.

Nikel, Johannes. *Der heilige Rock zu Trier und seine Geschichte*. Paderborn: Verlag von Ferdinand Schöningh, 1891.

Peilnetosi. *Der hl. Rock oder Jesuiten in Sicht! Sendschreiben an Bischof Korum*. Barmen: Wiemann, 1891.

Plater, Edward A. *The Holy Coat of Treves: A Sketch of Its History, Cultus, and Solemn Expositions; with Notes on Relics Generally*. London: R. Washbourne, 1891.

Reichard, Wilhelm. *Die Rockfahrt nach Trier Unter Aera Korum*. Trier: Druck und Verlag von A. Sonnenburg, 1891.

Reichensperger, Peter. *Kulturkampf oder Friede in Staat und Kirche*. Berlin: Verlag von Julius Springer, 1876.

Sauren, Josef. *Pilgerbüchlein zum heil. Rock in Trier*. Köln: Theissing, 1891.

Schettler A. *Der wahre Heilige Rock Jesu Christi. Ein Wort der Liebe an alle ernstgesinnten, frommen, christgläubigen Wallfahrer zum heiligen Rock in Trier*. Bonn: Johs. Schergens, 1891.

Schirmer, Wilhelm C. *Offenes Sendschreiben an die deutschen Bischöfe in Sachen des Sogennanten heiligen Rockes zu Trier*. Barmen: Druck und Verlag von D.B. Wiemann, 1891.

Schneider, Joseph. *Der heilige Rock unseres Herrn und Heilandes Jesu Christi in der Domkirche zu Trier ausgestellt im August und September 1891*. Aachen: Albert Jacobi & Co., 1891.

Schneidewin, Max. *Das zeitgeschichtliche Ereignis von Trier als ein Markstein zur Umschau über unsern religiösen Horizont*. Berlin: Stahn, 1891.

Scholl, Carl. *Die Rockfahrt nach Trier und die Judenverfolgungen in Rußland*. Nürnberg: Friese in Comm., 1891.

Schroeder, Arnold. *Das neue Lied von der Wallfahrt nach Trier: ein komisches Gedicht*. Oldenburg: Büttner, 1891.

Schütz, Paul. *Der Kampf gegen Rom das Wahrzeichen unsrer Zeit*. Barmen: Druck und Verlag von D.B. Wiemann, 1890.

Siebert, Erasmus. *Was will die römische Papstkirche mit der Trierer Rockausstellung?* Barmen: Druck und Verlag von D.B. Wiemann, 1891.

Stöck, Anton. *Die Wallfahrt nach Trier zum heiligen Rock des Herrn*. Dülmen bei Münster: A. Laumann'sche Verlagshandlung, 1891.

Stöck, Christian. *Aus Meinen Erinnerungen an die Besatzungszeit der Stadt Trier*. Trier: Druck und Verlag N. Besselich, 1930.

Thümmel, W. *Die Anbetung der "lückenhaften Stoffteile" in Trier: Eine Historisch-archäologische Untersuchung*. Barmen: D.B: Wiemann, 1891.

von Hammerstein, Ludwig. *Die Wallfahrt zum heiligen Rock in Trier im Jahr 1891*. Berlin: Verlag der Germania, 1891.

Waal, Anton de. *Das Kleid des Herrn auf den frühchristlichen Denkmälern*. Freiburg: Herder, 1891.

Wesendonck, Hermann. *Der sogenannte "hl. Rock" zu Trier, ein Betrug der Clerisei*. Leipzig: Carl Minde, 1891.

Willems, Christoph. *Der heilige Rock unseres Herrn Jesu Christi in Trier*. Halle:
   Verlag von Eugen Strien, 1891.
- *Der H. Rock zu Trier und Seine Gegner*. Trier: Verlag der Paulinus Druckerei, 1892.
- *Der Hl. Rock zu Trier Eine archaeologisch-historische Untersuchung
   herausgegeben im Auftrag des hochw. herrn Bischofs von Trier*. Trier: Verlag der
   Paulinus Druckerei, 1891.
- *Wallfahrt nach Prüm*. Trier: Paulinus Druckerei, 1896.
- *Wallfahrt nach Trier Geschichte des Hl Rockes nebst Anhang vor
   Andachtsübungen*. Trier: Verlag der Paulinus Druckerei, 1891.
Wilmowsky, Johann Nikolaus. *Die Schrift des hl Rhenanus: Eine Beleutung der,
   archäologischen Prüfung d. zwar Verküllung der Reliquie der Tunica des Erlösers
   verwendeten prachtreichen liturgischen Gewandes im Dom zur Trier*. Trier: Fr.
   Lintz'schen, 1877.

1933 Trier

Anders, G. "Plaudereien an Böhmischen Kaminen". *Katholiken-Korrespondenz* 9
   (1933): 180–9.
Anon. *Das gute, billige Volksbuch aus dem Verlag der Paulinus-Druckerei GmbH
   Trier*. Trier: Paulinus, 1933.
- "Der Verlauf der Wallfahrt zum hl. Rock". *St. Matthias Bote* 10 (October
   1933): 289–320.
- "Die Eröffnung der Wallfahrt zum Trier". *St. Matthias Bote* 9 (September
   1933): 257–62.
- *Die Wallfahrt zum Hl. Rock in Trier im Heiligen Jahr 1933 und die Genossenschaft
   der Barmherzigen Brüder von Trier*. Trier: Mutterhaus der Barmherziger
   Brüder, 1934.
- *Die Wallfahrt zum Hl. Rock in Trier 1933 und die Reichsbahn*. Koblenz:
   Nationalverlag GmbH, 1933.
- *Exposition of the Holy Robe of Our Lord in Treves from 23rd July to 10th
   September 1933*. Trier: Schaar u. Dathe, 1933.
- *Festnummer der Trierer Heimat-Glocken zur Ausstellung des hl. Rockes im Jahre
   1933*, 5. Jahrgang, 1. Heft.
- *Pfarrblatt St. Paulus* 39 (16 September 1934).
- *Pilger-Büchlein für die Wallfahrt zum Hl. Rock im Heiligen Jahre 1933*. Trier:
   Paulinus, 1933.
- "Sinnbild der Einheit und Mahnung zur Liebe". in: *Der Rufer zum Kreuzzug*
   9 (September 1933): 257–259.
- *Trier: Seine Heiligtümer und Sehenswürdigkeiten, nebst einem Stadtplan*. Trier:
   Schaaur u. Dathe, 1933.
- *Trier im Zeichen des heil Rockes 1933, Ante Romam Treveris Stetit Annis Mille
   Trecentis*. Wiesbaden: Walter Schwarz, 1933.

– *Trier und seine Sehenswürdigkeiten: Ein kurzer Führer mit Abbildungen und Stadtplan mit Straßenverzeichnis*. Trier: Jacob, Lintz, 1933?

– *Verehrung des hl. Rockes in Trier*. Kevelaer: Verlag Jos. Thum GmbH, 1933.

– *Wallfahrt zum Hl. Rock im hohen Dom zu Trier im Heiligen Jahre 1933 vom 23. Juli bis 10. September*. Trier: Paulinus, 1933.

– *Wallfahrt zum Hl. Rock im hohen Dom zu Trier im Heiligen Jahre 1933 vom 23. Juli bis 10. September*. Trier: Verkehrsamt und Reichsbahn, 1933.

– "Wohin geht die Fahrt? Nach Trier". *Der Rufer zum Kreuzzug* 10 (October 1933): 298–300.

B.P. "Schulungskursus mit Generalversammlung in Trier". *Akademische Missionsblätter* III/IV (1933): 2–6.

Dempf, Alois. "Wallfahrt nach Trier 1933 … 1844". *Das Wort in der Zeit* 3 (September 1933): 35–8.

Gansen, Jakob. *Andachtsbüchlein für die Wallfahrt nach Trier enthaltend die Geschichte d. heil. Rockes m. d. Ergebnis d. neuesten Untersuchungen*. Montabaur: Endris, 1933.

Franziska. "Die Simpelfelder Hauschronik berichtet folgendes." *Christrose* 3 (1933): 85–9.

Fuchs, Friedrich. "Vom heiligen Rock zu Trier". *Hochland* 1 (1933/4): 91–4.

H.M. "Wallfahrt zum Hl. Rock". *Der Hildegardiskreis* (October 1933): 11–13.

Haupt, Antonie. *Der heilige Rock, Erzählung aus den Tagen der Kaiserin Helena*. Trier: Paulinus-Druckerei, n.d.

Irsch, Nikolaus. *Die Wallfahrt zum Hl. Rock im Dome zu Trier 1933*. Trier: Paulinus-Druckerei GmbH, 1934.

Kammer, Karl. *Der hl. Rock in Trier*. Trier: Paulinus-Druckerei, 1933.

Kaufmann, Georg. *Die Legende vom heiligen ungenähten Rock in Trier und das Verbot der vierten Lateransynode*. Frankfurt a.M.: Neuer Frankfurter Verlag, 1904.

Keune, Johann Baptist. *Wallfahrt zum hl. Rock Trier 1933*. Trier: n.p., 1933.

Koths, Anton. *Der hl. Rock in Trier Ausstellungsjahr 1933*. Düsseldorf: Graf & Pflügge, 1933.

Kremer, Rosemarie. "Bundeswallfahrt nach Trier." *Jugendziele* 10 (October 1933): 151–3.

Lackas, Nikolaus. *Legenden vom Heiligen Trier*. Saarbrücken: Saarbrücker Druckerei und Verlag, 1933.

Massaretti, Jos. "3. Von der Trierer Wallfahrt". *Theologisch-praktische Quartalschrift* H. 86, Jg. H.4 (1933): 856–8.

Neurath, Nikolaus. *Zur Erinnerung an die Wallfahrt zum hl. Rock im Jahre 1933*. Trier: Verlag Koch, 1933.

Neurath, Nikolaus, and Peter Schroeder. *Vom hl. Rock in Trier*. Trier: Paulinus-Druckerei, 1933.

Pilgerkomittee Saaralben. *Die Wallfahrt der Lothringer Pilger zum Hl. Rock in Trier im August und September 1933*. Trier: Paulinus Dr., 1934.

Pinsk. "Die Wallfahrt zum Heiligen Rock in Trier". *Liturgische Zeitschrift* 6 (1932/3): 279–80.

- *Die Wallfahrt zum Heiligen Rock in Trier*. Regensburg: Pustet, 1933.

Schmitt, Jakob S.J. *Wallfahrt zum hl. Rock in Trier im Heiligen Jahr 1933: Skizzen zu Predigten für die Vorbereitung der Wallfahrt*. Trier: Paulinus, 1933.

Schneider, Siegfried O.F.M. "Wachset in der Liebe Christi / Sinn und Ziel der Verehrung des heiligen Rockes in Trier". *Santificatio Nostra*, H. 9 (September 1933): 385–90.

Schroeder, Peter. *Der helige Rock und die Sehenswürdigkeiten von Trier*. Trier: Victor Kowollik, 1933.

Schüller, Andreas. "Der Deutschkatholizismus in der Diözese Trier". *Pastor bonus* 44, Jg. 1933, H. 6, concluded in: *Pastor bonus*, Nr. 45, Jg. 1934, H. 1, 389–407, 48–58.

- "Deutschkatholische Ansätze in Koblenz und Umgegend". *Pastor bonus*, Nr. 46, Jg. 1935, H. 6, 177–86.

- "Pfarrer Peter Aloys Licht" in: *Pastor bonus* 44, Jg. 1933, H. 2, 151–8, concluded in H. 3, 433–6.

Stockhausen, Wilhelm. *Zwei Lieder für die Wallfahrt zum hl. Rock im Jahre 1933 komponiert von Domkapellmeister Msgr. Stockhausen*. Trier: Paulinus, 1933.

Wagner, J. "Der Hl. Rock von Trier auf Ehrenbreitstein". *Pastor bonus* 44, Jg. 1934, H. 3, 219–26.

Wirtz, Richard. *Der Trierer Hl. Rock und die Kaiserin Helena*. Trier: Paulinus-Druckerei, 1933.

Zell, Albert. *Der Heilige Rock Jesu Christi im Dom zu Trier*. Paderborn, Ferdinand Schöningh, 1933.

Trier (Miscellaneous)

Anon. *Bezirks-Wallfahrt der katholischen Gesellenvereine zum Grabe des heiligen Apostels Matthias verbunden mit Fahnenweihe des Gesellenvereins von St. Matthias: Fest- Programm, Sonntag, 6. September 1925*. Trier: Katholischer Gesellen-Verein, 1925.

Beck, Otto. *Beschreibung des Regierungsbezirks Trier*. Vol. 1. Trier: Lintz, 1868.

- *Beschreibung des Regierungsbezirks Trier*. Vol. 2. Trier: Lintz, 1869.

- *Beschreibung des Regierungsbezirks Trier*. Vol. 3. Trier: Lintz, 1871.

Evans, E.P. "Recent Recrudescence of Superstition." *Popular Science*, October 1895, 761–75.

- "Recent Recrudescence of Superstition II: Concluded." *Popular Science*, November 1895, 73–92.

Hommer, Joseph von. "Geschichte des heiligen Rockes unseres Heilandes," *Zeitschrift für Philosophie und katholische Theologie* 7, no. 25 (1838): 192–208.

Huxley, Thomas Henry. *The Advance of Science in the Last Half-Century*. New York: D. Appleton, 1898. First published in Thomas Humphry Ward, *The Reign of Queen Victoria: A Survey of Fifty Years of Progress*, 2:322–87. London: Smith, Elder, 1887.

Kann, Hans-Joachim. *Pilgrims' Guide and Area Trier*. Trier: Verlag Michael Weyand, 1996.

Ursula, Bartmann. *Ein "Reiseführer" zum Heiligen Rock: die bedeutensdste Relique im Dom zu Trier*. Trier: Paulinus, 2010.

Bibliography: Secondary Works

Articles

Allcock, John B. "Tourism as a Sacred Journey." *Loisir et Société* (1988): 33–48.
Anderson, Margaret Lavinia. "Interdenominationalism, Clericalism, Pluralism: The Zentrumsstreit and the Dilemma of Catholicism in Wilhelmine Germany." *Central European History* 21 (1988): 350–78.
– "The Kulturkampf and the Course of Germany History." *Central European History* 19, no. 1 (March 1986): 82–115.
– "The Limits of Secularization: On the Problem of the Catholic Revival in Nineteenth-Century Germany." *Historical Journal* 38, no. 3 (September 1995): 647–70.
– "Piety and Politics: Recent Work on German Catholicism." *Journal of Modern History* 63, no. 4 (December 1991): 681–716.
– "Voter, Junker, Landrat, Priest: The Old Authorities and the New Franchise in Imperial Germany." *American Historical Review* 5 (December 1993): 1448–74.
Anderson, Margaret Lavinia, and Kenneth Barkin. "The Myth of the Puttkamer Purge and the Reality of the Kulturkampf: Some Reflections on the Historiography of Imperial Germany." *The Journal of Modern History* 54, no. 4 (December 1982): 647–86.
Applegate, Celia. "Discussion – Metaphors of Continuity: The Promise and Perils of Taking the Long View." *German History* 27, no. 3 (2009): 433–9.
Arbeitskreis für kirchliche Zeitgeschichte (AKKZG), Münster. "Katholiken zwischen Tradition und Moderne. Das katholische Milieu als Forschungsaufgabe." *Westfälische Forschungen* 43 (1993): 588–654.
Aziz, Barbara Nimri. "Personal Dimensions of the Sacred Journey: What Pilgrims Say." *Religious Studies* 23, no. 2 (June 1987): 247–61.
Bennette, Rebecca Ayako. "Threatened Protestants: Confessional Conflict in the Rhine Province and Westphalia during the Nineteenth Century." *German History* 26, no. 2 (2008): 168–94.

318   Bibliography: Secondary Works

Blaschke, Olaf. "Das 19. Jahrhundert: Ein Zweites Konfessionelles Zeitalter?" *Geschichte und Gesellschaft* 26 (2000): 38–75.

Blackbourn, David. "Progress and Piety: Liberalism, Catholicism and the State in Imperial Germany." *History Workshop* 26 (Winter 1988): 57–78.

Borutta, Manuel. "Enemies at the Gate: The Moabit Klostersturm and the Kulturkampf: Germany." In *Culture Wars*, 227–54.

Cohen, Erik. "Authenticity and Commoditization in Tourism." *Annals of Tourism Research* 15 (1988): 371–86.

– "A Phenomenology of Tourist Experiences." *Sociology* 13 (1979): 179–201.

– "Pilgrimage and Tourism: Convergence and Divergence." In *Sacred Journeys: The Anthropology of Pilgrimage*, edited by E. Alan Morinis, 47–61. Westport, CT: Greenwood, 1992.

– "Who Is a Tourist? A Conceptual Clarification." *Sociological Review* 22, no. 4 (1974): 527–55.

Connolly, Daniel K. "Imagined Pilgrimage in the Itinerary Maps of Matthew Paris." *Art Bulletin* 81, no. 4 (December 1999): 598–622.

Constable, Giles. "Opposition to Pilgrimage in the Middle Ages," *Studia Gratiana; Post Octava Decreti Saeculari* 19 (1976): 123–46.

Corr, Rachel. "To Throw the Blessing: Poetics, Prayer, and Performance in the Andes." *Journal of Latin American Anthropology* 9, no. 2 (2004): 382–408.

Cucchiara, Martina. "The Bonds That Shame: Reconsidering the Foreign Exchange Trials of 1935–36 against the Catholic Church in Nazi Germany, *European History Quarterly* 45, no. 4 (2015): 689–714.

Dahlberg, Andrea. "The Body as a Principle of Holism: Three Pilgrimages to Lourdes." In *Contesting the Sacred: The Anthropology of Christian Pilgrimage*, edited by John Eade and Michael J. Sallnow, 30–50. Urbana: University of Illinois Press, 2000.

Doney, Skye. "Brown and Black Boundaries: Nazism and German Catholicism in the Summer of 1933." *Catholic Historical Review* (Spring 2018): 268–97.

– "Pilgrims and Presence: Distinguishing the Travelers of the Past." *Environment, Space, Place* 9, no. 2 (2017): 114–34.

– "The Sacred Economy: Devotional Objects as Sacred Presence for German Catholics in Aachen and Trier, 1832–1937." *International Journal of Religious Tourism and Pilgrimage* 1, no. 1 (2013): 62–71.

Donnelly, James S. "The Marian Shrine of Knock: The First Decade." *Ireland* 28 (1993): 55–99.

Drury, Marjule Anne. "Anti-Catholicism in Germany, Britain, and the United States: A Review and Critique of Recent Scholarship." *Church History* 70, no. 1 (March 2001): 98–131.

Eade, John. "Pilgrimage and Tourism at Lourdes, France." *Annals of Tourism Research* 19 (1992): 18–32.

Eliade, Mircea. "Yearning for Paradise in Primitive Tradition." In *Myth and Mythmaking*, edited by H.A. Murray, 61–75. New York: Braziller, 1960.

Elm, Susanna. "Perceptions of Jerusalem Pilgrimage as Reflected in Two Early Sources on Female Pilgrimage (3rd and 4th Centuries A.D.)." *Studia patristica* 20 (1987): 219–23.

Embach, Michael. "Die Trierer Heilig-Rock-Wallfahrt von 1844 im Spiegel ihrer Literarischen Rezeption." In Aretz et al., *Der Heilige Rock zu Trier*, 799–836.

Feldhay, Rivka. "Religion." In *The Cambridge History of Science*, Vol. 3, *Early Modern Science*, edited by Katharine Park and Lorraine Daston, 727–55. Cambridge: Cambridge University Press, 2006.

Fleischer, Aliza. "The Tourist behind the Pilgrim in the Holy Land." *International Journal of Hospitality Management* 19 (2000): 311–26.

Flury-Lemberg, Mechthild. "Das Reliquiar Für die Reliquie vom Heiligen Rock Christi." In Aretz et al., *Der Heilige Rock zu Trier*, 691–708.

Fröhlich, Anna Maria. "Die Wallfahrt der Maria Fröhlich aus Neuwied zum Hl. Rock in Trier im Jahre 1844." In Lichter, *Kurtrierisches Jahrbuch*, 86–104.

Frühwald, Wolfgang. "Die Wallfahrt nach Trier: Zur historischen Einordnung einer Streitschrift von Joseph Görres." In *Verführung zur Geschichte. Festschrift zum 500. Jahrestag der Eröffnung einer Universität in Trier 1473–1973*, edited by Georg Droege, Wolfgang Frühwald, and Ferdinand Pauly, 366–82. Trier: NCO-Verlag, 1973.

Geertz, Clifford. "'The Pinch of Destiny': Religion as Experience, Meaning, Identity, Power." *Raritan* 18, no. 3 (Winter 1999): 1–19.

Gentilcore, David. "Contesting Illness in Early Modern Naples: Miracolati, Physicians and the Congregation of Rites." *Past & Present* 148 (August 1995): 117–48.

Gesler, Wil. "Lourdes: Healing in a Place of Pilgrimage." *Health & Place* 2, no. 2 (1996): 95–105.

Goldberg, Alan. "Identity and Experience in Haitian Voodoo Shows." *Annals of Tourism Research* 10 (1983): 479–95.

Goldstein, Jan. "The Hysteria Diagnosis and the Politics of Anticlericalism in Late Nineteenth-Century France." *The Journal of Modern History* 54, no. 2 (June 1982): 209–39.

– "Moral Contagion: A Professional Ideology of Medicine and Psychiatry in Eighteenth- and Nineteenth-Century France." In *Professions and the French State, 1700–1900*, edited by Gerald L. Geison, 181–222. Philadelphia: University of Pennsylvania Press, 1984.

Gordon, Peter E. "The Place of the Sacred in the Absence of God: Charles Taylor's 'A Secular Age.'" *Journal of the History of Ideas* 69, no. 4 (October 2008): 647–73.

Gottfied, Korff. "Formierung der Frömmigkeit. Zur sozialpolitischen Intention der Trierer Rockwallfahrten 1891." *Geschichte und Gesellschaft* 3 (1977): 352–83.

– "Heiligenverehrung und soziale Frage: Zur Ideologisierung der populären Frömmigkeit im späten 19. Jahrhundert." *Kultureller Wandel im 19. Jahrhundert* (1978): 102–11.

Graburn, Nelson H. "Tourism: The Sacred Journey." In *Hosts and Guests: The Anthropology of Tourism*, edited by Valene L. Smith, 21–36. Philadelphia: University of Pennsylvania Press, 1989.

Graf, Friedrich Wilhelm. "Euro-Gott im starken Plural? Einige Fragestellungen für eine europäische Religionsgeschichte des 20. Jahrhunderts." *Journal of Modern European History* 3, no. 2 (2005): 231–56.

Gregory, Brad S. "The Other Confessional History: On Secular Bias in the Study of Religion." *History and Theory, Theme Issue* 45, no. 4 (2006): 132–49.

Gregory, Frederick. "Intersections of Physical Science and Western Religion in the Nineteenth and Twentieth Centuries." In Nye, *The Cambridge History of Science*, 36–53.

Gross, Jon. "The Souvenir and Sacrifice in the Tourist Mode of Consumption." In *Seductions of Place: Geographical Perspectives on Globalization and Touristed Landscapes*, edited by Carol L. Cartier and Alan A. Lew, 56–71. New York: Routledge, 2005.

Gross, Michael B. "Kulturkampf and Unification: German Liberalism and the War against the Jesuits." *Central European History* 30, no. 4 (1997): 545–66.

– "The Strange Case of the Nun in the Dungeon, or German Liberalism as a Convent Atrocity Story." *German Studies Review* 23, no. 1 (February 2000): 69–84.

Grosse, Wilhelm. "Adolf Glaßbrenner 'Herrn Buffey's Wallfahrt nach dem heiligen Rocke' ein politisches Genrebild des Deutschen Vormärz." *Zeitschrift für Germanistik* 1 (1981): 48–68.

Gumbrecht, Hans Ulrich. "Incarnation, Now: Five Brief Thoughts and a Non-Conclusive Ending." *Communication and Critical/Cultural Studies* 8, no. 2 (June 2011): 207–13.

Hagen, Joshua. "Parades, Public Space, and Propaganda: The Nazi Culture Parades in Munich." *Geografiska Annaler: Series B, Human Geography* 90, no. 4 (2008): 349–67.

Hastings, Derek K. "Fears of a Feminized Church: Catholicism, Clerical Celibacy, and the Crisis of Masculinity in Wilhelmine Germany." *European History Quarterly* 38, no. 1 (2008): 34–65.

Heilbronner, Oded. "From Ghetto to Ghetto: The Place of German Catholic Society in Recent Historiography." *The Journal of Modern History* 72 (June 2000): 453–95.

– "The Place of Catholic Historians and Catholic Historiography in Nazi Germany." *Historical Association and Blackwell Publishing* (2003): 280–92.

Heinz, Andreas. "Die Lieder vom Heiligen Rock im Trierer Diözesangesangbuch und ihr Verkündigungsgehalt." In Aretz et al., *Der Heilige Rock*, 525–45.

Hesse, Petra. "Die Restaurierung des Hl. Rockes in Trier 1890/91 Anhand Zeitgenössischer Quellen." In Aretz et al., *Der Heilige Rock zu Trier*, 335–46.

Hiort, Pontus. "Constructing Another Kind of German: Catholic Commemorations of German Unification in Baden, 1870–1876." *The Catholic Historical Review* 93, no. 1 (January 2007): 17–46.

Hunter, Dianne. "Hysteria, Psychoanalysis, and Feminism: The Case of Anna O." In *The (M)other Tongue*, 89–115.

Iserloh, Erwin. "Der Heilige Rock und die Wallfahrt nach Trier." In Aretz et al., *Der Heilige Rock zu Trier*, 163–73.

Jackowski, Antoni, and Valene L. Smith. "Polish Pilgrim-Tourists." *Annals of Tourism Research* 19 (1992): 92–106.

Jewson, N.D. "The Disappearance of the Sick-Man from Medical Cosmology, 1770–1870." *Sociology* 10 (1976): 225–44.

Jonas, Raymond. "Restoring a Sacred Center: Pilgrimage, Politics, and the Sacre Coeur." *Historical Reflections* 20, no. 1 (Winter 1994): 95–123.

Kann, Hans Joachim. "Heiligrock-Postkarten-Probleme und Möglichkeiten einer Materialauswertung." In Aretz et al., *Der Heilige Rock*, 625–68.

– "Trierer Wallfahrtspfeifen (St. Matthias und Dom)." *Neues Trierisches Jahrbuch* 2 (1991): 69–78.

– "Unedierte Metallene Heiligrock-Andenken (Medaillen, Anhänger, Plaketten, Schuberplaketten, Prägestöcke)." in Aretz et al., *Der Heilige Rock*, 669–87.

Kaufman, Suzanne. "Selling Lourdes: Pilgrimage, Tourism, and the Mass-Marketing of the Sacred in Nineteenth-Century France." In *Being Elsewhere: Tourism, Consumer Culture, and Identity in Modern Europe and North America*, edited by Shelley Baranowski and Ellen Furlough, 63–88. Ann Arbor: University of Michigan Press, 2001.

Kearns, Robin A., and Alun E. Joseph, "Space in Its Place: Developing the Link in Medical Geography." *Social Science Medicine* 37, no. 6 (1993): 711–17.

Kertesz, George. "A Rationalist Heresy as a Political Model: The Deutschkatholiken of the 1840s, the Democratic Movement and the Moderate Liberals." *Journal of Religious History* 13, no. 4 (December 1985): 355–69.

Kocka, Jürgen. "The European Pattern and the German Case." In Kocka and Mitchell, *Bourgeois Society*.

Kolbe, Günter. "Demokratische Opposition in religiösem Gewande. Zur Geschichte der deutschkatholischen Bewegung in Sachsen am Vorabend der Revolution von 1848/49." *Zeitschrift für Geschichtswissenschaft* 20 (1972): 1102–12.

Koshar, Rudy. "On the History of the Automobile in Everyday Life." *Contemporary European History* 10, no. 1 (March 2001): 143–54.

Köster, Kevin. "Wallfahrtsmedaillen und Pilgerandenken vom Heiligen Rock zu Trier." *Trierisches Jahrbuch* 10 (1959): 36–56.

Kojman, Tamar. "Germanness and Religious Universalism in the Aftermath of the 1844 Trier Pilgrimage." *Nations and Nationalism* (2021): 1–16.

Kretschmann, Carsten, and Henning Pahl. "Ein 'Zweites Konfessionelles Zeitalter'? Von Nutzen und Nachteil einer neuen Epochensignatur." *Historische Zeitschrift Band* 276 (2003): 369–92.

Kselman, Thomas. "Challenging Dechristianization: The Historiography of Religion in Modern France." *Church History* 75, no. 1 (March 2006): 130–9.

Kuhn, Annette. "Deutschkatholiken." In *Theologische Realenzyklopadie*, edited by Gerhard Müller, 559–66. Berlin: de Gruyter, 1981.

Ladner, Gerhart B. "*Homo Viator*: Mediaeval Ideas on Alienation and Order." *Speculum* 42, no. 2 (April 1967): 233–59.

Lanski, Noel. "Empresses in the Holy Land: The Creation of a Christian Utopia in Late Antique Palestine." In *Travel, Communication and Geography in Late Antiquity: Sacred and Profane*, edited by Linda Ellis and Frank Kidner, 114–24. Burlington, VT: Ashgate Publishing, 2004.

Laufner, Richard. "Logistische und Organisatorische, Finanzielle und Wirtschaftliche Aspecte bei den Hl.-Rock-Wallfahrten 1512 bis 1959." In Aretz et al., *Der Heilige Rock zu Trier*, 457–81.

Lehmann, Hartmut. "The History of Twentieth-Century Christianity as a Challenge for Historians." *Church History* 71, no. 3 (September 2002): 585–99.

Lill, Rudolf. "Kirche und Revolution: Zu den Anfängen der katholischen Bewegung im Jahrzehnt vor 1848." *Archiv für Sozialgeschichte* 18 (1978): 565–75.

Lins, Joseph. "Trier." *Catholic Encyclopedia* 15. New York: Robert Appleton, 1912.

Lüdtke, Alf. "The Role of State Violence in the Period of Transition to Industrial Capitalism: The Example of Prussia from 1815 to 1848." *Social History* 4, no. 4 (May 1979): 175–221.

Luhrmann, Tanya M., Howard Nusbaum, and Ronald Thisted. "The Absorption Hypothesis: Learning to Hear God in Evangelical Christianity." *American Anthropologist* 112, no. 1 (2010): 66–78.

MacCannell, Dean. "Staged Authenticity: Arrangements of Social Space in Tourist Settings." *American Journal of Sociology* 79, no. 3 (November 1973): 589–603.

Mallmann, Klaus-Michael. "'Maria hilf, vernichte unsere Feinde': Die Marienerscheinung von Marpingen 1876." In *Richtig Daheim Waren Wir Nie: Entdecungsreisen ins Saarrevier 1815–1955*, edited by Klaus-Michael Mallmann, Gerhard Paul, Ralph Schock, and Reinhard Klimmt, 48–50. Berlin/Bonn: Verlag J.H.W. Dietz, 1987.

McLeod, Hugh. "Weibliche Frömmigkeit – männliche Unglaube? Religion und Kirche im bürgerlichen 19. Jahrhundert." In *Bürgerinnen und Bürger.*

Geschlectsverhältnisse im 19. Jahrhundert, zwölf Beiträge, edited by Ute Frevert, 134–56. Göttingen: Vandenhoeck & Ruprecht, 1988.

Menozzi, Daniele. "Roman Catholicism." In *The Oxford Handbook of Nineteenth-Century Christian Thought*, edited by Joel D.S. Rasmussen, Judith Wolfe, and Johannes Zachhuber. Oxford: Oxford University Press, 2015.

Mergel, Thomas. "Ultramontanism, Liberalism, Moderation: Political Mentalities and Political Behavior of the German Catholic Bürgertum 1848–1914." *Central European History* 29, no. 2 (1996): 151–74.

Metzger, Franziska. "Konstruktionsmechanismen der katholischen Kommunikationsgemeinschaft." *Schweizerische Zeitschrift für Religions- und Kulturgeschichte* 99 (2005): 433–47.

Mitchell, Jon P. "A Moment with Christ: The Importance of Feelings in the Analysis of Belief." *Journal of the Royal Anthropological Institute* 3, no. 1 (March 1997): 79–94.

Myerhoff, Barbara G. "Return to Wirikuta: Ritual Reversal and Symbolic Continuity on the Peyote Hunt of the Huichol Indians" In Babcock, *The Reversible World*, 225–39.

Nash, David. "Reconnecting Religion with Social and Cultural History: Secularization's Failure as a Master Narrative." *Cultural and Social History* 1, no. 3 (2004): 302–25.

O'Sullivan, Michael E. "From Catholic Milieu to Lived Religion: The Social and Cultural History of Modern German Catholicism." *History Compass* 7, no. 3 (2009): 837–61.

Orsi, Robert. "The Center Out There, In Here, and Everywhere Else: The Nature of Pilgrimage to the Shrine of Saint Jude, 1929–1965." *Journal of Social History* 25, no. 2 (Winter 1991): 213–32.

– "The Cult of the Saints and the Reimagination of the Space and Time of Sickness in Twentieth-Century American Catholicism." *Literature and Medicine* 8 (1989): 63–77.

Paul, Harry W. "The Debate over the Bankruptcy of Science in 1895." *French Historical Studies* 5, no. 3 (Spring 1968): 299–327.

Pickstone, John V. "Establishment and Dissent in Nineteenth-Century Medicine: An Exploration of Some Correspondence and Connections between Religious and Medical Belief-Systems in Early Industrial England." In *The Church and Healing: Papers Read at the Twentieth Summer Meeting and the Twenty-First Winter Meeting of the Ecclesiastical History Society*, 165–89. Oxford: Published for the Ecclesiastical History Society by Basil Blackwell, 1982.

Porter, Roy. "The Patient's View: Doing Medical History from Below." *Theory and Society* 14 no. 2 (March 1985): 175–98.

Repgen, Konrad. "Christ und Geschichte," *Internationale Katholische Zeitschrift, Communio*, 11 (1982): 475–89.

Rinschede, Gisbert. "Forms of Religious Tourism." *Annals of Tourism Research* 19 (1992): 51–67.

– "The Pilgrimage Center of Fatima/Portugal." In *Pilgrimage in World Religions: Presented to Prof. Dr. Angelika Sievers on the Occasion of Her 75th Birthday*, edited by Surinder M. Bhardwaj and Gisbert Rinschede, 65–98. Berlin: Dietrich Reimer, 1988.

– "The Pilgrimage Town of Lourdes." *Journal of Cultural Geography* 7, no. 1 (1986): 21–34.

Robbins, Joel. "God Is Nothing but Talk: Modernity, Language, and Prayer in a Papua New Guinea Society." *American Anthropologist* 103, no. 4 (December 2001): 901–12.

Ronig, Franz. "Die Tunika Christi – 'Heiliger Rock' – in der Theologischen Literatur des Mittelalters." In Aretz et al., *Der Heilige Rock zu Trier*, 67–81.

Runia, Eelco. "Presence." *History and Theory* 45 (February 2006): 1–29.

Schaefer, Richard. "Program for a New Wissenschaft: Devotional Activism and Catholic Modernity in the Nineteenth Century." *Modern Intellectual History* 4, no. 3 (2007): 433–62.

Schilbrack, Kevin. "Religions, Models of, and Reality: Are We Through with Geertz?" *Journal of the American Academy of Religion* 73, no. 2 (June 2005): 429–52.

Schneider, Bernhard. "Feminisierung der Religion im 19. Jahrhundert: Perspektiven einer These im Kontext des deutschen Katholizismus." *Trierer Theologische Zeitschrift* 111, no. 2 (2002): 123–47.

– "Vergessene Welt? Religion, Kirche und Frömmigkeit als Thema der Deutschen Geschichtswissenscahft. Historiographische und Methodlogische Sondierungen." In *Wozu Historie heute?: Beiträge zu einer Standortbestimmung im fachübergreifenden Gespräch*, edited by Amalie Fössel and Christoph Kampmann, 45–79. Köln: Böhlau, 1996.

– "Wilhelm Arnoldi (1842–1864)." In *Die Bischöfe von Trier seit 1802: Festgabe für Bischof Dr. Hermann Josef Spital zum 70. Geburtstag am 31. Dezember 1995*, edited by Martin Persch and Michael Embach, 75–98. Trier: Paulinus Verlag, 1995.

Seibrich, Wolfgang. "Die Heilig-Rock-Ausstellungen und Heilig-Rock-Wallfahrten von 1512 bis 1765." In Aretz et al., *Der Heilige Rock zu Trier*, 175–218.

Shaw, David Gary. "Modernity between Us and Them: The Place of Religion within History." *History and Theory* 45, no. 4 (December 2006): 1–9.

Shoaps, Robin A. "'Pray Earnestly': The Textual Construction of Personal Involvement in Pentecostal Prayer and Song." *Journal of Linguistic Anthropology* 12, no. 1 (2002): 34–71.

Smith, Jonathan Z. "Acknowledgements: Morphology and History in Mircea Eliade's 'Patterns in Comparative Religion' (1949–1999), Part 2: The Texture of the Work." *History of Religions* 39, no. 4 (May 2000): 332–51.

Smith, Valene L. "Introduction: The Quest in Guest." *Annals of Tourism Research* 19 (1992): 1–17.

Soine, Aeleah. "The 'Gender Problem' in Nursing: Masculinity and Citizenship in Late Wilhelmine Germany." *German Studies Review* 42, no. 3 (October 2019): 447–68.

Spencer, Elaine Glovka. "Regimenting Revelry: Rhenish Carnival in the Early Nineteenth Century." *Central European History* 28, no. 4 (1995): 457–81.

Sperber, Jonathan. "Bürger, Bürgertum, Bürgerlichkeit, Bürgerliche Gesellschaft: Studies of the German (Upper) Middle Class and Its Sociocultural World." *The Journal of Modern History* 69, no. 2 (June 1997): 271–97.

– "Kirchengeschichte or the Social and Cultural History of Religion?" *Neue Politische Literatur* 43 (1998): 13–35.

– "The Transformation of Catholic Associations in the Northern Rhineland and Westphalia 1830–1870." *Journal of Social History* 15, no. 2 (Winter 1981): 253–63.

Springs, Jason A. "What Cultural Theorists of Religion Have to Learn from Wittgenstein: Or, How to Read Geertz as a Practice Theorist." *Journal of the American Academy of Religion* 76, no. 4 (December 2008): 934–69.

Stambolis, Barbara. "In den Steinbrücken 'lokaler' Erinnerungskultur: Karl der Große also Inbegriff 'denkwürdigen' Mittelalters in Paderborn." *Geschichte im Bistum Aachen* 7 (2003/2004): 1–30.

Staudenmaier, Peter. "Occultism, Race and Politics in German-Speaking Europe, 1880–1940: A Survey of the Historical Literature." *European History Quarterly* 39, no. 47 (2009): 47–70.

Steinhoff, Anthony J. "A Feminized Church? The Campaign for Women's Suffrage in Alsace-Lorraine's Protestant Churches, 1907–1914." *Central European History* 38, no. 2 (2005): 218–49.

– Review of "Michael B. Gross, The War against Catholicism: Liberalism and the Anti-Catholic Imagination in Nineteenth-Century Germany; Róisín Healy, The Jesuit Specter in Imperial Germany." *The Journal of Modern History* 78, no. 3 (September 2006): 756–758.

Steinruck, Josef. "Die Heilig-Rock-Wallfahrt von 1844 und Die Entstehung des Deutschkatholizismus." In Aretz et al., *Der Heilige Rock zu Trier*, 307–24.

Stephany, Erich. "Der Zusammenhang der Grossen Wallfahrtsorte An Rhein – Maas – Mosel." In *Kölner Domblatt Jahrbuch des Zentral Domvereins*, edited by Joseph Hoster, 163–79. Köln: Verlag J.P. Bachem, 1964.

Strathausen, Carsen. "A Rebel against Hermeneutics: On the Presence of Hans Ulrich Gumbrecht." *Theory and Event* 9, no. 1 (2006).

Studstill, Randall. "Eliade, Phenomenology, and the Sacred." *Religious Studies* 36, no. 2 (June 2000): 177–94.

Tebbe, Jason. "Landscapes of Remembrance: Home and Memory in the Nineteenth-Century Bürgertum." *Journal of Family History* 33, no. 2 (April 2008): 195–215.

Tenfelde, Klaus. "Mining Festivals in the Nineteenth Century." *Journal of Contemporary History* 13, no. 2 (April 1978): 377–412.

Thurston, Herbert. "Relics." In *The Catholic Encyclopedia*, vol. 12. New York: Robert Appleton, 1911.

Tilly, Richard. "Popular Disorders in Nineteenth-Century Germany: A Preliminary Survey." *Journal of Social History* 4, no. 1 (Autumn 1970): 1–40.

Toner, Patrick. "Eschatology." In *The Catholic Encyclopedia*. New York: Robert Appleton, 1909. https://www.newadvent.org/cathen/05528b.htm.

Turner, Victor. "Comments and Conclusions." In Babcock, *The Reversible World*, 276–96.

– "Liminal to Liminoid, in Play, Flow, and Ritual: An Essay in Comparative Symbology." *Rice University Studies* 60, no. 3 (Summer 1974): 53–94.

Tweed, Thomas A. "On Moving Across: Translocative Religion and the Interpreter's Position." *Journal of the American Academy of Religion* 70, no. 2 (June 2002): 253–77.

Van Osselaer, Tine. "Feminization Thesis: A Survey of International Historiography and a Probing of Belgian Grounds." *Revue d'histoire ecclésiastique* 103, no. 2 (2008): 497–544.

– "Sensitive but Sane: Male Visionaries and Their Emotional Display in Interwar Belgium." *Low Countries Historical Review* 127, no. 1 (2012): 127–49.

Wecker, Kurt Josef. "Heiligtumsfahrt 2014." *Pastoralblatt für die Diözesen Aachen, Berlin, Essen, Hildesheim, Köln, und Osnabrück* 66. Jahrgang (6 June 2014): 163–70.

Welter, Barbara. "The Feminization of American Religion: 1800–1860." In *Clio's Consciousness Raised: New Perspectives on the History of Women*, edited by Mary S. Hartman and Lois Banner, 137–57. New York: Octagon Books, 1976.

Williams, Anthony V., and Wilbur Zelinsky. "On Some Patterns in International Tourist Flows." *Economic Geography* 46, no. 4 (October 1970): 549–67.

Yonke, Eric. "The Problem of the Middle Class in German Catholic History: The Nineteenth-Century Rhineland Revisited." *Catholic Historical Review* 88, no. 2 (April 2002): 263–80.

Ziemann, Benjamin. "Der deutsche Katholizismus im späten 19. Und im 20. Jahrhundert: Forschungstendenzen auf dem Weg zu sozialgeschichtlicher Fundierung und Erweiterung," *Archiv für Sozialgeschichte* 40 (2000): 402–22.

Zimmer, Oliver. "Beneath the 'Culture War': Corpus Christi Processions and Mutual Accommodation in the Second German Empire." *The Journal of Modern History* 82 (June 2010): 288–334.

Books

Applegate, Celia. *A Nation of Provincials: The German Idea of Heimat*. Berkeley: University of California Press, 1990.

Aretz, Erich, Michael Embach, Martin Persch, and Franz Ronig. *Der Heilige Rock zu Trier: Studien zur Geschichte und Verehrung der Tunika Christi*. Trier: Paulinus Verlag, 1995.

Auslander, Leora. *Taste and Power: Furnishing Modern France*. Berkeley: University of California Press, 1996.

Babcock, Barbara, ed. *The Reversible World: Symbolic Inversion in Art and Society*. Ithaca, NY: Cornell University Press, 1978.

Baranowski, Shelley, and Ellen Furlough, eds. *Being Elsewhere: Tourism, Consumer Culture, and Identity in Modern Europe and North America*. Ann Arbor: University of Michigan Press, 2002.

Barnes, Timothy D. *Constantine and Eusebius*. Cambridge, MA: Harvard University Press, 1981.

Baumanns, Hans Leo. "'Die Aachener Heiligtumsfahrt 1937' Ein sozialgeschichtlicher Beitrag zur katholischen Volksoppositiom im III. Reich." Dissertation, Rheinisch- Westfälischen Technischen Hochschule, 1968.

Bergeron, Louis, François Furet, and Reinhart Koselleck. *Das Zeitalter der europäischen Revolutionen 1780–1848*. Frankfurt: Fischer Bücherei, 1969.

Bhardwaj, Surinder Mohan. *Hindu Places of Pilgrimage in India: A Study in Cultural Geography*. Los Angeles: University of California Press, 1973.

Bitton-Ashkelony, Brouria. *Encountering the Sacred: The Debate on Christian Pilgrimage in Late Antiquity*. Los Angeles: University of California Press, 2005.

Black, Monica. *Death in Berlin: From Weimar to Divided Germany*. Washington, DC: Cambridge University Press, 2010.

Blackbourn, David. *Marpingen: Apparitions of the Virgin Mary in Nineteenth-Century Germany*. New York: Knopf, 1994.

– *Populists and Patricians: Essays in Modern German History*. London: Allen & Unwin, 1987.

Blackbourn, David, and Richard J. Evans. *The German Bourgeoisie: Essays on the Social History of the German Middle Class from the Late Eighteenth to the Early Twentieth Century*. New York: Routledge, 1991.

Blaschke, Olaf, ed. *Konfessionen im Konflikt: Deutschland zwischen 1800 und 1970: ein zweites konfessionelles Zeitalter*. Göttingen: Vandenhoeck und Ruprecht, 2002.

Bloch, Marc. *The Royal Touch: Sacred Authority and Scrofula in England and France*. Translated by J.E. Anderson. London: Routledge & Kegan Paul, 1973.

Bredohl, Thomas M. *Class and Religious Identity: The Rhenish Center Party in Wilhelmine Germany*. Milwaukee, WI: Marquette University Press, 2000.

Brodie, Thomas. *German Catholicism at War, 1939–1945*. Oxford: Oxford University Press, 2018.

Brophy, James. *Popular Culture and the Public Sphere in the Rhineland, 1800–1850*. Cambridge: Cambridge University Press, 2007.

Brown, Peter. *The Cult of the Saints: Its Rise and Function in Latin Christianity*. Chicago: University of Chicago Press, 1981.

Burleigh, Michael. *Sacred Causes: The Clash of Religion and Politics, from the Great War to the War on Terror*. New York: HarperCollins, 2007.

Burrow, J.W. *The Crisis of Reason: European Thought, 1848–1914*. New Haven, CT: Yale University Press, 2000.

Busch, Norbert. *Katholische Frömmigkeit und Moderne: Die Sozial- und Mentalitätsgeschichte des Herz-Jesu-Kultes in Deutschland zwischen Kulturkampf und Erstem Weltkrieg*. Güttersloh: Chr. Kaiser, 1997.

Bynum, W.F. *Science and the Practice of Medicine in the Nineteenth Century*. New York: Cambridge University Press, 1994.

Cahan, David, ed. *From Natural Philosophy to the Sciences: Writing the History of Nineteenth-Century Science*. Chicago: University of Chicago Press, 2003.

– *Hermann von Helmholtz and the Foundations of Nineteenth-Century Science*. Berkeley: University of California Press, 1993.

Carroll, James. *Constantine's Sword: The Church and the Jews, a History*. New York: Houghton Mifflin, 2002.

Chapman, Alister, John Coffey, and Brad S. Gregory, eds. *Seeing Things Their Way: Intellectual History and the Return of Religion*. Notre Dame, IN: University of Notre Dame Press, 2009.

Chaucer, Geoffrey. *The Canterbury Tales*. New York: Bantam, 2006.

Childers, Thomas. *The Nazi Voter: The Social Foundations of Fascism in Germany, 1919–1933*. Chapel Hill: University of North Carolina Press, 1983.

Christian, William A., Jr. *Apparitions in Late Medieval and Renaissance Spain*. Princeton, NJ: Princeton University Press, 1981.

Clark, Christopher, and Wolfram Kaiser, eds. *Culture Wars: Secular-Catholic Conflict in Nineteenth-Century Europe*. New York: Cambridge University Press, 2003.

Collins-Kreiner, Noga, Nurit Kliot, Yoel Mansfeld, and Keren Sagi, eds. *Christian Tourism to the Holy Land: Pilgrimage during Security Crisis*. Burlington, VT: Ashgate Publishing, 2006.

Dalton, Margaret. *Catholicism, Popular Culture, and the Arts in Germany: 1880–1933*. Notre Dame, IN: University of Notre Dame Press, 2005.

Daum, Andreas. *Wissenschaftspopularisierung im 19. Jahrhundert: Bürgerliche Kultur, naturwissenschaftliche Bildung und die deutsche Öffentlichkeit, 1848–1914*. Munich: Oldenbourg Verlag GmbH, 1998.

Düding, Dieter, Peter Friedemann, and Paul Münch. *Öffentliche Festkultur: Politische Feste in Deutschland von der Aufklärung bis zum Ersten Weltkrieg*. Hamburg: Rowolhlt Taschenbuch Verlag GmbH, 1988.

Dühr, Elizabeth, and Markus Groß-Morgen. *Zwischen Andacht und Andenken: Kleinodien Religiöser Kunst und Wallfahrtsandenken aus Trierer Sammlungen*. Trier: Paulinus, 1992.

Egginton, William. *How the World Became a Stage: Presence, Theatricality, and the Question of Modernity*. Albany: State University of New York, 2003.

Eire, Carlos M.N. *War against the Idols: The Reformation of Worship from Erasmus to Calvin*. Cambridge: Cambridge University Press, 1989.

Ellis, Linda, and Frank. L. Kidner, eds. *Travel, Communication and Geography in Late Antiquity: Sacred and Profane*. Burlington, VT: Ashgate Publishing, 2004.

Evans, Ellen Lovell. *The German Center Party 1870–1933: A Study in Political Catholicism*. Edwardsville: Southern Illinois University Press, 1981.

Evans, Richard J. *The Third Reich in Power, 1933–1939*. New York: Penguin, 2005.

Fischer, Gert. *Wirtschaftliche Strukturen am Vorabend der Industrialisierung: Der Regierungsbezirk Trier 1820–1850*. Köln: Böhlau Verlag, 1990.

Forster, Marc R. *Catholic Germany from the Reformation to the Enlightenment*. New York: Palgrave Macmillan, 2007.

Frevert, Ute. *Women in German History: From Bourgeois Emancipation to Sexual Liberation*. New York: Berg, 1983.

Frey, Arthur. *Robert Blum als Mensch, Schriftsteller und Politiker*. Mannheim: J.P. Grohe, 1849.

Garner, Shirley Nelson, ed. *The (M)other Tongue: Essays in Feminist Psychoanalytic Interpretation*. Ithaca, NY: Cornell University Press, 1985.

Geertz, Clifford. *The Interpretation of Cultures: Selected Esssays by Clifford Geertz*. New York: Basic Books, 1973.

Gelbart, Nina Rattner. *The King's Midwife: A History and Mystery of Madame du Coudray*. Berkeley: University of California Press, 1998.

Gilman, Sander L., Helen King, Roy Porter, G.S. Rousseau, and Elaine Showalter, eds. *Hysteria Beyond Freud*. Los Angeles: University of California Press, 1993.

Graf, Friedrich Wilhelm. *Die Politisierung des religiösen Bewußtseins: Die bürgerlichen Religionsparteien im deutschen Vormärz: Das Beispiel des Deutschkatholizismus*. Stuttgart: Frommann Verlag Günther Holzboog, 1978.

Gregory, Frederick. *Scientific Materialism in Nineteenth-Century Germany*. Dordrecht: D. Reidel Publishing, 1977.

Grogan, Geraldine F. *The Noblest Agitator: Daniel O'Connell and the German Catholic Movement 1830–1850*. Dublin: Veritas Publications, 1991.

Gross, Michael B. *The War against Catholicism: Liberalism and the Anti-Catholic Imagination in Nineteenth-Century Germany*. Ann Arbor: University of Michigan Press, 2004.

Großbölting, Thomas. *Losing Heaven: Religion in Germany since 1945*. New York: Berghahn, 2017.

Gumbrecht, Hans Ulrich. *Making Sense in Life and Literature*. Translated by Glen Burns. Minneapolis: University of Minnesota Press, 1992.

– *The Production of Presence: What Meaning Cannot Convey*. Stanford, CA: Stanford University Press, 2004.

Hagen, Ursula. *Die Wallfahrtsmedaillen des Rheinlandes in Geschichte und Volksleben*. Köln: Rheinland-Verlag GmbH, 1973.

Hahn, Hans Joachim. *The 1848 Revolutions in German-Speaking Europe*. London: Pearson Education, 2001.

Harris, Ruth. *Lourdes: Body and Spirit in the Secular Age*. New York: Viking, 1999.

– *Murders and Madness: Medicine, Law, and Society in the fin de siècle*. New York: Oxford University Press, 1989.

Harrison, Peter, and John H. Roberts, eds. *Science without God? Rethinking the History of Scientific Naturalism*. Oxford: Oxford University Press, 2019.

Harvey, Susan Ashbrook, and David G. Hunter. *The Oxford Handbook of Early Christian Studies*. Oxford: Oxford University Press, 2008.

Hastings, Derek. *Catholicism and the Roots of Nazism: Religious Identity and National Socialism*. New York: Oxford University Press, 2010.

Healy, Róisín. *The Jesuit Specter in Imperial Germany*. Boston: Brill Academic Publishers, 2003.

Herbermann, Charles G., Edward A. Pace, Condé B. Pallen, Thomas J. Shahan, John J. Wynnn, eds. *The Catholic Encyclopedia: An International Work of Reference on the Constitution, Doctrine, Discipline, and History of the Catholic Church*. New York: Encyclopedia Press, 1913.

Hermand, Jost, ed. *Der deutsche Vormärz. Texte und Dokumente*. Stuttgart: Reclam, 1967.

Howard, Thomas A. *Protestant Theology and the Making of the Modern University*. New York: Oxford University Press, 2006.

Kane, Paula M. "'She Offered Herself Up': The Victim Soul and Victim Spirituality in Catholicism." *Church History* 71, no. 80 (March 2002): 80–119.

Kann, Hans-Joachim. *Pilgrims' Guide and Area Trier*. Trier: Verlag Michael Weyand, 1996.

Kaufman, Suzanne K. *Consuming Visions: Mass Culture and the Lourdes Shrine*. Ithaca, NY: Cornell University Press, 2005.

Kitchen, Martin. *A History of Modern Germany 1800–2000*. Malden, MA: Blackwell Publishing, 2006.

Kocka, Jürgen, and Allan Mitchell, eds. *Bourgeois Society in Nineteenth-Century Europe*. Providence, RI: Berg, 1993.

Kohl, Thomas. *Familie und soziale Schichtung: Zur historischen Demographie Triers 1730–1860*. Stuttgart: Ernst Klett Verlage GmbH, 1985.

Koshar, Rudy, ed., *Histories of Leisure: Leisure, Consumption, and Culture*. New York: Berg, 2002.

Kotulla, Andreas J. *"Nach Lourdes!": der französische Marienwallfahrtsort und die Katholiken im Deutschen Kaiserreich (1871–1914)*. Munich: Meidenbauer, 2006.

Krämer, Helmut. *Tunica Domini: eine Literaturdokumentation zur Geschichte der Trierer Heilig-Rock-Verehrung*. Trier, Trier Bibliothek des Bischöflichen Priesterseminars, 1991.

Kselman, Thomas. *Miracles & Prophecies in Nineteenth-Century France*. New Brunswick, NJ: Rutgers University Press, 1983.

Kurlander, Eric. *Hitler's Monsters: A Supernatural History of the Third Reich*. New Haven, CT: Yale University Press, 2017.

Lambertz, Josef. *Aachener Heiligtumsfahrten: zwischen Franzosenzeit und Nationalsozialismus*. Self-published, 2010.

Leclercq, Jean. *The Love of Learning and the Desire for God: A Study of Monastic Culture*. Translated by Catherine Misrahi. New York: Fordham University Press, 1982.

Lester, Rebecca J. *Jesus in Our Wombs: Embodying Modernity in a Mexican Convent*. Berkeley: University of California Press, 2005.

Lichter, Eduard, ed. *Kurtrierisches Jahrbuch*. Trier: Verein Kurtrierisches Jahrbuch e.V., 1978.

Lufer, Wolfgang. *Die Socialstruktur der Stadt Trier in der frühen Neuzeit*. Bonn: Ludwig Rohrscheid Verlag, 1973.

Macmullen, Ramsay. *Constantine*. New York: Croon Helm, 1987.

Marini-Bettòlo, G.B. *The Activity of the Pontifical Academy of Sciences 1936–1986*. Città del Vaticano: Pontificia Academia Scientiarum, 1987.

McGrath, Alister E., ed. *The Christian Theology Reader*. Malden, MA: Blackwell, 2007.

McLeod, Hugh, and Werner Ustorf, eds. *The Decline of Christendom in Western Europe, 1750–2000*. New York: Cambridge University Press, 2003.

Mergel, Thomas. *Zwischen Klasse und Konfession: Katholisches Bürgertum im Rheinland 1794–1914*. Göttingen: Vandenhoeck & Ruprecht, 1994.

Mitchell, Maria. *The Origins of Christian Democracy: Politics and Confession in Modern Germany*. Ann Arbor: University of Michigan Press, 2012.

Mosse, George L. *The Crisis of German Ideology: Intellectual Origins of the Third Reich*. Madison: University of Wisconsin Press, 2021.

– *The Image of Man: The Creation of Modern Masculinity*. New York: Oxford University Press, 1996.

Mueller, Volker. *Johannes Ronge und die freireligiöse Bewegung*. Neu-Isenburg: Angela Lenz Verlag, 2013.

Nelson, Bradley J. *The Persistence of Presence: Emblem and Ritual in Baroque Spain*. Toronto: University of Toronto Press, 2010.

Nipperdey, Thomas. *Germany from Napoleon to Bismarck: 1800–1866*. Translated by Daniel Nolan. Princeton, NJ: Princeton University Press, 1996. Originally 1983.

Nolan, Mary Lee, and Sidney Nolan. *Christian Pilgrimage in Modern Western Europe*. Chapel Hill: University of North Carolina Press, 1989.

Numbers, Ronald, ed. *Galileo Goes to Jail and Other Myths about Science and Religion*. Cambridge, MA: Harvard University Press, 2009.

Nye, Mary Jo, ed. *The Cambridge History of Science*. Vol. 5, *The Modern Physical and Mathematical Sciences*. Cambridge: Cambridge University Press, 2002.

Olenhusen, Irmtraud Götz von. "Die Feminisierung von Religion und Kirche im 19. und 20. Jahrhundert: Forschungsstand und Forschungsperspektiven." In *Frauen unter dem Patriarchat der Kirchen:*

Katholikinnen und Protestantinnen im 19. und 20. Jahrhundert, 8–21. Stuttgart: W. Kohlhammer, 1995.

– *Klerus und abweichendes Verhalten: Zur Sozialgeschichte katholischer Priester im 19. Jahrhundert: Die Erzdiözese Freiburg.* Göttingen: Vandenhoeck & Ruprecht, 1994.

Olson, Richard G. *Science and Scientism in Nineteenth-Century Europe.* Urbana: University of Illinois Press, 2008.

Ortner, Sherry B. *Sherpas through Their Rituals.* Cambridge: Cambridge University Press, 1978.

O'Sullivan, Michael E. *Disruptive Power: Catholic Women, Miracles, and Politics in Modern Germany, 1918–1965.* Toronto: University of Toronto Press, 2018.

Ozment, Steven E. *Mysticism and Dissent: Religious Ideology and Social Protest in the Sixteenth Century.* New Haven, CT: Yale University Press, 1973.

Paz, Dennis G. *Popular Anti-Catholicism in Mid-Victorian England.* Stanford, CA: Stanford University Press, 1992.

Petzholdt, Hans. *Trier 2000 Jahre Stadtenticklung.* Trier: Selbstverlag des Baudezernates der Stadt Trier, 1984.

Picht, Werner. *Trier: Geist und Gestalt.* Düsseldorf: Joachim Schilling Verlag, 1966.

Pilick, Eckhart. *Johannes Ronge: Vier Abhandlungen mit zeitgenössischen Illustrationen und ungedruckten Briefen Ronges.* Pfalz: Verlag Peter Guhl Rohrbach, 2015.

Poll, Bernhard, ed. *Geschichte Aachen in Daten.* Aachen: VDS-Verlagsdruckerei Schmidt, 2005.

Purvis, Zachary. *Theology and the University in Nineteenth-Century Germany.* Oxford: Oxford University Press, 2016.

Rauscher, Anton. *Deutscher Katholizismus und Revolution im frühen 19. Jahrhundert.* Paderborn: Ferdinand Schöningh, 1975.

Reardon, Bernard. *Religion in the Age of Romanticism: Studies in Early Nineteenth-Century Thought.* New York: Cambridge University Press, 1985.

Reinerding, J.H. *Glaubensbekenntniß von Johannes Ronge.* Münster: Theissing'schen Buchhandlung, 1844.

Ronge, Joahnn, and Bertha Ronge. *A Practical Guide to the English Kinder-Garten (Children's Garden) for the Use of Mothers, Governesses, and Infant Teachers.* London: A.N. Myers, 1871.

Ruff, Mark Edward. *The Battle for the Catholic Past in Germany, 1945–1980.* New York: Cambridge University Press, 2017.

Schieder, Wolfgang. "Church and Revolution: Aspects of the Social History of the Trier Pilgrimage of 1844." Edited by Clive Emsley. Translated by Richard Deveson. *Conflict and Stability in Europe.* London: Open University, 1979, 65–95.

– *Religion und Revolution: die Trierer Wallfahrt von 1844.* Vierow bei Greifswald: SH-Verlag, 1996.

Schmellekamp, Dieter. *"Richtiger Wegzeiger für die Reyss zu Land von Siegburg auf Trier": auf den Spuren der Pilger zum Grab des Heiligen Matthias*. Siegburg: Rheinlandia-Verl, 2002.

Schneider, Bernhard. *Wallfahrt und Kommunikation*. Mainz: Selbstverlag der Gesellschaft für mittelrheinische Kirchengeschichte, 2004.

Selung, Bruno, ed. *Heiligtumsfahrt Aachen 1937*. M.-Gladbach: B. Kühlen Kunst, 1937.

Shapin, Steven. *A Social History of Truth: Civility and Science in Seventeenth-Century England*. Chicago: University of Chicago Press, 1994.

Smith, Christian. *The Secular Revolution: Power, Interests, and Conflict in the Secularization of American Public Life*. Berkeley: University of California Press, 2003.

Smith, Helmut Walser. *The Continuities of German History: Nation, Religion, and Race across the Long Nineteenth Century*. New York: Cambridge University Press, 2008.

– *German Nationalism and Religious Conflict: Culture, Ideology, Politics, 1870–1914*. Princeton, NJ: Princeton University Press, 1995.

– *Protestants, Catholics and Jews in Germany 1800–1914*. New York: Berg, 2001.

Smith, Jonathan Z. *To Take Place: Toward Theory in Ritual*. Chicago: University of Chicago Press, 1992.

Sperber, Jonathan. *Popular Catholicism in Nineteenth-Century Germany*. Princeton, NJ: Princeton University Press, 1984.

– *Rhineland Radicals: The Democratic Movement and the Revolution of 1848–49*. Princeton, NJ: Princeton University Press, 1991.

Stayer, James M. *The German Peasants' War and Anabaptist Community of Goods*. Montreal: McGill-Queen's University Press, 1991.

Taylor, Charles. *Philosophical Arguments*. Cambridge, MA: Harvard University Press, 1995.

– *A Secular Age*. Cambridge, MA: Harvard University Press, 2007.

Treitel, Corinna. *A Science for the Soul: Occultism and the Genesis of the German Modern*. Baltimore, MD: Johns Hopkins University Press, 2004.

Treitz, Jakob. *Michael Felix Korum: Bischof von Trier 1840–1924*. Muenchen: Theatiner Verlag, 1925.

Turner, Victor. *Dramas, Fields, and Metaphors: Symbolic Action in Human Society*. Ithaca, NY: Cornell University Press, 1974.

Tweed, Thomas A. *Crossing and Dwelling: A Theory of Religion*. Cambridge, MA: Harvard University Press, 2006.

Ungureanu, James C. *Science, Religion, and the Protestant Tradition: Retracing the Origins of Conflict*. Pittsburgh, PA: University of Pittsburgh Press, 2019.

Volk, Wilhelm. *Die Berliner Gewerbeausstellung und die Ausstellung des heiligen Rockes in Trier mit besonderer Bezugnahme auf den Rongeschen Brief. Ein Brief aus Berlin von einem Protestanten*. Münster: Friedr. Regensberg, 1845.

Wandel, Lee Palmer. *The Eucharist in the Reformation: Incarnation and Liturgy*. New York: Cambridge University Press, 2006.

Weir, Todd. *Secularism and Religion in Nineteenth-Century Germany: The Rise of the Fourth Confession*. Cambridge: Cambridge University Press, 2014.

Wolffram, Heather. *The Stepchildren of Science: Psychical Research and Parapsychology in Germany, c. 1870–1939*. New York: Editions Rodopi B.V., 2009.

Wynands, Dieter J. *Zur Geschichte der Aachener Heiligtumsfahrt*. Aachen: Einhard Verlag, 2000.

Zalar, Jeffrey T. *Reading and Rebellion in Catholic Germany 1770–1914*. Cambridge: Cambridge University Press, 2018.

Zenz, Emil. *Geschichte der Stadt Trier im 19. Jahrhundert*. Trier: Paulinus-Druckerei GmbH, 1979.

Zimmer, Oliver. *Remaking the Rhythms of Life: German Communities in the Age of the Nation-State*. Oxford: Oxford University Press, 2013.

Index

German and European Studies

General Editor: Jennifer L. Jenkins